THE EUROPEAN UNION AFTER THE TREATY OF AMSTERDAM

Edited by

JÖRG MONAR

and

WOLFGANG WESSELS

CONTINUUM

London and New York

Continuum

The Tower Building, 11 York Road, London SE1 7NX

370 Lexington Avenue, New York, NY 10017-6503

First published 2001

British Library Cataloguing-in-Publication Data

A catalogue record for this book is available from the British Library.

ISBN 0-8264-4769-4 (hardback)
      0-8264-4770-8 (paperback)

Library of Congress Cataloging-in-Publication Data

The European Union after the Treaty of Amsterdam / edited by Jörg Monar and Wolfgang Wessels.

  p. cm.

Includes bibliographical references and index.

ISBN 0-8264-4769-4 (hardback)—ISBN 0-8264-4770-8 (paperback)

  1. European Union. 2. Treaty on European Union (1992). Protocols, etc., 1997 Oct. 2. I. Monar, Jörg, 1960– II. Wessels, Wolfgang.

JN30 .E9413 2000

341.242′2—dc21

                                                                00-056979

Typeset by CentraServe Ltd, Saffron Walden, Essex

Printed and bound in Great Britain by Biddles Ltd, Guildford and King's Lynn

CONTENTS

Part III   The reforms in major policy areas

Part IV   The Way ahead

THE CONTRIBUTORS

Monica den Boer Associate Professor of Public Administration, Centre for Law, Public Administration and Informatisation, Tilburg University

Elmar Brok Chair of the Committee on Foreign Affairs, Human Rights, Common Security and Defence Policy of the European Parliament, President of the Europa Union Deutschland, Representative of the European Parliament during the 1996/97 Intergovernmental Conference

Franklin Dehousse Professor of Law, University of Liège, Personal Representative of the Minister of Foreign Affairs of Belgium during the 1996/97 Intergovernmental Conference

Jan Grünhage PhD candidate, University of Bonn.

Jean-Victor Louis Professor of Law, European University Institute (Florence) and Institut d'études européennes, Université Libre de Bruxelles (Brussels)

Dieter Mahncke Alfried Krupp von Bohlen und Halbach Professor, Director of the Department of European Political and Administrative Studies, College of Europe (Bruges)

Andreas Maurer Research Fellow, Institut für politische Wissenschaft und europäische Fragen, University of Cologne

Jörg Monar Professor of Politics and Director of the Centre for European Politics and Institutions, University of Leicester, Professor at the College of Europe (Bruges)

Pier Carlo Padoan Professor of Economics and Head of the Department of European Economic Studies, College of Europe (Bruges), Professor at the University 'La Sapienza' (Rome)

Eric Philippart Research Associate at Fonds National de la Recherche Scientifique (Belgium), Associate Professor at Université Libre de Bruxelles, and part-time professor, College of Europe (Bruges)

Elfriede Regelsberger Deputy-Director of the Institut für Europäische Politik (Berlin)

Jacek Saryusz-Wolski Undersecretary of State for European Integration of the Republic of Poland

Uwe Schmalz Research Fellow at the Institut für Europäische Politik (Bonn)

Philippe de Schoutheete de Tervarent Ambassador, former Permanent Representative of Belgium to the European Union, Institut d'études européennes, Université Catholique de Louvain

Monika Sie Dhian Ho Senior Researcher, Scientific Council for Government Policy (The Hague)

Brendan Smith Post-doctoral Fellow at the Centre for European Studies, Harvard University

William Wallace, Lord Wallace of Saltaire Chairman of Sub-committee F of the House of Lords, Professor of International Relations at the London School of Economics

Wolfgang Wessels Jean Monnet Professor of Political Science, University of Cologne, and Chair of the Trans European Policy Studies Association (Brussels)

ABBREVIATIONS

AFSJ	Area of Freedom, Security and Justice
CEPI	Centre for European Politics and Institutions
CEPR	Centre for Economic Policy Research
CESDP	Common European Security and Defence Policy
CFSP	Common Foreign and Security Policy
CJHA	Cooperation in Justice and Home Affairs
CJTF	Combined Joint Task Force
CMS	candidate member state
COREPER	Committee of Permanent Representatives
COSAC	Conférence des organes spécialisées aux affaires communautaires
CSCE	Conference on Security and Cooperation in Europe
EC	European Community
ECA	European Court of Auditors
ECJ	European Court of Justice
ECOFIN	Council of Economics and Finance Ministers
ECOSOC	Economic and Social Committee
EEA	European Economic Area
EMU	Economic and Monetary Union
ENA	Ecole nationale d'administration
EP	European Parliament
EPC	European Political Cooperation
ETUC	European Union Confederation
EU	European Union
EUROPOL	European Police Organisation
EUI	European University Institute

FAWEU	Forces Answerable to Western European Union
FDI	Foreign direct investment
GATT	General Agreement on Tariffs and Trade
IGC	Intergovernmental Conference
JHA	Justice and Home Affairs
MEP	Member of the European Parliament
MS	Member State
NATO	North Atlantic Treaty Organization
NGO	non-governmental organization
PPEWU	Policy Planning and Early Warning Unit
OSCE	Organisation for Economic Cooperation and Development
QMV	Qualified Majority Voting
SEA	Single European Act
SIRENE	Supplementary Information Request at the National Entry
SIS	Schengen Information System
TEPSA	Trans European Policy Studies Association
TEC	Treaty establishing the European Community
TEU	Treaty on European Union
ToA	Treaty of Amsterdam
TREVI	Terrorisme, Radicalisme, Extrémisme et Violence Internationale
UNHCR	United Nations High Commissioner for Refugees
UNICE	Employer's Confederation of Europe
UNMIK	United Nations' Mission in Kosovo
WEU	Western European Union

FOREWORD

Dr Helmut Kohl

Europe has successfully entered into the new millennium. Behind that
success stand foremost all the great treaties in the history of European
unification. They were always more than mere stages in a cooperative
effort – they represent the increasingly greater steps in the process of
European unification. A year ago, at the beginning of 1999, we once again
made great progress in the construction of the House of Europe in an
important area, namely Economic and Monetary Union. After more than
a year since the introduction of the Euro one thing is now clear: the
common currency will bind Europe together in a very special way and
foster the development of a common European identity.

At the same time this is to be a Europe of diversity in which the citizen
stands at the centre. A Europe of the citizens must always tackle problems
in the best way to ensure they can be solved with the greatest prospect of
success. This has a profound affinity with the idea behind the principle of
subsidiarity. Brussels or Strasbourg should only intervene when a problem
area cannot be adequately dealt with on a lower level and when, at the
same time – and this is the decisive factor – it can be more effectively
dealt with on the European level.

Supra-regional action – and the shared solutions that go with it – will
appear in the area of justice and home affairs, a key chapter of the
Amsterdam Treaty. Here the European Council in Amsterdam has
achieved good results. They go beyond anything which could have been
expected at the beginning of the negotiations. Hence we have from our
point of view attained at least partially one of the central goals of the
Amsterdam Intergovernmental Conference.

The European Union can only counter the growing threat throughout
Europe from international organized crime, from the drugs mafia and
from terrorism by concerted action. It is therefore right that the powers of
Interpol have been strengthened. We also have been able to integrate the
Schengen Agreement into the framework of the European Union.

On the important questions of asylum and visa policy, of immigration

Dr Helmut Kohl served as Federal Chancellor of West Germany from 1982 and of the
united Germany from 1990 until 1998.

or in the cooperation of justice and customs authorities the Amsterdam Summit has set down crucial foundations for common and hence more effective action.

The experiences of Yugoslavia and most recently of Kosovo have once again made plain the necessity of a reinforcement of the European capacity to act in foreign and security affairs. The new treaty provisions will in practice ensure, if they are applied consistently, that the Europeans are in a position to adequately respond to challenges to peace and stability on their own continent.

Alongside the European Council's power to establish guidelines for the Common Foreign and Security Policy it proved possible to establish a window of opportunity in the Treaty of Amsterdam for the integration of the Western European Union into the European Union. And in addition Europe rises, with the 'Petersberg tasks', to the challenge of finally regarding humanitarian and peace-keeping measures as matters of its primary concern.

As regards institutional reforms we would have certainly wished for more. Nevertheless progress has been made in this area. The new President of the Commission, for example, has at his disposal very many more possibilities for making his leadership capacity felt in the Commission. A noticeable extension of the rights of co-decision of the European Parliament was possible, as were equally the simplification of the decision-making procedures, the improved participation of the national parliaments as well as the strengthening of the position of the Committee of the Regions.

The development towards an increased use of majority decisions has proved difficult. Majority decisions remain exceptions. The understandable interests of almost all Member States stood opposed to an extension of this principle – as did the common interest in maintaining diversity in Europe.

In this context flexibility is of paramount political significance: the further development of the Union can now also be driven by a particular grouping of its states. The Treaty of Amsterdam has shown that the unification of Europe is not to be held up or reversed, even by hesitant members. One can alter the tempo but the direction remains. The process of European unification has become irreversible.

The rules governing more flexibility in the European Union ensure for an extended Union with 20 or more members, and the possibility of pursuing further integration. One individual member can bring cooperation between several Member States into question only when vital national interests are in danger.

The Treaty of Amsterdam once more proves how the European Union is holding to its course even in difficult phases and it provides the foundations for meeting the challenges at the onset of the twenty-first century, with faith in the future and confidence in one's own judgement. No one could have believed that all the problems would have been solved at Amsterdam. In a historical context no one can achieve their ideal objectives. The round of the 15 makes compromises necessary.

The Europeans have now brought themselves into a stronger position than ever before by organizing their own affairs on their continent. The common house of Europe is not finished yet – the basic structure is right, but further construction is needed. The Treaty of Amsterdam opens the door – which is a decisive aspect for me – to the expansion of the European Union. For this reason it is so important that we do not now neglect to make the decisions still outstanding. Without our neighbours in Central and Eastern Europe, whose culture and traditions we share, the European Union remains merely a rump.

The unity of Europe should not be simply a matter of the intellect, it must also be a matter of emotions, of the heart. It means a vision with a spiritual and cultural dimension. This Europe, on which we continue to work, must remain aware of its spiritual foundations: its traditions, its history, its values and the heritage of antiquity of the Christian West. The shared culture of our continent is the source of the European idea – its core is the assurance of peace and freedom. From the beginnings of the Coal and Steel Community through the Single European Market to the European Union of our day this concept has consistently underpinned everything: the concept of a comprehensive structure of peace and freedom for our continent.

INTRODUCTION

ASSESSING THE TREATY OF AMSTERDAM: BEYOND CONVENTIONAL WISDOM

Jörg Monar and Wolfgang Wessels

RELEVANCE AND DIFFICULTIES: MORE SALIENT ... AND MORE COMPLEX

Conventional wisdom has a rather clear view on the Treaty of Amsterdam: after long and cumbersome negotiations[1] the Heads of State or Government failed in the core institutional issues to reform the Council and the Commission.[2] Thus, we are told, over two years of intense negotiations (if one includes the extensive preparatory work done since spring 1995) led to little more than a number of limited adaptations of the Amsterdam Treaty's much more important predecessor – the Maastricht Treaty on European Union. The contributions to this book – each from its own perspective and in its own field – develop a picture which is at the same time more differentiated and more positive.

The Treaty of Amsterdam, which came into effect on 1 May 1999, constitutes undoubtedly a significant new qualitative step in the evolution of the European construction. Its successes and failures will be crucial factors in the future development of the European Union, which will be driven forward – at least during the next five to ten years – both by the deepening effect of EMU and by the new challenges arising from the enlargement to an as yet unknown number of applicant countries in an open-ended process. The way the new treaty provisions are applied will decide how the Europeans are able to tackle 'vital' problems of their political, economic and social system. With the Treaty of Amsterdam the EU has now arrived at a political agenda which is in all but name similar to that of a state: there is now no major area of policy-making left outside of the scope of actual or potential action by the EU institutions. By ratifying this Treaty member states have again – and to an until then unknown degree – put their future into collective hands. The decisions on the 'Area of freedom, security and justice'[3] demonstrate that the negotiators of the new Treaty have even agreed on a substantial communitarization of major elements of their justice and home affairs, probably the last big *domaine réservé* of the European nation-state. And last but not least, the Treaty has also introduced important new elements in the areas of democratic control and accountability,[4] bringing the Union closer to a system of effective democratic governance than ever before.

All this is not to deny that the Treaty has a number of flaws, and indeed not minor ones: the Amsterdam negotiations left a number of old problems unresolved, especially in the institutional field,[5] the reforms of the Common Foreign and Security Policy[6] have fallen well short of the much more ambitious rhetorics of necessary change heard before the IGC and during the crisis in former Yugoslavia, and the massive introduction of 'flexibility' has created at least as many new risks and problems as it has created new opportunities.[7] One may also have different views on how much real progress has been achieved in the areas of employment and social policy,[8] areas which concern European citizens' interests much more directly than most of the other issues covered by the Amsterdam Treaty. Yet the overall balance sheet nevertheless comes out with significant elements of progress which provide the Union with new major opportunities and which are likely to generate a new dynamic of development over the next five to ten years.

With increasing salience, the EU has become ever more complex. The Treaty of Amsterdam does not lend itself to simple and straightforward anatomy, analysis and assessment. The 116 new articles, 13 protocols and 45 declarations (if we have counted correctly) do not only constitute a major challenge to implementation but also to the Union's much invoked need of becoming more transparent to European citizens. Even in its overhauled version the Treaty on European Union is difficult to understand and even more difficult to characterize with traditional interpretative labels. Although one legislative procedure (the cooperation procedure) has been almost completely eliminated and although the co-decision procedure has been simplified, the number of procedures has been extended again, and some – like the procedural rules applying to 'closer cooperation' – have become even more Byzantine.

The challenge is enormous: After Amsterdam we are governed to an even higher degree by a set of treaty provisions forming a constitutional whole which apparently could not be shaped in a more coherent and understandable way. Although a new Intergovernmental Conference is already in an advanced stage of preparation – with others to come – the Amsterdam version of the EU constitution will remain the major European political and legal framework within which a growing number of European citizens will have to live for many years to come.

AIMS OF THIS BOOK

Many critics of the EU use the growing gap between the ever-increasing political weight and role of the European construction and its ever-increasing complexity to add their arguments to the large literature on the democratic deficits of this polity. The editors and contributors of this volume did not want to succumb to this often rather resignative mood which easily obscures the Union's possibilities to move forward. We wanted to broaden our views by offering competing *readings* of the Amsterdam Treaty. Therefore most of the following chapters present *alternative views and interpretations*.

The contributors were asked to make a first *impact analysis* of the new provisions introduced by the Treaty in view of three criteria:

- The *effectiveness* of the Union to tackle major problems ahead: has the Amsterdam Treaty created adequate new instruments or adequately reformed existing instruments for the EU institutions in the different policy fields?
- The internal *efficiency*: does the Amsterdam Treaty offer new or extended possibilities for the institutions to achieve reasonable results within a reasonable period?
- The *legitimacy* of the Union: does the Amsterdam Treaty reduce complexity, increase transparency, promote parliamentary participation, judicial review, constitutional guarantees and democratic accountability?

At such an early stage after the signing and entry into force of the new Treaty such an effort of analysis has inevitably a speculative dimension. Yet all contributors have aimed to provide 'educated guesses' about the Amsterdam Treaty's impact in the light of the lessons which can be drawn from nearly five decades of EC and EU treaty revisions and their implementation. This also means that in assessing the Treaty one should not follow too closely what the 'treaty architects' tell us they wanted to achieve with one or other of the new provisions. As in the case of all constitutional texts the 'fathers' of this latest product of EU treaty engineering may also see their own considerations soon becoming largely irrelevant in a rapidly changing political context with new member states joining, new governments in power, the dynamics of economic globalization and new international challenges.

This book has been designed to be more than an ivory tower exercise: it has aimed at providing *concrete suggestions* how best to apply the new provisions (as most of the new provisions are open to different interpretations and practical regimes) and what might be necessary and realistic reforms to be undertaken during the next 'windows of opportunity' arising from future intergovernmental conferences. Yet it also wants to provide a new stimulus for the theoretical debate on the Amsterdam results[9] because we think that theoretical concepts can help to elucidate the place of this most complex Treaty in the overall context of European integration at the turn of the millennium.

SOME CAVEATS

In analysing and assessing the provisions of the Treaty of Amsterdam we must be careful not to fall into methodological traps which are quite common in debates about treaty changes and political events in general. Thus we should not trust our emotions after 'the end-game' in Amsterdam, which were largely based on past experiences and expectations: neither the disappointments over what has not been achieved ('if only this or that Head of Government had acted differently at a given moment', 'if they would have had more time etc. . . .') nor the surprises (be they good or bad) over what has nevertheless been agreed on ('never expected such an outcome') are helpful in analysing the possible impact on the future development of the Union. It would mean – in the words of John Osborne[10] – to spend our time 'mostly looking forward to the past'.

Similarly, it makes no sense to try to establish a balance about winners and losers. We are not referees at a beauty contest among politicians and the way in which they present us their achievements. We need to be careful about our yardsticks when applying the criteria. To compare the results of Amsterdam to an optimal model or even to a constitutional utopia (which are quite often deduced from political and constitutional concepts developed during the nineteenth century) might make us blind to the crucial elements of relative progress or possible regress.

In view of the contributions to this volume different assessments can be made. No single overall evaluation seems, however, possible. Even where there are some clearly discernible tendencies, such as those leading to further differentiation in the integration process, different interpretations and impact predictions can be fully justified. This volume of essays is thus part of an ongoing discourse which is as dynamic as the Union's own development. We decided to add a chapter on the new Treaty of Nice (agreed in December 2000) which in many ways continues and builds on the reforms introduced by the Treaty of Amsterdam.

Most of the contributions to this book were discussed at least once or twice in major international gatherings, especially in the context of the conference on the Treaty of Amsterdam organized by the Trans European Policy Studies Association (TEPSA) at the College of Europe in Bruges in

September 1997 and the UACES annual conference hosted by the Centre for European Politics and Institutions (CEPI) in Leicester in January 1998.

We would like to thank TEPSA for initiating and financing this project and CEPI for following it up and providing the necessary administrative support. The TEPSA network proved again its extraordinary usefulness in bringing together experts from different European countries and professional backgrounds for an interdisciplinary analysis and discussion of crucial issues of the integration process.

We owe special thanks to Barbara Bogusz, research associate at CEPI, for her extensive language proof-reading, reformatting and indexing work on what proved to be a demanding manuscript, and our copy editor at Continuum Andrew Mikolajski.

Leicester and Cologne
January 2001

NOTES

1. See on this point the chapter by Jan Grünhage.
2. For a vivid description of this failure see Chapter 3, by Franklin Dehousse.
3. See the chapters by Jörg Monar, Monica den Boer, and Brendan Smith and William Wallace.
4. See the chapter by Elmar Brok and Andreas Maurer.
5. See the chapter of Jean-Victor Louis.
6. See the chapters by Elfriede Regelsberger and Uwe Schmalz, and by Dieter Mahncke.
7. See the chapters by Philippe de Schoutheete and Eric Philippart.
8. See the chapter by Carlo Padoan.
9. See the chapter by Wolfgang Wessels.
10. In *Look back in Anger* (1956).

PART I

THE IGC 1996–97 NEGOTIATIONS AND THEIR OUTCOME

CHAPTER 1

THE 1996/97 INTERGOVERNMENTAL CONFERENCE: A SURVEY OF THE PROCESS

Jan Grünhage

INTRODUCTION

The Treaty of Amsterdam constitutes the third major treaty revision of what has become the European Union (EU) within little over a decade. Just like the Single European Act (1986) and the Maastricht Treaty on European Union (1992), the Amsterdam Treaty was negotiated in the framework of an intergovernmental conference (IGC), which – whatever may be its deficiencies – is the Union's current procedural framework for treaty revision. The aim of this chapter is to provide a succinct survey of the preparation, organization and development of the negotiations under the three Presidencies of this latest IGC.[1] It will focus on the main events in loose chronological order, trying to provide a useful background picture to the analysis of the Conference's results in the following chapters.

BACKGROUND AND AGENDA

The 1985 and 1991 IGCs, leading to the Single European Act and the Treaty on European Union respectively, had been driven by a momentum towards deeper integration in response to global economic challenges and geo-political changes, notably the end of the Cold War (Dinan, 1999: 292). In contrast, the 1996/97 IGC took place because it was stipulated in the Treaty on European Union. Article N(2) TEU stated that 'a conference of representatives of the member states shall be convened in 1996 to examine those provisions of this Treaty for which revision is provided'.

Beyond this formal requirement however other developments had their impact on the agenda and outcome of the conference. As Michiel Patijn (1997: 38), chairman of the IGC in the endphase of the conference, observes, soon after the ratification of the Maastricht Treaty expectations towards the next round of treaty reform were raised by three issues. First of all, both the governments of the EU Member states and the public at large were disappointed with the effectiveness of the Common Foreign and Security Policy (CFSP) after the civil war in Bosnia. This reinforced the desire to review Maastricht's second pillar in 1996. Secondly, the perspective of a wholesale expansion of the EU in the medium term, opened by the European Council in Copenhagen on 21/22 June 1993 (Presidency Conclusions, 1993a), provided those calling for institutional reform with an important argument in support of their demand. As the members of the IGC's preparatory committee, the Reflection Group, all agreed, the IGC was necessary 'to make enlargement possible' (Dinan, 1999: 294). Finally, the political debates in several Member States about the relevance of the Union to the ordinary citizens following the Maastricht ratification crisis had the seemingly paradoxical effect of simultaneously dispelling most of the Member States' enthusiasm for a new round of treaty reform while leading them to call for a strengthened Union closer to its citizens.

In the end, a number of states (notably the UK) started questioning the timing of the IGC. It was argued at the time that it was too soon to engage in another round of treaty reform for two reasons. First of all, doubts were raised that the functioning of the TEU could be adequately assessed only two and a half years after its ratification (Schmuck, 1996: 9). Secondly, it was argued that Austria, Finland and Sweden still lacked experience in the conduct of European affairs only one and a half year after their accession to the Union. In addition, the ratification crisis surrounding the TEU made the EU governments aware of an ever-growing critical public opinion *vis-à-vis* European integration (Dinan, 1998: 36). The end of Lindberg and Scheingold's (1970) 'permissive consensus' was declared. Therefore, some Member States called for a 'cooling-off' period. However, abandoning the follow-up IGC to the TEU was not only legally difficult, it was also politically risky (Dinan, 1999: 293). The IGC thus went ahead as planned.

Under the Maastricht Treaty, a number of questions had to be addressed at the 1996/97 IGC, including, *inter alia*, a possible extension of the co-decision procedure (Article 189b(8) TEC), the provisions relating to CFSP as well as defence issues (Article J.4 and Article J.10 TEU) and the possibility of extending the explicit competence of the Union to the areas of energy, tourism and civil protection (Declaration No. 1 TEU).

In addition, according to Article N(1) TEU the government of any Member State of the Union as well as the European Commission could submit proposals for treaty revision to the European Council. Consequently, various European Council meetings (Brussels December 1993, Corfu June 1994, Cannes June 1995) added numerous items to the agenda of the intergovernmental conference. Hence, the Brussels European Council mandated widespread institutional reform in light of the prospective enlargement of the Union to various countries in Central and Eastern Europe (Presidency Conclusions, 1993b). The Cannes European Council of June 1995 concluded that the IGC should further address questions which would allow the EU to respond to its citizens' anxieties, such as internal security, unemployment and environmental degradation (Presidency Conclusions, 1995a).

Another theme was added to the IGC agenda by a joint letter from Chancellor Helmut Kohl and President Jacques Chirac dated 6 December 1995. In view of prospective enlargement of the Union concerns were growing that the momentum of the European integration process could eventually come to a grinding halt, especially in light of the reluctance of some Member States to give up their veto rights in the two intergovernmental pillars of the EU. Thus, Kohl and Chirac demanded the examination by the intergovernmental conference of the possibility of endowing the Union with more flexible decision-making procedures (Kohl and Chirac, 1995).

Finally, after the practicalities as well as the opening date of the conference had been decided upon at the Madrid European Council of 15/16 December 1995 (see below), the Turin Summit of 29 March 1996 established the final mandate for the IGC and officially launched it. In the Presidency Conclusions, the Heads of State and Government considered that the Conference should, in view of the Report of the Reflection Group and in light of previous items agreed upon, concentrate primarily on the topics mandated by the TEU as well as by the subsequent European Council meetings, without prejudice to any other items added to the agenda during the Conference itself (Presidency Conclusions, 1996a).

Overall, the IGC's agenda had gradually moved from a relatively restricted list of items unfinished at Maastricht to a heavy workload, covering virtually all activities of the European Union with one exception. The area of Economic and Monetary Union (EMU) had been deliberately kept out as it was regarded as politically too sensitive in view of critical public opinion (interview with a Commission official). In addition, German Chancellor Helmut Kohl and his Finance minister Theo Waigel were strongly opposed to the inclusion of Maastricht's EMU provisions in the Conference's agenda, as they feared an erosion of the treaty's convergence criteria, designed to prevent inflation-prone Member States from entering into monetary union with Germany. In sum, the EU governments were in agreement about not opening what they considered a 'Pandora's Box'.

PREPARATION: VARIOUS INSTITUTIONAL REPORTS AND
THE REFLECTION GROUP

Of the four IGCs held since the relaunch of the European integration project in the mid-1980s, the 1996/97 Conference was undoubtedly the most thoroughly prepared. After the Maastricht Treaty, there had been a widespread feeling among the Member States that the two intergovernmental pillars of the TEU were less than satisfactory mainly because the IGC on political union had not been adequately prepared (Dinan, 1999: 294). Thus, in what may be described as a 'lesson from Maastricht' (Laursen, 1997), things were to be different in 1996/97.

The Heads of State and Government therefore took several decisions concerning the IGC at the Corfu European Council on 24/25 June 1994. Firstly, all institutions of the EC were asked to draw up reports on the functioning of the Maastricht Treaty. Secondly, it was decided to set up a Reflection Group to prepare the intergovernmental conference (Presidency Conclusions, 1994).

The Reflection Group was composed of personal representatives of the Foreign Ministers of the 15 Member States, a Member of the European Commission as well as two Members of the European Parliament (see Annex I). Dinan (1999: 295) reports how the European Parliament pressured the governments of the EU into letting it participate in the Reflection Group. It appears as if the EP managed to exploit a crisis over qualified majority voting in 1994. Dissatisfied with the 1994 Ioannina Compromise, the Parliament threatened to withhold its assent from the 1995 enlargement unless the Member States would involve it as fully as possible in the upcomming IGC. Of course it is doubtful that the EP would have in the end blocked enlargement over the issue, but it did give the parliamentarians some leverage over unsympathetic Member States (such as the United Kingdom and France). As a result the EP was thus granted two representatives in the Reflection Group.

At the Corfu European Council the Reflection Group was given the mandate to take position on the points which had to be dealt with at the IGC under the Maastricht Treaty, to think about further developments and possible improvements with respect to democracy and openness in the EU, and finally to scrutinize the functioning of the Maastricht Treaty on the basis of the various institutional reports. In addition, the Reflection Group was supposed to develop options for institutional reform in the context of enlargement. The Foreign Ministers, meeting in Messina on 2 June 1995, asked the Reflection Group to present its results to the European Council by the end of 1995 (Weidenfeld, 1998: 224–5).

The various institutional reports thus formed the basis for the work of the Reflection Group and 'provided a useful snapshot of the EU's functioning at the end of 1995' (Dinan, 1999: 295). All reports emphasized the need for greater openness, transparency, legitimacy, simplification and effectiveness of decision-making procedures in the Union (European Parliament, 1995; European Commission, 1995; Council, 1995; European Court of Justice, 1995). Beyond these rather general concerns however, the reports lacked 'any explicit theory or conceptual framework [. . .] which might help the citizens understand the rationale of the whole endeavour [of treaty reform]' (Laursen, 1997: 63).

On the basis of these reports, the Reflection Group began its work in Taormina (Sicily) on 3 June 1995. It was chaired by Carlos Westendorp, who was the Spanish Secretary of State for European Affairs at the time. In June and July 1995, the Spanish Presidency sent out questionnaires to the various delegations to get some initial feedback on the issues under consideration. On the basis of the responses to the questionnaires, the Presidency put forward an interim report on 5 September 1995 (Reflection Group, 1995a). The main suggestions of this interim report were that in cases of treaty revision unanimity should be kept and that the IGC should aim for the introduction of a sanction mechanism against Member States violating fundamental rights.

In total, the Reflection Group met 12 times in the 6 months of its existence (see Annex II). Following its mandate, the Group issued its final report on 5 December 1995. This document contained two parts (Reflection Group, 1995b). First of all, a general title on *A Strategy for Europe* underlined the necessity to make the EU more transparent and closer to the citizens. The Reflection Group argued that the Union fell short of being a proper state but that it was more than just a common market. As such it had to devote itself more to its citizens. With respect to enlargement the report stressed the need for institutional and procedural as well as structural adjustment and raised the possibility of flexible solutions. In addition, the Union was called to strengthen its capacity for external action and to display more external profile.

Secondly, an 'annotated agenda' provided a range of more detailed reform proposals. According to the report, the internal challenges of the Union, in particular the security concerns of the citizens, had to be met with a clear definition of goals. The Union had to acquire instruments to meet the main concerns of the citizens that were considered to be social exclusion and unemployment as well as environmental degradation. Also, the Union had to involve the citizen further by defining more precisely the protection of fundamental rights and Union citizenship in the treaty. With respect to institutional reform the report called for a reduction of decision-making procedures as well as for qualified majority voting to become the rule.

The role of the Reflection Group was to find an annotated agenda for the IGC through a process of brainstorming. As its name indicated, the purpose of the Group was reflection rather than hard diplomatic bargaining. This was also shown in the fact that the members of the Reflection Group were personal representatives of the Foreign Ministers of the Member States and of the Presidents of the Commission as well as the EP and did not necessarily hold official positions. Thus, some were retired officials or politicians, others university professors (see Annex I). The hope was that the Group could be more flexible in its reflection process than diplomats would be in an official negotiation. Yet, as McDonagh (1998: 39) asserts, national interests still prevailed in the course of the Reflection Group meetings and 'no national position of importance was conceded in the course of the work of the Reflection Group'.

The Report of the Reflection Group was officially submitted to the Madrid European Council meeting on 15/16 December 1995. The Heads of State and Government concluded that the Report by the Group constituted a 'sound basis for the work of the conference' (Presidency Conclusions, 1995b). However, beyond political rhetoric, the question about the real purpose of the work of the Reflection Group may be posed (Wessels, 1996).

The report of the Reflection Group was of course only a report setting out what issues were to be dealt with at the IGC. On most sensitive points, differences of view prevailed among the various delegations. As Kortenberg (1997: 711) comments, 'on quite a number of points, [the Report of the Reflection Group] constitutes more a statement of disagreement than a document of consensus'. This was illustrated in the Report by the use of formulations such as 'a broad majority', 'some members' or even 'one member' (generally meaning the UK) [author's translation].

Some observers have thus criticized the Reflection Group (Wessels, 1996; Bourlanges, 1997) and blamed its composition, arguing that the Reflection Group was still composed of too many junior ministers and high officials, who were all too wary of not upsetting their respective political superiors. Thus, it was concluded, a Committee of Wise Men would have been preferable. However, as Devuyst (1998: 618) argues, reports by individual Wise Men have never really yielded much influence in the Union, often for lack of political realism. He cites the examples of the Tindemans Report on European Union 1975, which 'simply ended up in government archives' and of the 1981 Genscher/Colombo initiative which 'merely resulted in a long-forgotten Solemn Declaration two years later'.

In the end, the Report did not become a formal reference document for the IGC. Any assessment of the work of the Reflection Group must however take into account the magnitude of the job it faced, as McDonagh

(1998: 41) contends. The importance and effectiveness of the Reflection Group should not be exaggerated. Nevertheless, it played a positive role in the preparation of the IGC. First of all, the Reflection Group clarified issues and forced all delegations to start thinking and developing positions on the points under consideration. Secondly, the Reflection Group facilitated good personal relationships, a factor not to be underestimated, especially in light of the fact that eight members of the Reflection Group were later reappointed to the IGC Representatives Group (see Annex III), which was the Group that did the bulk of the work of the IGC (see below). Finally, the Reflection Group started the process of 'diplomatic Darwinism', i.e. it identified issues not suited for the IGC, such as the idea of altering significantly the balance between the institutions to the detriment of the European Commission (McDonagh, 1998: 43).

Generally, the two Members of the European Parliament received praise from the other participants for their contribution to the work of the Reflection Group (interviews with members of the Reflection Group). This was due to a variety of factors. First of all, Elmar Brok (a German Christian Democrat) and Elisabeth Guigou (a French socialist) supplemented each other very well, as a close collaborator of Brok observed. Not only did they originate from the two dominating parties in the European Parliament, but Guigou's 'ENA-trained sharp intellect' complemented Brok, the 'instinct politician' very well (Interview with a Commission official). In addition, the EP had learnt from past mistakes. Marginalized at Maastricht by the Member States as a result of excessive demands, the two MEPs made sure that their demands and contributions to the Reflection Group always remained in the sphere of the realistic. On no occasion did the EP find itself in an isolated position in the Group, even if it demanded important steps forward, e.g. on institutional reform or on employment policy, as on each point at least some Member States supported the EP's positions. Thus, the two MEPs 'enjoyed a high degree of acceptance in the Reflection Group. On no occasion were they considered as foreign bodies' (interview with a Commission official).

Thus, the question was raised of the role of the European Parliament in the IGC itself. Lodge (1998: 486) reports that the European Parliament demanded a place at the conference table on the grounds that the IGC was convened to prepare the Union for enlargement. Since enlargement must be endorsed by the EP, the deputies argued, they could always withhold their assent unless they were granted a significant role in the IGC. In addition the MEPs claimed that since they were the only directly elected EC institution, their participation in the IGC would lend the whole process of treaty reform an increased degree of legitimacy.

Apart from the fact that granting the EP a formal role at the IGC would have posed legal problems (the 1996/97 IGC was conducted under the terms of Article N TEU which did not mention the European Parliament), France and the United Kingdom strongly resisted the demands of the EP and even vetoed suggestions by Benelux, Germany and Italy to allow the EP a status of permanent observer at the conference (Petite, 1997: 23). In the end, the Foreign Ministers, meeting in Brussels on 25 March 1996, agreed on the following compromise (European Parliament, 1995: 7):

- At the beginning of each ministerial session of the IGC, there would be an exchange of views with the EP President on the subjects on the agenda, in the presence of the representatives of the Parliament.
- Once a month and where the representatives of the Ministers considered it desirable, the Presidency of the Council would hold a working meeting on the occasion of the meetings of the IGC Representatives Group.
- The Presidency would keep the European Parliament informed, orally or in writing.

The reaction of the European Parliament was lukewarm. At a press conference, Klaus Hänsch, the President of the EP, stated that this compromise was 'reasonable' even though not 'formulated perfectly' (*Agence Europe*, 1996). Nevertheless, these provisions were endorsed by the Heads of State and Government at the Turin European Council on 29 March 1996. This extraordinary summit further established the final mandate for the IGC (see above) and solemnly launched the 1996/97 intergovernmental conference (Presidency Conclusions, 1996a). A deadline for the end of the IGC was not set however, but it was clear from the beginning that it would not conclude before the UK general election, due to be held in May 1997 at the latest (Schmuck, 1996: 14).

THE IGC: DEVELOPMENT UNDER THREE PRESIDENCIES

The practical arrangements of the IGC were decided at the Madrid European Council of 15/16 December 1995 (Presidency Conclusions, 1995b). Accordingly, the Conference met at four levels:

The *European Council* constituted the supreme decision-making body at which the key deals were struck. Some issues had such high political and constitutional importance that they could only (formally) be decided upon by the Heads of State and Government. This did of course not preclude previous broad agreement on certain issues, as was illustrated by the remaining question on the triggering mechanism for the use of closer cooperation, which reportedly was settled at the Amsterdam European Council in less than ten minutes (interviews with Commission official and Belgian diplomat).

The *Foreign Ministers* met throughout the conference on a monthly basis, typically on the brim of General Affairs Councils. In total, these ministers met 17 times between April 1996 and June 1997 (see Annex IV), not counting the various sessions held on the fringes of European Council meetings. In a way, the Foreign Ministers were sandwiched between the European Council and the IGC Group of Representatives. Their actual contribution to the IGC has thus been seriously questioned (interviews with Council official and Belgian diplomat) and the Foreign Ministers have been accused of only having restricted themselves to the use of 'meaningless *tours de table*' (interview with Council official), as the bulk of the IGC work was done by the Group of Representatives and the key political decisions were taken by the Heads of State and Government. Reportedly, the Foreign Ministers only really negotiated one IGC outcome themselves, the compromise on the use of majority voting in the second pillar (see below; interview with Council official). Nevertheless, the Foreign Ministers assumed the important task of ensuring the coherence and unity of the negotiations. This was precisely the reason why other Ministers did not formally convene in IGC meetings in the 1996/97 Conference.

The *IGC Representatives Group* met almost weekly throughout the conference, 33 times in total (see Annex V). It was composed of representatives of each Foreign Minister and of a representative of the President of the European Commission. As in the case of the IGC Reflection Group, the members of the Representatives Group held different functions in their respective Member States but enjoyed equal formal status within the Group (see Annex III). According to McDonagh (1998: 46), they represented an effective mix of technicians and politicians with different characters and backgrounds. A member of this Group estimates that approximately 60–70 per cent of the actual ToA was negotiated by the Representatives (interview), a view shared by other participants and observers of the IGC (interviews with Council official and German diplomat). The main reason for the predominance of this group in the 1996/97 IGC may be found in the complex technical nature of large parts of the negotiations. As a Director from the Council Secretariat observes, 'to handle all the technical details of dossiers like Schengen is just not possible at the level of ministers or even Heads of State and Government' (interview). It can thus be concluded that 'the IGC Representatives Group was the pivot around which negotiations turned' (McDonagh, 1998: 45).

Finally, some *working groups* were established in the course of the IGC. However, these were used rather sparingly, as most issues were considered as too political to be dealt with by pure bureaucrats (interview with Commission official). In addition, concerns about the continuity and unity of the negotiation were driving the EU governments not to delegate too much work below the level of the IGC Representatives (McDonagh, 1998: 21). Probably the most important working group established in the conference was the so-called *Friends of the Presidency* group, consisting of selected senior officials and chaired by the Dutchman Jaap de Zwaan. It was set up in the last week of May 1997 as the negotiations were drawing to a close. Its mandate was to cope with the volume of legal tidying up required in the run-up to the Amsterdam European Council. The Friends of the Presidency Group was so successful that it continues its work to the present day.

It should be recalled that the role of the Presidency is of crucial importance during an intergovernmental conference. In the regular daily business of the EC it is normally the European Commission that has the right of initiative. Things are different however during an IGC, because of the intergovernmental setting of the process. Together with the Council Secretariat, it is up to the Presidency to prepare and table papers or proposals for discussion in addition to its other more traditional tasks of setting the agendas for meetings as well as chairing these.

Things were no different at the 1996/97 IGC. Of course, individual delegations tabled papers as well, but according to McDonagh (1998: 23), Irish participant in the conference, these national propositions generally had much less influence as they were rarely used as a basis for discussion at the IGC. An example was the UK Government's memorandum of 22 July 1996 in which the UK Government demanded a restriction of the competencies of the European Court of Justice (United Kingdom, 1996). Nevertheless, there are exceptions, such as the Franco-German proposal on flexibility of 17 October 1996. In this paper, the French and German Foreign Ministers outlined the specific conditions for the use of flexibility, which were later broadly included as such in the Treaty of Amsterdam (Federal Republic of Germany and Republic of France, 1996).

The IGC began under the Italian Presidency on 29 March 1996 in Turin. The Presidency decided to proceed in the following way. Discussions were sub-divided into three broad areas: citizenship, institutional reform and external action. For every session, three to five documents were prepared (so-called *fiches*) by the Presidency, listing different options for each topic under discussion. In successive rounds of extensive *tours-de-table* each delegation would then comment on these *fiches* on the basis of which the Presidency would draw up possible compromises (Schmuck, 1996: 16). In the end, the Italian Presidency drafted a progress report, submitted to the Florence European Council of 22/23 June 1996. This report set out some options discussed at the IGC in the form of draft texts (for example on a possible employment chapter in the treaty), but progress was limited, as most parts of the report remained rather vague (Italian Presidency, 1996).

This had mainly to do with the fact that the Italian Presidency had a problem of timing (McDonagh, 1998: 53). For many delegations, there was a perceived lack of time pressure and therefore little incentive to begin with the real negotiations. Member States knew that the IGC would not be concluded before the UK general election which at the time lay more than a year in the future. Especially the smaller Member States were reluctant to take positions on institutional questions as they feared a shift of balance in favour of the larger Member states – concerns supported by the fact that France, Germany, the UK and Italy did indeed defend such reforms (European Parliament, 1996). Therefore, they tried to stall the negotiations as long as possible on these issues (interview with a Council official). The fact that no closing date for the IGC had been set clearly exacerbated these problems.

It was also at the Florence European Council that the following Presidency, the Irish, was given the mandate to prepare a draft treaty for the Dublin summit, scheduled to be held in December 1996. The Irish Presidency was thus facing an important challenge. It had to decide whether to aim for a draft treaty agreed upon by all delegations as well as, related to this, how much progress to strive for. Since the IGC would only be concluded under the Dutch Presidency, it was clear from the beginning that many issues would remain unresolved in the draft treaty. The *Financial Times* therefore described the task of the Irish Presidency as 'mission impossible' (as cited in McDonagh, 1998: 103).

Three broad phases can be distinguished under the Irish Presidency, in a process described by Noel Dorr, the Irish chairman of the IGC Representatives Group, as involving 'successive approximations' (as cited in McDonagh, 1998: 75). From July to September 1996 the Presidency tabled 'introductory notes' for discussion which summarized the issues and contained draft treaty language. Thus, for the first time during the IGC, specific wordings of treaty changes were actually discussed. From October to November 1996 papers were tabled as 'suggested approaches' with refined treaty language on the basis of the first round of discussions. Finally, in November and December 1996 the draft treaty was prepared for the Dublin European Council. This was done essentially at a four-day drafting session of the Presidency in Kildare, Ireland, with the help of officials from the Council Secretariat as well as the European Commission (McDonagh, 1998: 104, interview with a Council official).

The draft treaty was finally presented and discussed at the Dublin summit on 13/14 December 1996. It was distributed only shortly in advance of the Foreign Ministers' meeting of 6 December 1996. At the time, the Irish draft received some criticism for being too vague and demonstrating the lack of progress at the IGC (interview with a Commission official). Nevertheless, with the exception of the very contentious issues of institutional reform and flexibility, the draft contained concrete treaty language and possible alternatives (Irish Presidency, 1996, unpubli-shed government paper) and was thus 'already a pretty serious document to work with, reasonably advanced in many domains' (interview with a Council official). In addition, since it was widely distributed and included clear, easily understandable introductions before each chapter, the Irish draft treaty helped increase the IGC's transparency.

The principal challenge of the 1996/97 IGC, to conclude the conference, passed into the hands of the Dutch Government, which took over the IGC Presidency from Ireland on 1 January 1997. The deadline for the con-clusion of the conference in mid-1997 had been set at the Florence European Council of 21/22 June 1996 (Presidency Conclusions, 1996b) and reconfirmed at the Dublin summit of 13/14 December 1996 (Presi-dency Conclusions, 1996c). Consequently, as McDonagh (1998: 135/6) argues, the Dutch Presidency had essentially two weapons in its hands: the agreed target date for the end of the IGC plus the Irish draft treaty. Yet, on the most contentious issues at stake, there were still no draft treaty texts. In addition, the shape of the Dutch Presidency's programme was significantly influenced by the UK general election of May 1997, after which only about six weeks were left to conclude the IGC.

The Dutch Presidency had three broad phases (McDonagh, 1998: 137). From January to April 1997 the Dutch used the tactic of increasing the intensity of the negotiations in order to put delegations under pressure. Discussions were focused on the most difficult issues. The real nego-tiations began only after the general election in the United Kingdom, which ended 19 years of Conservative rule, thus bringing a new set of negotiators to the conference table. As de Schoutheete (1997) contends:

Of course previous work [...] allowed to clear the grounds, to settle a series of less important or less contentious problems, to test different hypotheses, to identify difficult problems and to outline possible solu-tions. Without this preliminary work, zealously pursued by the Italian, Irish and Dutch Presidencies, the conference would not have concluded. But on the crucial points, no delegation was prepared to enter into the realm of real concessions and decisions before knowing which British negotiator would sit around the table in the final phase.

In general, most participants in the IGC agree on the proposition that the three successive Presidencies, which closely collaborated throughout the conference, advanced the negotiations to the best of their capacities (interviews with various officials from the Council and the Commission). The process of giving shape to a draft treaty, which had begun in June 1995 with the establishment of the Reflection Group, took about two years. On 4 June 1997, the Dutch Presidency submitted to the IGC Representa-tives Group a final, consolidated draft treaty. It was divided into five parts: (1) Freedom, Security and Justice; (2) The Union and the Citizens; (3) An efficient and coherent Foreign Policy; (4) The Institutions of the Union; (5) Enhanced Cooperation.

The final and crucial phase of the Dutch Presidency, and arguably of the whole Intergovernmental Conference itself, was the Amsterdam European Council of 16/17 June 1997.

THE AMSTERDAM ENDGAME

The Heads of State and Government of the European Union met in Amsterdam on 16/17 June 1997 in order to conclude the IGC. Virtually all the time of that European Council meeting was scheduled to be devoted to the Conference. The battle-order had been laid out, by the Dutch Prime Minister Wim Kok, in the traditional pre-European Council letter from the Presidency to all participants. Discussions were thus to start with Section II of the Dutch draft treaty (*The Union and the citizens*), the remaining sections were thereafter to be dealt with in numerical order. As McDonagh contends (1998: 189), the Dutch Presidency's idea was to obtain that way the small psychological advantage of opening the negotiations with a relatively harmonious discussion in an area on which broad agreement had largely been reached previously.

A large number of contentious issues remained, however, the most important being:

- The decision-making mechanism in the new title on visa, asylum, immigration and the free movement of people as well as the degree of flexibility required in that title.
- The relationship between the WEU and the EU.
- External economic relations.
- The triggering mechanism for flexibility.
- The so-called triangle of institutional issues: the future composition of the European Commission, the question of the weighting of votes in the Council and the scope of the extension of majority voting as well as of the co-decision procedure.

Overall, the 'European Council would have to revisit every significant area of the work of the conference. Moreover, since nothing would be agreed until everything was agreed, there was nothing to prevent points which appeared to have been settled from being re-opened' (McDonagh, 1998: 190). The failure to reach agreement on more issues in advance of the Amsterdam summit thus resulted in a plethora of issues being left for discussion at the summit itself. Issues of minor importance to most delegations, such as, *inter alia*, specific declarations on churches or on public broadcasting, were on the agenda as well as highly contested questions of significant political importance to all delegations, such as the envisaged institutional reforms or the *terra incognita* of flexibility.

On 16 June 1997 negotiations opened as foreseen by Prime Minister Kok with Title II of the Dutch draft treaty. In turn, the Heads of State and Government discussed the employment chapter, social policy, environment, public health, outermost regions, public broadcasting, statistics and subsidiarity. As foreseen by the Dutch Presidency, none of these issues caused major controversy at the summit.

The European Council then turned its attention to Title I of the Dutch draft treaty on an 'area of freedom, security and justice'. The most difficult issue turned out to be the question of majority voting on asylum matters, to which German Chancellor Helmut Kohl was adamantly opposed. The first day of the Amsterdam summit concluded with an extensive discussion of CFSP-related issues, notably on the possibility of a common defence policy, the relationship between the European Union and the Western European Union, as well as the question of flexibility in Pillar II. No agreement could be reached on any of these dossiers. The Presidency hence announced it would review possible compromises overnight (Confidential documents).

Almost the whole morning of the second day of the Amsterdam summit was again devoted to Title I of the Dutch draft treaty with a focus on asylum questions and the integration of the Schengen *acquis* into the European Union. Agreement on these questions could finally be reached so that discussions moved to remaining issues in the afternoon (Confidential documents).

After a number of relatively minor questions, such as protocols on public broadcasting or on public credit institutions, were speedily agreed upon, the Heads of State and Government were only left with a few hours to finalize a number of very contentious issues, notably external economic relations as well as security and defence. The final part of the negotiations revolved around institutional reforms, which had in fact been one of the major *raisons d'être* of the conference. However, no agreement could be found between Member States. Most countries argued in favour of the introduction of a double majority system in the Council of Ministers while some, particularly France, Spain and the United Kingdom, favoured a simple reweighting of the votes in the Council. In addition, the question of reform of the European Commission proved too contentious to be solved at Amsterdam. Notably Spain raised last-minute concerns about insufficient compensation for its foreseeable loss of a second Commissioner. Discussions finally resulted in a protocol on institutional reform, which laid out future reform options, linking these to enlargement (Confidential documents).

In the end, the Amsterdam Council went on until the early hours of 18 June. As the summit was drawing to a close, the Presidency was under immense pressure to conclude the conference successfully. Over 3000 journalists were present at Amsterdam (Moravcsik and Nicolaïdis, 1999: 73) and anything other than a successful conclusion of the IGC would have represented a major blow to the political credibility of the European Union as a whole. As a result, the Presidency rushed through a large number of issues in the final hours of the summit, including flexibility, external economic relations, ECJ competencies for Europol and the question of granting the Union explicit legal personality (Confidential documents). Negotiations finally concluded at 3.35 a.m., despite the Presidency's original intention to bring the IGC to an end in the afternoon of 17 June (McDonagh, 1998: 194). For the Heads of State or Government it had been the longest end round of any IGC.

NOTES

1. In conducting research for this chapter, the author has been able to draw invaluable insight from a number of officials and diplomats involved in the negotiations leading to the Treaty of Amsterdam who generously agreed to be interviewed. For reasons of confidentiality, their names are not disclosed. The author would nevertheless like to express his gratitude, the persons concerned know who they are.

BIBLIOGRAPHY

Primary sources

Council of The European Union (1995), General Secretariat: *Report on the Functioning of the Treaty on European Union*. Luxembourg: Office of Official Publications.

European Commission (1995) *Report on the Operation of the Treaty on European Union*. SEC (95) final, Brussels, 10 May.

European Court of Justice (1995) *Report on Certain Aspects of the Application of the Treaty on European Union*. Luxembourg.

European Parliament (1995), Committee on Institutional Affairs: *Report on the Functioning of the Treaty on European Union with a view to the 1996 Intergovernmental Conference – Implementation and Development of the Union*. OJ C 151 19/07/1995.

European Parliament (1996) *White Paper on the 1996 IGC – Summary of Positions of the Member States*. Brussels.

Federal Republic of Germany and Republic of France (1996) *Franco-German Proposal on Flexibility*, 17 October 1996, CONF 3955/96.

Italian Presidency (1996) *Report of the Presidency on the State of the Negotiations in the Intergovernmental Conference*, 17 June 1996, CONF 3862/96.

Kohl, H. and J. Chirac (1995) *Common Letter to the President of the European Council*, 6 December 1995.

Presidency Conclusions (1993a) 'Copenhagen European Council', *Europe Documents*, No. 1844/45, 24 June.

Presidency Conclusions (1993b) 'Brussels European Council', *Agence Europe*, No. 6127, 12 December, 5–15.

Presidency Conclusions (1994) 'Corfu European Council', *Agence Europe*, No. 6259, 25 June, 5–17.

Presidency Conclusions (1995a) 'Cannes European Council', *Europe Documents*, No. 1942, 29 June.

Presidency Conclusions (1995b) 'Madrid European Council', *EU Bulletin*, 12, 9ff.

Presidency Conclusions (1996a) *Turin European Council*, General Secretariat of the Council of the European Union, REF: SN 100/96.

Presidency Conclusions (1996b) *Florence European Council*, General Secretariat of the Council of the European Union, REF: SN 300/96.

Presidency Conclusions (1996c) 'Dublin European Council (Dublin II)', *Agence Europe*, No. 6875, 15 December, 6–19.

Reflection Group (1995a) *Interim Report*, General Secretariat of the Council of the European Union, REF: SN 509/2/95 (REFLEX10) REV2.

Reflection Group (1995b) *Report*, General Secretariat of the Council of the European Union, REF: SN 520/1/95/REV1 (REFLEX 21).

United Kingdom (1996) *Memorandum of the United Kingdom on the European Court of Justice*, 22 July 1996, CONF 3883/96, LIMITE.

Secondary sources

Bourlanges, J-L. (1997) 'La Conférence intergouvernementale . . . ou comment s'en débarrasser?'. *Les Petites Affiches*, 33, 17 March, 19–22.

De Schoutheete de Tervarent, P. (1997) *L'avenir de l'Union: bilan et perspectives*. Speech given at a seminar organized by the Institute of European Studies of Louvain-la-Neuve on 5 December.

Devuyst, Y. (1998) 'Treaty reform in the European Union: the Amsterdam process'. *Journal of European Public Policy*, 615–31.

Dinan, D. (1998) 'Reflections on the IGCs'. In P-H. Laurent and M. Maresceau, *The State of the European Union, Vol. 4: Deepening and Widening*. Boulder, Co: Lynne Rienner Publishers.

Dinan, D. (1999) 'Treaty change in the European Union: the Amsterdam experience'. In L. Cram, D. Dinan and N. Nugent (eds), *Developments in the European Union*. London: Macmillan, 290–310.

Kortenberg, H. (1997) 'La négociation du Traité d'Amsterdam: Une vue cavalière'. *Revue Trimestrielle de Droit Européen*, 709–19.

Laursen, F. (1997) 'The lessons of Maastricht'. In G. Edwards and A. Pijpers, *The Politics of European Treaty Reform: The 1996 Intergovernmental Conference and Beyond*. London: Pinter.

Lindberg, L. and S. Scheingold (1970) *Europe's Would-be Polity: Patterns of Change in the European Community*. Englewood Cliffs, New Jersey: Prentice Hall.

Lodge, J. (1998) 'Negotiations in the European Union: the 1996 Intergovernmental Conference'. *International Negotiation*, 3, 481–505.

McDonagh, B. (1998) *Original Sin in a Brave New World: An Account of the Negotiation of the Treaty of Amsterdam*. Dublin: Institute of European Affairs.

Moravcsik, A. and Kalypso N. (1999) 'Explaining the Treaty of Amsterdam: interests, influence, institutions'. *Journal of Common Market Studies*, 37(1), 59–85.

Patijn, M. (1997) 'The Dutch Presidency'. In The European Policy Centre, *Making Sense of the Amsterdam Treaty*, Brussels.

Petite, M. (1997) 'Le traité d'Amsterdam: ambition et réalisme'. *Revue du March Unique Européen*, 17ff.

Schmuck, O. (1996) 'Die Regierungskonferenz 1996/97: Reformbedarf, Rechtsgrundlagen, Tagesordnung, Erwartungen'. In M. Jopp and O. Schmuck, *Die Reform der Europäischen Union: Analysen – Positionen – Dokumente zur Regierungskonferenz 1996/97*. Bonn: Europa Union Verlag.

Weidenfeld, W. (ed.) (1998) *Amsterdam in der Analyse*. Gütersloh: Bertelsmann Stiftung.

Wessels, W. (1996) 'Weder Vision noch Verhandlungspaket: der Bericht der Reflexionsgruppe im integrationspolitischen Trend'. *Integration*, 14–24.

Press

Agence Europe (1996) 'The arrangement for involving the EP in the IGC's work is sufficiently flexible to enable it to make its voice heard'. No. 6699, 30 March, p. 6.

ANNEXE I: MEMBERS OF THE IGC REFLECTION GROUP*

Ministers of State

Werner Hoyer	Germany
Carlos Westendorp	Chairman, Spain
Michel Barnier	France
Gay Mitchell	Ireland
Michiel Patijn	Netherlands
Gunnar Lund	Sweden
David Davis	United Kingdom

Member of the European Commission

Marcelino Oreja Aguirre	European Commission

Senior or retired officials or professors

Franklin Dehousse	Belgium	University Professor
Niels Ersboell	Denmark	Former Secr. Gen. of Council
Stephanos Statathos	Greece	Former Ambassador
Silvio Fagiolo	Italy	Foreign Ministry Official
Joseph Weyland	Luxembourg	Ambassador
Manfred Scheich	Austria	Permanent Rep. to the EU
André Gonçalves Pereira	Portugal	University Professor
Ingvar S. Melin	Finland	Former Minister

Members of the European Parliament

Elmar Brok	European People's Party
Elisabeth Guigou	Party of European Socialists

* Source: McDonagh (1998: 231)

ANNEXE II: MEETINGS OF THE IGC REFLECTION GROUP*

Date	Place
3 June 1995	Taormina
13/14 June 1995	Luxembourg
30 June/1 July 1995	Toledo
10/11 July 1995	Strasbourg
24/25 July 1995	Brussels
4/5 September 1995	Brussels
11/12 September 1995	Brussels
25/26 September 1995	Brussels
2/3 October 1995	Luxembourg
23/24 October 1995	Brussels
26 November 1995	Madrid
5/6 December 1995	Brussels

* Source: Weidenfeld (1998: 225–30)

ANNEXE III: MEMBERS OF THE IGC REPRESENTATIVES GROUP*

Ministers of State

Werner Hoyer   Germany
Michel Barnier[1]   France
Michiel Patijn   Chairman January to June 1997, Netherlands
Francisco Seixas da Costa   Portugal
Gunnar Lund   Sweden

Member of the European Commission

Marcelino Oreja Aguirre   European Commission

Permanent Representatives

Philippe de Schouteete de   Belgium
  Tervarent
Javier Elorza Cavengt   Spain
Jean-Jacques Kasel   Luxembourg
Manfred Scheich   Austria
Antti Satuli   Finland
Stephen Wall[2]   United Kingdom

Others

Niels Ersboell   Denmark
Yannis Kranidiotis MEP[3]   Greece
Noel Dorr   Chairman July to December 1996, Ireland
Silvio Fagiolo   Chairman March to June 1996, Italy

* Source: McDonagh (1998: 233)
1. Replaced by French Permanent Representative Pierre de Boissieu after the French general election in June 1997.
2. Replaced by Doug Henderson, Minister of State, after the UK general election in May 1997.
3. Later replaced by Stelios Perrakis, Secretary General for European Affairs at the Greek Foreign Ministry.

ANNEXE IV: MEETINGS OF THE FOREIGN MINISTERS*

Date	*Place*
20 April 1996	Luxembourg
13 May 1996	Brussels
17 June 1996	Rome
15 July 1996	Brussels
7/8 September 1996	Tralee
1 October 1996	Luxembourg
28 October 1996	Luxembourg
25 November 1996	Brussels
6 December 1996	Brussels
20 January 1997	Brussels
24 February 1997	Brussels
15/16 March 1997	Apeldoorn
25 March 1997	Rome
6/7 April 1997	Noordwijk
29/30 April 1997	Luxembourg
20 May 1997	The Hague
2/3 June 1997	Luxembourg

* Source: Weidenfeld (1998: 235–69)

ANNEXE V: MEETINGS OF THE IGC REPRESENTATIVES GROUP*

Date	Place
1/2 April 1996	Brussels
3 April 1996	Luxembourg
2/3 May 1996	Brussels
6/7 May 1996	Brussels
14/15 May 1996	Brussels
21/22 May 1996	Brussels
30/31 May 1996	Brussels
6/7 June 1996	Brussels
5/6/7 July 1996	Cork
16/17 July 1996	Brussels
22/23 July 1996	Brussels
3/4 September 1996	Brussels
16/17 September 1996	Brussels
23/24 September 1996	Brussels
7/8 October 1996	Brussels
15/16 October 1996	Brussels
21/22 October 1996	Brussels
12/13 November 1996	Brussels
18/19 November 1996	Brussels
3 December 1996	Brussels
13/14 January 1997	Amsterdam
27/28 January 1997	Brussels
10/11 February 1997	Brussels
17/18 February 1997	Brussels
3/4 March 1997	Brussels
10/11 March 1997	Brussels
14/15 April 1997	Brussels
21/22 April 1997	Brussels
5/6 May 1997	Brussels
16/17 May 1997	Maastricht
26/27/28 May 1997	Brussels
4/5 June 1997	Brussels
9/10 June 1997	Brussels

* Source: Weidenfeld (1998: 235–70)

CHAPTER 2

THE INSTITUTIONAL REFORMS OF AMSTERDAM: A VIEW FROM THE EUROPEAN PARLIAMENT

Elmar Brok

INTRODUCTION

Over the past few years, the attitude of individual citizens in some Member States towards the European Union has changed from benevolent indifference to a more fundamental scepticism. The ratification process of the Maastricht Treaty demonstrated that quite clearly. This change in public attitude was evident again in the 1999 elections to the European Parliament. Not only was the 49.9 per cent voter turnout lower than average, but domestic politics dominated the debate to the extent that European issues were sidelined. In view of the implementation of the Amsterdam Treaty, one has to ask the question whether this public attitude has changed once again, this time in favour of the European Union, or, if not, why the EU, which has provided us with more than 40 years of peace, freedom and prosperity, is being met with such scepticism by so many of its citizens? Or, to put the question the other way around, which conditions in politics are determinant factors for the acceptance of its actors, institutions and decisions, and how can these be influenced in a positive way?

My claim is that there are three essential determinants for acceptance. Well within the tradition of mathematical terms in European politics – just to mention core Europe, the Europe of concentric circles or the Europe of variable geometry – I would like to put my theory into an equation: transparency + democracy + efficiency = acceptance. Under the premise that the degree of acceptance of the European Union is relatively low, this equation means at the same time that the EU lacks these three factors: transparency, democracy and efficiency. Aware that a certain dilemma – on the one hand the aim of 'an ever closer union of the peoples of Europe', on the other hand the lack of acceptance by these peoples – had to be solved to prevent an erosion of the democratic base of the EU, the heads of state and government focused on the Intergovernmental Conference of

1996, making efficiency, transparency and democracy its priorities. The IGC thus aimed at scrutinizing the EU's institutions, decision-making procedures and politics and reforming them if appropriate.

THE SITUATION BEFORE AMSTERDAM

The lack of transparency is in several respects responsible for the acceptance problem. On the one hand, the nearly impenetrable labyrinth of competences, procedures and actors enabled the national and regional governments to sell EU politics to the public in a poor way. They tend to blame most of the 'negative' aspects of Community law on the EU, while claiming the credit for the positive impact of EU policies and regulations, which are, in any case, nationalized through their own implementation measures. When public contempt focuses on over-regulation, over-harmonization and autocracy from Brussels national politicians often conceal the fact that these directives and regulations are not the prerogative of a super-bureaucracy in Brussels, but do, in fact, represent the powers of the Council of Ministers, which, of course, is composed of government representatives of each member state. Europe's politicians also fail to adequately explain that the implementation of EU directives and regulations is the responsibility of Member States' governments and national parliaments, who may go well beyond the intended limits of a measure passed at the European level.

However, national politicians have this possibility of transferring their political toxic waste to Brussels only because the complicated institutional structure blocks the view on who is responsible for what and when in Europe. This makes European decisions unsuitable for media coverage, and this leads to little coherent information appearing during the various stages of legislation. Since information is scarce, the average citizen cannot follow the EU legislative process as he or she does in national affairs. The lack of personification, the absence of political cross-border personalities in Europe, makes it even more difficult for the citizens to understand the forming of the political will than it already is on the national level. The question of responsibility is not easy to answer at the European level. EU insiders, of course, can answer this, but the outsiders only see a faceless decision coming from Brussels, attributed to an anonymous super-techno structure. The person and even the exact institutional level responsible for a specific decision are left unclear. Therefore, the well-tried plot of dealing with exactly this person or level in national politics does not work on the European level. There is a void which is filled by ignorance. Ignorance breeds fear, and fear can be stirred by populists and opponents of

European integration so it becomes rejection – not only of a single regulation, but of the European Union as a whole.

On the other hand, a lack of publicity has frequently created prejudices and uncertainties. Secret diplomacy at intergovernmental conferences and summit meetings, vitally important decisions behind closed doors, cryptic laws the volume of a telephone directory – none of this adds to transparency of European politics and consequently to more acceptance.

The often mentioned democratic deficit is another 'negative factor' in our equation. Therefore, the 1996–7 IGC devoted a lot of time to the discussion of democratic control of the institution's actions. The importance of effective democratic scrutiny increases when the Member States vote by majority in the Council, because then Member States can be outvoted. For that reason, one of the main requests of the European Parliament in the IGC was to increase majority voting in the Council and to combine this with the use the co-decision procedure[1] under which the European Parliament decides on an equal basis with the Council.

Regarding the demand for efficiency, political developments play an important role, especially the significant change in the European security framework that has taken place since the fall of the Berlin wall in 1989, and its further repercussions. The East–West conflict, which demonstrated the necessity of close cooperation between Western European democracies, was once seen by citizens as a major *raison d'être* for European integration. So to many it now seems to be an issue that belongs more to the past than to the future. And at the same time, the war in the former Yugoslavia revealed a depressing powerlessness regarding the ability to end bloody conflicts in other parts of Europe. But in order to increase acceptance, it is most necessary to show clearly that the EU is an indispensable instrument for the successful solution of problems, even after the Cold War. This applies in areas that concern virtually every Member State: protecting peace and internal security, safeguarding common economic interests, fighting unemployment and protecting the environment. As the capacity to act is an indispensable factor in the legitimacy and the acceptance of the institutions, and as all these tasks have to be solved, it is most important that the EU is efficient, that there is an appropriate institutional framework. Efficiency therefore means overhauling the decision-making structures, especially the increase of majority votes in the Council. But also the aim of reducing and tightening of procedures played a major role during the IGC.

To increase efficiency, it was also important to abandon a failed path of European history – so-called 'intergovernmental cooperation'. Experiences with the Maastricht Treaty, which codified the extensive use of this method of policy-making outside the usual Community mechanisms, showed that this way a coherent and effective policy is not possible. That is why both of the intergovernmental policy areas – cooperation in justice and home affairs and foreign and security policy – were subject to extensive scrutiny in Amsterdam. Moreover, these policy areas are of particular importance to the citizens and therefore especially suited to influence acceptance positively.

THE 1996/97 IGC: THE EQUATION WORKS OUT

The IGC had a multiple task to perform. First of all, it was intended to correct some of the weak points in the Maastricht Treaty in the field of internal structures and procedures, and also in the field of legal and domestic policy, as well as in foreign and security policy. At the same time, it was intended to clear the way for enlarging the EU. The results thus have to be judged by the yardstick of these difficult and complex tasks. Being aware that acceptance by a majority of citizens is imperative in a democracy, the Heads of State or Government set out, above all, to increase transparency, democracy and efficiency via reforming institutions and decision-making procedures. They partly succeeded, and partly they failed.

Of special importance with regard to the *transparency* issue is the decrease of decision-making procedures by eliminating the cooperation procedure. In the future, it will be much easier for citizens to understand who is responsible for what. As was mentioned before, it had been quite usual for Member States to eliminate their toxic political waste via 'Brussels', even if one or more Member States had been responsible for a specific regulation. Because of the new transparency – generated by fewer and tightened procedures – this temptation will be reduced, because member states must now fear to be caught 'in the act'. It should also be noted that the Amsterdam Treaty now also provides the opportunity to get information about how every Member State voted in the Council. A new Article 207 was introduced into the EC Treaty, which concerns *inter alia* the access of the public to Council documents. It provides that when the Council acts in its legislative capacity, the results of votes and explanations of votes as well as statements in the minutes shall be made public.

The European Parliament will work for a new regulation within the framework of the new transparency article, which would introduce public protocols of the final sessions in the Council that clearly indicate who voted for what and why. The Amsterdam Treaty also brings about more direct improvements as far as openness and transparency are concerned. The principle of openness is now included in the general objectives of the Union, accompanied by a new legal basis granting access to Council,

Commission and Parliament documents, with the respective general rules and limits to be laid down with Parliament's co-decision within two years (Article 255 TEC). The EP will use this right to arrange for rules as generous and as unrestricted as possible.

As regards reducing the so-called *democratic deficit*, an extension of the co-decision procedure and a substantial improvement of the EP's rights were top priority. The Parliament indeed became the winner of the negotiations, getting 23 new cases of co-decision added to the only 15 cases under the Maastricht Treaty. A simplified co-decision procedure also makes Parliament and Council equal partners in the larger part of normal secondary legislation. The Parliament was also granted the 'power of the purse', in other words the right to adopt the budget and control its execution in the Common Foreign and Security Policy (CFSP), and the right of consent in appointing the Commission President as well as imposing sanctions on member states who violate human rights. In short: important decisions within the Union can no longer be taken without the Parliament in the future. The EP has thus finally gained the status of a full-blown Parliament. It will be important to emphasize this achievement at the national level since many people still have in mind a different picture of the EP which results from the days when today's Parliament was a 'European Parliamentary Assembly' with mere consultory functions and no decision-making power.

With regard to ameliorating *efficiency*, reforms of decision-making procedures and internal structures were agreed on. Efficiency is inseparably connected with the issue of institutional adjustments necessary for enlargement, because the Union's inner structures which had originally been designed for only six Member States would not withstand the pressure of 20 or more Member States. Many questions were at stake at the IGC: how can it be ensured that the Union can function properly with more members and more competences? What kind of working methods will be necessary, how many members should the EU institutions have, what rules are needed for their decision-making? How can an enlarged Union with more citizens be put on a more reliable democratic basis?

The Heads of State and Government agreed in Amsterdam on the following institutional adjustments.

The *Commission*, whose number of members was for the time being fixed at an upper limit of 20, was given a bigger potential through the strengthening of its President, who – as already mentioned – will be co-elected by the EP in the future (Article 214(2) TEC). These innovations will strengthen the President's democratic legitimation and make the role more that of a European chief of government. Election as such gets more political, because in the long run both of the big European party federations can even start their election campaign with an own candidate. The nomination of the other Commission members must now be done in agreement with the designated Commission President. The Commission will in the future have to work under the political leadership of the President, who has a wide area of discretion to divide and take back portfolios, and who will have, similar to the Federal Chancellor in Germany, the power to determine the policy guidelines. Given the crucial role of the Commission in pushing the European integration process, these reforms increase the potential of the Commission, whose efficiency depends rather on an improved internal structure than on its size.

Qualified majority voting in the *Council* has been extended on 11 new and five already existing treaty provisions, though not in decisive areas like taxation policy or the structural funds. This very limited extension was without doubt the most unsatisfying result of the IGC. The EP has always taken the view that only a substantial extension of the scope of majority voting without lifting (preferably even lowering) the threshold for a qualified majority will keep the Community from degenerating into some higher form of a free-trade-zone in the longer run, especially in view of enlargement. It is simply a matter of mathematical probability that the more Member States we have in the Union, the more likely it is that, whatever the particular subject, at least one country will exercise its veto, and if the Union is enlarged, there is a danger that ultimately no decisions will be possible any longer. In the Amsterdam negotiations the attempt to agree on a new weighting of votes in the Council failed altogether. Would the current weighting of votes be perpetuated beyond enlargement, majority voting would become unbalanced. It would be possible, for example, that a decision is taken with the majority of weighted votes, but that these votes represent a mere 50 per cent of the EU's population. This problem of democratic representativity could be addressed by either a new weighting of votes or the introduction of a 'double majority'. In the latter case, it would have also to be checked whether the votes represent a sufficient population majority. A decision one way or the other must be taken before the next enlargement round.

Important in view of efficiency is also the concept of so-called *closer cooperation* or *flexibility*, allowing a group of Member States to move ahead in line with the Union's objectives, within the Union's institutional framework and allowing non-participants to rejoin them whenever they are able and ready. The European Parliament has always insisted that this concept must not be used as a pretext for not moving ahead on the main institutional issues and must not threaten the *acquis communautaire*. In the end, the respective new treaty provisions are designed in a way that fears concerning a possible break-up of the Union's common legal order seem to be unfounded: the Commission plays a decisive role in the triggering-off and control of such cases, and the correct application of the relevant institutional treaty provisions for the respective field of action will be guaranteed by Parliament's participation in the decision-making, control by the European Court of Justice and the Court of Auditors. Besides Monetary Union, the only example of use so far is the inclusion of the Schengen Agreement into the Treaty without the United Kingdom and Ireland taking part, due to their special geographic situation. It remains to be seen whether there will be, under these restricted conditions, more cases of application.

Especially important, with view to acceptance, is the question of *internal security* in the EU. This problem becomes even bigger after enlargement towards the East. The transfer of important areas of Justice and Home Affairs from mere intergovernmental cooperation to the first pillar shows that the Heads of State and Government consider the community method to be in the end more effective than intergovernmental cooperation. Given the well-known reluctance by some national and regional authorities, especially in these areas, to transfer competences to another level than their own, it is unfortunate that unanimity is still required in these areas for the transfer to qualified majority voting after five years, rendering decision-making more difficult than the introduction of qualified majority voting now or an automatic transfer after a fixed period of time. It is however, more important to keep to the right method of improvements with a built-in follow-up in a next step than to reach limited progress without perspectives for further development in the future. The agreed communautarization as such is, therefore, a far more important step than, for example, the introduction of qualified majority voting under the rules of intergovernmental cooperation in the third pillar would have been. This is particularly true since the transfer into the first pillar, the Community sphere, brings new competences for the Commission – its right to initiate proposals taking into account the view of the Union as a whole, the European Court of Justice, and the European Parliament. It has been agreed that in five years a decision will have to be taken to transfer asylum, immigration and the other policy areas listed under new Title IV TEC[2] to the co-decision procedure. As far as the remaining third pillar is concerned, objectives, instruments and single fields of action have been defined in a much clearer way than before, including detailed provisions for development of operational competences for EUROPOL. A new instrument, the so-called 'framework decision' (Article 34(2)(b) TEU), has been introduced, which is similar to a community guideline and, with respect to the traditional ways of operating of police or justice forces, leaves the actual implementation of a measure to the national level.

Gaining the ability to act efficiently in foreign, security and defence policy is also an important task of the EU if it does not want to be regarded by its own citizens as a paper tiger. What the wars in former

Yugoslavia have clearly demonstrated is the fact that the EU has, despite its economic power, not enough strength in foreign and security affairs, not enough of a common will or the ability to react properly to a war in its immediate neighbourhood. This made Common Foreign and Security Policy (CFSP) an important issue on the agenda of the IGC, and, in fact, considerable progress has been made there. External representation of the Union can be enhanced by the new role of the Secretary General of the Council and the new Troika-formula, including – apart from the Secretary General and the respective national foreign minister of the Member State holding the presidency – the Commissioner responsible for foreign policy. These changes are a good basis for improving the continuity of the Union's external representation and the coherence between first and second pillar, i.e. foreign economic and foreign policy. The new Policy Planning and Early Warning unit may, if properly staffed and including Commission personnel, produce an added value by taking into account in its work the view and the interest of the Union as a whole and not only, as has too often been the case, basing proposals on the lowest common denominator of 15 independent foreign ministries with differing interests. To ensure this, staff for this unit should be selected under the responsibility of 'Mr CFSP' and the Commissioner responsible for the CFSP.

It is still premature to judge whether the revisions concerning the new decision-making procedures will in practice really produce the intended qualitative step forward. These procedures still do not prevent uncooperative Member States from blocking decisions. There is no way to effectively overcome any single Member State stiffly defending a 'national interest' up to the level of Heads of State and Governments. Other improvements could be undermined, if the governments of member states do not adapt their attitudes to the new treaty context. It will therefore depend on the way of application of the new regulatory framework and lastly on the political will for cooperation, whether or not the Union's external action will indeed gain in efficiency and visibility. In this context, one may regret that no agreement was found at the end to grant a legal personality to the European Union. As a minimal solution, the presidency can by unanimous vote be authorized to negotiate and conclude international agreements (Article 24 TEU).

On defence, links between WEU and EU have been tightened by including the so-called Petersberg-tasks of the WEU – humanitarian and peace-keeping actions – into the objectives of the EU treaty and thereby granting the European Council the power to determine the policy guidelines as regards the WEU. The aim of a possible future integration of the WEU into the EU is mentioned 'should the European Council so decide' (Article 17(1) TEU) by unanimity, as is the case for those Member States which see their common defence realized in NATO.

To get back to the already mentioned thought on the EU as a 'problem-solving instrument': with the new provisions on Justice and Home Affairs, and CFSP, the EU is clearly moving in the right direction by taking up appropriate structures and procedures that enhance its ability to act. There are other new provisions in the Treaty concerning issues which are especially relevant for the *citizens* of Europe, and therefore likely to increase acceptance if properly made use of. The Social Protocol has been fully integrated into the Treaty. An employment chapter has been introduced, the aim of which is, *inter alia*, to coordinate national employment policies, which is undoubtedly a vital issue (Title VIII TEU). As a result, employment policy has become one of the macro-economic objectives in the Union. Furthermore, the fact that the Council of Europe's Social Charter of 1961 and the European Council's Social Charter of 1989 have been included not merely in the preamble, but also in the Social Chapter itself, means that fundamental rights have become the foundation of Community legislation. In this way, it will be possible to monitor, on the basis of the law, whether they are being applied as a foundation of Community legislation and in its implementation. There has also been an enhancement of fundamental rights. Not only has the Council of Europe's Convention for the Protection of Human Rights and Fundamental Freedoms become a foundation for the Treaty, and an obligatory orientation for EU institutions, but some specific fundamental rights have also been introduced: an anti-discrimination clause covering sex, age, religion and disability; the equality of women and men even outside the world of work; data protection and so on (Article 13 TEC). The Treaty not only includes the commitment to respect Fundamental Rights, but also introduces the competence of the European Court of Justice and the possibility to impose sanctions on member states violating those rights. Thus there is now also an intra-Community instrument for monitoring whether all the member states do in fact comply with the Council of Europe's Convention.

These provisions, among others, turn the Treaty of Amsterdam into a treaty of social balance and alleviate the fears of those who saw in its predecessors mainly the work of economic institution builders in ivory towers without contact to the real world. There is a declaration assuring churches of non-intervention into their traditional status within Member States. The need for sustainable development, and better consumer protection, has been introduced into the 'objectives of the Union' and all Community policies. It will be easier in the future to introduce higher environmental standards within one member state than the Union as a whole. Moreover, there have been steps taken to strengthen existing community policies, like the safeguarding and supporting of cultural diversity, sports, voluntary services or animal protection in the Union.

Given the alarming employment situation in nearly all of the Member

States, and the fact that this problem is, naturally, one of the biggest concern of citizens, the new provisions on employment offer a big chance to convince citizens that the Union takes care of their worries. A high employment level is declared an objective of the Union (Article 2 TEC); the employment situation is to be considered when fixing the broad guidelines of the economic policies of the Member States; a legal basis for a coordinated employment strategy is being implemented into the Treaty; guidelines which the Member States shall take into account in their employment policies shall be drawn up each year, and there will be an annual report evaluating national measures (Article 28 TEC). The Council may adopt incentive measures designed to encourage cooperation between Member States and to support their action in the field of employment (Article 159 TEC). The latter proves that competence and responsibility for the employment situation rest with the Member States.

The new protocol on subsidiarity codifies a practice already followed since the Maastricht Treaty. The Union acts only if both of the following two conditions are met: a task cannot be adequately dealt with on the national/regional level; the Union can deal with this task question in a better way than lower levels of governance. As subsidiarity is a legally binding principle that concerns the relationship between the EU as an entity and the Member States as incumbents of national sovereignty, it touches the institutional structure of the Union at its very core. Perhaps more than anything else, the term 'subsidiarity' symbolizes democracy, transparency, efficiency and closeness to the citizens. Since its introduction into the Maastricht Treaty, there has arisen a great amount of controversy as to its definition and application between the levels involved. The new protocol now solves some of the interpretation problems of the principle by giving clear and detailed instructions as to how to examine intended legislation in view of its compatibility with the principle. The Treaty also includes, in a declaration to the protocol, that the division of competences within the Member States remains entirely at their disposition according to their constitutions and traditions. It also states that the implementation of community regulations shall in principle be the responsibility of Member States in accordance with their internal arrangements.

SUGGESTIONS FOR THE FUTURE

As long as the Amsterdam reforms have not yet been fully implemented it is too early to decide whether they improve transparency, democracy and efficiency, and therefore acceptance. Doubtless, the new treaty offers a remarkable potential in this respect. Whether the new provisions fulfil their tasks will depend considerably on the political will of Member States not to leave the improvements as mere lip services in the Treaty, but to fill them with life.

Immediately after the end of the negotiations in Amsterdam, the Heads of State or Government admitted that some important institutional questions had not been solved. Due to the existential importance of these reforms for the enlargement process, this remains to be done before the next enlargement. Those questions concern *inter alia* the weighting of votes in the Council, the scope of majority voting or the composition of the Commission. In a protocol to the Amsterdam Treaty, it was therefore fixed that at least one year before the membership of the European Union exceeds 20, another IGC shall be convened in order to carry out a comprehensive review of the Treaty provisions on the composition and functioning of the institutions. In a declaration to that protocol, Belgium, France and Italy observe that the Treaty does not meet the need for substantial progress towards reinforcing the institutions. Considering that such reinforcement is an indispensable condition for the conclusion of the first accession negotiations, they underline that a significant extension of qualified majority voting forms part of the relevant factors which should be taken into account.

The issue of extending majority voting in the Council is without doubt the decisive question as regards the capacity to act and efficiency. Without substantial improvements in this area, the Union will not be able to cope with enlargement. Especially when dealing with issues that have a financial impact, clinging to unanimity could be counterproductive, because it gives every Member State the opportunity to sell their consent at a high price. As a consequence, a wise allocation of funds is not possible.

The coming IGC will give the opportunity for further improvements regarding transparency, democracy and acceptance. First experiences with the new Treaty provisions will by then be made, and the degree of acceptance of the European Union and its policies will by then have been tested via opinion polls.

With regard to efficiency, transparency and democratization of the work of the institutions, there are already some perspectives for another reform of their internal structures.

The structure and working methods of the European Commission were established when the European Union had only six Member States. For a Union that consists of now 15, and soon 20 or more Member States, reforms have to be made. For example, it has to be considered how its efficiency can be increased in a way to achieve a better management of programmes. Its organizational structure must therefore be improved. Concerning the number of commissioners, 'junior commissioners' without portfolios could be appointed, or the posts of Directors-General could be upgraded to a similar level as that of the German state secretary. The necessity of such deliberations becomes obvious when regarding the current splitting of foreign affairs into several independent directorates – divided by geographical aspects, or by the type of work they are doing: development policy, humanitarian aid, foreign trade policy ... this needs to be rationalized. The question of the number of Commissioners is inseparably linked to a change of vote weighting in the Council. Theoretically, it is therefore possible that if an agreement on a new weighting of votes fails again, the number of Commissioners also will be left open.

There are similar problems with the future composition of the European Court of Justice and the European Court of Auditors. As it was the case with all European institutions, they had so far to have at least one member from every Member State. Every increase of members could burden the efficiency and functioning of these institutions. With view to the coming enlargement there are two possibilities being discussed: either increase the number of members while at the same time carry out internal reforms, or limit the number of members while at the same time introducing a system of rotation for the Member States. I prefer the first possibility because it is easier to achieve. Also, internal reforms always give the possibility of improving now and then outdated structures with a view to making them more efficient. The competences of the Court of Auditors are increased by the Amsterdam Treaty. This possibly demands a reform of working methods anyway, so that this can be combined with a reform regarding enlargement.

The European Parliament needs to work on how it determines its priorities. For the time being, it sometimes sets up priorities as if it was still 1980, the EP being still being the 'European Parliamentary Assembly' without decision-making power.

The Council is also in need of reforms. It is the least effective of all European organs. Improvements start with quite down-to-earth changes: is the current seating plan at square tables still appropriate? Shouldn't a parliamentary seating plan be chosen, as in the German Bundesrat or in the Swiss Ständerat, which would also change the form of the debates to a more parliamentary style. To enhance effectiveness and transparency, the General Affairs Council should be abandoned in favour of a Foreign Affairs Council and a Legislation Council. The European Parliament will try to see to it that, in the future, the minutes of the final Council session on a certain issue will be published so that everybody can see who voted how and why.

Finally, the form of Intergovernmental Conferences themselves must be reviewed. After two years of preparation and negotiation on the revision of the Maastricht Treaty, the question arises whether the method of Intergovernmental Conferences is still the most effective and otherwise appropriate way to initiate and conclude reforms to the Treaty. But, while the Treaty itself suggests an IGC as the means for reforms, the experience of the two-years-lasting IGC has clearly shown the limits of this method. With already 15 governments participating, the mere technical challenge for the presidencies and the secretariat is immense, and this will certainly increase after enlargement. Also, over long periods the negotiations are dominated by national officials, supervised by their ministries, doing a brilliant professional job, but still struggling with too many technocratic details and too strongly insisting that their national prerogatives should not be touched. In the future, these IGCs should become more political, i.e. by recruiting a third of its members from Member States' governments, a third from national members of parliament (weighted by the size of countries) and a third of European MEPs. This would be an important step to democratize IGCs.

A positive aspect of the outcome of the IGC are the advance in Justice and Home Affairs. The decision to 'communautarize' important parts of this policy area leads to more transparency through standardization of the methods of action, more democracy through the involvement of the EP and the other Community institutions and more efficiency through the use of the normal Community procedures.

In CFSP the increased use of majority voting, the reform of the Troika and the creation of the new Policy Planning and Early Warning Unit as well as appointing the Secretary General to exercise functions of the High Representative for CFSP will all together increase the Union's capacity to act, its continuity and manifestation as well as its united performance. The permanently changing representatives of CFSP did not enhance its credibility. Including the Commission and the Secretary General of the Council will ensure a European 'personalization' and its continuity. More-over, the inclusion of the Commission into the Troika and of Commission officials into the Policy Planning and Early Warning Unit will lead to a significantly increased consideration of the interests of the Union as a whole. The staff of the new Unit, for example, will observe international developments, report them to the Council and submit specific options for action. In the future, the foreign ministers will therefore be in possession of uniform dossiers with assessments of the status quo which carry also the mark of the independent Community institution, the Commission. They can thus start their deliberations from a uniform basis. This way, the new Unit could become the nucleus in which a common political will can develop. This big new potential must however be used by Member States in order to really achieve a common added value instead of the lowest common denominator of 15 separate analyses. Above all, a blockade through a single, non-cooperative Member State will be harder, although this still remains possible. It must be ensured, especially through the appointment of staff, that the new unit in fact represents the common added value, instead of becoming a 'Coreper III'.

Not only in CFSP, but in every other policy area that has been improved by Amsterdam, much will depend on the political will of Member States to take full advantage of the new provisions. Those necessary reforms that have been left unaccomplished in Amsterdam must be made up for in the next IGC. The most important reform is, as was said before, a substantial increase in majority voting. Without it, the effectiveness of all the other changes, improvements and innovations could be undermined. Even worse, the enlargement process could seriously hamper the integration process, if not paralyse it altogether. The European Union does not need new competences, but it is in urgent need of the instruments to make full and best possible use of its existing competences. With the ever-looming veto, this is impossible.

NOTES

1. Now Article 251 TEC.
2. On the 'area of freedom, security and justice'.

CHAPTER 3

AMSTERDAM: SUCCESS OR FAILURE? A PERSONAL VIEW

Franklin Dehousse

My memories about the Intergovernmental Conference (IGC) are quite distinct. I remember Carlos Westendorp presiding over the so-called Reflection Group and explaining in 1995 that 'it is indispensable to maintain the present institutional balance'. This sentence found its way directly in the report of the Group. I also remember Michiel Patijn, last president of the IGC group, asking me during the signing of the treaty in 1997, 'why did we fail?' The more I think about it, the more I believe we failed, at least in the institutional reform, precisely because all Member States (Belgium included) could not – and cannot yet – contemplate the idea of a new institutional balance. This reluctance was itself a reflection of a very conservative climate.

I am prejudiced, of course. From the start, I pleaded that it was necessary to envisage deep institutional changes. I repeatedly joked about the reflection group whose only ability was to present a reflection of the reality and not the reality. We were preparing a treaty that had to provide adequate instruments and mechanisms for the management of a single market, a single currency, an internal security system and a foreign policy on a continent divided by 2000 years of internecine wars. All this with 27 Member States (and probably more). It is sheer madness to believe that this is possible with an institutional setting created in 1957 mainly in order to manage a common market between six relatively homogeneous Member States.

This does not mean that the Amsterdam Treaty is a complete failure. It simply means that we have missed at least one of our objectives. Nevertheless, this failure is worrying since it concerns the most essential challenge of the future: enlargement. The European Council of Berlin in March 1999 revealed that, basically, the situation had not changed. Berlin was, as a matter of fact, a remake of Amsterdam. In Amsterdam, the Heads of State or Government failed to prepare the institutions for enlargement. In Berlin, they failed to prepare the policies. This indicates the depth of the problem.

To evaluate the impact of the Treaty, we need to take a long-term approach, examining the place of this treaty in the evolution of the European treaties. Four basic questions must consequently been examined: What has not changed? What has really changed? Why have some elements not changed? What must we do to prepare the future?

WHAT HAS NOT CHANGED?

Different starting points can be taken to evaluate the results of the IGC. It is a huge success when compared to the Maastricht provisions. Compared to the various positions of the member states in 1995, it is a qualified success. Compared to the institutional agenda, it is largely a failure. Finally, for those more interested in deepening the economic and social integration, some changes deserve to be mentioned.

It has been widely stated that the changes concerning foreign policy were rather weak. This is quite right (Monar, 1997; Remacle, 1998: 183–207; Dehousse, 1998a). As regards the communantarization of immigration and asylum in the EC Treaty, some comments have been more generous. Personally, I do not see this as a huge change. From a legal perspective, it is probably impressive. But from a realist political point of view, the results will not be important. Basically, some Member States did not want a reform at all. Others wanted a reform, but did not know what to do with it. Others, finally, knew what they wanted to do, but could not accept the idea of a communautarization. All this explains the legal mess we are in. Can this produce a new policy? Personally, I doubt it. We shall soon discover that the Tampere program of 1999 cannot be implemented.

The provisions about EMU have not changed at all, and this has some significance. The IGC had been foreseen in 1996 to correct the defects that could have emerged from the launch of the third phase of EMU. Meanwhile, the launch itself was reported and the sequence in time was reversed.

Finally, the institutional setting has not fundamentally changed. The provisions regarding the Commission and the Parliament have been modified. This will probably mean considerable change for the functioning of the Commission (see below), and certainly increase the weight of the European Parliament. We must not underestimate the importance of the provisions concerning the role of the Commission's President. Elsewhere, following the Reflection Group's rather silent approach, the institutional balance has been globally preserved.

WHAT HAS REALLY CHANGED?

In ten years, the most important progresses will probably look different. I anticipate the employment chapter being important one day. Of course, there is a lot of propaganda in these provisions. Nevertheless, it allows the development of new Community programmes by qualified majority decisions. There are limits, but the most important ones are defined by reference to the budget, and the budget can be changed. If the European Union needs to develop a redistributive system to accompany the EMU in the future, this would be useful. This could one day become the technical basis of a new Keynesian policy.

Other potentially important texts concern the area of crime. Measures against fraud can, henceforth, be taken by the Community with a qualified majority. This is an enormous change, which brings the Community into the realm of penal affairs (in spite of a few precautions). This is essential for the sake of the Community's future credibility. The European budgetary programmes have developed considerably, but the managerial teams have not. Consequently, there is a lot of external consultancy. I was amazed to discover that the Commission had even given a contract to a private company for the surveillance of the Russian elections! In such a context, fraud cannot be avoided. This is a disaster waiting to happen. The Community must acquire a real ability to fight against fraud, otherwise it will be strongly attacked by the public opinion.

The new provisions governing Europol are also important, from that point of view. During the negotiation, it was surprising to see how little these provisions were discussed. Nevertheless, they represent a huge change in comparison with the Europol Convention of 1995. However, it will not be possible to implement them correctly in the present institutional setting of the third pillar.

Finally, an essential provision concerns the choice and the powers of the Commission's President. The European Parliament will have a stronger voice in the appointment of the President and the Commission. More fundamentally, the President will have a strong role in the choice of the Commissionners and the repartition of portfolios. My personal view is that this provision could become the cornerstone of an in-depth reform. It will nevertheless depend a lot on the subtlety of the President and the wisdom of the Parliament. In any case, the collective resignation of the Santer Commission in March 1999 created a marvellous opportunity to use this provision to its maximum potential. That this was not used at all by Romano Prodi is a reflection of the weak potential of Prodi, and not of the position.

WHY WAS IT SO DIFFICULT TO REFORM?

It is important to understand why the IGC missed its fundamental objective. There were a lot of reasons, of course. Nevertheless, most of them present a structural character. Consequently, one can expect that they will not have disappeared by the time of the next IGC.

The political context

Let's face it: the negotiation of Amsterdam was full of hidden fears. Considering the doubtful mood of public opinion, many people feared a remake of the Maastricht debate. They also feared some side-effects on the launch of the single currency, and of a new British obstruction. The British Conservative government at the time had been waging some kind of theological war about all European issues.

Finally, all member states feared the consequences of the enlargement. In that context, the institutional debate in Amsterdam became a catastrophy. It looked like a Moroccan souk, with a lot of people who cried but did not even know how to measure the carpets correctly. No one was ready to make sacrifices for an enlargement which remained far away and which was often not very popular. There was, in general, no political project which could have justified some concessions. All this explains why the Amsterdam Treaty is long in words, and short in deeds, especially in the institutional domain.

The weight of the intergovernmental procedure

Another problem relates to the intergovernmental nature of the process.[1] This increases the fragmented approach of negotiation. The role of the supranational organs (the Commission and the European Parliament) is also more limited. There were many threats relating to the national ratification process in various Member States. The Danish example was contagious. The impulsion is much weaker, and so is the pressure to conclude. This was especially the case because the supranational institutions were not only legally but also politically weak. The Santer Commission was much weaker than the Delors Commission in the Maastricht negotiation. The European Parliament had difficulties in defining its institutional projects.

One must not overestimate the importance of the procedure of negotiation of the Amsterdam Treaty. There was a clear lack of ambition, which reduced the impact of procedural constraints. But the procedure of the next negotiation should be considered very carefully because this IGC will have to make fundamental decisions regarding the nature of the institutions themselves.

The absence of a global institutional perspective

The lack of a global institutional design was a huge problem during the negotiation. It was interesting to notice that the institutional balance – traditionally one of the 'holy cows' of IGCs – was not preserved. The European Council was absorbed by the EMU. The ECOFIN Council was clearly becoming more powerful. The Commission was steadily weakening. Some of these evolutions were accidental. Most of them were not. It was obvious that enlargement would increase this drift. Nevertheless, no one had a clear picture about the future design of the institutions.

It was consequently more difficult to reach a compromise. The institutional topics were debated, in a piecemeal approach, separated from each other. Some member states established some links, between the reweighting of votes and the reform of the Commission, between the reweighting of votes and the extension of qualified majority voting, and between the extension of qualified majority voting and the co-decision procedure. But there was no vision of the future institutional system. Two fundamental questions should have been discussed. Can a continental European Union with much enlarged tasks keep its original design? If not, which alternative design could be used?

The absence of a global institutional design also appeared in the debate about strengthened cooperation. The 'closer cooperation' project was invented by some member states who 'wanted to do more'. It is the institutional translation of the political concept of the 'hard core'. It became linked to the 'English problem', that is, the British obstruction under the Thatcher and Major governments. Basically, it is an ambiguous project. To allow some of the Member States to organize new initiatives, in the setting of the Union, is in fact a way to circumvent the requirement of unanimity for the revision of the Treaties. This was not widely admitted during the negotiation, as a matter of fact it was often not even realized.

The absence of a global design appears in the institutional protocol of the Amsterdam Treaty. This protocol establishes a link between the reweighting of the votes and the number of Commissioners (Article 1). This link indicates that, for many Member States, Commissioners are seen as national representatives. This is certainly not in line with the concept of the founding fathers. Furthermore, if one follows this line of reasoning, one must also take the European Parliament into consideration. But this was not done, which is an interesting limitation. Conceptually, the link is a bad link. Politically, it is also a bad link. A new negotiation strictly based on the institutional protocol is bound to create hostility, since it will strongly oppose big and small Member States. We cannot have a new IGC where small Member States can only lose. That is one of the reasons why the next IGC will be more difficult than most people anticipate.[2]

We need to find a way to extend the scope of the future institutional negotiation, to give to all Member States the opportunity to find (and publicly present in the national ratification debates) positive returns. That is why it will be so important to take a global institutional perspective. We must find new ways to balance the interests of big and small Member States. The small Member States must accept the fact that the size of the population must be represented somewhere. The big Member States must accept the fact that the equality of the Member States must be represented somewhere.

From that point of view, one must not forget that the most difficult debate in the Philadelphia Convention was already the balance between smaller and larger states in the federation. The revision of the provision of the American Constitution about the equal representation of the federated states in the Senate practically requires unanimity of the federated states. The Amsterdam IGC was especially difficult, among other things because it was the first time that such a topic was discussed since 1957.

The overall conservative approach

The absence of a global institutional approach resulted largely from the will 'to preserve the institutional balance'. Most Member States were totally opposed to deep change. In Freudian vocabulary, this could be described as a repressed refusal of enlargement. Everybody spoke about doing it, and nobody about how to do it. No one wanted to lose representation. No one wanted to lose budgets. No one wanted to abandon pet projects.

This conservative approach was also obvious at the technical level. The European Parliament wanted the extension of the co-decision procedure, for example, but could not manage the obvious consequences. The co-decision procedure is cumbersome. It will become even more cumbersome after the next enlargements. We cannot extend it on a general basis, without trying to simplify the role of the Parliament and without trying to limit its scope to general principles.

From that point of view, agriculture provided a very good illustration. It was obvious that the European Parliament would not be able to take all the required decisions. Consequently, it was to invent a new way to divide this matter. The Parliament tried, but not very convincingly. This of course strengthened the opposition against its intervention in this domain.

The mechanical approach was also obvious as regards qualified majority voting. Generally, it was simply proposed to substitute unanimity by qualified majority voting. The solution is not so simple. Since the Treaties of Rome, provisions requiring qualified majority voting have generally been drafted with much more precision than provisions requiring unanimity. This distinction in drafting is of course very logical, since the Member States retain much more control on the use of provisions with unanimity.

The coordination of national social security systems provides a good example. It was obvious that general harmonization by qualified majority would create a threatening perspective. In this case, the scope of the provision should have been limited by the objective of facilitating the free movement of workers. However, this was not explored.

Basically, all new ideas were welcomed in this negotiation with strong suspicion. Even in Belgium (sometimes seen as the cradle of revolution by other Member States), many of my propositions were immediately discarded: the Commissioners' individual responsibility, the limitation of legislation to essential principles, the abandoning of minor and complementary competences of the Union, the use of super qualified majority for secondary treaty provisions.

The question of the individual responsibility of the Commissioners is especially interesting from that point of view. It was obvious that the collective responsibility of the Commission had become the perfect shield for mediocrity – or worse. In a rather mathematical way, each enlargement of the Union was going to dilute the individual responsibility. A collective dismissal motion by the European Parliament was the atomic bomb that nobody dared to use. After hearing (justified) objections about the need to protect the collegiality principle inside the Commission, I had devised a mechanism allowing the President of the Commission to determine whether a dismissal motion directed against a Commissioner was a matter of principle for the Commission or not. In this last case, the attacked Commissionner could be sacrificed to the European Parliament. This solution presented the added advantage to strengthen the President. It is interesting to note that myself and Michiel Patijn, were alone to defend such a principle in the so-called 'Reflection Group', which never had a serious debate about this. It is also interesting to note that the project was later buried by the head of the Belgian diplomacy, for political reasons that had absolutely nothing to do with the correct functioning of the institutions – but everything with the pure will to preserve the status quo (the final argument being – of course – that this would 'upset the institutional balance', which had precisely already been upset). After the collective resignation of the Santer Commission, the Belgian position suddenly changed. Everyone, needless to say, had suddenly forgotten that such an idea had ever been discussed.

WHAT MUST WE DO IN THE FUTURE?

The next IGC is coming, even if many Member States are not eager to contemplate this perspective. It will not correctly prepare the Union for enlargement, but it can hopefully reduce the structural mess we are in. The danger of failure is high (even if we do what we did in Amsterdam and Berlin: fail and declare success).

A real reflection about the implications of the enlargement

The implications of enlargement are underestimated everywhere. We need at least a serious analysis on this issue. This will be useful for negotiations, but also for national public opinion. This being said, such an analysis will be difficult to obtain. Most people who are or have been involved in the European circuit start from a bad position. Outsiders' opinions will not be easily accepted. We nevertheless know what is *not* needed: a report from the COREPER or a so-called Reflection Group whose members follow strictly the instructions of their government.

The impact of the next enlargement is heavily underestimated. The European institutions are already functioning badly. All institutions currently have serious managerial problems. The Agenda 2000 was a good illustration of these problems. The Council was unable to coordinate the debate correctly. Files were negotiated separately in the General Affairs Council, in the ECOFIN and in the Agriculture Council. Some meetings of the General Affairs Council were organized just for the sake of proving that this Council was still coordinating. The legitimacy of the Commission was decreasing constantly. During the last months of the negotiation, it became quasi non-existent. The European Parliament was unable to define, at the end of the process, a coordinated position on the Agenda 2000 amongst different parliamentary commissions involved.

The first result of all this is the tremendous growth of influence of the European Council. This growth is increasingly compromising the normal functioning of the institutions, among other things because everything is decided by consensus at that level. The result was obvious in Berlin. The love for pet projects and Christmas tree presents for everyone was still more ardent than in Amsterdam. Nevertheless, a second long-term tendency is the growth of influence of the European Parliament. This one is mechanical. It is the result of the Maastricht and the Amsterdam treaties. The problem of the Parliament is precisely to manage this increasing influence.

These are real difficulties, but there are still others. We have not yet seen the full implications of the single currency and of the Amsterdam

Treaty. To multiply both the Member States and the tasks of the European Union in such a context, without drastic reform, is the perfect recipe for disaster.

A more coordinated procedure

It will not be possible to find a way out of the constraints of Article 48 TEU. Unanimity and national ratification will be needed for all revisions. It is still possible to introduce greater coherence in the process by giving more technical responsibilities to the institutions which represent the Community's interests, i.e. the Parliament and the Commission.

In that context, it will also be important to associate the national Parliaments. Enlargement requires a fundamental reform of the institutions, especially concerning the representation of the Member States. Some governments will try, for understandable reasons, to present this as a 'technical revision'. This is nonsense. The representation of the Member States in the institutions is the hard core of the institutional system. This is as fundamental for the national sovereignty as the use of qualified majority voting. It is an illusion to imagine that this will be negotiated without major political debates in the Member States. There is therefore a need for strong coordination between the European Parliament and the national Parliaments on this issue.

A new institutional design: 'focus'!

Finally, we must come back to the two basic questions. Must we keep the original institutional design of the beginning? Is there an alternative design? My personal view is that the original institutional design cannot be maintained, for various political and technical reasons.

From the political point of view, the European Union has become the most important decision-making centre in all Member States. It has a constant direct impact on the daily life of citizens and enterprises. We cannot go on pretending this is basically a technical project managed according to diplomatic processes. In such a fundamental system, an institution needs democratic legitimacy – and democratic processes. The growth of influence of the European Council and the European Parliament is no happenstance. The first reason, therefore, why we cannot preserve the original institutional design is that it is already changing now.

From the technical point of view, the institutional system needs a strong managerial rebalancing. This may sound too much like a businesslike approach, but it would be very interesting to commission a report from McKinsey & Company (international management consultants) on the

European Union. I would even suggest a motto: 'Focus, Focus, Focus!' The motto applies to all institutions, and more generally to the Union.

The Council must ensure the representation of the Member States. This means, by the way, that any modification of the reweighting of the votes must be discussed very carefully by the small Member States. Qualified majority decision must become the rule, even in minor treaty matters. The Council should concentrate on the legislation. The executive regulatory measures should be transferred to the Commission, provided a general control procedure allows the Council to annul some decisions.

The European Parliament must ensure the representation of the population. This means that a reweighting of the seats should be accepted by the small Member States. The rationalization of the parliamentary function is vital. The Parliament cannot micromanage a European Union with 370 and later 500 million people. We have absolutely no need of an assembly government. Consequently, the generalization of the co-decision procedure must be traded in for the abandoning of regulatory details to the Commission. The Parliament should also concentrate more on the budget and the administration. It should consequently have a veto on all executive regulatory measures having an impact on the budget.

The European Commission must ensure that it can fulfil its executive function. Its regulatory powers should be strengthened (provided the control of the Council and the Parliament is also strengthened). Its control powers should also be strengthened. This means that local antennas of the Commission should be created in the Member States. Everything in the single market cannot be monitored from Brussels. To improve the level of management, there is a need for an individual responsibility of the Commissioners (along the line suggested above). There is also the need for a collective responsibility toward the European Council (two thirds of the Member States should be the ceiling for a dismissal). More responsibility is essential to prevent strong scepticism in the public opinion. This is the trend in the Member States, and the European Union is no exception.

At the judicial level, the European Court of Justice should become a full constitutional court. Secondary decisions should be systematically sent to the tribunal. Minor decisions should be systematically left to the national courts.

The European Union itself must refocus. Limited competences without regulatory meaning (like health, vocational training, culture, etc.), without strong budgetary funding, and without qualified majority voting, should be abandoned. Very often, for the sake of political symbolism, we have substituted the possibility to spend, by the establishment of qualified majority voting. The Commission is now consequently the quartermaster of a limitless flotilla of scattered, weak and inefficient budgetary programmes.

Seen in such a long-term perspective, some strategic priorities in the negotiation of the Amsterdam Treaty may be better understood. It was vital not to modify the weighting of votes without more progress on qualified majority voting and the European Parliament. An inbalance had to be compensated by another balance, to keep the steam in the institutional debate alive. It was also vital to strengthen the President before modifying the composition of the Commission. Otherwise, the pressure to strengthen the President would have become much weaker later.

But, needless to say, such a long-term perspective was absolutely absent in Amsterdam. The reformers were weak. The political context was bad. The agenda was too heavy. Thus, paradoxically, from that perspective, the postponement of the final institutional trade-offs must be seen as a success – a strategical retreat, with quite a few tactical gains. I sometimes ventured to compare this experience with 'an Echternach procession on the Titanic'. One step forward, one step backward in a beautiful setting ... but right towards the iceberg. We corrected the course of the ship a little bit, but certainly not enough to prevent the collision. The iceberg is still there and it is getting even closer.

NOTES

1. It is very revealing to discover the description by someone else involved in the negotiations: see McDonagh (1998) *Original Sin in a Brave New World*. Dublin: Institute for European Affairs (though the title 'New sin in a grey old world' would have been more to the point). My personal feeling is that McDonagh's description underestimates strongly the irrationality of the process.
2. Very interestingly, McDonagh also indicates that this will be the nexus of the next negotiation (McDonagh, 1998: 228–9). According to him, 'the balance [between large and small Member States] will always be preserved'. I suspect that this will not be possible any more, at least with the same principles.

CHAPTER 4

THE REFORMED EUROPEAN UNION AND THE CHALLENGE OF ENLARGEMENT

Jacek Saryusz-Wolski

INTRODUCTION

This chapter will focus on the evaluation of the Amsterdam Treaty from the candidate countries' perspective. A thorough analysis of the Treaty will not be provided since this has already been done in the preceding chapters. Reference to the Treaty is unavoidable as its impact on the accession process will be commented upon. One can be accused of simplistic criticism while judging the Treaty; nevertheless it seems worthwhile to indulge in a constructive critique in order to reach any enlightening conclusions concerning enlargement. Assessment of the ToA from the candidate countries' point of view is difficult, as the analysis of the current situation must take into account an inherent contradiction between formality and reality. The conclusions of the Amsterdam Council read as follows:

> The European Council on 16 and 17 June successfully concluded the IGC ... This opens the way for the launching of the enlargement process in accordance with the conclusions of the Madrid European Council.[1]

Thus the European Union officially fulfilled the only condition it had set up for itself at the Madrid European Council in 1995 – the internal reform was judged to be sufficient in order to inaugurate the enlargement process. Yet if one makes an effort to evaluate the results of the Treaty, taking into account the real degree of the European Union's preparedness for the challenge of enlargement, the conclusion is bound to be much more sombre.

The assessment of the Treaty based on a subjective set of priorities might lead to radically different conclusions, therefore it seems more reasonable to evaluate it in the light of the tasks that were established by the Member States themselves. The Reflection Group (1995: 77) has unanimously stated that:

The 1996 reform must adjust the instruments of the Union so as to guarantee the improvement in their operation in the Union as it is now and the Union that emerges from next enlargement. The reform is already necessary now, but the prospect of enlargement makes it imperative. The results of the conference will have to be judged in this light.

Since the fundamental reform of the institutions was not on the agenda (Timmermans, 1996), it was more a question of the adjustment of the existing structures to the sufficient degree. It should be reiterated that enlargement does not necessitate any radical reorganization of the European Union's polity, but on the other hand, it cannot be based on an incremental extrapolation of the existing arrangements. Therefore, even though from the general perspective to call the Treaty a failure would be largely unfounded, especially in the view of the substantial progress in the area of justice and home affairs, from the perspective of enlargement the Treaty may be labelled as 'unsatisfactory', as most of the institutional dilemmas were left unresolved.

The outcome of the Amsterdam Treaty negotiations demonstrate very clearly the absence of a driving force behind enlargement. A palpable lack of common vision, divergence of objectives blended with short-term political calculation rendered a coherent far-reaching result difficult if not impossible. The behaviour of policy-makers during the IGC negotiations proved that they did not perceive enlargement as a grand, imminent objective commensurate to that of common market completion or to constructing the foundations of political union. The pre- or post-election political uncertainty in some of the Member States only added to the general feeling of inertia. Enlargement seen by a majority as indispensable, was not, however, situated in the immediate perspective. The policy-makers, instead of tackling the indispensable reform agenda, concentrated on concocting appetising half-solutions in other domains. The agenda of the conference was fluctuating, some issues were added, others under-scored. A visible crisis of leadership in combination with the preoccupation with objectives other than enlargement itself led the way to the postponement of the essential institutional reform.

The radical shift of priorities constituted the main feature of the concluding sessions of the 1996–7 IGC. That phenomenon contributed to the lukewarm reception of the new Treaty in the candidate countries. There is no doubt that employment should be one of the Union's priorities, but the chapter introduced in the Treaty of Amsterdam would not resolve the problem by itself, a concerted action in that field on the part of the Member States is still required. The Amsterdam provisions severely limit the Union's operational capacity for incentive measures designed to encourage cooperation between the Member States (Article 129 (formerly

Article 109r)). Of course, in the light of the Luxembourg Employment Council it is now clear that national governments exhibit a strong will to foster such cooperation, not necessarily along the lines of a strict application of the Amsterdam provisions. Yet the fact remains that the Amsterdam Treaty dealt more with the sensitivities of national electorates rather than with the demands of reality.

INSTITUTIONAL REFORM

Before the IGC the majority of the Member States claimed that an increase in qualified majority voting constituted an indispensable condition for successful enlargement, as unanimity among 30 or more Member States would be immensely difficult to attain. It seemed that only the scope of the necessary changes was to become a source of controversy. The majority opted for retaining unanimity for issues of a quasi-constitutional character (Reflection Group, 1995). One could have expected that the problem of extending QMV was going to be resolved at the IGC, especially with the more constructive attitude of the new British government.[2] The reform was, however, almost entirely blocked. Before the IGC the majority of the Reflection Group postulated 19 fields in which QMV should be introduced. The Project of the Treaty prepared by the Dutch Presidency, the so-called Addendum to the Irish draft, limited the number of fields to 11. The Amsterdam Treaty was, however, even more conservative in that respect. It is very striking that the reform was blocked by Germany, which had always been one of the most ardent supporters of deeper integration. Chancellor Kohl had to yield to the demands of the Länder on the issue of QMV extension in exchange for their support for the EMU, otherwise the issue of monetary union could have been voted down in the Bundesrat, which would have had grave political implications. A question to be considered is whether the unreserved belief in 'snowball effect' is still justified: one should not be as certain as Helmut Kohl that further economic integration will simultaneously lead to the formation of a true political union. Anyhow, the German fixation on EMU, along with the election perspective, prevented to a large extent the success of the institutional reform.

The issue of QMV extension was quite crucial enough as such, but during the last stage of the IGC it gained in importance as it was linked to the remainder of the institutional reform. None of the institutional reforms could be resolved in a vacuum, they are all interconnected and dependent on one another. With a great degree of simplification one could say that some smaller states were ready to discuss other indispensable institutional reforms only after the extension of QMV. Larger states, on the other hand, did not want to renounce their second Commissioner without the reweighting of the votes in the Council.

It is quite difficult to imagine enlargement without the reform of the composition of the Commission. Commissioners cannot be added infinitely without influencing the effectiveness of the institution. In order to make enlargement feasible it seemed inevitable that their right to nominate Commissioners would have to be reconsidered, or that the larger states would have to be denied the second one. The answer to that question cannot, however, be agreed upon without the decision on how to reweigh the votes in the Council. The smaller Member States are over-represented in the Council, which as such does not pose any controversy; the degree of over-representation, is however, quite controversial. The next enlargement is going to encompass a great number of smaller states (with an exception of Poland). After accepting the six newcomers from the first wave who already started the accession negotiations, larger states (with Spain and Poland) would represent 77 per cent of the Union's population but having only 50 per cent of the votes in the Council. On the other hand, new smaller members (without Poland) would represent only 5.6 per cent of Union's population but would have 15 per cent of the votes in the Council. Moreover, along with enlargement, if the present system is not changed, the relative power of the big states is going to be diminished, whereas that of the smaller states is going to get enhanced. It is clear that such a situation needs to be remedied if there is to be progress on the road to accession. Unfortunately, along with the blockage of the QMV extension, none of those crucial questions was resolved. The policy-makers concentrated on other issues during the last round of negotiations, and there was simply no time left to focus on that highly divisive part of the agenda. Therefore, the suggestion of Chancellor Kohl to postpone the institutional reform made at the informal Summit in Noordwijk was met with relief and acceptance.

Regardless of the relative failure to tackle the institutional reform one should not underestimate the changes which were after all introduced by the new Treaty, even though they were not directly linked to enlargement.[3] Most importantly, the trend towards the strengthening of the European Parliament has continued. The Amsterdam Treaty introduced a significant, further increase of the number of provisions to which the co-decision procedure – Article 251 (formerly Article 189b) – applies.[4] As a general rule, all those provisions that were regulated by the cooperation procedure will now be ruled by co-decision.[5] Co-decision was also introduced into a number of important new provisions of the Amsterdam Treaty, such as employment incentive measures (Article 129 (formerly Article 109r)), social exclusion measures (Article 137 (formerly Article 118(2))), social policy (Article 141 (formerly Article 119)), transparency

(Article 255 (formerly Article 191a)), countering fraud (Article 280 (formerly Article 209a)) and customs cooperation (Article 135 (formerly Article 116)). Moreover, along with the simplification of the former co-decision the European Parliament was put on an equal footing with the Council. Even though there remains a number of important issues on which the Parliament is merely consulted or excluded from the decision process, an effort to strengthen the position of the EP was clearly undertaken. As regards the European Parliament the ToA also introduced a change which has resulted from the upcoming enlargement – a ceiling of 700 members was established to prevent the EP from expanding indefinitely (Article 189 (formerly Article 137)).

The ToA also strengthened the position of the President of the Commission. The Member States will have to consult the nominations for Commissioners with the nominee for the President (Article 214 (formerly Article 158(2) para. 2)). Moreover, the Commission will work under the political guidance of its President (Article 219 (formerly Article 163)), who according to the declaration attached to the Treaty will have a broad discretion in the allocation of portfolios. The reinforcement of the Commission's President is of crucial importance for the future and for the coherent workings of that institution and may facilitate other indispensable changes within it. Of course, from the point of view of enlargement every effort which has the objective of enhancing the Communities' institutions effectiveness has to be assessed positively. Nevertheless, it should be stressed that the Amsterdam Treaty only has made a step in the right direction.

The Amsterdam Treaty did not resolve the most important institutional questions, but it did narrow the scope for compromise, sketching out a clear direction in which the Union's institutional set-up should evolve. In the Protocol on the Institutions which was added to the Amsterdam Treaty the Member States decided to limit the number of Commissioners to one for each state

> provided that by that date, the weighting of the Council has been modified, whether by reweighting of the votes or by dual majority in a manner acceptable to the all Member States ..., notably compensating those Member States which give up the possibility of nominating a second member of the Commission.[6]

If, however, the number of the Member States were to exceed 20 a new IGC will be convened to carry out a comprehensive institutional reform. Just after the IGC France, Italy and Belgium published a declaration in which they opted for convening a new IGC before enlargement, as they see the fulfilment of the institutional reform as an indispensable condition for the success of the accession process. A similar sentiment was shared by the Commission in the Agenda 2000 and in the letter to the British Presidency published by Chancellor Helmut Kohl and President Jacques Chirac. As there are six countries in the first group (a renewed application of Malta may change that number to seven) it is clear that a new IGC concerning the institutional reform will need to be carried out before enlargement, and preparations have indeed started under the German Presidency of 1999.

What consequences for the accession negotiations does the procrastination of the institutional debate produce? That is, no doubt, the most fundamental question which is asked within the acceding countries. The IGC of 1996 was to clear the path for the enlargement process. After dealing with the most sensitive issue of institutional adaptation the Member States could have focused, with a considerable weight off their shoulders, on other no less delicate questions which in their mind will require a solution before enlargement. Unfortunately, because of the Amsterdam handicap, that is now not going to happen. It seemed that a logical thing to do would be to close the institutional debate before plunging into the midst of controversies that surround such appallingly difficult issues as the future of Common Agricultural Policy, structural funds and last but definitely not least the Union's future finances.

The Member States face an extremely difficult debate – as an unresolved institutional question is going to get entangled in a net of the Member States' interests concerning the reform of the most sensitive of Union's policies. Package deals undeniably constitute an intrinsic part of intra-community bargaining, but possible trade-offs within such a complicated agenda are going to be very hard to agree upon. It would be naive to expect that it is going to be easier to resolve the institutional dilemma in such a truly labyrinthine context. Unless suddenly it will appear trifling in the face of the challenges of redistribution. The acceding countries are understandably most worried that the enlargement process could become a hostage of the unresolved institutional question. The most reticent can use the issue of the Union's insufficient degree of preparedness as a pretext for delaying the negotiations or accession itself. There is not much else to do, however, and I strongly believe that such fears are largely unfounded.

CLOSER COOPERATION

Closer cooperation or flexibility constituted a true leitmotif of the 1996–7 IGC. There was an undeniable need to provide the Member States with 'a means of organizing diversity in an increasingly heterogeneous Europe, while at the same time preserving an integration dynamic' (Wallace and de la Serre, 1997). Flexible arrangements were introduced in the Maastricht Treaty, and they also existed outside of the Treaties in the form of the Schengen Agreement and Western European Union. Along with the increase of the divergence within the Union the need to sanction flexibility became more and more urgent. Flexibility as such presents a difficult dilemma as an *à la carte* Europe could easily lead to disintegration, but in present political reality a complex web of variable arrangements may be unavoidable. In that context effective multi-speed arrangements would anyway be required for a successful management of enlargement, and this prospect provided a special impetus to the debate. The majority of the Member States wanted to avoid fragmentation, but since the reality did not permit consensus on every point of the Union's agenda there was a necessity to create an instrument that would prevent the more integrationist-minded states to seek for further cooperation outside of the Treaties. Some perceived it as a panacea for all the ills, some saw it as a pragmatic solution, better and more coherent than *ad hoc* opting out. Candidate Countries, on the other hand, were most anxious not to witness an emergence of the two-tier Europe, which would create two categories of membership.

The ToA introduced the concept of closer cooperation in a quite reserved manner as the very nature and sheer number of safeguards make it difficult to be employed in practice. From candidate countries' perspective it is most important that it is open to all Member States, 'allowing them to become parties to the co-operation at any time, provided that they comply with the basic decisions taken within its framework' (Article 43(g) TEU (formerly Article K 15(g)); thus fears of a hermetic nature of the new provision were largely eliminated. Other safeguards, however, regardless of the fact whether they are logical or not,[7] limit the potential of closer cooperation. It is quite understandable that it should further the objectives of the Union (Article 43(a) TEU) and that it should not affect the *acquis communautaire* (Article 43(e) TEU); it seems reasonable that it should concern at least the majority of the Member States (Article 43(d) TEU) and that it should not concern areas which fall under the exclusive competence of the Community within the First Pillar (Article 11(a) (formerly Article 5a (a))). In practice, it is quite difficult to imagine how closer cooperation can avoid affecting Community policies, actions and programmes in any way (Article 11(b) TEU), or how can we be sure that it will not affect the interests of those Member States which do not participate therein (Article 43(f) TEU). Since the Commission will also have to make sure that closer cooperation is used as a last resort (Article 43(c) TEU), it is quite clear that it might become a 'dead letter' before it is even used. Many authors have already paid due attention to the danger of the revival of the old Luxembourg compromise, but it should be reiterated that putting it explicitly in the Treaty can be potentially more dangerous than scrapping the closer cooperation clause altogether (Editorial comment, 1997). Since other flexible arrangements have been used in the case of the Third Pillar, Schengen Agreement, and Monetary Union and since the Second Pillar was purposely excluded from the realm of closer cooperation, the immediate demand for it might as well have been eliminated.

It is important to stress, in that context, that the Acceding Countries had expected that they may be treated with a certain degree of flexibility. No one reasonable in Central and Eastern Europe denies the fact that *acquis communautaire* should be treated as a target, and that the prospective Member States should accept it in its integrity. Nevertheless, it seems reasonable to introduce a certain degree of flexibility into the negotiations. Unfortunately, such hopes are not easily materialized. The eighth article of the Protocol Integrating the Schengen *acquis* into the Framework of the European Union states that the Schengen *acquis* must be accepted in full by all candidate countries before admission. The reasons for that provision are quite easy to understand, but nevertheless the current Member States should refrain from pre-empting the accession negotiations, especially in the domain where such preposterously framed derogations were granted to certain members. Moreover, it seems that a strict application of the Schengen Protocol in principle would not allow for keeping the special arrangements that some of the Candidate Countries have with their neighbours. It is particularly important in the context of the border between the Czech Republic and Slovakia, as well as between Estonia and Latvia, provided that these countries would accede to the Union at a different time. This problem, however, is bound to be short-term, whereas an issue of special border and visa arrangements between Poland and its eastern neighbours clearly is not. The Union should employ some flexibility in that respect to prevent the creation of a new division line in Europe. The accession of Poland to the EU should help in reinforcing and facilitating the formation of special relations between the enlarged European Union and the countries of the former Soviet Union, rather than undermine the potential of special relations Poland developed with its eastern neighbours. That would allow for stabilizing influence and beneficial demonstration of successful political and economic transformation. It is true that the countries from Central and Eastern Europe strive towards European Union membership and not the other way round, but preemption is not the best incentive for creating the atmosphere of mutual understanding which should be the basis of the accession process. Unfortunately, both the Amsterdam Treaty and, to an even greater degree, Agenda 2000 are not very promising in that respect.

TRANSPARENCY

In the light of the declarations of the Member States, adding a greater degree of transparency to the European Union's highly complicated framework should have been one of the fundamental goals of the new Treaty, as granting a freer access to the Communities' documents is clearly not sufficient. The Union needs enhanced democratic legitimacy and that cannot be achieved without clarity of design – a set of provisions which are difficult to comprehend, half solutions which leave space for arbitrary and sometimes even contradicting interpretations, will not command crucial public respect, and without public respect the European integration loses its *raison d'être*. It might have been unrealistic to expect a fully coherent, transparent result as complication constitutes an intrinsic feature of the Union's legal order but the Amsterdam Treaty disappointed the high hopes voiced during the 1996–7 IGC. The new Treaty remains arcane even for the trained specialists, its structure is indecipherable for the experts, let alone ordinary citizens. Apart from the simplification of the co-decision procedure and the consolidation of the Treaties, which at the beginning will produce more evil than good, absolutely nothing has been done to allow the public to understand what has really happened in Amsterdam.

The complicated structure of the new Treaty has its consequences also for enlargement. Without rationalization the current state of affairs is devoid of legal certainty. The new Treaty alone necessitates a few 'screening' sessions in order to explain its content. It remains to be seen who would undertake such a quixotic task. One may use only one example, as was rightly pointed out (Kortenberg, 1998):

> the difficulty in distinguishing in the longer term measures arising from Title VI of the TEU and further development of Schengen acquis may be a source of disputes since the legal arrangements are different.

Moreover, there is a realistic threat that the interpretation of such loopholes and inconsistencies within the Treaty is going to be influenced by the political interests of the Member States and that it might have a detrimental effect on the accession negotiations. The candidate countries must be given a chance to understand the nature of their obligations, there should be no room for arbitrariness as negotiations are much more similar to the game of bridge than to the game of poker – competence is much more important than luck and there should be no bluffing because it may mislead the partner.

THE INTERGOVERNMENTAL PILLARS

A coherent and effective Common Foreign and Security Policy of the European Union is in the interest of the candidate countries. In the future it will also include their national sensitivities and allow them to influence world politics to the extent they have never experienced before. It seemed clear that the CFSP should be made more effective before enlargement, as it will be increasingly difficult to manage. Fostering the Union's identity in the field of foreign policy and giving it a greater capacity for external action was one of the goals of the 1996–7 IGC. Even though the evolution of a true common foreign and security policy is determined more by political will based on a firm perception of common destiny than by a mere institutional building, the institutions may facilitate the CFSP formation. In the light of the quite ambitious proposals which were submitted just before and throughout the 1996–7 IGC the changes introduced by the Treaty in the realm of the second pillar are quite modest. There are, however, at least three modifications which should be assessed positively. The Amsterdam Treaty witnesses a further extension of qualified majority in that field: if joint actions are going to be agreed in the framework of a newly established instrument of common strategies, which had been unanimously established beforehand, they may be decided upon by majority (Article 23(2) TEU (formerly Article J.13 (2))). It is doubtful, however, if such a possibility is going to be employed in reality. Other positive developments include the introduction of constructive abstention (Article 23(1) TEU (formerly Article J.13 (1)) and the setting up of the Policy Planning and Early Warning Unit.[8] A constructive abstention, even though largely constrained by the Luxembourg compromise, is one of the most promising developments as it adds to the CFSP's flexibility which can positively influence the effectiveness of the common policy. The establishment of the Planning Unit is also crucially important because it will finally provide the Union with a capacity to plan ahead, analyse and anticipate without which the CFSP had a largely static and reactive character.

There is absolutely no doubt that a progressive creation of an area of freedom, security and justice – new Title IV (formerly Title IIIa) of the Treaty establishing the European Community – constitutes the biggest achievement of the 1996 IGC. Thus, a large part of the intergovernmental third pillar – all the provisions which concern visas, asylum, immigration and other policies related to free movement of persons (Articles from 61 to 69 (formerly Article 73i-73q)) along with Title X TEC (formerly Title VIIa) customs co-operation (Article 135 (formerly Article 116)) – were incorporated into the first pillar. Within a period of five years all of those issues are going to be regulated by the Community method. Due to that fact that in these areas the cumbersome system of intergovernmental cooperation was abolished the number of decision-making levels will be reduced. Community legal instruments will be employed, an overlap between the first and third pillars largely eliminated. All of those developments will undoubtedly increase the effectiveness of common policies in that area, even though the insistence of certain countries on retaining unanimity prevailed. The above described development is a perfect example of the phenomenon described as 'creeping communitarization' (Laffan, 1997). Finally the Commission's right of initiative will be extended to the domain of internal security, the consultative role of the European Parliament will be somewhat more pronounced and the Court of Justice will gain jurisdiction, however limited, in that respect.

The Amsterdam Treaty also introduces certain modifications within the realm of the third pillar itself – provisions on police and judicial cooperation in criminal matters – Title VI TEU (Articles 29–42 TEU (formerly Article K.1-K.14)). First of all, it explicitly enumerates the objectives of common actions initiated in each of the fields of cooperation which adds clarity to the design (Article 30 and 31 TEU (formerly Article K.2 and K.3)). It also provides police cooperation with a limited operational capacity (Article 30 (2) TEU (formerly Article K.2 (2)), introduces a new decision-making instrument (framework decisions) which will have a similar role to directives (Article 34b TEU (formerly Article K.6b)), also allows for a limited jurisdiction of the European Court of Justice (Article 35 TEU (formerly Article K.7)) and simplifies the modalities for the adoption of conventions (Article 34d TEU (formerly Article K.6d)). The Treaty explicitly provides for enhanced cooperation in that field, making it a subject of the ECJ's jurisdiction (Article 40 TEU (formerly Article K.12)), which will allow the Member States that wish to do so to initiate closer cooperation in that field within the Union's institutional framework.

The above mentioned developments, along with the incorporation of the Schengen *acquis* into the Treaty, must be assessed positively from the perspective of the candidate countries. They represent the best way of dealing with a perceived lack of internal security in the Member States. There is a quite common fear within the European Union that the countries of Eastern and Central Europe may become exporters of internal instability as they clearly suffer from a deficit in that area. Therefore, a closer cooperation in that field is indispensable to mitigate those exaggerated misgivings. One must, however, pay closer attention to the nature of *ad hoc* derogations which were granted to certain Member States, as they obfuscate the clear, transparent picture which should have been aimed for. The derogation of Denmark is in that light the most curious example as it may produce legal obligations in international, not community, law, which in itself represents a legal hybrid. One is left to wonder whether an eternal multiplication of *ad hoc* opt-outs represents the best way of dealing with the unavoidable challenge posed by flexibility.

CONCLUSION

The assessment of the Amsterdam Treaty from the perspective of the candidate countries is bound to be ambivalent. On the one hand, it introduces quite a number of modifications which can be evaluated positively, on the other hand, it fails on account of institutional reform, which may have a detrimental effect on the accession negotiations. The Belgian Deputy Prime-Minister, at the time Elio di Rupo, in his speech delivered at the College of Europe Natolin in October 1998 claimed that the institutional reform should be conducted in parallel to enlargement and that it will not interfere with the process.[9] There is not much else left to do but believe that this is going to be the case. Nevertheless, it should be stressed that the Member States did not adapt the European Union for the biggest challenge it faces in years. As it is not a mere charity initiative but a considerable investment into the future the reluctance to face it well prepared is astonishing. Apart from a possibility to suspend a Member State in its rights deriving from the Treaty in the case of a serious and persistent breach of one of the basic principles on which the Union is founded (Article 7 TEU (formerly Article F.1)) and setting up of a limit of the MEPs, it seems that none of the reforms introduced by the new Treaty was really prompted by the prospect of enlargement. It represents a certain paradox that, according to many declarations, it was to provide a stimulus for the internal reform but that, in the end, it clearly did not do so to a sufficient degree. It is very doubtful whether the postponement of the most indispensable reforms is going to be beneficial, as the resolution of all the sensitive issues left over by Amsterdam along the accession negotiations may prove to be even more difficult. It is a truism to say that the negotiations between the Member States are often much more heated than the negotiations between the Union and the candidate countries, but as the current situation indicates that the proportions of that discrepancy may even be increased, it is hard to believe that it will have a propitious effect on the smoothness of the process.

The outcome of the 1996–7 IGC leads one to ponder on the nature of its preparation phase. It was postulated by many that the Treaty revision of such dimension should have a different form. The Westendorp group's report had a visibly intergovernmental character and therefore it lacked coherence, in many of its points it was just a protocol of substantial divergence of opinions. Moreover, too many issues were left to be resolved by the Heads of State or Government at the last minute. As Joseph Weiler (1997) commented:

It was an Intergovernmental Conference which should never have started ... there was no shared agenda and no mobilizing force behind the exercise ... It was, too, an Intergovernmental Conference which should never have ended ... This was a technocratic blunder: there were simply too many open agenda items to be discussed and negotiated seriously in the ludicrously short time available at the Summit.

In spite of this succinct criticism one has to admit that the formal closure of the IGC allowed for the opening of the accession negotiations, even though it is a fact that the most important agenda items were left open-ended as the time available to resolve them was truly ludicrously short. Concluding, one should agree with the President Jacques Chirac who said: *'Dans certains domaines, je suis frustré, dans d'autres je suis satisfait. Mais, au total, c'est un pas raisonnable qui nous permet de commencer l'élargissement ...'* (Le Monde, 1997).

NOTES

1. The Amsterdam Council Conclusions. Bull. EU 6–1997.
2. Blair's government opted for unanimity only as regards immigration and the Social Charter.
3. With an exception of the limit of MEPs.
4. Fifteen existing Treaty provisions are going to be additionally ruled by co-decision.
5. With an exception of the field of EMU where cooperation will be still applicable in the following new articles: 99(5), 102(2), 103(2), 106(2).
6. Protocol on the Institutions with the Prospect of Enlargement of the European Union.
7. See Helmut Kortenberg's (1998) argument in 'Closer Co-operation in the Treaty of Amsterdam'.
8. A Declaration no. 11 on the creation of Policy Planning and Early Warning Unit annexed to the Treaty.
9. Rupo di, E. 'La vision belge de l'élargissement de l'Union Européenne'. Speech delivered at the College of Europe Natolin on 20 October 1998.

BIBLIOGRAPHY

Bulletin of the European Union (1997), The Amsterdam Council Conclusions. No. 6.
Editorial comment (1997) 'The Treaty of Amsterdam: neither a bang nor a whimper'. *Common Market Law Review*, 34.

Kortenberg, H. (1998) 'Closer co-operation in the Treaty of Amsterdam'. *Common Market Law Review*, 35, August.

Laffan, B. (1997) 'The governance of the Union'. In B. Tonra, (ed.), *Amsterdam, What the Treaty Means*. Dublin.

Le Monde, 19 June 1997.

Reflection Group (1995) *The Reflection Group Report*. Brussels.

Timmermans, C. W. A. (1996) 'General institutional questions: the effectiveness and simplification of decision-making'. In J. A. Winter *et al.*, (ed.), *Reforming the Treaty on European Union*. The Hague.

Wallace, H. and de la Serre, F. (1997) *Flexibility and Enhanced Cooperation in the European Union: Placebo rather than Panacea*. Paris.

Weiler, J. H. H. (1997) editorial, *European Law Journal*, 3(4).

CHAPTER 5

THE AMSTERDAM TREATY IN THEORETICAL PERSPECTIVES: WHICH DYNAMICS AT WORK?

Wolfgang Wessels

THE RELEVANCE OF THE 'ACQUIS ACADÉMIQUE'

Why we need to discuss 'theories' at all!

Ever since Plato moved his Academia out of Athens theoretical reflections about the polity have been criticized for being out of touch with realities. Also in the context of European integration the label 'useless' or even 'disturbing' has been put on works of a more general and systematic character. What we might call in analogy to the *acquis communautaire*, the EC collection of all binding texts, the 'acquis académique', a less clearly defined though existing list of major approaches and lines of argument, seems to have a life beside and often unconnected with what is happening in the arenas and corridors of power.

Theories represent, however, more than just a playground for academics in 'ivory towers' following a different logic than the 'real' life. Academic reflections are not only a game for university people but they are also of high political relevance for all those with responsibility in committee and council rooms.Political and administrative actors are working and discussing with and within a conceptional 'luggage' of considerable impact. Those who proclaim to be pure pragmatists are slaves of concepts handed down from long outdated theorists (to paraphrase Keynes). Everyday references to terms like 'sovereignty' or 'federalism' demonstrate the risk of unreflected rhetorics. Even more: major parts of the 'acquis académique' have sunk deeply into the political memory and consciousness. Thus, also in the Council building, christened by the name of the humanistic Professor Justus Lipsius, politicians and civil servants are discussing on the basis of conceptual assumptions of a more general nature than those actors are aware.

The Amsterdam Treaty is no exception to this rule. Architects of the Treaty reflect about their own activities within their political paradigms and expect that their decisions work in the direction they expect. The articles of the Treaty document a relationship between the objectives the masters of the Treaty had in mind and the rules they fixed to achieve them. They are also hoping or worrying about some overall effect these Treaty amendments might have on their own role and the states they represent.

Given these assumptions of a rather general nature, integration-related theories are helpful to discuss and reflect about a certain part of reality. While the issues of specific policy fields and institutions are treated in other chapters of this volume, I would like to pursue a more comprehensive macropolitical approach looking at the evolution of the rather strange construction nowadays called EU in a middle range perspective (Merton, 1968). My major question is therefore: how does the Amsterdam Treaty fit into the basic patterns and trends of the integration process over the last 50 years?

Which approach to pursue

To develop answers to this question we need to use categories for description of this construction, i.e. we need to work with integration indicators, which can identify and grasp the process. I would like to use criteria with which the evolution of a political system can be observed (Wessels, 1997); thus, we should look at:

- the evolution of the scope of public policies which are earmarked in one way or other for being dealt within the EU;
- the legal and constitutional transfer of competencies and instruments from the national to the EU level;
- the institutional growth, especially in terms of actors involved; and
- the evolution of procedures by which the EU institutions prepare, make, implement and control binding decisions.

My approach thus stresses a dynamic approach in contrast to a static snap-shot that only captures the moment, or a comparative static approach that deals with consecutive big bargains among Member States as a recurrent pattern (Moravscik and Nicolaidis, 1999).

Implied into medium-term perspectives are also – involuntarily or on purpose – basic principles and models of the way our polity should be constructed. In the tradition of Aristotle the theoretical debate is also one about how we want to organize our commonwealth and, thus, legitimize our endeavour. Teleological considerations about the 'finalité politique' are major parts of this trend analysis.

Implied in these considerations are also options for future strategies: for action to be taken by politicians and administrations theories can broaden the view and the range of available options. Predictions will not be made though we present some educated guesses about possible scenarios of the implementation and follow up to the Amsterdam Treaty.

Thus, this macropolitical dynamic approach offers certain benefits: it tries to put the Amsterdam Treaty into a broader and medium-term perspective.

The Amsterdam Treaty in theoretical perspectives:
sets of possible explanations and predictions

Following this dynamic approach, we might start with alternative views of how the process towards the Amsterdam EU has evolved and might develop from this stage of treaty making. Using the 'acquis académique' of integration-related theories (Taylor, 1981; Jachtenfuchs and Kohler-Koch, 1996: 15–44)[1] and views different readings of the Amsterdam Treaty are offered.

From the traditional neo-functional (Haas, 1958; Hallstein, 1979; Schmitter, 1969; Keohane and Hoffmann, 1990: 276–300; Moravscik and Nicolaidis, 1999) or neo-federal (Pinder, 1986; Schneider, 1994: 21–50) points of view, we would expect some kind of linear growth of the integration process as measured by the integration indicators, i.e. a rather smooth process 'upwards' to some sort of final stage of a 'federal union' with a strengthening of the EP as core institution. In contrast to the original concept of federalism in the early Spinelli version (Spinelli, 1958), new federalism claims that constitutional projects such as treaty revisions do not provide for qualitative jumps but constitute incremental steps forward to a real constitution similar to a 'Bundesstaat' (Hallstein, 1979) or to the 'United States of Europe' (see Monnet, 1955). The historical changes of 1989 have not diminished but strengthened the case for even more federation-building. The Amsterdam Treaty would be another step within this incremental process.

In a related view neo-functionalist thinking might claim that the Amsterdam Treaty by itself and even in major parts could be best explained by spill-over processes (Haas, 1968; Schmitter, 1996: 211–44) or 'Sachlogik' (Hallstein, 1979) of several kinds. A built-in integration logic has worked again in the Amsterdam case and the new EU set of rules will even reinforce endogenous dynamics.

With all respect to some specifities the Amsterdam Treaty in general or at least its major results would be a satisfactory test for the validity of that mechanism. Further steps would then be in the making. Amsterdam would not constitute the final point but an important step.

In contrast to this school of thought, explanations based on realist theories (Grieco, 1988; Link, 1998; Meyers, 1977; Thatcher, 1989: 411–18) or on liberal intergovernmentalism (Moravcsik and Nicolaidis, 1999) will stress the role and interest of member states. They would claim that again member governments have proven their status as 'masters of the treaty'[2] and have created only some additional forms of some kind of cooperation among sovereign nation states. Three variants might be discerned.

In the most radical view, the geopolitical revolution of 1989 and the subsequent radical transformation of the political context in the international and the European system have left west European integration as a child of the Cold War. From this perspective, the Maastricht Treaty was already outdated at the time of its signature (Mearsheimer, 1990). In line with this reasoning we would need to find clear traces of decline and disintegration that would ultimately lead to the renaissance of the traditional nation-state. Amsterdam would signal a clear step of a return to the nation-state and an intra-European conflictual balance of power. The transfer of competencies would go back and downwards to the national level; the scope of common policies would be reduced to low politics issues, the institutional and procedural set-up would be clearly geared to a hierarchy under national control.

A neo-realist view would, however, explain the EU after the end of the Cold War as an exercise aimed at an integrative balancing of the united Germany and a co-operative balancing *vis à vis* the only remaining superpower, that of the United States (Link, 1998). As for the indicators used the major issue of the approach is the final control of the Member States as the masters of the treaties; the Amsterdam Treaty should thus be a document which is not only negotiated by governments in an intergovernmental conference, but in which and by which national control over supranational bodies is reinforced even if the scope might be enlarged and competencies shifted.

A third variant, the liberal intergovernmentalism, stresses the role of national preferences, asymmetrical bargaining among states and the bounded commitments and hybrid solutions in the institutional fields (Moravcsik and Nicolaidis, 1999).

In a third school of thought linked to governance approaches (Bulmer, 1994; Caporaso, 1996; Wallace and Wallace, 1996; Jachtenfuchs and Kohler-Koch, 1996), the importance of constitutional amendments and revisions is downgraded. In non-hierarchical networks actors prepare decisions with only limited attention to formal rules. Within a broad framework the pendulum metaphor assumes some kind of cyclical up and down between 'fusion' and 'diffusion' (Wallace, 1996: 3–36). With Maastricht as a more permanent fixture (Jachtenfuchs and Kohler-Koch, 1996) this to-ing and fro-ing leads to an 'unstable equilibrium' (Wallace, 1996: 439–460). The Amsterdam provisions would then be characterized by a mixed result on the list of integration indicators with no major step forward.

My own argument is that we can witness long-term trends of considerable scope as regards enlargement, transfer of competencies, institutional growth and procedural differentiation. In this process the Amsterdam Treaty would be part of a ratchet effect: on a certain level some indicators would stay at a local optimum for a certain period and then move up to a new plateau (Wessels, Maurer and Mittag, 2000). The major feature of this process is a 'fusion' (Wessels, 1997) of public instruments from several state levels linked with the respective Europeanization of national actors and institutions. For some kind of verification, the Amsterdam Treaty would have to demonstrate that member states use the EU for solving key problems and simultaneously strengthening their own involvement as those of supranational bodies. Procedural differentiation would lead to a higher degree of complexity. The Amsterdam Treaty would constitute a higher level, at which for a certain period relative stagnation would occur. Contrary to the neo-federal view no clear 'finalité politique' along conventional lines of traditional state building can be expected, but a new yet highly ambiguous stage in the evolution of European states can.

Table 1 shows the expectation according to the theories.

AN ANALYSIS OF THE TREATY TEXT: TESTING THE THEORIES

Scope enlargement

One way to look at the EU system and its evolution is an analysis of the changes in the scope of public policies. In regard to this indicator the findings are rather clear: the Amsterdam Treaty has again extended the Union's areas of policies bringing the Union close to the level of a state-like agenda. There are nearly no subjects of public interest, no national 'domaines reservées' that remain outside the Union's objectives. Seen from a historical perspective this extension is remarkable, given the difficulties to get the term 'defence' into the Treaty and looking at the start of the Trevi group (Wallace, 1996) outside any treaty framework in the areas of justice and home affairs (Müller-Graff, 1998: 656–70).

With its amendments the Amsterdam Treaty forms a triptych with the Single European Act (SEA) and the Maastricht Treaty. Its contribution to fill the EU list of activities in terms of policy priorities is to add more detailed subjects – e.g. fundamental rights (Article 6 TEU), discrimination (Article 13 TEC), 'humanitarian and rescue tasks, peacekeeping tasks and tasks of combat forces in crisis management' – the so-called Petersberg tasks – (Article 17 TEU), 'offences against children' (Article 29 TEU),

Table 5.1   The Amsterdam Treaty in the view of different theoretical approaches

Schools of thought	Indicators			
	Scope of enlargement	Transfer of instruments and competencies	Institutional growth	Procedural evolution
Neo-functionalism	+	+	+ (Commission)	technocracy
Neo-federalism	+	+	+ (European Parliament)	democratization by parliamentarization
Realism	−	−	+ (European Council)	−
Neo-realism	+	−	+ (European Council)	−
Liberal intergovernmentalism	+	−	+	+
Governance	+ and −	+ and −	networks	differentiation
Fusion	+	+	+ (Council and European Parliament)	strong differentiation

'protection of individuals with regard to the processing of personal data' (Article 286 TEC) and employment policy (Title VII TEC), animal welfare (protocol 24), public radio (protocol 23). A major point in the overall set-up will be the area of freedom, security and justice which reinforces the Union's tasks in the vital area of 'internal' policies. Such an enlargement of topics is due to the Christmas tree effect:[3] each state wanted to have its priorities or sensibilities put into the Treaty;[4] Thus Member State governments reinforced the role of the Union to deal with those problems dear to their national priorities without really debating if the EU level is the appropriate one.[5]

Transfer of legal instruments and competencies

Looking at the evolution of the instruments which the Member States have shifted to the EU level, the Amsterdam Treaty documents demonstrate again one major feature of integration trends – that of a constitutionalization in form of a communitarization.[6] More competencies and instruments of public policies are now ruled by the procedures characteristic of the EC 'first pillar' – even if we observe forms of incomplete and imperfect communitarization. Despite exceptions for Member States (incomplete communitarization) and imperfect roles for the Court, the Commission and the EP (imperfect communitarization), these provisions of the Amsterdam Treaty underline that the Community method is more than just one choice among others, thus on the same level as intergovernmental cooperation, but that it evolved into the dominating approach within the Union's overall construction. The unique roles of the Commission, the EP and especially the Court are extended to further policy fields to establish a set of rules of a clearly supranational nature.[7]

A major proof for this assessment is the as yet imperfect and incomplete communitarization of the area of freedom, security and justice. In spite of major shortcomings (Müller-Graff, 1998; Monar, 1997; Duff, 1997)[8] the new instruments are a major historical 'victory' for the supranational method if one compares them to the rather slow intergovernmental development in this area since the 1970s.

The integration of the Social Protocol reinforces this argument in so far as the first pillar is concerned. The smooth and unspectacular complete communitarization of this major problem issue of the Maastricht Treaty points to a step by step integration and tells us the lesson that an imperfect and incomplete communitarization of a hitherto national policy field might be a better choice for integrationists than to press for the perfect solution at once with the high risk of a total blockage.

One often neglected form of using essential elements of the supranational method is the quasi-communitarization of the remainder of the third pillar.[9] The distance of this set of rules to procedures in the EC has been considerably reduced. Major innovations are the extension of the functions of the Court, the creation of quasi-directives and the introduction of majority voting.

There are also formulas which are less in line with this argument; the new provisions for trade in services and intellectual property (Article 133(5) TEC) (Monar, 1997) are mentioned as one sign of imperfect communitarization. Some, however, argue that this Article 308 (former Article 235) TEC-like rule might be more flexible than the alternative on the table, namely to sketch a long list of exceptions in a protocol which would have been more difficult to get out of the Treaty.

Also other instruments need to be discussed in view of their nature. With the employment chapter, the Amsterdam summit has created additional forms of soft co-ordination, i.e. Title VIII (there will be only a procedural follow up and then a loss of 'reputation' as 'penalty', whereas the stability pact signed at the same time is of a 'hard' nature as violations of these rules are punished by budgetary sanctions against Member States).

The almost completely new formulation of the Common Foreign and Security Policy (the 'second pillar') needs a specific reference (Regelsberger, 1998: 237–44). With several steps towards what might be called a 'rationalized intergovernmentalism' (Wessels, 1997) the chapter on the CFSP offers a certain though limited extension of the Union's capacity.[10] The introduction of the Petersberg tasks is a considerable extension of the scope and competence of the EU. The new instrument of 'common strategies' and the now more clearly defined instruments of 'common positions' and 'joint-actions' are steps to a more legalized foreign policy. The new 'policy planning and early warning unit' as well as the creation of a 'Mr CFSP' will increase the human resources in the Brussels arena, but the real roles will be established only by the first trial and error processes.[11] This set-up might prove to be a further secretariat in the hand of the presidency of the day and thus just of limited impact on the nature of the CFSP or it might turn into the nucleus of a real European Foreign Office. The Treaty procedures are clearly pointing at the first interpretation.

The overall assessment of the CFSP chapter tends to support the views of the neo-realists: Member States as masters of the treaties have only marginally modified their central role as decision makers in the day-to-day activities. In this vital area of high politics member governments and especially diplomats have not transferred the competence of their national instruments. The 'common' policy will remain a 'coordinated' one at the best. Credible commitments via an institutional reinforcement have not been made.

The overall trend towards communitarization in line with neo-functionalist functional logic arguments is paradoxically even documented by the attempts to draw clear lines for EC competencies and prevent uncontrolled spill-overs. The protocol on subsidiarity, similar to some other concretely formulated limitations of EC action (such as in the employment chapter), look like rather helpless attempts to stop the Union's propensity to attract Member States' preferences for actions in the EU arena. The architects of the Amsterdam Treaty were not able or rather were unwilling to design a clear vertical division of competencies between the national and the European level.

Institutional and procedural evolutions

Looking at the 'institutional balance' (the term has been inserted into the Treaty by the Protocol (No. 21) on the application of the principles of subsidiarity and proportionality),[12] a perhaps surprising impression is that all EU-organs and bodies have extended their functions and their fields of competencies. A clear shift between the institutions into either the supranational trend as the neo-federalists and the neo-functionalists claim or into the intergovernmental direction of the neo-realists cannot be deduced from the provisions of the Treaty. Though both can point at decisions in line with their specific arguments, no global institutional design was pursued.[13]

The European Council (quite often neglected in such an analysis) has now constitutionalized some of its (so far *de facto*) powers. Besides stressing its role to give general and specific guidelines also in the EC Treaty (employment chapter) it also installed itself officially in an 'appellation' and 'referee' position (when dealing with national vetoes). At the same time, the European Council's actions remain outside the control by the Court and thus outside the checks and balances of the EC system. The enormous gain of control[14] of the Heads of State or Government via the backdoor might become a major issue for the EU's constitutional set-up, at least from the point of view of conventional standards.

The Council (of Ministers) has kept and reinforced its role as gate keeper, e.g. with Article 133 TEC and Article 8 TEU, in the area of freedom, security and justice and by keeping unanimity in many areas.

The treaty architects have again extended the powers of the EP (Schmuck, 1998: 79–86; Maurer, 1999).[15] By the extension and simplification of the co-decision procedure and a two-step procedure for (co-) electing the President and the Commission, the treaty provisions document a dynamic towards an equal partner in a two-chamber system. It will however remain difficult to clearly identify the accountable bodies and politicians; such a diffusion of responsibilities (Scharpf, 1988) is a typical feature of a bicameral legislature.

The reforms of the Commission (Rometsch, 1998: 71–8) will lead to a basic change in the internal interaction style – away from a collegial-system to a prime-ministerial system. If used properly the Commission might increase its weight and efficiency – even with more members. Being granted new essential functions in internal policy fields – such as immigration, or also in the employment chapter – the Commission has seen its considerable powers reinforced also in additional areas of traditional national policies.

Often neglected in political science assessments, the Court also will extend its role as a constitutional guarantor for a Union state of law.

Except for major parts of the 'common provisions' (including the European Council) and the discrete and discretionary field of the CFSP (where Courts normally did not play any role in national systems) most of the EU will be subject to legal control and therefore to constitutional checks and balances. The limits and ambiguities set by the Treaty to judicial review of the actions in the area for security, freedom and justice[16] indicate the need to improve those constitutional guarantees.

The Treaty has also extended the scope of policy fields for the Court of Auditors as well as the ECOSOC and the Committee of Regions (Hrbek, 1998: 105–10). An upgrading of these 'grand committees' in terms of their decision-making powers has however not taken place. The COSAC, the committee of the European committees of national parliaments, has been mentioned but it has not been put into the policy cycle of the EU.[17] The treaty architects – including the parliaments of the member states themselves – have not given any incentive to further the 'Bruxellisation' of national deputies, though after Maastricht national parliaments gained additional powers in the national cycle of the EU system. They arrived at only limited access to the European arena, yet their new responsibilities[18] might lead to a further increase in the degree of complexity.

As regards the set of decision-making rules, the trend towards procedural differentiation has again been reinforced. Against all proclaimed intentions the architects of the Treaty have increased the number of rules and their complexity. The abolishment of one legislative procedure – that of the cooperation procedure (except for the EMU chapter) – and the simplification of the co-decision procedure are more than counterbalanced by additional and ever more complicated procedures in all three pillars. They all document the dilemma of Member States: as masters of the treaties they have to find an adequate balance between the intention to improve the efficiency of the EU institutions on one hand and to keep an effective say for themselves on the other. Two 'innovative' rules are examples of this tension: the procedures to provide opportunities for an 'enhanced cooperation' are highly Byzantine.[19] In a strange coalition between the defenders of Community orthodoxy and those of national interests, the rules for flexibility have produced a high degree of inflexibility: they will offer very limited chances only in those cases where a cooperative approach among all members can be found.

The other case is the introduction of a modified version of the Luxembourg compromise in two procedures, enhanced cooperation in the EC and majority voting in the CFSP.[20] Somehow the treaty architects wanted to increase the Union's capacity to take decisions but then they wanted to install a fall back clause – just for the case they need to safeguard important interests. In political reality the logic of such a procedure might lie in its anticipatory effects: if a member government threatens with a veto only behind the scene no other governmental actor might then be willing to push the issue as the path to be used is full of legal and political obstacles.

As we have to take the growing complexity of procedures into account, the diffusion of political responsibility has and will continue. Accountability is difficult to establish. The rules for transparency might be helpful for some academic research, but few effects can be expected for the average or even interested citizen of Europe.

REVISITING THE THEORETICAL PERSPECTIVES: AMSTERDAM AS A STEP TOWARDS FUSION

In revisiting the theoretical perspectives with a preliminary validity check, we could present arguments for each of the competing approaches. A reading of the Amsterdam Treaty does not simply falsify or verify one of these theories.

Though they are the most criticized, adherents to neo-functionalism and to neo-federalism could point to many elements of the Amsterdam Treaty supporting their assumptions and expectations – such as the functional and legal spill-over from the Internal Market to the area of freedom, security and justice and the institutional upgrading of the European Parliament and the Court. From that view the still imperfect communitarizations, the remaining intergovernmental methods, especially in the CFSP, and the priority given to the subsidiarity protocol can be interpreted as some kind of rearguard action of national governments, which will in time disappear because of the built-in logic of the integration process.

Those articles and provisions stressing the role of the European Council, the Council and national actors (especially in regard to the CFSP) could be invoked by the neo-realists. Their arguments become, however, less and less convincing. As in Maastricht, communitarization has not stopped at low politics but has been again extended to high politics, touching core areas of national sovereignty. At least these two treaties on the European Union have clearly falsified some basic assumptions of the traditional realists who expected a decline of the EU as a consequence of its loss in function after the end of the Cold War.

The governance or pendulum view can point at mixed records of more or less progress; however, to put Maastricht and Amsterdam into a broad corridor without identifying trends and differences is difficult. In the Amsterdam Treaty we do not find traces of a spill back or diffusion. The steps taken might not be as far-reaching as the neo-functionalists have expected; the communitarization might be incomplete and imperfect, but seen in dynamic perspective in no area or procedure could we identify some kind of down-swing. Liberal intergovernmentalists can point at package dealing among national preferences and hybrid institutional solutions.

The major provisions of the Amsterdam Treaty (like that of the Maastricht Treaty) clearly indicate that the masters of the Treaty have again (as often in the European post-World War II history) perceived the need to solve basic problems (and some minor ones) via a common framework. They also realized that to fulfil these functions in the interest of their states they need efficient and legitimized Community methods – while simultaneously keeping a strong role for national governments. The members of the European Council, as the architects of the Amsterdam Treaty, did not desire to abolish their states but to strengthen them by pooling national and Community resources and also by upgrading Community methods. Amsterdam is another ratchet step within long-term trends: a fusion with an open *finalité politique*. The Amsterdam Treaty is neither a constitutional *saut qualitatif* into a new era of the Union, nor a step towards an intergovernmental set-up under the control of member states, but it is in many ways a continuation and reinforcement of fundamental evolutions within the post-war integration history. As such it is part of a medium term (Braudel, 1986) development of the European polity.

Given its built-in complexities reflecting the fundamental dilemmas of Member States, these treaty provisions will invite the present and the future Member States to look at further amendments and revisions – probably again not in the sense of radical reforms. The upcoming Nice Treaty might be a follow-up in the line of this argument. If we take this analysis seriously, we should not expect any innovative way to get to a more efficient and democratic 'real' constitution.[21] Thus the preparation for the enlargement will be suboptimal in terms of the institutional streamlining.[22]

NOTES

1. See e.g. Moravscik and Nicolaidis (1999).
2. Judgement of the Federal Constitutional Court from 1993 about the constitutional appeal against the treaty of Maastricht (1993), Judgement of October 12 1993, in Oppenheimer (1994).
3. See Chapter 6, J.-V. Louis, 'The European Union's constitutional muddle: Which way forward?'
4. See Chapter 1, J. Grünhage, 'The 1996/97 Intergovernmental Conference'.
5. See Chapter 11, P. C. Padoan, 'EU employment and social policy after Amsterdam: too little or too much?'
6. See Chapter 6.

7. This interpretation is not shared by all commentators. See the chapters by Jörg Monar and Monica den Boer in this volume.
8. See Chapter 8, B. Smith, and W. Wallace, 'Constitutional deficits of EU justice and home affairs: transparency, accountability and judicial control'.
9. *Ibid*.
10. See Chapter 13, Regelsberger and Schmalz, 'The Common Foreign and Security Policy of the Amsterdam Treaty: towards an improved EU identity on the international scene?'
11. See Chapter 2, E. Brok,: 'The institutional reforms of Amsterdam'.
12. See Chapter 3, F. Dehousse, 'Amsterdam: success or failure? A personal view'.
13. *Ibid*.
14. *Ibid*.
15. See Chapter 7, A. Maurer, 'Democratic governance in the European Union: the institutional terrain after Maastricht'.
16. See Chapter 8.
17. See Chapter 7.
18. *Ibid*.
19. See Philippe de Schoutheete (Chapter 9) and Eric Philippart and Monika Sie Dhian Ho (Chapter 10) in this volume.
20. *Ibid*.
21. See Chapter 6.
22. See Chapter 4, J. Saryusz-Wolski, 'The reformed European Union and the challenge of enlargement'.

BIBLIOGRAPHY

Braudel, F. (1986) *Sozialgeschichte des 15–18. Jahrhunderts, Aufbruch zur Weltwirtschaft*. Munich.

Bulmer, S. (1994) 'The governance of the European Union: a new institutionalist approach'. *Journal of Public Policy*, 4, 351–80.

Caporaso, J. (1996) 'The European Union and forms of the state, Westphalian, regulatory or post modern?' *Journal of Common Market Studies*, 1, 29–52.

Duff, A. (1997) *The Treaty of Amsterdam: Text and Commentary*. London.

Engel, C. (1998) 'Der Europäische Rat'. In W. Weidenfeld and W. Wessels (eds), *Jahrbuch der Europäischen Integration 1997/98*. Bonn.

Grieco, J. M. (1988) 'Anarchy and the limits of cooperation: a realist critique of the newest liberal institutionalism'. *International Organization*, 3, 485–507.

Grünhage, J. (2000) 'The 1996/97 Intergovernmental Conference', in this volume.

Haas, E. B. (1968) *The Uniting of Europe: Political, Social and Economic Forces, 1950–1957*. Stanford.

Hallstein, W. (1979) *Die Europäische Gemeinschaft*. 5th edn., Düsseldorf.

Hrbek, R. (1998) 'Der Ausschuß der Regionen'. In W. Weidenfeld and W. Wessels (eds), *Jahrbuch der Europäischen Integration 1997/98*. Bonn.

Jachtenfuchs, M. and B. Kohler-Koch (1996) 'Regieren im dynamischen Mehrebenensystem'. In M. Jachtenfuchs and B. Kohler-Koch (eds), *Europäische Integration*. Opladen.

Keohane, R.O. and Hoffmann, S. (1990) 'Conclusions: community politics and institutional change'. In W. Wallace (ed.), *The Dynamics of European Integration*. London.

Link, W. (1998) *Die Neuordnung der Weltpolitik, Grundprobleme globaler Politik an der Schwelle zum 21. Jahrhundert*, Munich.

Louis, J-V. (2000) 'The European Union's constitutional muddle: which way forward?, in this volume.

Magiera, S. and M. Niedobitek (1998) 'Der Gerichtshof'. In W. Weidenfeld and W. Wessels, (eds), *Jahrbuch der Europäischen Integration 1997/98*. Bonn.

Maurer, A. (1999) *What Next for the European Parliament? Future of European Parliamentary Democracy Series II*. London.

Maurer, A. (2000) 'Democratic governance in the European Union: the institutional terrain after Amsterdam', in this volume.

Mearsheimer, J. J. (1990) 'Back to the future, instability in Europe after Cold War'. *International Security*, 1, 5–56.

Merton, R. K. (1968) *Social Theory and Social Structure*. 3rd edn, New York.

Meyers, R. (1977) *Weltpolitik in Grundbegriffen*. Bonn.

Monar, J. (1997) 'The European Union's Foreign Affairs system after the Treaty of Amsterdam: a strengthened capacity for external action?' *European Foreign Affairs Review*, 2, 413–36.

Monnet, Jean (1955) *Les Etats-Unis d'Europe ont commencé: la Communauté, du charbon et l'acin, discours et allocations, 1952–1954*. Paris.

Moravcsik, A. (1994) 'Preferences and power in the European Community: a Liberal intergovernmentalist approach'. *Journal of Common Market Studies*, 31, 473–24.

Moravcsik, A. (1999) *The Choice for Europe: Social Purpose and State Power from Messina to Maastricht*. London.

Moravcsik, A. and K. Nicolaidis (1999) 'Explaining the Treaty of Amsterdam: interest, influence, institutions'. *Journal of Common Market Studies*, 1, 59–85.

Müller-Graff, P-C. (1998) 'Justiz und Inneres nach Amsterdam: Die Neuerungen in erster und dritter Säule'. In R. Hrbek *et al.* (eds), *Die Europäische Union als Prozeß*. Bonn.

Office for Official Publications of the European Communities (1997) *European Union, Consolidated Versions of the Treaty on European Union and the Treaty establishing the European Community*. Luxembourg.

Oppenheimer, A. (ed.) (1994) *The Relationship between European Community Law and National Law: The Cases*. Cambridge.

Padoan, P. C. (2000) 'The new provisions on employment. Too little or too much social policy?', in this volume.

Pinder, J. (1986) 'European Community and Nation-State: a case for a neo-federalism'. *International Affairs*, 1, 41–54.

Regelsberger, E. (1998) 'Gemeinsame Außen- und Sicherheitspolitik'. In W. Weidenfeld and W. Wessels (eds), *Jahrbuch der Europäischen Integration 1997/98*. Bonn.

Regelsberger, E. and M. Jopp (1997) 'Und sie bewegt sich doch! Die Gemeinsame Außen- und Sicherheitspolitik nach den Bestimmungen des Amsterdamer Vertrages'. *Integration*, 4, 255–63.

Regelsberger, E. and U. Schmalz (2000) 'The Common Foreign and Security Policy of the Amsterdam Treaty: towards an improved EU identity on the international scene?' in this volume.

Regelsberger, E. and W. Wessels (1996) 'The CSFP Institutions and Procedures, a third way for the Second Pillar'. *European Foreign Affairs Review*, 1, 29–54.

Rometsch, D. (1998) 'Die Europäische Kommission'. In W. Weidenfeld and W. Wessels (eds), *Jahrbuch der Europäischen Integration 1997/98*. Bonn.

Saryusz-Wolski, J. (2000) 'The reformed European Union and the challenge of enlargement', in this volume.

Scharpf, F. W. (1988) 'The joint-decision trap: lessons from German Federalism and European integration'. *Public Administration*, 66, 229–78.

Schmitter, P. C. (1969) 'Three neo-functional hypotheses about international integration'. *International Organization*, 23, 161–7.

Schmitter, P. C. (1996) 'If the nation-state were to wither away in Europe, what might replace it?' In S. Gustavsson and L. Lewin (eds), *The Future of the Nation-State: Essays on Cultural Pluralism and Political Integration*. Stockholm.

Schmuck, O. (1998) 'Das Europäische Parlament'. In W. Weidenfeld and W. Wessels (eds), *Jahrbuch der Europäischen Integration 1997/98*. Bonn.

Schneider, H. (1994) 'Föderale Verfassungspolitik für eine Europäische Union'. In H. Schneider and W. Wessels (eds), *Föderale Union: Zukunft Europas? Analysen, Kontroversen, Perspektiven*. Munich.

Smith, B. and W. Wallace (2000) 'Consitutional deficits of EU justice and home affairs transparency, accountability and judicial control', in this volume.

Spinelli, A. (1958) *Manifest der Europäischen Föderalisten*. Frankfurt.

Taylor, P. (1981) 'The European Communities and the obligation of membership: Claims and Counter Claims'. *International Affairs*, 2, 236–53.

Thatcher, M. (1989) 'Rede vor dem Europa-Kolleg in Brügge am 20. September 1988'. In W. Weidenfeld and W. Wessels (eds), *Jahrbuch der Europäischen Integration 1988/89*. Bonn.

Wallace, H. (1996) 'Politics and policy in the EU: the challenge of governance'. In H. Wallace and W. Wallace (eds), *Policy-making in the European Union*, 3rd edn, Oxford.

Wallace, H. and W. Wallace (eds) (1996) *Policy-making in the European Union*, 3rd edn., Oxford.

Wallace, W. (1996) 'Government without statehood: the unstable equilibrium'. In H. Wallace and W. Wallace (eds) (1996) *Policy-making in the European Union*, 3rd edn., Oxford.

Weidenfeld, W. and W. Wessels (eds) (1989) *Jahrbuch der Europäischen Integration 1988/89*. Bonn.

Wessels, W. (1997) 'An ever closer fusion? a dynamic macropolitical view on integration process'. *Journal of Common Market Studies*, 2, 267–99.

Wessels, W. (1998) 'Verstärkte Zusammenarbeit: Eine neue Variante flexibler Integration'. In M. Jopp, A. Maurer and O. Schmuck (eds), *Die Europäische Union nach Amsterdam, Analysen und Stellungnahmen zum neuen EU-Vertrag*. Bonn.

Wessels, W. (1999) 'Das politische System der Europäischen Union'. In W. Ismayr (ed.), *Die politischen Systeme Westeuropas*, 2nd edn, Opladen.

Wessels, W., Maurer, A. and J. Mittag (eds) (2000) *Fifteen into One? The European Union and Its Member States*. Manchester.

Westlake, M. (ed.) (1998) *The European Union beyond Amsterdam: New Concepts of European Integration*. London.

PART II

CONSTITUTIONAL AND INSTITUTIONAL REFORMS

CHAPTER 6

THE EUROPEAN UNION'S CONSTITUTIONAL MUDDLE: WHICH WAY FORWARD?[1]

Jean-Victor Louis

INTRODUCTION

The predecessor to the Amsterdam Treaty, the Treaty on the European Union (TEU), signed at Maastricht, has allowed the European Union to make an important step forward towards the realization of Economic and Monetary Union (EMU). However, it has, at the same time, created an institutional disorder in the Union which has been rightly criticized (Curtin, 1993: 17–69). The pillar system and the opt-outs consented to the United Kingdom have altered the coherence of the Community legal order.

As pointed out by Ulrich Everling (1998), the Amsterdam Treaty, besides introducing some important new elements in the integration process, brings also some consolidation by clearing some formal and material weaknesses from the Treaty. Particularly noticeable in this respect is the suppression of the British exception concerning the social protocol, the accent on fundamental rights and general principles, the integration of the Schengen agreement and the improvement in terms of both efficiency and effectiveness of the third pillar,[2] not to mention the – rather limited – operation of simplification of the treaties.

The Amsterdam Treaty marks a step forward in the progressive constitutionalization process.[3] To quote Ulrich Everling again, these elements of progress is 'wie alle vorhergehenden, begrenzt und unvollkommen und bedürfen der Fortführung'.[4]

What kind of reform would actually be needed in order to strengthen and democratize the constitutional structure of the Union in order to allow it to cope with its new responsibilities under the EMU, and in the world, and to be ready for the enlargement? Whatever the importance of the content of the prospected reform of the Constitution of the Union, the process of the reform, which has been up to now based on the intergovernmental procedure of Article 48 TEU (former Article N TEU and 236 TEC), has to be considered as a priority.

THE REFORM PROCESS

After Maastricht, it has repeatedly been said that the 1991–1992 Conference would be the last big IGC, conducted behind closed doors as a
classical diplomatic negotiation. Nevertheless, in a very large measure, the
1996–1997 IGC has been a repetition of the Maastricht process, which was
based on previous experiences. The limited originality of the latest IGC in
this respect comes from the establishment of the Reflection Group, chaired
by Carlos Westendorp. This should have represented for the political
union what the Delors Committee was for the Economic and Monetary
Union in the Maastricht Treaty, but the composition of the Group, based
on completely different grounds, was perhaps a handicap in that respect[5]
– and in the modalities of association of the European Parliament which
have varied from one conference to another.[6] Of course, the main reason
for this continuity is to be found in the absence of revision of the Treaty
article governing the revision procedure itself, but the provision allows
for some imaginative formulae within the existing legal framework, if the
political will is there. For example, there is nothing in the Treaty that
places an obligation to follow the order of succession of presidencies
according to the six months rule applicable to the Council, and the
modalities of association of the European Parliament depend only on the
conception of the role which it has agreed to grant to this institution.
Many views have been expressed to explain the failure of the IGC to
achieve what it was assigned to do, that is, to re-equilibrate the treaties in
order to develop their political features (development of the second and
third pillars) and prepare the Union for enlargement.

There were indeed circumstantial factors that explain why there has
been so little real negotiation during a large part of the Conference and,
in the end, no significant will to achieve important institutional results.
There was a feeling of absence of time constraint during parts of the
Conference. There were, indeed, good reasons to expect the results of the
British elections in the spring of 1997. On the other hand, it was not easy
to combine the difficulties of the negotiation of a new treaty with the
problems of the transition to the single currency (Kortenberg, 1998: 1–10).
Perhaps, and this was an important psychological and political element,
enlargement was conceived as a distant prospect, which did not justify
early concessions (Kortenberg, 1998: 10). As a diplomat closely involved
in the negotiation observed 'in the absence of time constraints, there is
little if any incentive for delegations to begin to engage in negotiations'
(McDonagh, 1998: 53).

Lengthy sessions of the IGC were devoted to endless 'tours de table'.[7] It
gave national delegations time to prepare 'a large number of disparate

and relatively unimportant proposals'. This led to the adoption of a number of declarations and protocols, creating what has been called a 'Christmas tree effect' which did 'add neither to the coherence nor to the readability of the Treaty' (McDonagh, 1998: 220) but, as has also been pointed out, created 'new heights of complexity and opacity' (Toulemon, 1998: 119). In a way, the lack of concern for substantial political reform has resulted in a number of rather minor initiatives that have been considered as being able to capture the sympathy of different sectors of the civil society.

A large part of responsibility for the lacunae of the Amsterdam Treaty can be attributed to the loose and open-ended mandate adopted by the European Council in Turin in March 1996. Its resolution was, indeed, more a listing of problems than an assignment of objectives. Without clear political guidance, the IGC was unable to make a success of the negotiation of many of the points included in the Turin mandate. This lack of political orientation from the European Council reflects the limited degree of consensus among the Member States on the objectives of the European construction. Apart from those circumstantial elements, which explain the slow pace, and eventually, the limited output of the IGC on some crucial matters, the main excuse advocated by the diplomats to justify the limitations of the Amsterdam Treaty rests, as for preceding IGCs, in the unanimity requirement. Bobby McDonagh (1998: 71) for example, stated that:

The obvious fact that unanimous agreement was necessary at every stage of the Conference is worth recalling only because there is apparently no shortage of armchair visionaries who could have written a better Treaty of Amsterdam before breakfast.

This observation is not without grounds, but aiming at consensus for the sake of it, as could be observed in the last part of the negotiations, led to the excesses of what has been called the 'polder technique', by reference to the role of the Dutch Presidency, i.e. the search for the emergence of areas of consensus, with a minimum concern for their actual content and their coherence with some global principles. This can run against the clarity and the effectiveness of the output (Labayle, 1998: 173). The fragmentation of the rules, with the large number of exceptions and special regimes, is particularly evident in the new title on freedom, security and justice and in the new third pillar (see Chapter 14, below; Monar, 1998: 320–35). For some, far from having only inconvenience, the unanimity requirement represented a guarantee of success for the Conference. Martin Westlake refers, in this context, to the 100 per cent success rate the IGCs have enjoyed to date. They have achieved 'the best possible results' due to four factors: the spreading of amendments, the creation of complex package deals, the championing of Heads of State or Government and the linkage to the success of the enterprise as a whole (Westlake, 1998: 25). The European civil servant who signed an article on the Amsterdam Treaty under the pseudonym of Helmut Kortenberg seems to share this view when referring to the number of amendments to the Constitution of the United States that have failed to be adopted due to their lack of realism and final consensus (Kortenberg, 1998: 11). One can object to this pragmatism when historical challenges are at stake, the possibility of a crisis should not be systematically ruled out. This was the European Movement's position when he suggested that Governments that were convinced of the necessity of a substantial reform should consider the recourse to exceptional procedures in order to avoid the consequences of a veto of one or more Member States. This way has not been pursued, with the consequence that a new IGC will have to be called in order to achieve the required reform. The 'Protocol on the institutions with the prospect of enlargement', annexed to the ToA provides in its second paragraph for a complete re-examination of the provisions of the Treaty concerning the composition and the functioning of the institutions, at least one year before the Union counts more than 20 Member States. There are different views on the possible content of such a new reform which was set to be negotiated during 2000. We will come back later on some of these questions.

The implementation of the provisions of the Maastricht Treaty concerning Monetary Union was given priority over its revision. Nobody was prepared for a crisis which could have endangered the process of realization of the EMU. This setting of priorities was perfectly understandable. On the other hand, one should not forget that the necessity of reaching a unanimous agreement for the revision has caused a disruption of the Community legal order by the Amsterdam Treaty. The concession of the two opt-outs to the United Kingdom and the special regimes for Denmark would not have been agreed in the absence of the unanimity rule for the revision, which is indeed, as observed by Koen Lenaerts, 'a powerful means to protect their [the Member States] autonomy and national identity' (Lenaerts, 1998: 787).

The next IGC will take place under the same provision of the Treaty. That does not prevent Member States and the institutions from providing greater participation of the European Parliament in the Conference in order allow for a wider political debate. This is indeed of the utmost importance for the creation of the conditions for an open and in-depth confrontation of views. This should not be left solely to regular press meetings held by the Presidency of the IGC. A form of constitutional co-decision procedure should be the final goal of the reform. A first step in this direction would involve the compulsory examination by the IGC of the suggestions for amendments made by the European Parliament.

An inescapable matter for negotiation at the next Intergovernmental Conference should be the revision procedure itself. In order to avoid the difficulties created by the unanimity requirement for any revision whatever its importance, a possible 'deconstitutionalization' of some parts of the Treaties should be considered, allowing for revision by legislative acts of the Community adopted with a strengthened majority. If the unanimity rule has to be preserved due to imperious political reasons, at least for the revision of some 'constitutional' provisions, the possibility of opting out from the Union should be left open for dissenting Member States in those cases which are of the utmost importance for them and for the Union.

To conclude this section, there is an important lesson from the past: an IGC has a greater chance of concluding with satisfactory results if there is a clear political mandate given by the Heads of State or Government. That was the case for both the Single Market in 1985 and the EMU in 1990. The Turin European Council failed to give such impulse to the 1996 IGC. The opening of a constitutional debate, with the participation of the civil society, can help to identify and to clarify the issues at stake.

THE ORIENTATION OF THE REFORM

Contrary to what is often said by some opponents to progress towards a European Political Union, the aims of the reform and of the integration process itself are not equivalent to the building of a European State. The Union is characterized – and so it will remain – by a *sui generis* institutional architecture (Majone, 1998: 8), but the development of the Union's competencies and responsibilities is such that a major institutional reform is needed. It is indeed important to realize that if enlargement constitutes the main motor of reform, the latter was already justified by the qualitative step the Union made with the Maastricht Treaty. The new competencies which have been conferred to the Union are all very similar to the ones which Member States have been responsible for so far but that they are unable to exercise any more in a very changing world. This transfer – with varying degrees of importance according to the subject – of national prerogatives to a central institution underlines the already actual features of federalism which are discernible in the constitution of the Union (Lenaerts, 1998: 751–2). The rejection of this reality leads to inadequate intergovernmental formulae. It is true that there has always been an 'impossibility of mapping functions onto specific institutions' (Majone, 1998: 8). The question is not to define *in abstracto* a Government for the Union, but to designate the existing or new institution(s) for the Union, which will be in charge of executive and legislative functions in the fields where these functions are required.

The EMU is a case in point. The existing asymmetry between economic union and monetary union, on the one hand, and between the competencies of the Council and of the Central Bank, on the other hand, are often underlined. It seems very unrealistic to believe that the ECOFIN and its Presidency are able to cope with the responsibilities generally allocated to the executive branch of power in such matters at the national level and on the international scene. An intermittent institution with a rotating Presidency has neither the authority nor the possibility to rapidly react to unexpected shocks, and could not possibly be an effective counterpart to what represents the most independent Central Bank which has ever existed. It would be a major handicap for the Union and for its partners if one of the most important currencies in the World economy and in the international monetary system would be managed in a suboptimal way, or at least less coherently than in the US or in Japan.

In the legislative field, co-decision between the Council and the Parliament, with the participation of the Commission, has to be generalized, for the adoption of the budget. It is very important to realize that democracy has to be understood as a requirement not only at the Community level but also at national level (Verhoeven, 1998). On the other hand, competencies lost by national parliaments should be exercised with sufficient parliamentary control at Community level. We do not believe in the merits of the alternative, consisting in the introduction of legislative referenda which coincide with the European elections, as proposed by Joseph Weiler (1998: 39). In our view, referenda should be reserved for constitutional issues.

The definition of what is legislation and what may be left to the Commission, in its capacity of executive, is clearly needed in order to avoid the interferences of both branches of the legislature in the implementation field. That raises the question of a clear comitology procedure which would combine efficiency, transparency and democratic control (Dehousse, 1998a).

A kind of co-decision should also be provided for the conclusion of international agreements in order to remedy this unacceptable situation where the competencies lost by national parliaments are exercised in some case (for example, as regards trade agreements) without any kind of parliamentary control.

There is no shortage of ideas concerning the possible shape of the constitutional structure of the Union. The Spinelli and the Herman drafts, as well as many resolutions of the European Parliament and suggestions by governments, comprise food for thought. What is needed is a sense of urgency and a shared conviction that things have to move on.

These are some of the arguments that have led the European Movement, an organization which, by its very nature, has to be concerned with the future orientation of European integration, to propose a so-called 'Constitutional pact'.[8]

This exercise would have different purposes. It would constitute a restatement of the objectives and basic principles of the Union in one fundamental text. It would legitimize the development, and provide limits on the powers of the Union in matters concerning the sovereignty of the States and the citizens' rights. The Pact would provide a sound basis for the direct links between the Union and its citizens and reunite them around common visions and undertaking.[9] In this context a paragraph from a recent publication on a Human Rights Agenda for the EU merits quotation.

> There is something terribly wrong with a polity which acts vigorously to realise its economic ambitions, as it clearly should, but which, at the same time, conspicuously neglects its parallel ethical and legal obligations to ensure that those policies result in the fullest possible enjoyment of human rights.[10]

The Constitutional pact should include the principles and the objectives of the Union, the basic principles of its organization and of the allocation of competencies between the Union and its Member States, [11] the principles governing the relations among the institutions, the citizenship of the Union and the rights and obligations of its Member States. It would be a concise and clear text that could be a substitute for the preambles, common provisions and other preliminary articles of the Treaties. The Pact could have the same formal rank and nature as the Treaties but its content will confer to it a superior political and moral value.

In order to establish more firmly its value this text, adopted following the modalities of a Treaty revision, could be submitted to a European referendum. The recourse to a referendum would be justified, considering the historical and constitutional significance of the Pact.[12] The suggested Pact does not intend to exclude such or such country. It should be conceived in the interest of the present, as of the prospective members, of the Union.

It is essential to begin in the near future with the necessary constitutional debate. A clear orientation should emerge after the start of the new legislative period of the European Parliament. It should be mentioned in this regard that the informal European Council of Pörtschach (24–25 October 1998) constitutes an interesting move towards the elaboration of a convincing concept for the reforms of the Treaties.[13]

NOTES

1. The present text was written in November 1998; the views expressed in it remain valid after the IGC 2000. They are related to the inefficiency of the intergovernmental way of revising the treaties and the necessity to aim at new

forms of revision – less diplomatic and more democratic. The Union needs a government, EMU having been built on an asymmetry between the monetary and political branches of power. A hierarchy of norms should be introduced. A consititutional pact should reaffirm common values and give the union the clear and efficient structure it needs.

2. See in the same direction, the comments of Lenaerts (1998: 773).
3. Prof. Mouton and Torsten Stein have coined it as a constitutional process of an evolutionary nature (1997: 27).
4. *Op. cit.* 'As all their predecessors, they are limited, imperfect and need to be followed by others'.
5. Petite (1997: 17 *et seq.*), observes that 'as the members of the group were, for a great number of them, the future negotiators, all the options evoked by one or another delegation find their place in the report, without neither indication of priorities nor elimination of the more improbable'.
6. In 1991, interinstitutional meetings between the sessions of the IGC; in 1996–1997, participation of two Parliaments' delegates to official meetings of personal representatives.
7. See also Kortenberg (1998: 5) and Petite (1997: 23).
8. See the report of the European Movement for the Hague Congress of 8 to 10 May 1998 *'Let us build together a Europe for the XXIst Century'* (Jean-Guy Giraud).
9. In the context of the defence of democratic values, see Verhoeven (1998: 217–34): 'a common core of democratic values needs to be further developed and affirmed'. This author underlines the role of the Court at this regard but the 'thorough debate' she asks for is evidently a political and constitutional one.
10. *Leading by Example*: Cassese, Lalumière, Leuprecht and Robinson (1998: 35).
11. In that context, the subsidiarity principle – which, in the Treaty, concerns the exercise and not the allocation of competencies – is very often mentioned. The Amsterdam Treaty has developed through a protocol – which takes over most of the Birmingham resolution on subsidiarity, a kind of code of conduct for the use of Article 3B of the Maastricht Treaty. It is very doubtful that one could achieve more on this subject. Any attempt at definition of exclusive competencies would be a perilous exercise.
12. Such constitutional referenda, organized at the level of the Union, should remain exceptional. We do not share the view of the proponents of the institution of legislative referenda; compare with Weiler (1998). See also *Le référendum européen* (1997), and Epiney and Siegwart (1997).
13. See, in particular, the declaration of Mr Schröder on the objectives for the months to come; *Bulletin Europe* (1998).

BIBLIOGRAPHY

Bulletin Europe (1998), 26–27 October.

Cassese, A., Lalumière, C., Leuprecht, P. and M. Robinson (1998) *A Human Rights Agenda for the European Union for the Year 2000*. Agenda of the Comité des Sages and Final Project Report. EUI, Academy of European Law.

Curtin, D. (1993) 'The constitutional structure of the Union: a Europe of bits and pieces'. *Common Market Law Review*, 17–69.

Dehousse, F. (1997) 'Les résultats de la Conférence intergouvernementale'. *Cahiers du Centre de Recherches socio-politiques*, No. 1565–1566.

Dehousse, F. (1998) 'Les enjeux de l'élargissement'. *Cahiers du CRISP*, No. 1600.

Dehousse, R. (1998a) 'Citizens' rights and the reform of comitology procedures: the case for a pluralist approach'. Florence, The Robert Schuman Centre, EUI, Policy Paper 98/4.

Dehousse, R. (1998b), 'Institutional architecture after Amsterdam: parliamentary system or regulatory structure?' *Common Market Law Review*, 595–627.

Epiney, A. and K. Siegwart (eds) (1997), *Direkte Demokratie und Europäische Union. Démocratie directe et Union européenne*. Fribourg: Editions Universitaires.

European Movement (1998) *Let Us Build Together a Europe for the XXIst Century*. Report for the Hague Congress of 8 to 10 May 1998 (Jean-Guy Giraud).

Everling, U. (1998) 'Folgerungen aus dem Amsterdamer Vertrag für die Einheit der Europäischen Union und Gemeinschaften-Zusammenfassende Bewertung der Tagungsbeiträge'. In A. von Bogdandy and C. D. Ehlermann (eds), *Konsolidierung und Kohärenz des Primärrechts nach Amsterdam*. Europarecht, Beihefte.

Flauss, J. F. (1995) 'Vers un droit constitutionnel européen. Quel droit constitutionnel européen?' *Revue universelle des droits de l'homme*, 357–468.

Kortenberg, H. (1998) 'La négociation du Traité. Une vue cavalière'. In *Le Traité d'Amsterdam*. Paris: Dalloz.

Labayle, H. (1998) 'Un espace de sécurité, de liberté et de justice'. In *Le Traité d'Amsterdam*. Paris: Dalloz.

Lenaerts, K. (1998) 'Federalism: essential concepts in evolution: the case of the European Union'. *Fordham International Law Journal*, 746–98.

Le Référendum européen, (1997) Brussels: Bruylant.

Majone, G. D., (1998) 'Europe's democratic deficit: the question of standards'. *European Law Journal*, 5–28.

Mattera, A. (ed.) (1996) *La Conférence intergouvernementale sur l'Union européenne: répondre aux défis du XXIe siècle*. Paris: Clément Juglar.

McDonagh, B. (1998) *Original Sin in a Brave New World. An Account of the Negotiation of the Treaty of Amsterdam*. Dublin: Institute of European Affairs.

Monar, J. (1998) 'Justice and home affairs in the Treaty of Amsterdam: reform at the price of fragmentation', *European Law Review*, 23, 320–35.

Mouton, J. D. and T. Stein (eds) (1997) Vers une nouvelle constitution pour l'Union européenne? La Conférence intergouvernementale de 1996. Bonn: Bundesanzeiger.

Petite, M. (1997) 'Le traité d'Amsterdam: ambition et réalisme'. *Revue du Marché unique européen*, 17.

Snyder, F. (1998) 'EMU revisited: are we making a constitution? What constitution are we making?' *EUI Working Papers*, Law 98/6, Florence.

Toulemon, R. (1998), in M. Westlake (ed.), *The European Union beyond Amsterdam*. London: Routledge.

Verhoeven, A. (1998) 'How democratic need European Union members be? Some thoughts after Amsterdam'. *European Law Review*, 217–34.

Weiler, J. (1998) 'L'Europe: du pain et des jeux'. In *Six opinions sur l'euro et sur l'Europe*. Florence: Centre Robert Schuman.

Westlake, M. (ed.) (1998) *The European Union beyond Amsterdam*. London: Routledge.

CHAPTER 7

DEMOCRATIC GOVERNANCE IN THE EUROPEAN UNION: THE INSTITUTIONAL TERRAIN AFTER AMSTERDAM

Andreas Maurer

INTRODUCTION

While each of the European Union (EU) Member States enjoys some kind of a democratic government, the EU as a political system is widely perceived to suffer from what is called a 'democratic deficit'. Like the previous Intergovernmental Conferences (IGC), the Amsterdam process was meant not only to reform the Union's policy agenda, but also to strengthen the democratic nature of its institutional basis. The alliteration of the democratic deficit focuses mainly on the role of institutions which are designed to represent the different interests of the citizens and to establish different forms of linkage, and interest mediation in and for a given polity. In this context, the notion of the 'democratic deficit' means that during the European integration process, legislative competencies have constantly been shifted from a national parliamentary level towards the Council of Ministers without including the European Parliament as an equal partner in the EC/EU legislative process at the same time.[1] Of course, those stressing that national sovereignty may resist European integration would argue that decision-making in the EU rests primarily upon the Member States and the Council of Ministers and, since Maastricht, upon the European Council. Accordingly they would ascribe only a minor role to the European Parliament.[2] However, since the entry into force of the Single European Act (SEA) and the introduction of the cooperation as well as the assent procedure, the real distribution of powers between the institutions goes far beyond this conceptualization of the Union. Within the sphere of the European Communities, the Treaty revisions from 1986 onwards reveal a tendency towards a multi-level polity where competencies are not only shared between the Members of the Council but also between the Council and the European Parliament.

Nevertheless, even if the SEA and the Maastricht Treaty (TEU) opened new opportunities for an original kind of parliamentary democracy in the EC/EU, they left considerable gaps in parliamentary involvement and control in many policy areas, which directly affect the way of living of the Union's citizens.

Hence, whereas the legitimacy of democratic and representative policy-making is not fundamentally challenged within each of its Member States, the EU's institutions and their national counterparts face a multitude of questions as to how representative the system of multi-level governance is, in which way the Union's quasi-executive branches are accountable to a directly legitimated body and how democratic the decision-making procedures between the Union's legislative authorities are. Moreover, and with regard to other than parliamentary or formal mechanisms of linkage between the political authority established by the Union and its citizenry, many scholars in integration studies highlight the fact that the EU is lacking broader societal consent. As Weiler (1992: 11–41) pointed out, formal legitimacy requires that the evolving structure of power and authority should have been approved by democratically elected parliaments. In this sense, every stage of the integration process is legitimate when and insofar as it has been settled in a document of EU primary law and after 'being ratified by all the member states in accordance with their respective constitutional requirements' (Article 48 TEU). In addition, a political system which is entitled to limit national sovereignty and which is enabled to take decisions directly binding the residents of its constituent members without the prior and individual assent of each national government requires more than the formal approval of founding treaties and their subsequent amendments. In Weiler's terms, such a political system – like the European Union – needs social legitimacy: 'the willingness of minorities to accept the decisions of the majority within the boundaries of the EU's polity' (Shackleton, 1998: 130–4). In other words, social legitimacy supposes that decisions which are not taken by unanimity at all levels of and at every stage in the policy cycle have to be based on a broad acceptance of the system. Even if the citizenry of the EU polity is not fully aware of or interested in the way binding decisions about their way of life are taken, the system and the institutions which deliver the law must be aware of the risk that the public attitude towards it can shift from some kind of a 'permissive consensus' or – in Elmar Brok's words – 'benevolent indifference' (see Chapter 2) to fundamental scepticism.

And indeed, with regard to the 1996/1997 IGC, many if not all of the directly involved 'collective actors'[3] argued for the need to enhance democracy in and the legitimacy of the EU. Although Member State governments, parliaments, parties and EU institutions recognized the need to achieve a higher degree of polity-acceptance by the Union's population, most of the proposals concentrated on reforming already existing forms and instruments of the EU's 'input-legitimacy' (Scharpf, 1975) and its observed problems: decision-making procedures, institutions and inter-institutional arrangements.

Interestingly, the IGC attracted greater attention, interest and expectations in the parliaments of the EU Member States than any of the revisions of the Treaties establishing the EC carried out hitherto. Unlike the negotiations leading to the SEA and the Treaty on European Union (TEU), the Amsterdam deal was prepared and set in a relatively transparent space. Every institution produced its own document on the functioning of the Maastricht Treaty in order to fulfil the requirement of the then Article N TEU. In addition, every Member State government – with the exception of Germany, where position papers were produced only in the format of 'Franco-German' or 'Italo-German' declarations or letters to the Presidency of the Union – published some kind of memorandum on institutional reform. Due to Swedish constitutional requirements to make every document forwarded by the Government to the Riksdag available for the people, not only the papers circulating around the Reflection group but also those of the Member State delegations in the IGC were open to discussion for the interested citizenry. The European Parliament created a Task Force on the IGC which produced and updated systematic briefings summarizing the positions on every issue on the IGC's agenda. Like the synoptic reports of the French National Assembly and the British House of Commons during the IGC, the European Parliament's briefings and summaries were open to the public. Yet public opinion did not concentrate on institutional issues like the reweighting of votes in the Council, nor did it really focus on the extension of areas covered by majority voting and co-decision.

In general, IGCs, as the Amsterdam process, are conceived by their political rather than institutional objectives.[4] Consequently, during the process of treaty reforms, new or adjusted policy areas reveal higher interest and motivation than institutional or procedural questions. In turn, those actors which orient their argumentation towards mass media, public opinion and the electorate capture the issue of democracy and legitimacy in and of the EU, and its policy-making structure mainly by referring to its problem-solving capacity in specific policy areas. The EU has been seen as some kind of a regulatory regime (Majone, 1994; Majone, 1996: 263–77) or a 'special purpose organisation' (Dehousse, 1998: 1), which is less dependant on its parliamentary legitimacy than on efficiently oriented policies. In this perspective, the 'output-legitimacy' of the Union 'depends on its capacity to achieve the citizen's goals and solve their problems effectively and efficiently: The higher this capacity, the more legitimate the system' (Schimmelpfennig, 1996: 19; Bogdandy, 1993).

By contrast to this approach, elitist attention and interest with regard to the Amsterdam process were closely tied with the question of what institutional role both the European Parliament and the national parliaments will have to play in the future of the Union. Thus, parliamentary democracy within the institutional terrain of the EU became a central element of institutional reform. One may argue that Amsterdam – both the negotiations and the new Treaty itself – reflect a focal point of reference for the discussion on appropriate models of parliamentary and representative democracy in the European Union.

THE CHALLENGE: DEFICITS IN PARLIAMENTARY DEMOCRACY AFTER MAASTRICHT

The Maastricht Treaty introduced several important changes concerning the role and position of the European Parliament. On the basis of the positive experiences gained with the cooperation procedure since the entry into force of the SEA, the TEU widened its scope of application and in addition created the so-called co-decision procedure, consisting of three readings, at most. Herewith, the European Parliament got the right to block a proposed legislative act without the Council having the right to outvote the Parliament at the end. The conciliation committee was set up as the nucleus and new major element of the co-decision procedure. Composed of an equal number of representatives of the Council and the Parliament it has been given the task of reaching an agreement on a joint compromise text within six weeks after being convened. It can safely be said that with co-decision, the Parliament has gained a nearly equal say at least in vetoing a legislative act. But unlike the Council, the European Parliament was, however, not able to bypass resistance in the Council against a certain legislative act and to subsequently adopt the act without having the approval of the Council. Apart from co-decision, the TEU extended the assent procedure to a wider range of international agreements and other sectors of legislative nature.

Concerning Parliament's elective function, the TEU granted the European Parliament with the right to be consulted on the Member State's choice of the President of the European Commission and to approve the European Commission. Furthermore, the Treaty also provided Parliament to be consulted on the President of the European Monetary Institute and, once the EMU is established, on the appointment of the President, Vice-presidents and the members of the Board of the European Central Bank. Especially Parliament's right to vote on a motion of censure on the Commission raised and backed the Parliament's attempts to increase its influence in the appointment of the Commission. Appointments reflect a dynamic system of checks and balances or, in the language of the European Court of Justice, a system of loyal cooperation such as it derives from Article 5 (now Article 10 TEC) (OJ C246/81 1451). In political terms and given the EU's structure of indirect interest representation through its institutions, appointments create a relationship of accountability and responsiveness between the appointing and the appointed institution. However, until Maastricht, the European Parliament acted in a paradoxical situation: under Article 144 TEC (Article 27-2 of the Merger Treaty), the Commission could be dismissed as a collegiate body by Parliament. Given that since June 1979 the European Parliament is the only directly legitimated body in the EC, it would have been consequential that the institution which has the sole right to censure the Commission should also have the right to appoint the members of this body. Yet contrary to this thought the original right to nominate and to approve the Commission was held by the Member States alone. A new step in the direction of Parliament's elective function was made with the introduction of Article 158 (2) TEC by the TEU. With the entry into force of the TEU, the Commission's mandate was aligned with the Parliament's mandate. Consequently, the right of approval could not only be perceived as a formal act, but also as a design for a genuine political decision. Accordingly, the European Parliament sent, by amending its Rules of Procedure in September 1993, a clear signal that it insists on this right and regards it as an essential part of its competencies. Thus, the new mechanism became a very important element for the strengthening of the Commission's formal legitimacy and the European Parliament's visibility towards its electorate.

Given the Maastricht provisions on the European Parliament's new opportunities to 'co-govern' within the inter-institutional framework of the Union, it could be argued that its position and role were considerably strengthened. And indeed, many commentators underlined the importance of the upgraded Parliament with regard to its legislative, its control and its elective functions (Maurer, 1996: 15–38; Raworth, 1994). Some even concluded that the European Parliament 'was perhaps the largest net beneficiary of the institutional changes in the TEU' (Wallace, 1996: 63) and that 'Maastricht marks the point in the Community's development at which the Parliament became the first chamber of a real legislature; and the Council is obliged to act from time to time like a second legislative chamber rather than a ministerial directorate' (Duff, 1995: 253–4). Hence, through the introduction of the co-decision procedure, the European Parliament gained more control in the legislation process (it can prevent the enactment of legislation) and acquired more means of input into the binding EC legislation (the final text requires the EP's approval).

Nevertheless several structural deficits concerning the state reached in the execution of parliamentary democracy remained and lead to a controversial dispute about the pros and cons of Maastricht not only with regard to the European Parliament but also to the national parliaments in the EU Member States (Kohler-Koch, 1997; Nickel, 1993; Pliakos, 1995; Reich, 1992; Smith, 1996). Whereas most of the early commentaries held that the European Parliament is still lacking 'true legislative capabilities' (Thomas, 1992: 4) or that it could generally be 'regarded as a somewhat ineffective institution' (Nugent, 1994: 174), the German Constitutional Court's Maastricht ruling lead to a more general critique of the EU's parliamentary model. The basic assumption of the Court and later on of its protagonist commentators was that a polity presupposes a demos in ethno-national or ethno-cultural terms (the 'Volk' instead of the 'Gesellschaft' or 'Gemeinschaft'), and that without a single European people sharing heritage, language, culture and ethnic background, that without a European public space of communication that could shape the wills and opinion of the population, no European statehood could be founded. For those who adopted this view, it was logical to deny the pre-constitutional conditions for further integration and therefore to conclude that in the absence of a demos there cannot be real democracy at the European level (Weiler *et al.*, 1995; Weiler, 1997; Craig, 1997). Given that a socio-political entity which is willing to produce democratic forms of governance cannot simply dictate structural prerequisites and pre-constitutional elements of the future polity, one could argue that any attempt of institutional and procedural reform is senseless unless the different European demoi are not identifying themselves as part of an emerging European demos. Consequently, if one adopts this perspective, the European Parliament remains an artefact of elitist integration and cannot be considered as a 'Vollparlament' (Lübbe, 1994: 147; Schröder, 1994: 318), a fully fledged or 'real' parliament. Therefore, strengthening the European Parliament by means of institutional and procedural reforms would not lead to any kind of a democratic system. The Constitutional Court, however, opened another window for reforming the Union: it argued that in the absence of a truly European demos, democratic governance is mainly secured by the peoples of the Member States via their nationally elected representative bodies. Thus, democratizing the Union would mean strengthening the roles and powers of national parliaments and not, or only in the second instance, of the European Parliament.

Apart from this general condemnation of the Union's constitutional structure and its incapability to develop further more democratic modes of governance, other commentators and involved actors criticized the Maastricht Treaty as moving in the right direction but not far enough. In this regard, criticism occurred because the co-decision procedure has only been conceived for 15 out of 162 EC and 11 EU articles containing procedural arrangements (Table 1).[5] In approximately 140 possible cases these articles deal with original binding secondary legislation whereas the

Table 7.1 European Parliament and Council decision-making powers (1.11.1993 until 30.4.1999)

Council participation of EP	Unanimity in Council		QMV in Council		Simple majority in Council		Special majorities other than QMV		Sum	
	Σ of cases	%	Σ of cases	%	Σ of cases	%	Σ of cases	%	Σ of cases	%
Information	1	0.617	7	4.32	0	0	0	0	8	4.93
Consultation	27	16.66	21	12.96	0	0	4	2.46	52	32.09
Co-operation	0	0	16	9.87	0	0	0	0	16	9.87
Co-decision	2	1.23	13	8.02	0	0	0	0	15	9.25
Assent	3	1.85	2	1.23	0	0	1	0.617	6	3.70
None	24 EC	14.81	37	22.82	1	0.617	3	1.85	65 EC	40.12
	8 EU	72.72	3	27.27					11 EU	100.00
Sum (Σ)	57 EC	35.18	96 EC	59.26	1	0.617	8	4.93	162 EC	100.00
	8 EU	72.72	3 EU	27.27					11 EU	100.00

Author's calculation; *Source: Treaty on European Union*, 1993

remaining provisions concern quasi-constitutional questions such as enlargement or Treaty reform. In other words, only 9.25 per cent of the EC Treaty arrangements were conceived for co-decision and another 9.87 per cent for co-operation. By contrast, more than one-third of the EC's procedural articles contained an opportunity for the Council to adopt binding secondary legislation without any participation of the European Parliament, out of which 38 cases (22.43 per cent) were considered for simple or qualified majority voting (QMV).

Those policy areas where co-decision applied were considered to be rather limited (Gosalbo Bono, 1995: 22; Tsinisizelis and Chryssochoou, 1996). More specifically, it was argued, that 'the granting of co-decision rights regarding internal market legislation is only of limited significance, given that such legislation should have been adopted by 1992 and that Articles 100a and 100b [TEC] would no longer serve a purpose after that date' (Corbett, 1994: 209). However, focusing on the implementation of the Maastricht Treaty, we observe that 106 cases or 60.0 per cent of the 166 procedures concluded up to the end of June 1999 were based on Article 100a (now Article 95 TEC). In addition 18 other directives (10.0 per cent) were concluded on a combination of Articles 49, 57, 66 and 100a (now Articles 40, 47, 55 and 95 TEC). On the other hand Article 100b was never applied in order to adopt mutual recognition measures in the field of the internal market.[6] Moreover, only 18.7 percent (31 cases) of the procedures were based on articles originally incorporated into the Maastricht Treaty together with the co-decision procedure (Article 126 – Education and Youth (now Article 149 TEC); Article 128 – Culture (now Article 151 TEC); Article 129 – Health (now Article 152 TEC); Article 129a – Consumer Protection (now Article 153 TEC); Article 129d – Trans European Networks (now Article 156 TEC)) (Maurer, 1999). With regard to the impact of the European Parliament on the EU's legislative output, and therefore the potential of its 'output-legitimacy', the co-decision procedure itself was interpreted as being (too) complex, lengthy, cumbersome and protracted (Earnshaw and Judge, 1996: 109; Westlake, 1994: 119; Nugent, 1998: 119). Indeed, the procedure described in the then Article 189b TEC (now 251), could well be interpreted as symptomatic for the 'general trade-off' between the efficiency of EU decision-making on the one hand and parliamentary involvement on the other. As Scharpf puts it: 'Expanding the legislative ... powers of the European Parliament could render European decision processes, already too complicated and time-consuming, even more cumbersome' (Scharpf, 1994: 220; Wessels, 1996: 58). Consequently, with regard to the Amsterdam IGC, one could propose either to make co-decision more efficient and to cut off those parts of the procedure which in practice were only rarely used, or to delimit co-decision to those policy areas where inefficiency is less visible and therefore acceptable for those directly involved. However it has to be noted, that unlike the above-mentioned fears, co-decision did not appear to have led to serious delays in the final adoption of EC legislation. Detailed analysis even indicates that the average duration of co-decision fell dramatically from 769 days in 1994 to 344 days for proposals published in 1997 and adopted in 1997 or 1998. The average duration for all legislative acts adopted under the co-decision procedure until June 1999 was 738 days. This is four days more than the total average duration for all the acts hitherto adopted under the cooperation procedure, which is 734 days (Maurer, 1999).

Besides those innovations introduced in the framework of the TEC, the new fields of intergovernmental cooperation and co-ordination – Common Foreign and Security Policy (CFSP) and Co-operation in the fields of Justice and Home Affairs (CJHA) – constituted what was probably the EU's most obvious parliamentary democratic deficit. The inadequacy of Parliament's powers of control was all the more serious, since many governments escaped any kind of parliamentary scrutiny at the national level. When acting under the CFSP, the European Parliament obtained the right to ask questions, to put forward recommendations to the Council and to be informed by the Council Presidency. In addition, the Commission too had to inform Parliament about the progress made in CFSP. The scrutiny rights of Parliament were, however, severely limited since its general participation in CFSP activities was specified neither in the Treaty provisions on common positions nor on the adoption of joint actions. In sum, the European Parliament's right to be consulted was limited to the main aspects and basic choices of the CFSP, although the Council Presidency alone decided on the scale, content and timing of the information provided. Consequently, Parliament's active participation in shaping the substance of the CFSP depended entirely on the political will of the governments of the member states. Where Justice and Home Affairs were concerned, the Treaty provisions on the European Parliament's role in CJHA corresponded very largely to the CFSP. A positive factor for Parliament in this context was the fact that the Commission was at least given a right of initiative in the areas listed under the then Article K.1 (1) to (6) TEU, although it had to share this right with the member states. The latter, on the other hand, obtained the sole right of initiative in judicial cooperation on criminal matters, customs cooperation and police cooperation. There was thus a specific and effective opportunity for monitoring and censuring the Commission, but not the Council of Ministers.

The complexity of the EU system: a challenge and result of institutional reform

With its evolving structure of a dynamic multi-level governance (Marks, 1993: 391–411; Bulmer, 1994; Kohler-Koch, 1995), the EU is neither comparable with national constitutional systems nor with international organizations or associations. Its autonomous development depends on the process of the growth and differentiation of policy areas, institutions and procedures which is not yet complete and might well not be in the near future. The nature of the EU has been characterized by a continuing extension of its responsibilities and authorities which have enlarged the total range of policy areas community-wide. Simultaneously, more and more competencies have been partly transferred from the exclusive national to a supranational level. Finally and in order to reconcile the management of growing responsibilities successfully with the demands for real and functional participation of the political actors involved, new institutions have been established and the already existing institutional framework has been altered (Wessels, 1996; Wessels, 1997). As regards the Maastricht Treaty, the decision-making procedures, and especially the rules applied within and between the institutions of the EU, were often characterized as opaque and too complex. Of course, the complexity of the EU is a result of the huge number of its duties, legislative processes and implementation procedures and, at times, the unfathomable nature of the procedures and the roles of the actors involved. Basically, under the Maastricht Treaty, the EU institutions utilized four different procedures (consultation, cooperation, co-decision, assent). Above these four principal procedures, the Treaties and other inter-institutional agreements offer further decision-making courses depending on the voting rules of the

Council and the participation of other institutions (Committee of the Regions, Economic and Social Committee, European Central Bank). The complex structure of the Community becomes visible in this variety of procedures. The decision-making methods differ both across the areas of application and across the institutions and bodies involved.[7] Furthermore, Maastricht introduced new institutions (Committee of the Regions, European Monetary Institute, which has been transformed into a European Central Bank with the beginning of the third phase to the EMU). This development – further enhanced in the Amsterdam Treaty by the creation of new institutions (Employment Committee, Mr/Mrs CFSP, Policy Planning and Early Warning Unit) is an expression of the dynamic of growth and differentiation of European integration. Of course, new institutions are not established in order to swell even further the institutional structure of the EU, but because they are needed to deal with new monetary or social policy duties of the Union, to give the EU a single voice or interface for dealing with third countries and organizations, or – with regard to the Committee of the Regions – to become the EU's feedback towards the regional and local level of governance. Hence, new institutions do not operate in a political vacuum but in a closely connected system of power distribution in which the architects of the Treaty have implemented them. Whenever new institutions gain autonomy, they do not use it in isolation but in a framework of already established rules and bodies of political power. Concomitantly this process of institutional growth automatically attains a higher degree of complexity. This is obvious for players involved in this decision-making process, but for the citizens of the EU it is not.

THERAPY AND ACHIEVEMENTS

Comparing the documents produced during the IGC process (Istituto Affari Internazionali, 1994–6; European Parliament, 1996; Pijpers and Edwards, 1997; Griller *et al.*, 1996; Jopp and Schmuck, 1996; Jopp, Maurer, and Schmuck, 1996; Piepenschneider, 1996), the proposals made under the headings of 'democratization' can be classified as follows:

1. Democratization by reforming the decision-making procedures through an extension of the areas covered by the co-decision procedure according to the following four strategies:

(a) A systematic conjunction of the different types of decision-making procedures and the institutions to be involved on the one hand and the nature of the different legal acts at the EC/EU's disposal on the other. This approach would have suggested that some kind of a hierarchy of norms like it might be derived from the legal definition of the Council acting as legislator (OJ L304/7 of 10 December 1993).[8] Originally, the joint declaration of the then German and Italian Foreign Affairs Ministers Kinkel and Agnelli was strongly in favour of classifying the decision-making system of the Union according to this approach.[9] During the negotiations, the Commission, on 3 July 1996, published a comprehensive report on the method of extending the coverage of co-decision based on the definition of EC legislation (European Commission, 1996). The European Parliament, in its Bourlanges/De Giovanni report of 7 November 1996, largely welcomed this approach but suggested a more coherent way for separating 'legislative' from 'non-legislative' acts (European Parliament, 1996). The main variable for identifying an area as subject to co-decision was the legal nature of legislation, its scope and its implications. However, apart from Germany, Greece and Italy, the Member States delegations' did not further develop this approach.

(b) A systematic association of decision-making mechanisms in the Council of Ministers and decision-making procedures between the Council and the European Parliament. Protagonists of this approach suggested the introduction of co-decision in all cases where the Council decides by qualified majority. Consequently, the success of this strategy largely depended on the reform of the Council's own decision-making regime. The fact that after Maastricht the Council in the field of the EC's binding secondary legislation still had to decide unanimously in 57 TEC cases (see Table 7.2) seemed to be characteristic for the incapability of acting as one Union of 15 Member states. The unanimity requirement in the Council of Ministers serves as a serious obstacle to efficient policy making. The refusal strategy of the British government in the 'BSE/mad-cow disease conflict' in the preliminary stage of the Florence European Council highlighted this problem to a remarkable extent. However, negotiations on the reform of the Council's voting mechanisms and on the extension of the areas governed by the Damocles-sword of majority voting were not successful. The Member States discussed the possibility of an extension of qualified majority voting by referring to power (or status) oriented linkages between their personal representation in the EU institutions (namely with regard to the Commission), the representation of states by the weight of votes and the maintenance of Member State veto power with regard to the threshold for qualified majorities and blocking minorities. Since no compromise could be found between the larger and the smaller Member States, the IGC postponed the whole issue of adjusting these representative aspects of institutional reform to the next enlargement round (McDonagh, 1998: 151–64; Duff, 1997; Laffan, 1997). The 'Protocol on the institutions with the prospect of enlargement of the European Union' concludes that upon the next enlargement of the Union, Member States which actually nominate two Commissioners will have to give up one of these posting rights. However, this reform is conditioned by the need of a reorganization of the weighting of votes within the Council in order to compensate those states which stand to lose one of the two Commissioners to which they are entitled. The protocol thus reflects a strong cleavage between larger and smaller Member States and admits the failure of Amsterdam in this respect. Consequently, in the absence of a solution to this cleavage, an extension of co-decision depending on the voting requirements in the Council was not achievable.

(c) The simple transfer of the existing co-operation procedures into co-decision procedures. Right from the beginning of the preparatory 'reflection' phase on the IGC, Austria, Belgium, Germany, Italy, Luxembourg, the Netherlands and Portugal argued strongly in favour of deleting the co-operation procedure and its replacement by the co-decision procedure. During the negotiations between the Member States' delegations, this approach attracted the highest degree of sympathy. However, since an early agreement could be found not to reopen the Treaty provisions on EMU, it was very likely that four cooperation procedures would be retained.

(d) A policy oriented and single (national) interest guided re-ordering of decision-making procedures. Protagonists of such an approach looked at the European Parliament as a potential winning coalition partner in order to enforce or to block decision in specific policy areas. Given their general attitude of reforming the procedural set-up of the Union on a case-by-case basis, the governments of Finland, Ireland, Portugal and Sweden preferred this approach. Especially Sweden, where a majority of the political parties in government were reluctant *vis-à-vis* a general strengthening of the European Parliament, linked its 'parliamentarization' suggestions to proposals on the improvement of policy areas such as environmental and social affairs.

2. The second option for democratization concerned the intergovernmental EU pillars (CFSP and CJHA). Proposals varied between (a) the full-scale or partial integration of one or both pillars into the EC Treaty and its procedural as well as institutional obligations, and (b) the introduction of more legally binding – similar to the EC Treaty – procedures and more participatory as well as control powers for the European Parliament and/or the national parliaments within the remaining EU pillars.[10]

3. A third option for democratization of EC/EU decision-making procedures was discussed with regard to the roles of the national parliaments. Proposals varied between those who opted for: (a) the introduction of direct participatory or control powers for national parliaments within the legal framework of the EC/EU, (b) the introduction of a provision within the EC/EU Treaty framework guaranteeing national parliaments some unilateral control mechanisms *vis-à-vis* their respective governments, and

Table 7.2 Coverage of co-decision after Amsterdam

Treaty articles on co-decision between the European Parliament and the Council			
Article	Subject	Council decides by	Comment
12.2	Prohibition of discrimination	QM	Previously cooperation procedure
18.2	Citizens' rights	U	Previously cooperation procedure
40	Free movement of workers	QM	Co-decision since Maastricht
42	Social security for migrant workers	U	Previously cooperation procedure
44	Right of establishment	QM	Co-decision since Maastricht
46	Provisions concerning treatment of foreign nationals	QM	Co-decision since Maastricht
47.1	Mutual recognition of diplomas	QM	Co-decision since Maastricht
47.2	Provisions for the self-employed	U	Co-decision since Maastricht
55	Provision of services	QM	Co-decision since Maastricht
62.2bii	Visa procedures and conditions	U → QM automatically	Co-decision five years after entry into force of Amsterdam
62.2biv	Visa uniformity rules	U → QM automatically	Co-decision five years after entry into force of Amsterdam
71	Transport policy	QM	Previously cooperation procedure
80.2	Sea and air transport	QM	Previously cooperation procedure
95	Internal market – harmonization measures	QM	Co-decision since Maastricht
Ex-Art. 100b	Internal market – mutual recognition	Deleted	Co-decision since Maastricht; never applied
129	Incentive measures in the field of employment	QM	New
135	Customs cooperation	QM	New

Article	Policy	Voting	Notes
137.2	Equal opportunities women/men	QM	Previously cooperation procedure
141.3	Equal treatment women/men	QM	New
148	European Social Fund – operation	QM	Previously cooperation procedure
149	Education and youth policy	QM	Co-decision since Maastricht
150	Vocational training policy	QM	Previously cooperation procedure
151	Cultural policy	U	Co-decision since Maastricht
152.4	Health policy	QM	Co-decision since Maastricht
152.4.a	Minimum requirements regarding quality and safety of organs	QM	New: previously treated under ex-Art. 43: Agricultural policy
152.4b	Veterinary/phytosanitary health policy	QM	New: previously treated under ex-Art. 43: Agricultural policy
153.4	Consumer protection	QM	Co-decision since Maastricht
156	Trans-European networks – guidelines	QM	Co-decision since Maastricht
156	Trans-European networks – actions	QM	Previously cooperation procedure
162	European Regional Funds – operation	QM	Previously cooperation procedure
166	Research and technology framework programme	QM	Co-decision since Maastricht; previously treated by unanimity in the Council
172.2	Joint undertakings in RTD	QM	Previously cooperation procedure
175.1	Environment policy – actions	QM	Previously cooperation procedure
175.3	Environment policy – action programmes	QM	Co-decision since Maastricht
179	Development policy	QM	Previously cooperation procedure
255	Right of access to EU documents	QM	New
280	Combating fraud	QM	New
285	Statistics	QM	New
286	Creation of data protection unit	QM	New

QMV: qualified majority voting in the Council; U: unanimity in the Council; ex-Art. = old Article of the Maastricht Treaty

(c) the formal upgrading of existing multilateral scrutiny regimes bringing together members from both the European Parliament and the national parliaments. Several ideas had been suggested to institutionalize national parliaments in the European policy process. The French parliament considered that the establishment of a European Senate or an interparliamentary committee, made up of an equal number of representatives from each Member State, could represent the national parliaments in respect of the EU decision-making process. The vast majority of parliaments were against those ideas, arguing that the creation of new bodies leads to an overload of both the institutional framework of the Union and of the parliaments in the Member States. However, parliaments and governments in the United Kingdom and Denmark suggested to at least upgrade the Conference of European Affairs Committees (COSAC) in a pragmatic fashion in relation to the application of the principle of subsidiarity and the second and third pillars.

4. The fourth option for democratization of the EU concentrated on the structural prerequisites of the Union, and on how to provide opportunities for democratic and legitimate governance through the introduction or the reinforcement of new or more visible fundamental rights within the EC/EU Treaty set-up, of new information and deliberation rights for the citizenry or through the introduction of certain direct participation rights in the Treaties (Zürn, 1996; Abromeit, 1998).

Achievements

If, from an institutionalist perspective, the centrality of the European Parliament as the main actor securing indirect democracy in the European Union is accepted, then the Treaty of Amsterdam means a greatly improved setting. It widens the scope of application of the co-decision procedure extensively both with respect to those policy areas which it newly introduces into the EC sphere and with respect to policy areas which were already covered by the cooperation procedure. In future, the bulk of the EC's original secondary legislation will be adopted following the co-decision procedure.

Apart from those areas where co-decision will apply right after the entry into force of Amsterdam, it will automatically be extended to measures on the procedures and conditions for issuing visas by Member States as well as to rules on uniform visa formats after five years. The assent procedure was extended to the new TEU provision on sanctions in the event of a serious and persistent breach of fundamental rights by a Member State. Finally, the scope of application of the consultation procedure has been expanded by nine treaty provisions. As a result, this

Table 7.3 European Parliament and Council decision-making powers after Amsterdam (1.5.1999–approx. 2002)

Participation of the EP	Unanimity in Council		QMV in Council		Simple majority in Council		Special majorities other than QMV		Sum	
	Σ	%	Σ	%	Σ	%	Σ	%	Σ	%
Consultation	33 EC	17.09	23 EC	11.91	1 EC	0.518	2 EC	1.03	59 EC	30.57
	4 EU	13.79	1 EU	3.44	1 EU	3.44	1 EU	3.44	7 EU	24.13
Cooperation	0 EC	0	4 EC	2.07	0 EC	0	0 EC	0	4 EC	2.07
Co-decision	5 EC	2.59	33 EC	17.14	0 EC	0	0 EC	0	38 EC	19.67
Assent	6 EC	3.10	2 EC	1.03	1 EC	0.518	2 EC	1.03	11 EC	5.69
	2 EU	6.89							2 EU	6.89
Information	1 EC	0.518	8 EC	4.14	0 EC	0	0 EC	0	9 EC	4.66
No participation	31 EC	16.06	31 EC	16.06	4 EC	2.07	6 EC	3.10	72 EC	37.30
	9 EU	31.03	3 EU	10.34	3 EU	10.34	5 EU	17.24	20 EU	68.96
Sum (Σ)	76 EC	39.38	101 EC	52.33	6 EC	3.10	10 EC	5.18	193 EC	100.00
	15 EU	51.72	4 EU	13.79	4 EU	13.79	6 EU	20.68	29 EU	100.00

Author's calculation; *Source: Treaty of Amsterdam*, 1997

procedure will cover an overall figure of 59 EC and 9 EU cases after the entry into force of the Amsterdam Treaty (see Table 7.3).

Considering the potential coverage of all these new provisions with regard to the implementation of the Treaty, the 'virtual' co-decision statistics produced by the European Parliament's Conciliation Secretariat in July 1997 underlined that 'if the provisions of the draft Amsterdam Treaty were to be applied to the legislative procedures completed between 1 November 1993 and 7 July 1997, the number of co-decision procedures would be increased from 80 to 192. The same exercise with regard to legislative procedures in progress would increase the number of co-decision procedures from 110 to 193' (European Parliament, 1997). As a result of the Amsterdam process, many core issues of European integration will be added to decision-making procedures providing the European Parliament with considerable powers *vis-à-vis* the Council of Ministers and the European Commission.

The European Parliament maintains to be excluded from dynamic and 'costly' policy areas such as agriculture (Article 37 TEC), tax harmonization (Article 93 TEC) and trade policy (Article 133 TEC). Consequently, the effects of Amsterdam will be less visible than Table 7.2 suggests. In this regard, the findings of Fligstein and McNichol (1998) are highly illustrative: The overall proportion of 'legislation' (the sum of secondary legislation and implementing measures) passed in these fields between 1992 and 1994 was 49.4 per cent. Yet agriculture alone covered 45.1 per cent of EC legislation with an average of 777.7 decisions per year. By contrast, the proportion of legislation adopted in the framework of the internal market in the same time period was 6.1 per cent or 106 decisions on average per year. Of course, these numbers have to be qualified in the light of the nature of the legislative output concerned. Whereas the bulk of agriculture policy concerns regulatory implementing decisions of the Commission within the price-stability system, internal market measures are considered as secondary legislative acts which cover a wider range of issues and directly affect a much broader part of the citizenry in the Union.

Apart from the extension of co-decision, the procedure itself has been considerably simplified in four ways.

Firstly, it now provides for the adoption of a legislative text at first reading phase if the European Parliament does not propose any amendment at first reading or if the Council agrees with all of the European Parliament's first reading amendments. The importance of this reform becomes clear when looking into the practice of co-decision. Out of the 96 procedures concluded until mid 1997, 67 cases could have been closed after the first reading stage, either because the Council accepted all first reading amendments of the European Parliament (24 times), because Parliament accepted the common position of the Council (35 times), or because both Parliament and Council adopted the original Commission's proposals as final text (8 times) (European Parliament, Delegations to the Conciliation Committee, 1997). The new first reading phase offers a chance for accelerating, rationalizing and simplifying the EC's legislative process. Given the new legal bases where co-decision will apply (see Table 7.2), the possibility of conclusion after the first reading may lead to saving time for the higher number of legislative proposals.

Secondly, the phase whereby the European Parliament could vote on its intention to reject the Council's common position has been dropped. Consequently, in future the European Parliament can go straight to a vote of rejection and the draft proposal will fail. This part of the procedure's reform largely corresponds to the practice of co-decision. Until August 1998, Parliament used this option only once. Thus, during the negotiations, both the Member States' delegations as well as the Parliament and the Commission declared this part of the procedure as senseless and, therefore, as subject to total abolition.

Thirdly, the so-called third reading, whereby the Council could seek to impose the common position after a breakdown of conciliation, unless the European Parliament could overrule it by an absolute majority of its members, has been dropped too. During the negotiations, some of the

Member States opposed this abolition because it would appear to change the institutional balance between the institutions. The Juppé government in France especially opposed any changes to the procedural set-up of the Union that could change the institutional balance – precisely between the European Parliament and the Council (Assemblée Nationale, 1996). Thus, the elimination of the third reading was the most controversial question. In the end, France accepted the new procedure for two reasons. First, the French proposals for strengthening the role of national parliaments in the Union were successful in that Amsterdam provides for a new, legally binding protocol on the powers offered to these actors. Secondly, unlike its Gaullist predecessor, not only the French Socialist Party as such, but also the new Red–Green coalition lead by Lionel Jospin, has a more positive attitude towards the European Parliament. As one of the most important achievements of Amsterdam, the new procedure now provides for the proposal to have failed in the absence of agreement in conciliation. This deletion of the third-reading phase means that Parliament is put on an equal footing with the Council at every stage of the procedure. In more concrete terms, this provision will have important effects for how the Parliament is seen from the outside world: under the Maastricht rules, the Council could easily make the Parliament responsible for the failure of a draft legislative act. With the entry into force of Amsterdam, both the Council and the Parliament will take the shared responsibility for the adoption as well as for the failure of a proposed legislative act. Both institutions anticipated this reform in March 1998, when no agreement on the Comitology issue could be found within the conciliation committee on the draft directives 93/6/EEC and 93/22/EEC. Instead of reshuffling the draft according to the Maastricht Treaty provisions, the two institutions declared the failure of the procedure after conciliation (European Parliament, 1998).

In addition, Article 251(4) TEC seeks to prevent too much flexibility in the consideration of European Parliament amendments in conciliation by stating 'in fulfilling this task, the Conciliation Committee should address the common position on the basis of the amendments proposed by the European Parliament'. This provision will certainly lead to more self-discipline in both the Council and the Parliament, because it leads to a higher degree of programming amendments before conciliation takes place. Finally, the new procedure also provides stricter time limits than at present. If – according to Article 251(3) TEC – the Council does not approve all of the European Parliament's amendments in second reading, the meeting of the Conciliation Committee has to be convened within six weeks, extendable to eight weeks if necessary. In close connection to this, the non-binding declaration No. 34 annexed to the Amsterdam Treaty states that 'in no case should the actual period between the second reading by the European Parliament and the outcome of the Conciliation Committee exceed 9 months'. These two provisions together with the broader application and the simplification of the procedure will certainly lead (1) to new workload for some of the European Parliament's committees and of the Commission's Directorates General, and (2), as a consequence, to new inter-institutional or even informal arrangements between the institutions.

Improvements in Amsterdam were also made with regard to the European Parliament's elective function (Article 214 TEC). From the 1999 European Elections onwards, not only the Commission as a collegiate body, but also the future President of the European Commission alone was subject to a vote of approval by the European Parliament. This innovation may have unexpected and far-reaching implications for the future style of governance in the Union. One can imagine the European political parties deciding to put up in their electoral campaigns for the European Parliament's elections a top candidate for the Commission presidency. Consequently, the elections would be brought more alive and enriched through a kind of personalization of the Union's governing institutions. Moreover, provided that each of the European parties presents its contest candidate for the post in question, not only the election campaign, but also the day-to-day life in Brussels and Strasbourg could induce politicizing and mobilizing effects for the Union's citizenry. In other words, there is a realistic chance that political parties at the European level will become a renewed source of legitimacy (Notre Europe – European Steering Committee, 1998; Notre Europe – European Steering Committee and Padoa-Schioppa, 1998; Padoa-Schioppa, 1998; Hix, 1995).[11] However, assuming that the European parties would gain in autonomy by introducing such a mechanism, national parties will not automatically like the idea. Secondly, Member State governments may not admit the idea too, since the optional mechanism could restrict their autonomy in putting forward a candidate for the Commission's Presidency (Nickel, 1997).

As far as the institutional-procedural democratization of CJHA is concerned, the Amsterdam Treaty introduces the European Parliament for the first time as a consultative body within the new Title covering the 'Area of Freedom, Security and Justice' (AFSJ). Moreover, the Treaty stipulates a phasing of Parliament's involvement with regard to AFSJ in general. While for five years after ratification of the new Treaty the European Parliament will only be consulted, Article 67(2) TEC allows the Council to introduce the co-decision procedure after the end of this transitional period. For those two areas which remain in the third pillar (police cooperation and judicial cooperation in criminal matters) the European Parliament shall be consulted when framework decisions, decisions and conventions are adopted. Similar progress could not be achieved in the

CFSP area. However, the Amsterdam Treaty introduced an inter-institutional agreement between the Parliament, the Council and the European Commission confirming Parliament's role in scrutinizing CFSP expenditure which will continue to be regarded as non-compulsory.

Considering the above-mentioned features of the Amsterdam reform, it could be argued that parliamentary democracy has been considerably strengthened by the new Treaty. However, some serious deficits in the parliamentary dimension of the future European Union are as obvious as the positive achievements. As regards the assent procedure, Amsterdam failed to extend it to cover all international agreements (Articles 133, 300 and 301 TEC), the decisions over the EC's own financial resources (Article 269 TEC), the extension of the authority of the institutions in pursuit of Treaty objectives (implied powers Article 308 TEC) and finally the amendment of the TEU itself (Art. 48 TEU). With regard to Justice and Home Affairs, several structural weaknesses remain: free movement of persons which formerly could have been implemented on the basis of Article 95 TEC (co-decision with QMV in the Council) will now be decided following the Article 67 procedure of the TEC (consultation and unanimity for five years after ratification). This constitutes not only a considerable backlash for the concept of an area without internal frontiers but also – if one agrees that parliamentary democracy is possible beyond the state – for the democratic legitimacy of its realization. Moreover, the consultation mechanism in Article 39 TEU gives Parliament only a very limited power insofar as the Council may lay down a time-limit of at least three months. This in fact deprives the consultation procedure of its main impact for Parliament, namely to influence the Council's position by postponing its opinion. Furthermore, the provisions on the transfer of the Schengen *acquis* into the area of the EC/EU competencies do not foresee any involvement of either the European Parliament or the parliaments of the Member States. This in fact goes against any democratic principle, since the Schengen *acquis* contains not only the ratified Schengen Agreements but also a vast corpus of decisions exclusively adopted by the Schengen Executive Committee. Finally, the Council will decide to introduce closer cooperation between certain Member States by qualified majority. By virtue of Article 40 TEU, the request of the Member States concerned will be forwarded to the European Parliament. Yet neither the actual decision on closer cooperation nor the decision allowing a non-participating Member to opt in requires any parliamentary involvement. As far as the future CFSP is concerned, the European Parliament's role maintains to be restricted to information. The revised CFSP Title emphasizes the predominant position of the European Council as a quasi-legislative body. As the common strategies of the European Council form the basis of joint actions and other measures to be decided by the Council of Ministers, the

European Council will have a *de facto* right of initiative which is not open to censure. Thus, Parliament's active participation in shaping the substance of the CFSP rests at the entire discretion of the Member States' governments. Given the efficiency criterion with respect to foreign and security policy decisions, it seems acceptable, especially at times of crisis, that the European Parliament should be informed only after joint actions have been adopted. What is incomprehensible from a democratic standpoint, on the other hand, is that Parliament should not have a mandatory right to be consulted on the formulation of general guidelines and common strategies (European Parliament, PE 211.022/fin; European Parliament, PE 211.310).

The new responsibility of national parliaments

The IGC led to the insertion of a 'Protocol on the role of National Parliaments in the European Union' (PNP) into the Amsterdam Treaty, which addresses both the scope and the timing of parliamentary scrutiny (Maurer, 2000). Following proposals made by the French, British and Danish delegations to the IGC as well as the Dublin COSAC meeting of 16 October 1996 which for the first time adopted conclusions on the reinforcement of Declaration No. 13 of the Maastricht Treaty, the PNP now holds that national parliaments shall receive all Commission consultation documents as well as green and white papers or communications. On the other hand, the PNP implicitly excludes the following types of document for the transmission of legislative proposals to national parliaments: all documents falling under the CFSP pillar, all documents concerning the entry into closer cooperation, all documents prepared by Member States for the European Council, and all documents falling under the procedure of the 'Protocol on integration the Schengen *acquis* into the framework of the European Union'. However, once the Schengen *acquis* is integrated into the first or third pillar, the appropriate legislative and scrutiny procedures for both the European Parliament and the national parliaments will apply. The 'Protocol on the role of national parliaments in the European Union' (PNP) includes a commitment of timing addressed to the Commission and the Council. Firstly, the Commission shall ensure that the legislative proposal is 'made available in good time'. Secondly a six-week period between issuing a 'legislative proposal or a measure to be adopted under Title VI' TEU and its discussion or adoption by the Council has to elapse. Of course, these provisions are geared to allow the governments to inform their parliaments on the proposal and leave parliaments time for discussion. However, the protocol does not commit the governments to really use the time provided by the Community institutions for informing their parliaments. Thus it remains up to the parliaments and their governments to negotiate on the content and the procedures to be applied for the implementation of the PNP.

Besides the provisions on the improvement of national parliamentary scrutiny mechanisms, the PNP also recognizes COSAC as a means to contribute to the lack of parliamentary scrutiny in EC and EU Affairs on a multilateral basis. The PNP specifies three areas for deliberation within the COSAC framework: according to Articles 5 and 6 of the PNP, COSAC may examine 'any legislative proposal or initiative in relation to the establishment of an area or freedom, security and justice', 'legislative activities of the Union, notably in relation to the application of the principle of subsidiarity' and 'questions regarding fundamental rights'. Thus the text leads to the question, whether COSAC is the appropriate body for these issues. The fact that the PNP focuses on the area of freedom, security and justice and on the fundamental rights policies reflects the political and legal sensibility on this issue in the EU Member States. If we add this specification in the PNP to the new consultative role provided for the European Parliament in the context of the policy area concerned, we observe the introduction of a certain kind of 'three-level-scrutiny-mechanism' with regard to judicial and home affairs in the framework of the future EU: Firstly, the EP will control – of course to a limited extent – the European level of decision-making in the first and the third pillar. Secondly, provided that they organize their scrutiny mechanism effectively, the national parliaments may monitor unilaterally the stance of their governments on matters falling under this area. Thirdly, COSAC will become able to deliberate these issues between the European Parliament and the national parliaments of the Member States. However, at least three shortcomings will certainly occur: firstly, the PNP does not improve the lack of parliamentary control with regard to the CFSP pillar. Given that the European Union's Foreign and Security policy may not be simply conceived as a 'domaine réservé' of the executives of the Member States and given that the EP's budgetary power is limited to the framing of CFSP's financial aspects on a yearly basis, it is not understandable why democratic control of action in this field is completely excluded. Secondly, neither the EP nor the national parliaments and COSAC are given a right to monitor the process of transferring the Schengen *acquis* into the EC/EU area. If this lack of democratic control may be reduced due to further negotiations on both the European and the national level, a third structural problem will certainly not be resolved in the next years. By definition COSAC delegations are constituted by the parliamentarians of the Committees responsible for handling EC/EU affairs and not of the Committees on civil liberties, justice and/ or home affairs. Therefore, it is hardly conceivable how parliamentarians dealing mainly with horizontal issues of European integration will become able to deliberate effectively on matters falling under the area of freedom, security and justice.

CONCLUSIONS

Assessing the overall development of the EU after Amsterdam with regard to its institutional and procedural democratization leads to an ambiguous picture. On the one hand, the European Parliament's potential for influence in the preparation, adoption, implementation and control of legislative binding acts has been considerably strengthened in the sphere of the EC. In addition, Amsterdam marks a significant effort to strengthen the accountability of the executive with regard to the Commission. Moreover, Parliament's involvement in Justice and Home Affairs has been relatively increased. On the other hand, the basic principles of the budgetary procedure were not reformed and Parliament will remain excluded from framing compulsory expenditures in the EC. Furthermore, the fact that unanimity in the Council and consultation of the European Parliament still dominate the matters of justice and home affairs falling under Title VI TEU and under the Title IV TEC reflects a strong reservation in the majority of the Member States against a wider recourse to genuinely supranational means of decision-making in these sensitive but – for the population living inside and outside the Union – important spheres. This reluctance seems to be confirmed with the new provisions on the integration of the Schengen *acquis* into the Union and the provisions ruling the decision-making in the CFSP. The unwillingness to introduce more supranational and parliamentary decision-making procedures in these areas might certainly stem from the fact that they are considered to constitute the core elements of national sovereignty. This argument was widely defended not only during the Amsterdam process but also at the 1991 IGC leading to the Maastricht Treaty and during its ratification.

The Amsterdam Treaty marks another step forward in the move of the EU from an economic problem-solving arena to an original polity. However, the institutional and procedural arrangements of the EU remain complex, fragmented and opaque. The new Treaty does not contain a definition of a hierarchy of rules which could offer a distinction between those of a legislative nature and those which have a rather regulatory function and which might help to simplify the complexity of the Union on the basis of transparent criteria for associating policies with procedures and actors. The next revision of the Treaty should try to solve this problem. In the absence of such an exercise, every reform of the Union's legal foundations will remain dominated by short-term interests of Governments and their representatives.

Amsterdam certainly provides new and important offers for strengthening parliamentary democracy in the Union. Seen from an institutionalist perspective, the process of 'parliamentarization' is impressive in its continuity (Dehousse, 1998: 9). Since the SEA, the Parliament has considerably developed – with regard to the formal revision as well as to the implementation of the subsequent reforms – from a rather 'decorative' (Wallace, 1996: 63) to a fully fledged legislative institution. The question however remains if these improvements will also provide new ground for enhancing the legitimacy and proximity of European governance towards the citizens of the Union. Hence, due to the exclusive nature of IGCs, active participation of the citizenry and the general acceptance of the Union can hardly be achieved. Thus, it is up to the implementation of the new Treaty and in the hands of the actors then involved to offer appropriate means for the involvement of the Union's demoi in shaping the conditions for their way of living. More precisely, the national parliaments and the national political parties will have the difficult task of proving that they are able and willing to provide channels for communication across the boundaries of the Union's Member States. The greater involvement of the national parliaments in the Union's policy process may help to render Governments more accountable for what they do in the Council of Ministers and its subordinated working mechanisms. However, one should also bear in mind that the simple formalization of COSAC within the realm of the new Treaty also renders the Union more complex and less understandable. A citizen may ask: if the (directly elected) European Parliament represents the peoples of the Union, the Council of Ministers the Member States through (elected) governments, the European Economic and Social Committee some of the most important interest groups of the Union, and the Committee of the Regions the (elected) representatives of some of the Union's regional and local communities, what is the surplus of a body bringing together some members of the European Parliament with some members of the national parliaments? Of course, it is difficult to abolish established institutions. However, the next Treaty reform should discuss appropriate ways for a more coherent and clear-cut organization of interest representation and mediation in an enlarged Union.

NOTES

1. For the original definition of the democratic deficit see the so-called Vedel report of the European Commission (1972: 4) and the Toussaint par Michel Toussaint, PE DOC A 2276/87 of 1 February 1988.
2. In this regard, the IGC blueprint of the former British Government is highly illustrative: Foreign and Commonwealth Office (1996) 'A Partnership of

Nations: the British Approach to the European Union Intergovernmental Conference 1996', presented to Parliament, March 1996.

3. For the use of the term see Haftendorn (1990: 401–23)

4. For public and published opinion, the Single European Act (SEA) has been the discovery of the internal market programme, the Maastricht Treaty has been about economic and monetary union and the introduction of a single currency. And the Amsterdam Treaty was mainly considered as a reform on employment and social policy, CFSP and the establishment of an area of freedom, security and justice.

5. For a general discussion on the legal aspects of the different decision-making procedures see: Kapteyn and Verloren van Themaat (1998: 408–46); Schoo (1997).

6. Consequently, the Amsterdam Treaty deletes article 100b in the consolidated version of the TEC.

7. For example, only the EC Treaty chapters on EMU contain nine different decision-making procedures: assent of Parliament and unanimity of the Council (two times); cooperation procedure (four times); consultation of Parliament and unanimity of the Council (seven times); consultation of Parliament and qualified majority voting of the Council (seven times); information of Parliament and qualified majority voting of the Council (six times); information of Parliament and unanimity of the Council (two times); unanimity in the Council without any participation of Parliament (three times) qualified majority voting in the Council without Parliament's participation (nine times); two thirds majority of weighted votes of the Council without Parliament's participation (once).

8. See Rules of Procedure of the Council of Ministers, Annex.

9. See *Bulletin des Presse: und Informationsamtes der Bundesregierung*, 1995.

10. For CFSP reform see Chapter 13, by Elfriede Regelsberger and Uwe Schmalz in this volume; for CJHA, see Chapter 14, by Jörg Monar, in this volume.

11. The idea of creating a politicized linkage between the Commission and the Parliament is not as new as it seems; see Jacqué (1989: 217–25).

BIBLIOGRAPHY

Assemblée Nationale (1996) *Déclaration du Gouvernement sur la préparation et les perspectives de la Conférence intergouvernementale*. Assemblée Nationale, Compte rendu analytique officiel, 1ère Séance du 13 Mars 1996.

European Commission (1972) 'Rapport du groupe ad hoc pour l'examen du problème de l'accroissement des compétences du Parlement européen'. *Bulletin des Communautés européennes*, 4.

European Commission (1996) *Report on the Co-decision Procedure*. Doc. SEC(96) 1225 fin. of 3 July 1996.

European Parliament (1995) *Opinion of the Committee on Foreign Affairs, Security and Defence Policy for the Committee on Institutional Affairs on the Operation of the Treaty on European Union with a View to the Intergovernmental Conference in 1996*. Rapporteur: Enrique Barón Crespo, PE 211.022/fin., 21 February 1995.

European Parliament, Committee on Institutional Affairs (1995) *Working Document on the CFSP process*. Rapporteur: Raymonde Dury, PE 211.310.

European Parliament (1988) *Rapport fait au nom de la Commission institutionnelle sur le déficit démocratique des Communautés européennes*. Par Michel Toussaint, PE DOC A 2276/87 of 1 February 1988.

European Parliament: Task Force 'IGC 1996/1997' (1996) *White Paper on the IGC, Vol. I to III*. Luxembourg.

European Parliament (1996) *Report on the Report of the Commission*. SEC(96) 1225 fin., Doc. A4–0361/96 of 7 November 1996.

European Parliament, Delegations to the Conciliation Committee (1997) Progress report 1 August 1996 to 31 July 1997 on the Delegations to the Conciliation Committee. Annex 2, pp. 3–4.

European Parliament (1997) Reply to Question No. 39/97 by Richard Corbett. DOC PE 259.385/BUR.

European Parliament (1997) *Conciliation Stop Press*, 9 July.

European Parliament (1998) *Conciliation Procedures: Stop Press*, 18 (March).

Abromeit, H. (1998) 'Ein Vorschlag zur Demokratisierung des europäischen Entscheidungssystems'. *Politische Vierteljahresschrift*, 1, 80–90.

Bogdandy, A. von. (1993) 'Supranationale Union als neuer Herrschaftstypus: Entstaatlichung und Vergemeinschaftung aus staatstheoretischer Perspektive'. *Integration*, 4, 210–24.

Bulletin des Presse: und Informationsamtes der Bundesregierung (1995) 'Deutsch-Italienische Gemeinsame Erklärung, Porto Santo Stefano, 15 July', No. 60, 587.

Bulmer, S. (1994) 'The governance of the European Union. A new institutionalist approach'. *Journal of Public Policy*, 4, 351–80.

Corbett, R. (1994) 'Representing the people'. In A. Duff, J. Pinder and R. Pryce, (eds), *Maastricht and Beyond: Building the European Union*. London: Routledge.

Craig, P. (1997) 'Democracy and rulemaking within the EC: an empirical and normative assessment'. *European Law Journal*, 3, 105–30.

Dehousse, R. (1998) 'European institutional architecture after Amsterdam: Parliamentary system or regulatory structure?' RSC No 98/11, *EUI Working Papers*, Florence.

Duff, A. (1995) 'Building a Parliamentary Europe'. In M. Télo (ed.), *Démocratie et Construction Européenne*. Edition de l'Université de Bruxelles.

Duff, A. (1997) *The Treaty of Amsterdam, Text and Commentary*. London: Sweet & Maxwell.

Earnshaw, D. and D. Judge (1996) 'From cooperation to codecision: the European Parliament's path to legislative power'. In J. Richardson (ed.), *Policy Making in the European Union*. London: Routledge.

Fligstein, N. and J. McNichol (1998) 'The institutional terrain of the European Union'. In W. Sandholtz and A. Stone Sweet (eds), *European Integration and Supranational Governance*. Oxford: Oxford University Press.

Foreign and Commonwealth Office (1996) 'A Partnership of Nations: the British Approach to the European Union Intergovernmental Conference 1996', presented to Parliament, March 1996.

Gosalbo Bono, R. (1995), 'Co-decision: an appraisal of the experience of the European Parliament as co-legislator'. In *Yearbook of European Law*. Oxford: Clarendon Press.

Griller *et al.* (1996) 'Regierungskonferenz 1996: Ausgangspositionen.' *Working Paper* No. 20 of the Forschungsinstitut für Europafragen. Vienna.

Haftendorn, H. (1990) 'Zur Theorie außenpolitischer Entscheidungsprozesse'. In V. Rittberger (ed.), *Theorien der Internationalen Beziehungen. Bestandsaufnahme und Forschungsperspektiven, Politische Vierteljahresschrift, Sonderheft 21/1990.* Opladen: Westdeutscher Verlag.

Hix, S. (1995) 'Parties at the European level as an alternative source of legitimacy'. *Journal of Common Market Studies*, 4.

Istituto Affari Internazionali (ed.), *Maastricht-Watch*. 1994–6.

Jacqué, J. (1989) 'Strategien für das Europäische Parlament: Abschied von nationalen Konfliktlinien'. In O. Schmuck and W. Wessels (eds), *Das Europäische Parlament im dynamischen Integrationsprozeß: Auf der Suche nach einem zeitgemäßen Leitbild.* Bonn: Europa Union Verlag.

Jopp, M. and O. Schmuck (eds) (1996) *Die Reform der Europäischen Union. Analysen: Positionen: Dokumente zur Regierungskonferenz 1996/97.* Bonn: Europa Union Verlag.

Jopp, M., A. Maurer, and O. Schmuck (eds) (1998) *Die Europäische Union nach Amsterdam: Analysen und Stellungnahmen zum neuen EU-Vertrag.* Bonn: Europa Union Verlag.

Kapteyn, P. J. G. and P. VerLoren van Themaat (1998) *Introduction to the Law of the European Communities*, 3rd (edn) by L. W. Gormley. London: Kluwer.

Kohler-Koch, B. (1995) 'The strength of weakness: the transformation of governance in the EU'. AB III/No. 10, *MZES Working Papers*. Mannheim.

Kohler-Koch, B. (1997) 'Die Europäisierung nationaler Demokratien: Verschleiß eines europäischen Kulturerbes?'. In M. Greven (ed.), *Demokratie: eine Kultur des Westens? 20. Wissenschaftlicher Kongreß der Deutschen Vereinigung für Politische Wissenschaft.* Opladen: Leske & Budrich.

Laffan, B. (1997) 'The governance of the Union'. In B. Tonra (ed.), *Amsterdam: What the Treaty Means.* Dublin: IEA.

Lübbe, H. (1994), *Abschied vom Superstaat: Die Vereinigten Staaten von Europa wird es nicht geben.* Berlin: Siedler.

Majone, G. (1994) 'The rise of the regulatory state in Europe'. *West European Politics*, 3, 78–102.

Majone, G. A. (1996) 'European regulatory state?'. In J. Richardson (ed.), *European Union: Power and Policy-Making.* London: Routledge.

Marks, G. (1993) 'Structural policy and multilevel governance in the EC'. In A. W. Cafruny and G. G. Rosentahl (eds), *The State of the European Community*, Vol. 2. Boulder, Colo: Rienner.

Maurer, A. (1996) 'Die Demokratisierung der Europäischen Union: Perspektiven für das Europäische Parlament'. In A. Maurer and B. Thiele (eds), *Legitimationsprobleme und Demokratisierung der Europäischen Union, Schüren.* Marburg.

Maurer, A. (1999) *(Co)-Governing after Maastricht: The European Parliament's Institutional Performance 1994–1998.* Working paper (Research Project No. IV/98/13) prepared for the European Parliament, Luxembourg/Brussels.

Maurer, A. (2001) *National Parliaments after Amsterdam: Losers, Latecomers or Adapters?* Baden-Baden: Normos.

McDonagh, B. (1998) *Original Sin in a Brave New World: An Account of the Negotiation of the Treaty of Amsterdam.* Dublin: IEA.

Nickel, D. (1993) 'Le Traité de Maastricht et le Parlement européen: le nouveau paysage politique et la procédure de l'article 189b'. In J. Monar, W. Ungerer and W. Wessels (eds), *The Maastricht Treaty on European Union*. Brussels: EIP.

Nickel, D. (1997) *The Amsterdam Treaty: A Shift in the Balance between the Institutions!?* Paper submitted for a lecture at the Harvard Law School.

Nugent, N. (1994) *The Government and Politics of the European Union*. Durham, NC: Duke University Press.

Nugent, N. (1998) 'Decision-making procedures'. In D. Dinan (ed.), *Encyclopedia of the European Union*. Boulder, Colo.: Lynne Rienner Publishers.

Notre Europe – European Steering Committee (1998) 'Politicising the European Debate'. *Agence Europe* 2089, 27 May 1998.

Notre Europe – European Steering Committee and A. Padoa-Schioppa (1998) 'From the Single Currency to the Single Ballot-Box'. *Agence Europe* 2089, 27 May 1998.

Padoa-Schioppa, A. (1998) 'The institutional reforms of the Amsterdam Treaty'. *The Federalist*, 1.

Piepenschneider, M. (1996), Regierungskonferenz 1996, *Synopse der Reformvorschläge zur Europäischen Union*, 2. Auflage, *Sankt Augustin*.

Pijpers, A. and G. Edwards (eds) (1997) *The Politics of European Treaty Reform: The 1996 Intergovernmental Conference and Beyond*. London: Pinter.

Pliakos, A. (1995) 'L'Union européenne et le Parlement européen: y a-t-il vraiment un déficit démocratique?' *Révue du droit public et de la science politique et France et à l'Étranger*, No. 3.

Raworth, P. (1994) 'A timid step forwards: Maastricht and the democratisation of the European Community'. *European Law Review*, 1.

Reich, C. (1992) 'Le Traité sur l'Union européenne et le Parlement européen'. *Revue du Marché Commun*, 357.

Shackleton, M. (1998) 'Democratic deficit'. In D. Dinan (ed.), *Encylopedia of the European Union*. Boulder, Colo.: Lynne Rienner Publishers.

Scharpf, F. W. (1975) *Demokratie zwischen Utopie und Anpassung*. 2nd edn, Kronberg (Taurus).

Scharpf, F. W. (1994) 'Community and autonomy: multi-level policy-making in the European Union'. *Journal of European Public Policy*, 1, 220.

Schimmelpfennig, F. (1996) 'Legitimate rule in the European Union: the academic debate'. *Tübinger Arbeitspapiere zur Internationalen Politik und Friedensforschung*. 27.

Schoo, J. (1997) 'Kommentar zu Art. 189b–189c'. In H. von der Groeben, J. Thiesing and C.-D. Ehlermann (eds), *Kommentar zum EU/EG-Vertrag, Band 4 (Art. 137–209a EGV)*. Baden-Baden: Nomos.

Schröder, M. (1994), 'Das Bundesverfassungsgericht als Hüter des Staates im Prozeß der europäischen Integration'. *Deutsches Verwaltungsblatt*, 6.

Scully, R. (1997) 'Institutional change in the European Union: Maastricht and the European Parliament' (unpublished paper). *ECSA Fifth Biennial Conference*, *Seattle*, 29 May–1 June 1997.

Smith, M. (1996) 'Democratic legitimacy in the European Union: fulfilling the institutional logic'. *Journal of Legislative Studies*, 4.

Thomas, S. (1992) 'Assessing MEPs' influence on British EC policy'. *Government in Opposition*, 1.

Tsinisizelis, M. and D. Chryssochoou (1996) 'From "Gesellschaft" to "Gemeinschaft"? Confederal Consociation and Democracy in the European Union'. *Current Politics and Economics of Europe*, 4.

Wallace, H. (1996) 'Politics and Policy in the EU: the Challenge of Governance'. In H. Wallace and W. Wallace (eds), *Policy-Making in the European Union*. 3rd edn. Oxford: Oxford University Press.

Weiler, J. (1992) 'After Maastricht: community legitimacy in post-1992 Europe'. In W. J. Adams (ed.), *Singular Europe: Economy and Polity of the European Community after 1992*. Ann Arbor: University of Michigan Press.

Weiler, J., Haltern, U. and F. Mayer (1995) 'European democracy and its critique'. *West European Politics*, 4, 24–33.

Weiler, J. (1997) 'Legitimacy and democracy of Union governance'. In A. Pijpers and G. Edwards (eds), *The Politics of European Treaty Reform. The 1996 Intergovernmental Conference and Beyond*. London: Pinter.

Wessels, W. (1996) 'The modern West European state and the European Union: democratic erosion or a new kind of polity?'. In S. S. Andersen and K. A. Eliassen (eds), *The European Union: How Democratic Is It?* London: Sage.

Wessels, W. (1997) 'An ever closer fusion? A dynamic macropolitical view on integration processes'. *Journal of Common Market Studies*, 2.

Westlake, M. (1994) *A Modern Guide to the European Parliament*. London: Pinter.

Zürn, M. (1996) 'Über den Staat und die Demokratie im europäischen Mehrebenensystem'. *Politische Vierteljahresschrift*, 1, 27–55.

CHAPTER 8

CONSTITUTIONAL DEFICITS OF EU JUSTICE AND HOME AFFAIRS: TRANSPARENCY, ACCOUNTABILITY AND JUDICIAL CONTROL

Brendan Smith and William Wallace

INTRODUCTION

Border control, asylum procedures, and criminal and political intelligence are among the sensitive areas of state sovereignty and state security. Cooperation among police forces, intelligence services, customs and immigration services and their supervising ministries therefore grew up in the 1970s and 1980s firmly under inter-governmental control. Cross-border cooperation among the forces of law and order however also touches on sensitive issues of civil liberty and political accountability. The culture of police cooperation favours informal networks over bureaucratic procedures and controls (Anderson *et al.*, 1995: ch. 7). Distinctive structures of national agencies for law enforcement, and different definitions of citizenship, are rooted in state development and history. As over the past 10 to 15 years the intensity of cross-border cooperation has grown, therefore, governments have struggled with the underlying tension between executive secrecy, sovereign statehood, harmonization of rules and procedures, and accountability. Establishment of an area of 'Freedom, Security and Justice', the declared aim of Article 2 of the Treaty on European Union (as amended by the Amsterdam Treaty), demonstrates the tensions inherent in this field. Security as an objective is not easy to reconcile with freedom and justice.

The Maastricht treaty formalized cooperation in justice and home affairs (JHA) as the third inter-governmental pillar of the European Union: with minimal oversight by the European Court of Justice (ECJ) and the European Parliament (EP), with the European Commission playing a marginal role (Bieber and Monar, 1995). The emerging structure of committees and working groups, serviced by the Council Secretariat, reporting to infrequent meetings of the Council of Ministers (JHA), also proved resistant to scrutiny by national Parliaments (House of Lords Select Committee on the European Communities, 1997a). The shocks of the Maastricht ratification process left many member governments painfully aware of the need to make EU policy-making less opaque. As the IGC approached, various pressures combined to raise questions of improving accountability and judicial control in the third pillar. Members of the European Parliament were determined to extend the parliament's influence and sphere of scrutiny on such matters. Civil liberties groups were monitoring the growth of activities which were beyond the range of effective national accountability yet still excluded from parliamentary or judicial oversight at the European level. Some within national governments were concerned about the long-term acceptability of secretive activity through committees of officials in this highly sensitive area. The anomalous position of the Schengen Agreement, overlapping with EU competencies in such matters as free movement and police and judicial cooperation, added to the confusion within which common policies were pursued. The aim of this chapter is to examine how far the Amsterdam Treaty has responded to these calls for greater democratic accountability and judicial oversight.

FROM MAASTRICHT TO TURIN

The primary objective of the follow-on IGC to which the signatories were committed by Article N(2) of the Maastricht Treaty was to be a strengthening of CFSP. The emergence of justice and home affairs as a major theme of Amsterdam resulted from a combination of circumstances. The end of the Cold War, with the opening of frontiers on the EU's eastern flank creating new flows of migrants and of criminal activities, coincided with a rise in the flow of asylum seekers from Africa and the South. The flood of refugees from the Balkans conflict brought home to several governments, particularly the German and Dutch, the need for a common and co-ordinated approach on asylum and refugee policy. The tightening of German criteria for asylum, in July 1993, saw the number of asylum seekers plummeting from around 37,000 per month to 10,000.[1] The knock-on effects of these changes to the Basic Law included a switch in the flow of asylum seekers to the Netherlands.[2] Such issues of burden sharing and dealing with applications from third countries had already been addressed in other forums, through for example the Dublin Convention of June 1990 that established an EU-wide arrangement to deal with the complications of applying for asylum. Rising flows of people and of goods across the EU's internal borders – and therefore also of trans-national crime – required closer cooperation among national law enforcement agencies and the transformation of the European Drugs Unit into EUROPOL, supplementing the slow procedures of INTERPOL. More intensive patterns of working together, with new multilateral conventions and new institutions, necessitated government attention to reassure their publics about these new developments.

Even without these changes within the EU and along its borders, it would have been clear that the system under the third pillar lacked transparency and democratic credibility. Article K.6 TEU had provided for the European Parliament to be 'regularly' informed and consulted on the principal aspects of activities under the third pillar. But the erratic pace at which policies moved from proposals to decisions in a system managed by the Presidency and the Council Secretariat meant that the European Parliament was on occasions left almost entirely uninformed, for example on asylum policy.[3] National Parliaments, in the nature of the case, were no better informed. The extent of the European Parliament's dissatisfaction at its limited role was reflected in its own internal assessments of the third pillar. A draft inter-institutional agreement in December 1993 requested a greater role for the Parliament (Monar, 1995). At the end of 1996 the Committee on Civil Liberties adopted the draft resolution by Michele Lindeperg (PES, F) on progress made in 1996 in implementing the 'third pillar' on cooperation in Justice and Home affairs. The resolution criticized the lack of transparency in the Council before going on to claim that the Council on several occasions had failed to inform the Parliament of agreements that it had concluded, some of them major, such as extending the powers of EUROPOL's drugs squad and adoption of a work programme for 1996–1998 (PE Doc 207.806).

The Court of Justice had potentially a more influential role under Title VI than was initially apparent. Looking strictly at Title VI its role was restricted to Article K.3(2)(c). However Article M TEU made clear that Title VI was not to affect 'the Treaties establishing the European Communities or the subsequent Treaties and Acts modifying or supplementing them' (Article M TEU) (Foster, 1990: 104). Therefore Article M, pursuant to Article L, provided the Court of Justice with a role in ensuring that the implementation of Title VI did not encroach on Community competence (*Commission v Council* Case C-170/96 (The Air Transport Case)). This provided for the possibility of resorting to the then Article 173 TEC (now Article 230 TEC) and in certain instances Article 177 TEC (now Article 234) (Neuwahl, 1995; Christian and Müller-Graff, 1994: 500 and 504; Eaton, 1996: 221; Neuwahl, 1996: 245). Yet the language of Article L was stark in restricting the Court's role to Article K.3(2)(c).

FROM TURIN TO AMSTERDAM[4]

An early momentum gathered on reforming the third pillar in preparation for the 1996–7 IGC. The emphasis on an EU that does more for the citizen, is more relevant for the citizen and closer to the citizen drew attention both to civil order and to civil liberties. Increases in transborder crime, in illegal immigration and in asylum seekers and refugees gave the area greater political saliency. The increase in activities in this field itself demanded a response. Yet the process through which the IGC eventually delivered reforms, itself reflected the problems of lack of transparency and openness, the very issues which negotiators were committed to address. The negotiations smacked of confusion. At the crucial meetings of the personal representatives there was no recording either from the Presidency or the Council Secretariat, agreeing to what was discussed at a particular session and outlining the state of progress on the issue at hand. Each national delegation recorded their own notes on the meeting. While attempts to reach some sort of agreement on the contents of an actual meeting would have been difficult and perhaps even counter-productive it did leave the way open for a degree of repetition, divergence in interpretation and understanding and ultimately confusion (McDonagh, 1998: 17–28). Not even the multiple press conferences were sufficient to suggest a transparent and open process.

The confusion as regards the negotiating objectives of the Member States resulted from a number of factors. Firstly the difficulties of ratifying the Maastricht Treaty and the evidence of popular resistance to further moves towards integration had left governments cautious about new initiatives. Secondly, domestic politics in several Member States hampered constructive preparations. The Italian Presidency was handicapped by government collapse, while French elections in early June 1997 required some refocusing of the negotiations in the final critical stages.[5] It was however the timing of the British general election that most distorted the process of negotiations (Parker, 1996). The defence of sovereignty, defined in terms of retaining the veto, had become one of the major themes of the debilitated Conservative government, leading to increasingly sharp confrontations with its continental partners. Michael Howard, one of the strongest 'Eurosceptics' in the British Cabinet, was as Home Secretary principally responsible for the dossier on justice and home affairs; the likelihood of another confrontation with the UK on this dossier seemed high. The result was the postponement of hard bargaining, in the expectation that Conservative defeat would allow consensus-building in the final stages (Peston, 1997; *Financial Times*, 1997; Barber and Buckley, 1997; Parker, 1996; *International Herald Tribune*, 1997; Buerkle, 1997a; *Irish Times*,

1997c). The Irish Presidency did have some success in finding common ground. Through 'successive approximation' it laid the initial groundwork that would eventually culminate in title IV TEC on Visas, Asylum, Immigration.[6] However the key issues as regards where any new title on JHA would be placed, the role of the institutions and the decision-making procedures were not addressed in any substantive manner (*Agence Europe*, 1996g; European Report No. 2176 – November 20, 1996 I, pp. 1–2; CONF 2500/96, pp. 19–28).

This drift in negotiations had a negative impact on the three issues of transparency, democracy and judicial control. There was in principle universal support from Member States and institutions on the need for a more transparent treaty in general, ranging from support regarding a simplification and codification of the treaties to a clearer process of decision-making to a greater access for the public to certain documents.[7] Yet a confused negotiating process, with governments unsure of the positions they would adopt at the final meeting at Amsterdam, did not augur well for a transparent treaty. The overall issue of transparency, as regards both integrating the principle into the Treaty and a general access to information, was discussed on several occasions at the level of personal representatives.[8] There were however few references to the issue in JHA papers presented by the Irish and Dutch Presidencies, as well as those from most Member States.[9] Other papers dealing with a general simplification and codification of the treaties and clarity in all legislative acts did, in a more indirect manner, touch on transparency. An exception to this approach were the papers from the Finnish and Swedish delegations, the Finnish paper calling for a new Article 192a TEC on transparency, with a right of access to documents, specifically mentioning the possibility of an extension to the third pillar through the then Article K.8 TEU.[10]

For the Dutch Presidency, most of all for Michel Patijn, the priority on the agenda was incorporation of the Schengen *acquis*.[11] The reaction from many of the other delegations as well as from the Council and Commission secretariat was one of bewilderment. No agreed text of the Schengen *acquis* was provided, in spite of repeated requests from the Irish delegation; negotiations thus proceeded over a document which had not been tabled. Patijn's commitment to incorporating the *acquis* was such that the Presidency readily drafted complicated opt-out clauses, necessary to accommodate the Nordic Travel Area and the British and hence Irish resistance, to abandoning frontier controls (Dutch Non-paper CONF/3806/97; CONF/3823/97 (Dutch Presidency)). At the same time there was much suspicion among other delegations about how far the French were really committed to some of their ambitious proposals, e.g. Commission re-sizing, the role of the ECJ in a revised third pillar and the immediate recourse to QMV in any new title of freedom, security and justice.[12] This was further to the doubts about Helmut Kohl's ability to deliver his government's consent on treaty changes in general in the face of domestic constraints.[13] As in the Maastricht IGC, a confused negotiating process hindered a transparent result.

Member governments differed widely on whether and how far to strengthen the position of the European Parliament, national parliaments and the Court of Justice in this field. For example the Benelux called for an extended role for the European parliament in the third pillar, particularly where the Council adopted decisions of a legislative nature.[14] The Danish government, late in the negotiations, added to its earlier emphasis providing implicit support for a stronger role for the European Parliament, when it called for a greater role for national parliaments (Danish Foreign Ministry, 1995).[15] The German government's position expressed support for a strong role for the European Parliament, while the Spanish document favoured setting up 'joint committees' of the European Parliament and the national parliaments on subjects related to the third pillar.[16] The French government in its guidelines for the IGC proposed a role for a 'High Parliamentary Council' – a body made up of representatives from national parliaments – where proposed legislation affected civil or criminal law (*Le Figaro*, 1996). The British Conservative government's White Paper called for maintenance of the status quo (UK Government, 1996).

At the first meeting of the personal representatives to the Conference in early April 1996 the German and Benelux delegations called for the Court of Justice to be given a more extensive jurisdiction in the third pillar. The Spanish delegation requested that the ECJ's role be limited to communitarized areas; the Swedish and Irish negotiators suggested a case-by-case approach. The Benelux in their proposed treaty title of 22 November 1996 on the third pillar claimed that bringing immigration and asylum into the Community framework would make for more effective action, giving the EP and ECJ clear roles. It proposed that under the new Title VI – 'Police and Judicial Cooperation' – the ECJ would rule on disputes between Member States or between Member States and the Commission (*Agence Europe*, 1996h). The Irish draft was non-committal on a role for the ECJ and the EP under its new title on 'Free movement of persons, asylum and immigration'. Article G stated that it was a matter that needed to be considered further (CONF 2500/96, p. 28). Article K.3(2) TEU provided for a mere consultation of the Parliament (CONF 2500/96, p. 36.).

The confusion among officials and observers as regards the progress and objectives of the negotiations makes it particularly difficult to trace any momentum to support a stronger role for both institutions. Yet certain submissions and meetings between delegations did provide a degree of promise for change. The Dutch Presidency's February 1997 submission followed by the March amendments to the Irish draft proposed a limited and loosely defined expansion of roles for both the Parliament and the Court (CONF/3823/97; CONF/2500/96 ADD.1). The French government's paper was mixed, confining a role for the Court, though a fairly robust one, to Chapter 3 on Security and Safety of Persons under the reformed Title VI TEU, while giving little extra authority to the European Parliament under Article G on decision-making procedures in the proposed new Title IIIa (now Title IV TEC) and on decision-making pursuant to Article K.3 TEU (CONF 382/97). The Italian government's paper was much more ambitious. Its newly created title under pillar I called for co-decision for the European Parliament and a full role for the Court of Justice (CONF 3840/97).

THE TREATY OUTCOME – TRANSPARENCY OR OBSCURITY?

The potential of the new Title IV TEC and the revamped Title VI TEU to provide for a greater transparency will only become apparent when the treaty is implemented and tested through practice, both in the courts and through parliamentary activity. It is necessary firstly to define what is meant by the term transparency and secondly to consider the treaty changes based on this definition. A useful approach in arriving at a definition is to pose the question as to what one would have expected from a transparent JHA in an ideal situation. Firstly there should be clarity as regards the treaty objectives, the means for implementing these objectives and the treaty language. Secondly a transparent process should have an effective and recognizable system of accountability within the whole framework. This is examined through a consideration of the role provided for the European Parliament and national parliaments under both titles. Thirdly and lastly there needs to be legal certainty and predictability as regards resolving any difficulties or disputes that may arise in the operation of the treaty.

Maintaining a balance

Article 2 of the consolidated Treaty of European Union, setting out the objectives of the Union, was amended to add a fourth paragraph, which neatly displays the underlying tensions and potential contradictions of the Amsterdam Treaty in this field:

> to maintain and develop the Union as an area of freedom, security and justice, in which the free movement of persons is assured *in conjunction with appropriate* measures with respect to border controls, asylum,

immigration and the prevention and combating of crime. (Article 2, Title I, Consolidated Treaty on European Union)

To realize this objective it is necessary to strike a balance between the opposing principles of freedom and security. The delicacy of that balance is increased by the further distinction between the first and third pillars, and the potential for conflict and confusion between them. (This is considered below.) A further balance had to be struck between the commitment of the Benelux states to the complete abolition of internal frontier controls, and the conditions the French and others wished to attach. The text of the treaty thus incorporates a number of reservations held by different states. The likely difficulty of the Court in carving out a role for itself in the matter of internal border controls under Title IV, given the wording of Article 68(2) TEU, leaves absent a necessary degree of impartiality in striking a (fair) balance between freedom and security. As the following examples show the Member States are left to determine this balance.

Article 64 TEC, for example, limits the commitment to common rules for internal free movement set out in the previous three articles by reserving (in its first paragraph) 'the exercise of the responsibilities incumbent on member states with regard to the maintenance of law and order and the safeguarding of internal security'. This reservation is reinforced by the second paragraph, permitting the Council to adopt provisional measures in the event of an 'emergency' in one or more Member States, but 'without prejudice to paragraph 1' (Article 64, Title IV, Consolidated Treaty on European Union). Declaration 19 muddies the waters further by allowing Member States to take into account foreign policy considerations 'when exercising their responsibilities under Article 64 (1) of the Treaty establishing the European Community'.[17]

The language of Article 64 TEC is repeated in Title VI in Article 33 TEU (formerly Article K.2(2) of the Maastricht Treaty), again providing the Member States with a potential let-out from implementing in a balanced manner the principles of security and freedom. The French government has already shown its willingness to use such clauses in relation to Schengen. By virtue of Article 2(2) of the Schengen Convention and in the interests of French security the French government has maintained controls on its border with Belgium.[18] Article 35 TEU gives the Court of Justice limited powers to review the actions of Member States; though 35(5) TEU, in a similar manner to Article 68(2), explicitly excludes from its jurisdiction actions justified 'with regard to the maintenance of law and order and the safeguarding of internal security'. There is room for further manoeuvring over interpretation and over the conditions under which such justifications must be accepted by other states. As discussed below it will be for the ECJ to interpret the scope of its jurisdiction under these provisions. Whether this should provide for a degree of certainty and predictability as regards striking a fair balance between freedom and security only practice will tell.

Conflicts and confusion

Some of the resulting confusion is inherent in the pillar approach adopted at Maastricht, and confirmed at Amsterdam. It was, after all, rooted in French and British resistance to handing over crucial areas of national sovereignty to the supra-national institutions of the EC: specifically, to exclude the Court of Justice from ruling on most matters reserved to inter-governmental negotiation, and to limit the involvement of the Commission and the European Parliament. This left unavoidable tensions between different forms of action within different pillars, and unavoidable areas of overlap, not just between the first and third pillars but also between the first and second. For example, at Maastricht the overhaul of EPC and the creation of CFSP saw certain tensions and fears that pillar I would 'contaminate' pillar II or vice versa. In turn this influenced the role and effectiveness of the Commission. After being granted the right of initiative it was reluctant to use it for these very reasons (Ginsberg, 1997).

A re-allocation of powers between the first and third pillars, rather than full incorporation of the Maastricht third pillar into the TEC, unavoidably left legal and political obscurities that reflected compromises between national positions. In a similar fashion to Title IV TEC, Title VI TEU refers to 'an area of freedom, security and justice' but rather than establishing such an area, it aims 'to provide citizens with a high level of safety' and the means to achieve this is by 'developing common action among the Member States in the fields of police and judicial cooperation in criminal matters and by preventing and combating racism and xenophobia' (Article 29 of TEU).

Therefore, at first instance, the boundary between the two titles seems relatively clear. However, there are overlaps and potential jurisdictional problems. While Title IV TEC aims to establish an area of free movement, this is also to include flanking measures 'with respect to external border controls, asylum and immigration . . .'. Title VI TEU provides for further flanking measures and the framework in which to guarantee safety within the new area of freedom, security and justice. Article 61(a) TEC calls for the adoption of measures to combat crime in accordance with the provisions of Article 31(e) TEU. Article 61(e) TEC suggests a further fight against crime by adopting 'measures in the field of police and judicial co-operation in criminal matters aimed at a high level of security'. However this must be in accordance with the provisions of the Treaty on European

Union. Article 29 TEU in a similar manner refers to providing for 'a high level of safety . . .' but 'without prejudice to the powers of the European Community . . .' (Article 29 of TEU). Again the precise meaning and effects of such saving phrases will only be established with implementation. There are few provisions for dealing with potential jurisdictional conflicts between the two pillars. Should a jurisdictional conflict arise it is again questionable whether there are sufficient means to resolve such matters in a clear and predictable manner; though Article 47 TEU (ex-Article M TEU) repeats the reservation that 'nothing in this Treaty shall affect the Treaties establishing the European Communities or the subsequent Treaties and Acts modifying or supplementing them' (Article 29 of TEU).

There are further difficulties as regards the approach to be taken under both pillars in realizing the competing objectives of freedom and security. The cooperation that grew up in the 1970s and 1980s among police forces, intelligence services, customs and immigration services and their supervising ministries was firmly under inter-governmental control. One of the defining characteristics of this cross-border cooperation was the emphasis on an approach that favoured informal networks over bureaucratic procedures and controls (Anderson *et al.*, 1995: ch. 7). The Maastricht Treaty through the 'third pillar' attempted to bring order, coherency and formalization to this *ad hoc*, extensive and overlapping network of trans-governmental cooperation. Raising the profile and visibility of such cooperation did not however otherwise mark a dramatic change from the previous means of cooperation; it was essentially a consolidation and regularization, maintaining the defining feature of intergovernmental cooperation. Amsterdam has changed this. The movement of cooperation on visas, asylum and immigration into the first pillar provides for cooperation according to modified Community procedures, alongside the continued intergovernmental cooperation under Title VI.

There is, however, a risk that a black hole of accountability and responsibility may open up between the third pillar mechanisms of national oversight and the first pillar mechanisms of Community oversight, with informal operational practices and inter-governmental working groups beyond the reach of either national or Community-level scrutiny – and for much of the time beyond the attention-span of ministers who retain formal responsibility. At the time of writing it is not clear how large a staff the Commission will be allowed to recruit to manage its new responsibilities under Title IV TEC, or even whether this will become the responsibility of a new Directorate-General. The Council Secretariat, reinforced through incorporation of the Schengen Secretariat, is likely to play a larger role in this field, servicing an extensive network of committees through which decisions are made beyond the effective reach of public, parliamentary or judicial view.

Incorporation of the Schengen *acquis* adds a further layer of complexity to this already-obscure framework. Unpublished documents, to be allocated between the two pillars from a list the exact extent of which had not been agreed a year after the Amsterdam Treaty had been signed, have the potential to make either judicial review or parliamentary scrutiny almost impossible. The British House of Lords protested in the summer of 1998 that:

> the presentation of the draft Decisions and Explanatory Memoranda [are] inadequate. Columns of numbers listed without descriptions or explanations are as unhelpful a way of providing information as we can think of. In order to make any sense of the draft Decisions as presented to Parliament it is necessary to have open the Decisions themselves, the EC Treaty, the Treaty on European Union, the Schengen Protocol and the Schengen Convention. (para.101)

The British Government's response to this strongly worded Committee Report, delivered to Parliament 15 months after the Amsterdam Treaty had been signed, and after most Parliaments had completed the process of ratification, declared that: 'It would . . . appear premature to publish a series of texts purporting to form the Schengen *acquis*' (House of Lords, 1999: para. 10). Negotiations on what had been decided at Amsterdam thus seemed likely to continue well beyond the coming into force of the Treaty, without sufficient legal clarity to enable those outside the process to grasp the political implications of this still-expanding pattern of cooperation among governments.

Treaty language

The lack of transparency is not confined to the relations between the two titles or the potential conflict between free movement and a secure Union. The language of a much greater number of articles is obscure, hiding underlying disagreements between national positions and carefully crafted compromises. It expresses the hesitations of negotiators and the compromises they struck – looking over their shoulders to domestic reactions, not focusing on clear rules for efficient operation. This was not confined to the two pillars but extended to the Schengen *acquis* (described in more detail in Chapter 15). The Heads of Government signed the Treaty without a prior agreement on what the Schengen *acquis* contained, and without non-members of Schengen being allowed to see even a draft outline of the *acquis*. Declaration 44 commits the signatories to

> adopt all the necessary measures referred to in Article 2 of the Protocol integrating the Schengen *acquis* into the framework of the European Union upon the date of entry into force of the Treaty of Amsterdam. To

that end the *necessary preparatory work shall be undertaken in due time in order to be completed prior to that date.* [italics added]

This meant that there would be no less than three rounds of negotiations: first on the treaty iself, then a further negotiation to discover what the treaty commitments entailed, and thereafter another one to allocate those commitments to relevant articles in Title IV TEC and Title VI TEU. Governments agreed that their Parliaments would ratify the treaty without having an explanation of what these clauses implied. This was an astonishing abdication of responsibility, a denial of the principles of transparency and accountability in this field, an acceptance that officials in working groups would define law and practice in the 12 to 18 months after the Amsterdam text had been signed, largely without ministerial oversight or reference to parliaments.

Returning to Title VI, Articles 30(2)(a) and (b) TEU on Europol's role come close to contradicting each other, reflecting unresolved differences over how far Europol should be allowed to develop an autonomous operational capacity. Paragraph (a) seeks 'to enable Europol to facilitate and support the preparation, and encourage the coordination and carrying out of specific investigative actions by the competent authorities of the Member States, *including operational actions of joint teams comprising representatives of Europol in a support capacity*' [italics added]. However, the composition of joint teams, and the exact role of Europol representatives in operational actions, is left for further negotiation between Member States in the Council, or for the development of practical experience. The language of paragraph (b) more hesitantly commits the Council to 'adopt measures *allowing Europol* to ask the competent authorities of the Member States to conduct and co-ordinate their investigations in specific cases . . .', while Europol itself is only 'to develop specific expertise which may be put at the disposal of Member States to *assist* them in investigating . . .'. (italics added)

Lack of clarity, reflecting unresolved differences – or insufficient time to refine loosely agreed commitments, and willingness to leave clarification to post-treaty negotiation – runs through the whole of Title VI. The relationship between the Co-ordinating Committee (the former 'K.4 committee') and Coreper is left unclear; Article 36 gives this group of senior officials 'the task . . . to give opinions for the attention of the Council', and 'contribute, without prejudice to Article 207 of the Treaty establishing the European Community, to the preparation of the Council's discussions . . .' – though Article 207 TEC states boldly that Coreper 'shall be responsible for preparing the work of the Council'. Here, as elsewhere, the relationship in practice between consultations under pillar three and pillar one will depend on goodwill among officials and among national delegations.

Article 40 allows for 'closer cooperation' within the third pillar among a number of Member States, building on the general clauses on closer cooperation contained in Title VII (Articles 43–45 TEU). The clause is peppered with saving phrases: 'provided that the cooperation proposed . . . respects the powers of the European Community' and 'has the aim of enabling the Union to develop more rapidly into an area of freedom, security and justice', and 'without prejudice to the Provisions of the Protocol integrating the Schengen *acquis* into the framework of the European Union'. The exact effects of such wordings, perhaps even proving beneficial, will only be determined in practice. For now their implications remain unclear.

However there are exceptions. Article 34 TEU provides a much clearer framework for 'the appropriate form and procedures' for measures agreed under Title VI. 'Common positions', and 'decisions', are familiar European Community language, though with different meanings under the TEC. Member States could draw up 'Conventions' after the Maastricht treaty under the then Article K.3 of the TEU, while the new concept of 'framework decision' is reasonably well defined under Article 34(b) TEU. These categorizations provide a distinctive bases for formal cooperation. Article 42 repeats the Maastricht Treaty's *passerelle*, allowing for the transfer of third pillar actions to the first pillar by unanimous consent; though without mentioning that post-treaty negotiations on the allocation of the Schengen *acquis* are likely to do more to determine the balance between the pillars than any explicit and unanimous decisions to move already settled practices from one to the other.

A LIMITED ROLE FOR EUROPEAN AND NATIONAL PARLIAMENTS

In the immediate aftermath of Amsterdam the European Parliament was widely considered as a clear-cut winner from the treaty.[19] However within the European Parliament itself there was considerable criticism of the limited influence the Parliament had gained over justice and home affairs (interviews with MEPs and EP officials). Member States' capability in emergency situations to resort to restrictive measures on free movement, for example, in Article 64(2) TEC, is subject to the approval of the Council, without any further reference to the Parliament. Article 67 limits the role of the European Parliament in this field to 'consultation', not only during the 'transitional period of five years following the entry into force of the treaty' but for an indefinite time thereafter. Paragraph 2 permits the Council, 'acting unanimously after consulting the European Parliament', to decide to transfer 'all or parts of the areas covered by this Title to be governed by the procedure referred to in Article 251' (which sets out the co-decision procedure). Until such unanimous agreement, however, consultation without co-decision will remain the parliamentary rule. The European Parliament is thus left with a much more restricted role in this field than in almost all other areas of policy included under pillar one. Articles 62 and 63 TEC specify that it is these Article 67 procedures which will apply to visa policy, and to policy on asylum and immigration.

As elsewhere domestic pressures on member governments shaped these limitations. The French government's paper of February 1997 proposed to lengthen the transitional period to five years, with a unanimous decision being required to bring it to an end, in line with traditional Gaullist opposition to supranational encroachments on national sovereignty.[20] Chancellor Kohl, previously sympathetic to the strengthening of Community institutions, was pressed by the *Länder* governments to insist on a unanimous change-over after five years, in order to protect the regional levels of government from an undue centralization of decision-making capacity.[21] Previous experience suggests nevertheless that the European Parliament will seek to exploit every opportunity to extend its influence, and to bring as much of the area allocated to the first pillar under its scrutiny as possible (see below). Under the third pillar the role of the European Parliament is more tightly limited. Article 39 TEU presents one significant advancement for the Parliament over the comparable Maastricht clauses, with the requirement that 'the Council shall consult the European Parliament', rather than the Presidency on 'the principal aspects of activities'. Yet even this modest extension of influence is limited to paragraphs (b), (c) and (d) of Article 34: the adoption of framework decisions, decisions and conventions. Otherwise the language of Article 39 repeats that of Maastricht. Paragraph 2 requires 'the Presidency of the Council and the Commission to regularly inform the European Parliament of discussions in the areas covered by this Title'. Paragraph 3 is shorter than its Maastricht equivalent, permitting the EP to ask questions of the Council, to make recommendations to it, and to hold an annual debate 'on the progress made in the areas referred to in this Title'. Article 40, on the possibility of moving towards 'closer cooperation' under Title VI, provides the European Parliament with an even more marginal role; the Council will merely 'forward' requests for closer cooperation to it, without any obligation to await or to consider its response.

The political and constitutional delicacy of cooperation in Justice and Home Affairs thus led to another tangle of governmental reservations and inter-governmental decision-making procedures, in which democratic accountability has been left at the margin. The European Parliament will undoubtedly seek to expand its influence and scrutiny over this field.

In this it may find an ally in the European Court of Justice, as the following section suggests.[22] But substantial obstacles, of national government resistance, and of secrecy, will remain. National parliaments in most Member States have themselves exerted only limited control over such key executive agencies of the state as police and intelligence services, considering major legislative changes but rarely monitoring regular activities. The European Parliament is therefore attempting to establish a position that many national governments have only reluctantly conceded to their own legislatures.

The role of national parliaments in scrutinizing issues of the third pillar has been difficult. The Declaration on their role in an annexe to the Maastricht treaty was limited. Mention was only made of ensuring 'that national Parliaments receive Commission proposals for legislation in good time . . .'. Within the EC framework, the flow of paper is sufficiently regular for scrutiny to operate. Where Commission initiative is the rule, proposals emerge, and are circulated to national governments and parliaments. Under the second and third pillars initiatives emerged from Member States or the Presidency, often taking formal shape as a fully drafted proposal only at a fairly late stage in inter-governmental discussions. The Commission did not play the leading role. The British House of Lords had repeatedly protested between 1994 and 1997 about the late delivery of third pillar documents for scrutiny, making it almost impossible to consider their implications before the Council had adopted them (House of Lords Select Committee on the European Communities, 1997). Pleas from national scrutiny committees for advance notice of draft agendas for JHA Councils, and for early delivery of negotiating texts, have come up against the informal working practices of this field and the pressures under which successive Presidencies operate to rush through priority proposals before six months are out. The Conference of committees of scrutiny of national parliaments (COSAC) discussed this problem at meetings under the Luxembourg and British Presidencies in 1997–8, without discovering better ways to bring pressure on their respective governments to release draft documents earlier than exchanging information among clerks. However, the Amsterdam treaty introduces changes that may enhance the role of national parliaments under both titles. Firstly the Commission has seen a potential strengthening in its position as regards making proposals under Article 67 TEC and Article 34(2) TEU. Therefore any proposals that it submits to the Council under both titles should ensure that the national parliaments are kept well informed. Secondly the Protocol on the Role of National Parliaments in the European Union permits COSAC to 'make any contribution it deems appropriate for the attention of the institutions of the European Union'. More significantly it 'may examine any legislative proposal or initiative in relation to the establishment of an area of freedom, security and justice'. The institutions are to be informed of any 'contribution' that COSAC may make on such matters or indeed on any legislative activities of the Union on freedom, security and justice.

A STRONGER ROLE FOR THE EUROPEAN COURT OF JUSTICE?

The Court of Justice pursuant to Article 68 TEC has been granted a potentially strong and influential role in Title IV of the EC Treaty. However, it is possible to overstate the importance of these new powers. Article L and M TEU (now Article 46 and 47 TEU) provided the Court with the potential to hold a Community act within the JHA pillar in breach of the TEC (*Commission v Council* Case C-170/96 (The Air Transport Case)). Yet the changes have very real benefits since it was unlikely that Article 47 could be extended so far as to allow the court to interpret the actual articles of Title VI of the TEU.[23] As with its predecessor, Article M, it is concerned with ensuring that measures adopted under the third pillar do not encroach on areas of Community competence.

The first paragraph of Article 68 introduces the preliminary reference procedure under Article 234 powers (formerly Article 177) into the title. This provides for effective judicial control that extends far beyond the ECJ, to the system of national courts across the participating Member States. Article 234 has been one of the ECJ's primary tools and strategies in engendering good relations with national courts to maintain an effective system of EC law (Weiler, 1987: 366). In the interest of safeguarding the uniform application of EC law the court has held that the provision does not permit national courts to declare a Community act invalid, though they have the power to declare them valid. It is the national court that decides if and when to seek guidance, subject to the requirements set out in the treaty. Equally it is the national courts that ultimately decide the cases, the ECJ interprets the relevant provision of EC law, leaving it for the national court to apply the ruling given by the ECJ to the facts of the case (Hartley, 1994: 266). Maintaining an effective system of EC law has been a team effort. Therefore given the nature of the preliminary reference procedure effective judicial scrutiny of the actions and decisions of the institutions, in particular under Title IV, seems possible.

Yet there are restrictions. The principal restriction is based in Article 68(2) TEC on measures 'relating to the maintenance of law and order and the safeguarding of internal security'. However, the Court has alternatives open to it in minimizing the application of the Article. The vagueness of the article leaves it open as to the extent of its application and this will most probably see the court being called upon to provide an interpretation. Given the sensitivities surrounding such issues as internal security and law and order the Court of Justice may find it necessary to be somewhat constrained as regards its interpretation. Anything that may be construed by the governments of certain Member States as strengthening the hand of the ECJ may be met by a backlash against the court similar to that expressed by some governments during this IGC, particularly in the pre-negotiation stage.[24] A more subtle approach restricting the effects of Article 68(2) may be secured by the Court availing itself of any opportunities that may arise to give an interpretation of Article 62(1) TEC that emphasizes its importance in ensuring the free movement of persons, while at the same time limiting its use as a legal basis for the very measures or decisions as suggested under Article 68(2). This, in turn, would reduce the number of measures or decisions that would be exclusively confined to interpretation by the national courts, thereby limiting the possibility of a diversity within the case-law that could undermine the uniformity of EC law. This would also ensure that the freedoms guaranteed are not undermined by the equally important requirements on security, ensuring that a balance is maintained.

As with Title IV TEC judicial scrutiny of the institutions activities under Title VI TEU (particularly those pursuant to Article 34(2) TEU) is for the greater part guaranteed by the preliminary rulings procedure. However, pursuant to Article 35(2) TEU Member States were left to make individual declarations that they would accept the ECJ's jurisdiction to give preliminary rulings in this area. This freedom to choose was necessary to accommodate the few opposed to a strong role for the court in the third pillar, notably the British government. Yet with the signing of Amsterdam it seems that only Austria, Germany, Greece and the Benelux made such declarations providing for some form of a role for the Court of Justice (OJ 97/C 340/05). The absence of any time limit on making a declaration pursuant to Article 35(2) TEU has meant that some Member States have avoided confronting the issue. However, as Title VI is implemented the moral obligation and practical benefits of signing up to a role for the Court – providing for a clarity and uniformity on interpreting decisions, conventions and implementing measures – should lead to further declarations. The confusion that would follow from having 'ins' and 'outs' on what is in any case a restricted role for the Court would undermine the effectiveness of Title VI and prove detrimental to all Member States.

There are other restrictions to the Court's role on top of the 'opt in-or-out' feature. The lack of direct effect for decisions and framework decisions under Article 34 may see a reduction in the number of preliminary rulings, given that it will not be possible for an individual to bring a case before a national court seeking to enforce a right against a Member

State, where it has failed to implement the framework decision or decision.[25] Article 35(6) TEU, which is closely modelled on Article 230 TEC (formerly Article 173), restricts the privilege of initiating action to Member States and the Commission. Natural or legal persons cannot institute proceedings.[26] As is likely to be the case with the absence of direct effect this is set to limit the number of cases brought before the ECJ and ultimately its ability to scrutinize the various decisions.

The equivalent of Article 68(2) TEC can be found in Article 35(5) TEU. It has two parts. The first states the ECJ has no jurisdiction as regards 'the validity or proportionality of operations carried out by the police or other law enforcement agencies of a Member State'. This confirms the restriction of judicial review to the national courts as outlined by the Declaration on Article 30. Interestingly, though, the Declaration provided for national judicial review of Europol while failing to mention Europol in the restriction of the ECJ's role pursuant to Article 35(5) TEU. Confusion therefore surrounds the precise role of the Court of Justice regarding its ability to review Europol's actions. This proves even more difficult given that much of Europol's activities are in a support capacity to national forces.[27] The second part of Article 35(5) throws out a much wider net, excluding the ECJ from the sensitive issues of law and order and the safeguarding of internal security. Such provisions operate in tandem with Article 33 TEU. However, as is the case in the first pillar, the ECJ may provide a narrow and restricted interpretation of the Articles themselves, in the interests of ensuring that any security measures are fairly balanced with the need to maintain the freedom guaranteed under Title IV TEC and the respect for fundamental human rights under Title I of the TEU.[28]

Even the cooperation between national judicial authorities – subject to the Council's adoption of specific measures on, for example, criminal matters under Article 31 and 32 TEU – may have negative implications on the effectiveness of judicial scrutiny, failing to promote a harmonized EU-wide system under the supervision of the ECJ. Declaration No. 7 on Article 30 TEU provides for the appropriate judicial review in each Member State as regards the 'action in the field of police cooperation' under the same article. This reflects the sensitive nature of an issue such as police cooperation and hence the desire for exclusive national control on such matters. However, the cooperation that Article 30 seeks to engender may very well be jeopardized by the strong likelihood of national courts allowing a diversity in the forms of police cooperation (between Member States and involving Europol), pursuant to Declaration No. 7. To maintain an effective and relatively harmonized approach on police cooperation the option should have been provided for an Article 234 TEC referral to the ECJ allowing for a standard interpretation on the vague and self-contradictory paragraphs of Article 30.

The Court of Justice is at its strongest under Article 40. Article 40(4) TEU provides a similar role for the Court on closer/enhanced cooperation as would be the case under the TEC. The granting of full powers epitomizes the concern of all the member governments on the manner in which flexibility will be used under Article 40. Greater powers of scrutiny for the Court of Justice, it is hoped, will ensure that a balanced and fair approach is taken by the governments in deciding whether to go ahead with closer cooperation and extending at a later stage the number of participating Member States. One can expect the Court to ensure that 'the powers of the European Community' are respected with any closer cooperation.

The position and influence of the Court under both pillars have been significantly improved. As regards the restrictions and uncertainties on its role and jurisdiction, in similar situations in the past the Court of Justice has not shied away from developing its own powers and those of the European parliament with a range of legal interpretative techniques.[29] This has the potential of providing for a treaty in which the institutions are more accountable and one where a fair balance between the objectives of freedom and security can be maintained.

CONCLUSIONS

On justice and home affairs the European Union remains a long way from the safeguards of constitutional democracy. To an even greater extent than in earlier Inter-governmental Conferences, the post-negotiation stage of the Amsterdam Treaty has left the Member States attempting to regain their bearings after passing through the eye of a two-day storm in June 1997. Much was left undecided; internal disagreements within member governments, and unresolved differences of perspective among member governments, made for obscure and ambiguous language and for underlying differences of interpretation. Absence of legal certainty, of clarity and of transparency, was epitomized by the agreement to incorporate into the treaty the Schengen *acquis*, without having first defined what that *acquis* contained or how it was to be allocated among the different clauses of the TEC and TEU – without even allowing non-members of Schengen to see the purported text before the treaty was signed. Specific clauses in both Title IV TEC and Title VI TEU limited the capacity of the EP and the ECJ to oversee the development of policy and of practice. As with other sensitive and contentious areas of European cooperation, a great deal has been left to be worked out through experience, or to be renegotiated in the light of that experience at the next IGC.

Executive power within nation-states has traditionally extended further over policing, border controls, exchange of sensitive information with other governments, intelligence services, the granting of asylum and the expulsion of undesirable aliens than over most other fields of domestic politics. The growth of European cooperation in these areas has multilateralized the operation of national executive agencies, removing their activities further from parliamentary accountability and public understanding. The slow accumulation of conventions for judicial cooperation, for broad rules of asylum, for the conditions under which national forces operate on each other's territory, are providing a transparent legal framework for some aspects of these rapidly expanding activities. The European Parliament, and the Court of Justice, have extended their authority to a limited extent over such matters. But there remains a large gap – a black hole – between what national parliaments are able to review and what the European Parliament yet scrutinizes; and a smaller, though still worrying, gap, between the reach of national courts and the authority of the European Court of Justice. That constitutes a constitutional, and a democratic deficit, which remains to be tackled at the next IGC.

NOTES

1. Kohl described this move to a more restrictive approach 'as an important precondition for the fact that Germany can fully participate in a common European immigration and asylum policy'. See Uçarer (1997: 289) and *International Intelligence Report* (1994).
2. *Ibid.*
3. 'Examples of such occasions can be found on the adoption of Joint Action 96/747/JHA Official Journal L 342, 31 December 1996; Joint Action 96/748/JHA Official Journal L 342, 31 December 1996.
4. A meeting between Heads of State or Government in late March 1996 at Turin formally convened the IGC.
5. Barry (1997: 9); Buerkle (1997a); Buerkle (1997c). For an alternative position see Smyth (1997); *Agence Europe* (1997); Davidson (1997). For Italian domestic political situation see McCarthy (1997).
6. This related to an approach that attempted to reach final agreement through a series of phases, gradually bringing the Member States along. For detailed discussion on the concept see McDonagh (1998: 75–7). Also see Svensson (1998: 21).
7. For a general call from the various governments of the Member States for a more transparent treaty see Reflection Group Report (SN 519/95 Reflex 20), pp. 24–6; Government policy paper addressed to the Belgian Parliament on the 1996 IGC; Memorandum on the IGC from the Governments of Belgium, Luxembourg and the Netherlands, 7 March 1996; European Cooperation in the fields of Justice and Home Affairs. Third Memorandum for the 1996 Intergovernmental Conference (23 May 1995); Communication of March 1996: 'From Madrid to Turin: the Netherlands' priorities for the 1996 IGC'; Germany's

objectives for the Intergovernmental Conference, 26 March 1996; CDU, CSU and FDP coalition agreement for the current legislative period. Point VIII on 'Europe and Foreign Policy – Security and Defence', 11 November 1994; Joint declaration of 15 July 1995 by the German and Italian Foreign Ministers regarding the 1996 Intergovernmental Conference; Position of the Italian Government on the IGC for the revision of the Treaties, 18 March 1996; Austria's positions of principle on the Intergovernmental Conference: Austrian Government document of 26 March 1996; Portugal and the IGC for the revision of the Treaty on European Union – Foreign Ministry document, March 1996; Communication of the Swedish Government of 30 November 1995 on the 1996 IGC; Agenda for Europe: the 1996 Intergovernmental Conference. Report of the Danish Foreign Ministry, June 1995; Bases for negotiations: an open Europe. The 1996 IGC. Memorandum of the Danish Government, 11 December 1995; *Agence Europe* (1995e); *Agence Europe* (1995f); 'Towards a citizens' Europe – democracy and development': Memorandum for the 1996 IGC, January 1995; Memorandum of the Greek Government of 24 January 1996 on the IGC: Greece's positions and comments; 'The 1996 Intergovernmental Conference: starting points for a discussion', 2 March 1995; 'Elements for a Spanish position at the 1996 Intergovernmental Conference', 28 March 1996; *Le Figaro* (1996); White Paper on Foreign Policy: 'External challenges and opportunities', 26 March 1996; Luxembourg Government memorandum of 30 June 1995 on the 1996 Intergovernmental Conference; Memorandum of the Foreign Ministry of 18 September 1995 on the views of the Finnish Government concerning the 1996 Intergovernmental Conference; Finland's starting-points and objectives for the 1996 IGC – report of the Finnish Government, 27 February 1996.

8. See *Agence Europe* (1996c), *Agence Europe* (1996d), and *Agence Europe* (1996e).
9. For example of major papers see CONF 3918/96 (UK Proposal); CONF/3866/96 (Irish Presidency); CONF/3976/96 (Irish Presidency); CONF 2500/96 (Irish Draft); CONF/3823/97 (Dutch Presidency); CONF 3824/97 (French Proposal); CONF 3840/97 (Italian Proposal); CONF/3862/97 (Greek Proposal).
10. CONF/3865/97 (Finnish Proposal); CONF/3853/96 (Swedish Proposal).
11. Michel Patijn was Secretary of State for European Affairs.
12. CONF 3824/97 (French Proposal).
13. Interviews conducted in the French, Dutch, British, Irish and German foreign ministries. See also *Economist* (1997b); *Irish Times* (1997a); *Irish Times* (1997d).
14. *Memorandum on the IGC from the Governments of Belgium, Luxembourg and the Netherlands*, 7 March 1996.
15. *The Role of National Parliaments in Relation to Cooperation on Justice and Home Affairs*, 16 May 1997.
16. *Germany's objectives for the Intergovernmental Conference*, 26 March 1996; *Elements for a Spanish position at the 1996 Intergovernmental Conference*, 28 March 1996.
17. Declaration on Article 64 of the Treaty establishing the European Community, Consolidated Treaty on European Union.
18. See *Agence Europe* 20 April 1995; *Agence Europe* (1995d). See in relation to Schengen *Agence Europe* (1995b); *Agence Europe* (1996b).
19. Interviews at European Parliament, July 1997.
20. CONF 3824/97 p. 2 and Article G, p. 6. The Irish draft had proposed an amendment to Article B of the TEU suggesting this to take place by 2001. At

the same time Article B of the new title proposed that the actual measures 'on ensuring the absence of any controls on persons when crossing internal borders' and measures regarding the 'external borders' should be taken within a year after the entry into force of the treaty.

21. For details on domestic constraints on Kohl and federal government see Gillespie (1997); *Irish Times* (1997c); *Economist* (1997a); *Economist* (1997b); *Economist* (1997c); *Economist* (1997d); Stüdemann (1997); *Agence Europe* (1996a).

22. See also the following series of cases for an account of the development of the European Parliament's powers under the then Article 173, now Article 250; *European Parliament* v *Council*, Case 13/83 (Transport case), [1985] ECR 1513; *European Parliament* v *Council*, Case 302/87 (Comitology Case), [1988] ECR 5616; *European Parliament* v *Council*, Case C-70/88 (Chernobyl case), [1990] ECR I-2041. See Hartley (1994: 397–9).

23. See Neuwahl (1995: 302) on the equivalent Article M, TEU.

24. See Rice (1996); Kampfner (1996); Harding (1996); *Agence Europe* (1995c); *Agence Europe* (1996f).

25. Direct effect, in its vertical form, confers rights on individuals against the state and when of a horizontal nature imposes obligations on individuals in favour of the state or other individuals. See Hartley (1994: 216–222).

26. It should be noted that even under Article 230 TEC the circumstances when an individual or firm can challenge a measure is restricted.

27. The Florence European Council in June 1996 claimed to have resolved a long-term dispute regarding EUROPOL that enabled the Court of Justice of the European Communities to give a preliminary ruling on the interpretation of the Europol Convention. The question is how this relates to Declaration No. 7 and Article 35(5).

28. It should be noted that Article 35 does not provide the ECJ with the freedom to give preliminary rulings on the actual treaty articles of Title VI TEU. However, in interpreting a decision recourse may have to be made to the actual treaty articles thereby providing for some form of interpretation. On the Court's willingness to be liberal in its interpretation see Rasmussen (1986). See also Cappelletti (1987: 3–17).

29. *Op. cit.*, 22.

BIBLIOGRAPHY

Agence Europe (1995a), 20 April.

Agence Europe (1995b) 'France Reintroduces Controls, at Airports, of Passengers Travelling in the Schengen Area', 28 July.

Agence Europe (1995c) 'German Constitutional Court Judge Criticizes EU Court of Justice', 22 August.

Agence Europe (1995d) 'Strengthening of Anti-Terrorist Measures Requested by France has been Accepted', 6 September.

Agence Europe (1995e) 'Visit by Danish Parliamentarians to Luxembourg: The Problem of Transparency', 19 October.

Agence Europe (1995f) 'Mr. Ersbell, Member of the Reflection Group, Emphasizes Transparency and Defends the Role of the Commission', 23 November.

Agence Europe (1996a) 'German Länder Welcome the Assurance of their Presence in the German Delegation at the IGC', 25 January.

Agence Europe (1996b) 'France Abolishes Border Controls with Germany and Spain but not with Benelux (Because of Drugs)', 25 March.

Agence Europe (1996c), 15–16 April.

Agence Europe (1996d), 22–23 May.

Agence Europe (1996e) 'Transparency: Presidency Proposals, Especially with a View to Integrating this Principle in the Treaty', 30 July.

Agence Europe (1996f) 'British Memorandum on the Court of Justice Recommends a Number of Changes in the Working of the Court: Details on Proposals', 28 August.

Agence Europe (1996g) 'EU/IGC–Dorr Group Examines Different Issues Related to Third Pillar and Legal Personality of the Union on the Basis of Drafts by the Presidency', 20 November.

Agence Europe (1996h) 'Proposals by Benelux on Crossing of External Borders, Immigration and Asylum, EU Financial Interests and Penalties for Violation of Community Law: Belgian Proposal on Police and Judicial Co-operation', 23 November.

Agence Europe (1997) 'Mr. Van Mierlo Does not Believe French Elections Will Influence Timing of the IGC', 2 June.

Anderson, M, den Boer, M., Cullen, P, and Gilmore, W. (1995) *Policing the European Union: Theory, Law and Practice.* Oxford: Oxford University Press.

Barber, L. and N. Buckley (1997) 'European Union: delight in Brussels as Britain turns on charm', *Financial Times*, 6 May.

Barry, J. (1997) 'Right faces living with the Left', *International Herald Tribune*, 26 May.

Bieber, R. and J. Monar (eds) (1995) *Justice and Home Affairs in the European Union.* Brussels: European Interuniversity Press.

Buerkle, T. (1997a) 'A gamble that could backfire, Europe says', *International Herald Tribune*, 22 April.

Buerkle, T. (1997b) 'Hopes rise that Britain will warm to Europe', *International Herald Tribune*, 3 May.

Buerkle, T. (1997c) 'Stakes are high as EU leaders gather for Summit: cautious optimism for deal to save Euro', *International Herald Tribune*, 16 June.

Cappelletti, M. (1987) 'Is the European Court of Justice "running wild"?', *European Law Review*, 12, 3–17.

Christian, P. and G. Müller-Graft (1994) 'Legal bases of the Third Pillar and its position in the framework of the Union Treaty', *Common Market Law Review*, 31, 493–510.

Danish Foreign Ministry (1995) *Agenda for Europe: The 1996 Intergovernmental Conference.* June.

Davidson, I. (1997) 'Lunatic instability', *Financial Times*, 11 June.

Eaton, M. R. (1996) 'Common Foreign and Security Policy'. In D. O'Keefe and P. Twomey (eds), *Legal Issues of the Maastricht Treaty.* Wiley.

Economist (1997a) 'Germany decides who is German' and 'Who is a German?', 5 April.

Economist (1997b) 'Battling on, for Germany and for Europe', 12 April.

Economist (1997c) 'Euro-Division: Germany's unloved politicians', 14 June.

Economist (1997d) 'The Princes are revolting: Germany: Helmut Kohl v Germany's States', 28 June.

Financial Times (1997) 'Euro-strategy for Mr Blair', 24 May.

Foreign and Commonwealth Office (1996) *A Partnership of Nations*, UK White Paper of 12 March 1996 on the IGC.

Foster, N. G. (1990) *EC Legislation*. London: Blackstone Press.

Gillespie, P. (1997) 'Kohl is too weak in Germany, but he is too strong in Europe', *Irish Times*, 21 June.

Ginsberg, R. H. (1997) 'The EU's CFSP: the politics of procedure'. In M. Holland (ed.), *Common Foreign and Security Policy: The Records and Reforms*. London: Pinter.

Harding, J. (1996) 'Howard's call to curb European Court splits Cabinet', *Financial Times*, 18 May.

Hartley, T. C. (1994) *The Foundations of European Community Law*, 3rd edn. Oxford: Clarendon Press.

House of Lords Select Committee on the European Communities (1997) *Enhancing Parliamentary Scrutiny of the Third Pillar*. Session 1997–98, 6th Report, HL paper 25. London: HMSO.

House of Lords Select Committee on the European Communities (1998) *Incorporating the Schengen Acquis into the European Union*. Session 1997–8, 31st Report, HL Paper 139. London: HMSO.

House of Lords Select Committee on the European Communities (1999) *Correspondence with Ministers*. Session 1998–9, 4th Report, HL Paper 24. London: HMSO.

International Herald Tribune (1997) 'Britain signals new era with EU', 6 May.

International Intelligence Report (1994) 'Kohl views 1993 achievements, 1994 asks', 3 January.

Irish Times (1997a) 'Poll shows lack of support for Kohl's re-election', 5 April.

Irish Times (1997b) 'Ending Britain's self-imposed exclusion', 23 May.

Irish Times (1997c) 'Moving down the EU road', 19 June.

Irish Times (1997d) 'Trouble at home reduces EU heavyweight', 21 June.

Le Figaro (1996) 'Memorandum on France's guidelines for the 1996 IGC', 20 February.

Kampfner, J. (1996) 'Working time directive: court ruling puts ministers in fighting mood', *Financial Times*, 13 November.

McCarthy, P. (1997) 'Italy at a turning point', *Current History*, March.

McDonagh, B. (1998) *Original Sin in a Brave New World*. Dublin: Institute for European Affairs.

Monar, J. (1995) 'Democratic control of Justice and Home Affairs: the European Parliament and the National Parliaments'. In R. Bieber and J. Monar (eds), *Justice and Home Affairs in the European Union*. Brussels: European Interuniversity Press.

Neuwahl, N. A. E. M. (1995) 'Judicial control in matters of Justice and Home Affairs: what role for the Court of Justice'. In R. Bieber and J. Monar, (eds), *Justice and Home Affairs in the European Union*. Brussels: European Interuniversity Press.

Neuwahl, N. A. E. M. (1996) 'Foreign and security policy and the implementation of the requirement of "consistency" under the Treaty on European Union'. In D. O'Keefe and P. Twomey (eds), *Legal Issues of the Maastricht Treaty*. Wiley.

Parker, G. (1996) 'Maastricht: Rifkind says EU talks "on hold until election"', *Financial Times*, 28 December.

Peston, R. (1997) 'Blair: British interests come "first, second and last" ', *Financial Times*, 10 May.

Rasmussen, H. (1986) *On Law and Policy in the European Court of Justice*, Dordrecht, Netherlands: Martinus Nijhoff.

Rice, R. (1996) 'Business and the law: guns lock on old target: Robert Rice on fresh UK efforts to reform the European Court of Justice', *Financial Times*, 26 November.

Smyth, P. (1997) 'French poll date to save Euro', *Irish Times*, 23 April.

Stüdemann, F. (1997) 'Germany: States miss budget targets', *Financial Times*, 3 May.

Svensson, A-C. (1998) *The IGC 1996–97: The Role of the Presidency, Presented at 26th ECPR*, Warwick, 23–8 March.

Uçarer, E. M. (1997) 'Europe's search for policy: the harmonization of asylum policy and European integration'. In E. Uçarer and D. J. Puchala (eds), *Immigration into Western Societies: Problems and Policies*. London: Pinter.

UK Government (1996) White Paper on Foreign Policy: 'External challenges and opportunities', 26 March.

Weiler, J. H. (1987) 'The European Court, national courts and references for preliminary rulings'. In H. G. Schermers *et al.* (ed.), *Article 177 EEC: Experiences and Problems*. North-Holland.

Weiler, J. H. (1987) 'The Court of Justice', *Common Market Law Review*, 24, 555–89.

CASES

European Parliament v *Council*, Case 13/83 (Transport Case), [1985] ECR 1513.

European Parliament v *Council*, Case 302/87 (Comitology Case), [1988] ECR 5616.

European Parliament v *Council*, Case C-70/88 (Chernobyl Case), [1990] ECR I-2041.

Commission v *Council*, Case C-170/96 (The Air Transport Case).

CHAPTER 9

CLOSER COOPERATION: POLITICAL BACKGROUND AND ISSUES IN THE NEGOTIATION

Philippe de Schoutheete

THE ORIGINS OF A CONCEPT

Outsiders seem frequently to consider the European Community as a massive fortress of uniform rules and regulations, a pyramidal structure constraining Member States in a legal straitjacket, enforced by a rigid institutional framework. Insiders know that, in fact, it is, and always has been, much more flexible. Over the years it has devised a variety of ways to accommodate different situations and differing views. It accepts that change is a gradual process, and that time and flexibility are needed to accomplish it. It grows in bits and pieces, on the basis of frequently ambiguous texts. 'The Community political system', says Stanley Hoffmann (1990: 282), 'can best be visualised as an elaborate set of networks, closely linked in some ways, partially decomposed in others, whose results depend on the political style in the ascendant at the moment.' That is why, today, it seems so complex, so difficult to describe and to put in categories.

In the mid-1970s, shortly after the first enlargement, it became clear that the entry of Britain, Denmark and Ireland, however desirable in itself, was changing the conceptual basis on which the Community had been originally based. The level of commitment, the aspiration towards further integration, was no longer equal among Member States. Willy Brandt, then Chancellor of the Federal Republic, began talking about *'abgestufte Integration'*. Leo Tindemans, then Prime Minister of Belgium, noted in the report on European Union which he submitted to the other heads of government in the first days of 1976, that it was impossible to submit a credible programme of action if it was deemed necessary that all stages be reached by all states at the same time: 'progress as regards economic and monetary policy may be sought initially between certain States'.

Brandt and Tindemans were addressing a Community of nine Member States. By 1985 it was growing to 12 members and Helen Wallace, writing on the 'Challenge of Diversity', pointed out that 'labels for strategies to respond to heterogeneity have proliferated: variable geometry, two speed/two tier Community, *l'Europe à la carte*, differentiation, *abgestufte Integration*' (Wallace, 1985: 3). In fact, but nobody could be sure of that, the Community was then on the verge of breathtaking new steps in integration through the implementation of the single market, from 1985 to 1992, and the establishment of monetary union, from 1992 to 1999. The realization of these goals implied, as Helen Wallace indicated, that the Community would need to face the challenge of diversity.

In this respect, as in many others, the Treaty of Maastricht seems, with hindsight, to have marked a watershed. The single most important aim of the negotiators, i.e. economic and monetary union, clearly necessitated a flexible approach, as Tindemans had pointed out 15 years before. The Treaty articles concerning economic and monetary union organize this approach by formulating objective criteria and procedures for the accession to monetary union, rules and voting arrangements for its further development, and conditions for its ultimate extension to all Member States. What we have in the Treaty itself is in conformity with the concept of a two-speed Community which had by then become part of accepted doctrine, even for the purists: the goal is common to all Member States (Article B, new Article 2 TEU), its realization is escalated in time (Article109 J, new Article 121 TEC), those who fail at the first test are encouraged to catch up (Article 109 K, new Article 122 TEC).

But in the last hours of negotiations between ministers and heads of government, and under the pressure of John Major, two new developments were agreed, and found their place in protocols annexed to the treaty. One indicated that Britain and Denmark were free *not* to participate in the final phase of monetary union even if all relevant criteria were fulfilled (Protocols 11 and 12). The other organized the possibility of legislation on social policy as between 11 Member States, Britain excluded (Protocol 14). In both cases we are beyond the (orthodox) framework of the two-speed concept: the ultimate objective is no longer common. We are in the (unorthodox) field of variable geometry: two Member States choose not to participate in a common policy.

This new development of the concept of flexibility in legally binding texts linked to the Maastricht Treaty was greeted with sharp criticism from several quarters, notably in the European Parliament. Claus Dieter Ehlermann, who had long been an authority on flexibility in Community affairs, considered that these clauses were 'revolutionary' (Ehlermann, 1995). The obvious but inglorious answer was that this had been necessary to ensure overall agreement, and the meanders of the Danish ratification process were to show how true this was.

Nevertheless many of the negotiators and most Member States were not happy with the results. The social protocol, in particular, bore clear signs of hasty drafting. For this or other reasons its legislative clauses were scarcely used in the years intervening between Maastricht and Amsterdam. The majority opinion was that the relevant protocols were blemishes on the Maastricht Treaty. This was demonstrated in the course of the accession negotiations with Austria, Finland, Norway and Sweden, conducted in the aftermath of the Maastricht ratification process. All four countries were told, in clear terms, that there would be no opt-out for them: they would need to subscribe to the social protocol and to accept entry into the third phase of monetary union when the criteria were fulfilled (an obligation which Sweden has managed to evade). The position taken in the negotiation was not inspired simply by the will to restore traditional orthodoxy; it was an effort to maintain in the Union the basic elements of legal and political coherence without which there was a risk of it drifting apart.

But even if misgivings or afterthoughts were not absent from the Community scene, the situation with respect to flexibility, in 1995, at the moment when a new intergovernmental conference was on the point of convening, was determined by the Maastricht Treaty: EMU as a major new development in the two-speed approach, British and Danish opt-outs breaking new ground by going beyond that approach.

A NEW IMPULSE FOR FLEXIBILITY

The concept of flexibility played an important role in the intergovernmental conference leading to the Treaty of Amsterdam. Under various denominations (flexibility, differentiation, enhanced cooperation, reinforced integration) it was present in many contributions, coming from Member States or from institutions. Debated at length, and with much confusion, at various moments of the conference, it was finally formulated in treaty provisions that are among the most controversial (and certainly not the simplest or clearest) parts of that Treaty. Two preliminary remarks can shed some light.

Firstly the debate, in the way it was conducted, was new. On this occasion, closer cooperation was discussed not as a practical solution to a given problem (like monetary union or social policy), but as a new concept, to be introduced as such into the treaties, and applied in future, under certain conditions, across the board, in various pillars and in circumstances as yet unforeseen.

Conceptual debates are intellectually stimulating but they are not the rule in intergovernmental conferences. The closest parallel to this one would be, to my mind, the debates, also lengthy and sometimes confused, on the concept of subsidiarity in the Maastricht negotiation. In both cases the discussion was interesting because it was new, and because it led to a real debate, in the sense that the position of many participants changed as ideas became clearer, dangers or opportunities more apparent, motives better understood. The concepts of subsidiarity and closer cooperation are not unrelated because both concern the exercise of power (including legislative power) at different levels of authority.[1] Closer cooperation, says Article 43 TEU, is a means of last resort: it is justified by incapacity or ineffectiveness at Community level just as Community action is justified by incapacity or ineffectiveness at national level. In both cases action is only appropriate at one level if action at the other level is blocked or ineffective. Enhanced cooperation can then be seen as a new form of subsidiarity.[2]

But intellectual debate, however important the result may be, is not the job of professional negotiators. Some are good at it and others not. A few have a liking for, and many a deep dislike for, this sort of exercise. Some presumably have strict instructions to avoid it at all costs. In those circumstances, and in a relatively short period of time, the results cannot be wholly satisfactory, as the Amsterdam Treaty clauses amply demonstrate.

A second point worth making is that, in the Amsterdam negotiation, the advocates of flexibility came from an unexpected quarter. Some sub-systems in the Community, making use of this concept, have always had, of course, long-standing and impeccable credentials (De Schoutheete, 1990: 106–24). Nevertheless, in previous years, the strongest arguments in favour had been formulated by countries like Britain or Denmark, or by political leaders like Margaret Thatcher who were concerned by the (in their view) excessive ambitions of their partners. The justification was to avoid what Helen Wallace called the Community's malady: 'namely that of seeking to apply excessively and unrealistically strict common goals and disciplines to countries which in fact are strikingly diverse in endowments, policy needs and political character' (Wallace, 1985: 3). A typical example of this approach is the William and Mary lecture given by John Major at Leyden in September 1994 (Major, 1984). Now in the course of the Amsterdam negotiation proposals for some sort of flexibility came from practically all delegations. But I believe it can safely be documented that the strongest advocates were, on the one hand, France and Germany, who made specific joint proposals in various instances, and, on the other hand, a group round the Benelux countries, including Italy, Finland and Austria. The United Kingdom, Denmark and Sweden should be counted among the more reticent Member States. The fact that the drive towards flexibility came from countries normally identified with high ambitions for the European Union and strict orthodoxy in Community matters is significant. A member of the Irish delegation, then in the chair, notes, with some regret: 'The positive support for flexibility from several of the players who traditionally defend the community method ... meant that the most likely natural counterweight to the impulse for flexibility was unlikely to develop' (McDonagh, 1998: 142). Up to then flexibility had been accepted as a fact of life but had not been defended as a basic principle.

This leads us to a consideration of the motives of the different partners.

A VARIETY OF MOTIVES

It is always dangerous to try to ascribe motives to the negotiating positions of governments. In some cases motives are publicly proclaimed but not entirely credible, in others motives are hidden, or even denied, but nevertheless very real. Moreover national positions are quite frequently the result of internal compromise between conflicting views and contradictory motivations. Diplomacy needs to be effective, but it does not have to be entirely rational.

For the analyst, however, it is important to identify the reasoning underlying national positions in a given negotiation. In the case of 'enhanced cooperation' in the Amsterdam Treaty, and with the systemic reservations just mentioned, I would tend to underline four trends of thought which, isolated or in combination, seem to have been present in the arguments put forward. In one way or another Member States were recognizing the following needs:

- to avoid unacceptable blockage by one or two Member States,
- to adapt decision-making to a much larger and more heterogeneous Union,
- to allow participants in EMU to implement decisions made necessary as a consequence of monetary union,
- to avoid the consolidation and the proliferation of parallel sub-systems (such as Schengen or 'contact groups') outside the institutional framework of the Union.

Blockage

The letter jointly signed by President Chirac and Chancellor Kohl on 6 December 1995 states: 'les difficultés momentanées de l'un des partenaires à suivre la marche en avant ne devraient pas faire obstacle à la capacité d'action et de progrès de l'Union'.[3] This was the most obvious motive and the easiest one to understand. As soon as it was mentioned eyes turned to

London, and it is true that in the latter years of the Conservative government there was competition among British ministers as to who had more categorically vetoed one or more proposals from partners or the Commission. Press conferences were called by the British delegation to highlight these refusals even more. Irritation provoked by this attitude has caused lasting damage to British influence on European affairs, but London was by no means the only capital that came to mind. The idiosyncratic behaviour of the Greek delegation on some regional issues was well remembered. And for those who had participated in the Maastricht negotiation the case of Denmark was perhaps the most instructive.

What would have happened if, in December 1992, the second Danish referendum had been negative? Denmark might have decided to leave the Community, even if no treaty article allows this option, but most probably it would not have wanted to leave. So, what could have been done? Scrapping a treaty to which several Heads of State or Government had the highest personal and political commitment? Certainly not! To renegotiate in depth in order to accommodate Denmark? Very difficult and potentially destructive! So perhaps a flexibility clause allowing, in future, the majority to pursue its chosen course in the absence of the reluctant partner made sense. Cases of this sort might occur more frequently in an enlarged Union. Moreover the existence of such a clause might in itself have a beneficial effect, just as the threat of majority voting breeds consensus: 'evidence of the willingness of some member governments to proceed by enhanced cooperation, and their ability to use a legal formula to do so, might have the powerful effect of provoking the more reluctant to join in rather than be left behind' (De la Serre and Wallace, 1997: 9).

Enlargement

The Benelux memorandum of March 1996 indicated that the three countries 'in no way reject a differentiated approach which will most probably become inevitable in an enlarged Union' (*L'Union politique de l'Europe*, 1998: 422). Similarly, the detailed proposals on enhanced cooperation put forward by France and Germany, in October of the same year, were justified primarily by the perspective of enlargement.[4] These governments were picking up trends that had been openly discussed, inside and outside official circles, for several years. The idea that a partial solution to the institutional problems of an enlarged, and therefore more heterogeneous Union could be sought in the direction of enhanced cooperation was widely accepted before the beginning of the intergovernmental conference. The report of the Reflection Group, chaired by Carlos Westendorp, prior to the beginning of the Intergovernmental Conference links flexibility to the perspective of enlargement. The 'Club de Florence', bringing together a group of personalities around Max Kohnstamm, the former assistant of Jean Monnet, wrote in 1996: 'In truth, the choice is not between different forms of differentiation, but between differentiation and chaos [*éparpillement*]' (Club de Florence, 1996: 238).

Economic and monetary union

More controversial, at least in the initial stages of the conference, was the idea that participants in EMU might need such a clause to enable them to adopt specific rules as a consequence of monetary union. Already in the Maastricht negotiation it had been argued by some that the Treaty clauses were exceedingly specific on the monetary side but rather vague on the economic component of EMU. They argued that monetary union implied the acceptance of common rules on budget discipline. Something similar might in future be needed in fields like taxation, social policy or the environment, and a provision should therefore be made to enable participants in EMU to act together when necessary and under certain conditions.

This line of reasoning was badly received by those Member States who expected that they would not, for whatever reason, take part in monetary union. It was assimilated to the 'hard core' concept that had provoked considerable emotion when it had been initially put forward, in 1994, by the CDU/CSU fraction of the Bundestag (the 'Schäuble Lamers' paper). But as time went by the argument based on EMU gained ground for two reasons which had no direct link to the negotiation itself. In the first place it became apparent during the winter of 1996–7 that a considerable number of Member States would probably, in due course, qualify for the third phase of monetary union. Countries which previously had considered themselves as being outside the 'core' now took a different view. And in the second place the debate over the stability pact, requested by Germany to ensure future budget orthodoxy in the monetary union, showed that the problem was not purely speculative. Discussions, held at the highest level under the Irish Presidency, were difficult. Part of the difficulty came from the lack of legal solutions in the existing Treaty to accommodate what was, in fact, a question of enhanced cooperation. The risk of disrupting the normal work, and diminishing the responsibility, of the Council by a succession of *ad hoc* solutions with dubious legal bases, was a matter of concern for all Member States, irrespective of their prospective relationship to monetary union. Without convincing everybody, the proposal to have a flexibility clause in the first pillar, which had been discarded by the Reflection Group, was, from then on, better understood and gained in credibility.

Sub-systems

The Maastricht Treaty had gone some way towards bringing together the various fora in which Member States of the Community were active. The pillar structure of the Union organized the co-existence in a single institutional framework of Community activities, based on *integration*, with activities in the fields of foreign policy, police and justice, which had gradually evolved over the years on the basis of intergovernmental *cooperation*. Opinions differed as to the operational capacity of this hybrid solution but there was a general feeling that it made sense to strive for coherence in various activities through what Tindemans, years before, had called a single decision-making centre.

A new Intergovernmental Conference opened up the possibility of going further down that road, and two structures seemed obvious candidates for incorporation into the Union: the Western European Union and Schengen. Both cases were difficult, for different reasons, but they had one thing in common: given the position of neutral countries on defence, and the position of Britain on free circulation of third country nationals, a solution could only be found on the basis of differentiation. This then became one of the arguments in favour of flexibility.

Towards the end of the Maastricht negotiation the absorption of WEU by the European Union had seemed a realistic possibility in the future, and this is precisely what six governments proposed in March 1997. The reaction was strongly negative both from Britain and from the neutrals. 'This is not merely an institutional question, but rather a fundamental disagreement about which responsibilities to attribute to the EU, about the future development of European defence, and about how it should be configured *vis à vis* NATO' (De la Serre and Wallace, 1997: 26).

The case of Schengen seemed not only more promising but also more instructive. It concerned a Community objective, the free circulation of persons, but had developed outside the Community framework because one Member State did not accept that third country nationals were 'persons' in the sense of Article 7A of the EC Treaty. This implied that internal border controls would need to remain in place, indefinitely, in order to control third country nationals. Schengen was about strengthening external border controls in order to do *without* internal border controls. These two different approaches could not easily be accommodated inside the existing Community framework.

The Franco-German document of 18 October 1996 made the point that a flexibility clause would make it possible to practise within the Treaty forms of enhanced cooperation which otherwise would need to happen outside. Speaking in Madrid a few days later, the Belgian Prime Minister Jean-Luc Dehaene was even more specific in talking about Schengen: 'if a general differentiation clause had existed in the treaty we would not have been compelled to develop a cooperation outside of the treaty in order subsequently to import it in the treaty'.[5]

The argument was not simply one of abstract institutional coherence. Schengen was developing, out of necessity, an administrative apparatus based on the Benelux secretariat in Brussels. Staff were already significant in number and growing fast. It seemed obvious that if nothing happened we would end up with two sizeable and competing international bureaucracies in Brussels, both dealing, on different legal bases, with free circulation of persons. The very real difficulties that the Council Secretariat has encountered, after Amsterdam, in absorbing the staff of Schengen, confirm that it was high time to halt parallel development in this specific field and, if possible, avoid similar occurrences in future.

DEVELOPMENT OF THE NEGOTIATION

Because the debate around flexibility and enhanced cooperation was a new one, it needed ample time and progressed slowly, in two successive stages. In the Reflection Group and during the Italian Presidency it was largely conceptual: partners were trying to develop their understanding of the concept and of each other's views and motives. Real negotiation, in the sense of textual proposals, began in the second half of the Irish Presidency (autumn 1996) and accelerated under the Dutch Presidency. The finishing touches were given at Amsterdam itself, at the level of heads of government.[6]

The issue was debated on several occasions in 1995 in the Reflection Group, not least because both the contribution of the Commission and that of the European Parliament underlined the necessity of looking at different speeds of integration. Views within the Group were far from unanimous and some, including significantly the Spanish member, were taking defensive positions. The final report is dubious about the whole concept ('It may also mean that flexible solutions will have to be found'), strict on the conditions which have to be met (last resort, temporary, no exclusion, single institutional framework, respecting the *acquis communautaire*, etc.) and indicates that such solutions are more appropriate in the second and third pillar than in the first. But despite the reluctance of some members it was clear, from then on, that the debate was going to be a central one in the incoming IGC.

By the time the European Council met in Turin in March 1996 to launch the conference several new documents were on the table. Two of them have been already mentioned and are significant in view of the way the subsequent negotiation was to evolve: the Chirac–Kohl letter of December

1995 and the Benelux memorandum of March 1996. In the last case the concept of 'differentiated approach' is put at the forefront of the document. The mandate given by the European Council is cautious in its formulation. The conference should 'examine whether and how to introduce rules either of a general nature or in specific areas to enable a certain number of Member States to develop strengthened cooperation', and that should be done under conditions which are close to those indicated by the report of the Reflection Group.

The Italian Presidency proceeded, in this field as in others, by putting questions to Member States, and this procedure indicated that national positions were completely at variance and not always well elaborated. There was a large ground for misunderstandings and mutual suspicion. This was not very encouraging for the incoming Irish Presidency, who proceeded with extreme caution in what was, for Ireland also, a difficult subject. The negotiation received a new impulse on 17 October with a Franco-German document proposing a general enabling clause and specific flexibility clauses in all three pillars. This presentation was to be the focus of discussions for the rest of the conference.

The general outline for a draft revision of the treaties presented by the Irish Presidency to the European council meeting in Dublin on 5 December did not present draft articles concerning this issue. It recognized that what had come to be called 'flexibility', 'enhanced cooperation' or 'differentiated integration' was one of the most important issues of the conference but considered that it would be premature to put forward draft texts. The presidency did, however, provide a very useful analysis of the points under discussion and possible solutions. Among the latter it made a distinction between:

- case-by-case flexibility, constructive abstention is an example
- flexibility in a predetermined specific area, Schengen, for instance
- a more general approach with enabling clauses.

The Dublin document very correctly identified what were to be the main points of discussion in the following months.

On this occasion the European Council invited the conference to give particular attention to enhanced cooperation and under the Dutch Presidency the debate was very actively pursued at personal representative level. By now it was clear that some flexibility clause would need to be put in the Treaty and negotiations began to concentrate on the issues of trigger mechanisms and differences between pillars which were to remain open until the end. Representatives attempted to define the scope of a future flexibility clause by drafting positive lists (cases where it could be applied) and negative lists (cases where it could never apply), but the exercise was frustrating and finally abandoned. Camps began to be clarified. France and Germany were obviously in favour but left much of the campaigning to an activist group composed of the Benelux countries, Italy, Finland, Austria and frequently Ireland. Britain, Denmark and Sweden were clearly reluctant while Greece, Portugal and Spain were at least doubtful.

MAJOR ISSUES OF DEBATE

Given the variety of underlying motives, the existence of different 'pillars' and of widely divergent views, it comes as no surprise that the debate was frequently repetitive, sometimes meandering and confused. But basically the main points at issue can be regrouped under two headings:

- the *scope* for flexibility in each pillar,
- the *trigger mechanism*, including the number of participants and the role of Community institutions.

The scope

In the first pillar it became apparent relatively early in the negotiation that some sort of flexibility clause would be included in the Treaty. The debate then concentrated, as indicated above, on positive or negative lists. Although the Treaty goes more in the direction of conditions to be fulfilled than a case list, there is no doubt that it is the negative school that has prevailed. The conditions formulated in Article 11 TEC are such that it is open to reasonable doubt whether, in fact, they can ever be fulfilled in strictly legal terms.

In the third pillar the debate was slightly different. Given that the Schengen agreements would, in one way or another, probably be incorporated in the Treaty, was there a need for a separate 'enhanced cooperation' clause? Although some doubts were expressed, by the end of the negotiation the answer to this question was broadly positive. Most delegations were in favour of the possibility of enhanced cooperation in police and justice affairs and this is reflected in Article 40 TEU.

In the second pillar the debate was both open and full of contradictory undercurrents. On the one hand it was perhaps the sector where blockage by one Member State was felt as most detrimental to the Union. But, of course, constructive abstention, if correctly applied, could, at least in theory, take care of that, without a systemic clause on enhanced cooperation. On the other hand, *de facto* enhanced cooperation between the bigger Member States, in various caucuses and contact groups outside of the treaty, was already a fact of life. Most of the smaller Member States considered this evolution to be negative, and potentially destructive of common foreign policy. Would a flexibility clause eliminate this practice or discourage it? Or would it be legitimized by a Treaty article? Supposing some type of enhanced cooperation were in future to take place within the treaty framework, would this give some influence to the non-participants? Or would this in fact bind them to so-called Union policies on which they had had no say? Who would pay for 'enhanced coopera-tion' policies? These and other questions remained largely unanswered.

In the specific case of defence, a enhanced cooperation clause did not seem really necessary, since the Western European Union already offered, outside of the Treaty, whatever flexibility was needed. An effort, led by France and Germany, to incorporate the WEU in the Treaty was met with absolute opposition from Britain. To pursue the matter did not seem promising.

My understanding is that by the time of the Amsterdam European Council most Member States had come to the conclusion that, on balance, there was more to be lost than to be gained by a enhanced cooperation clause in the second pillar. The bigger Member States did not want to be in any way constrained in their 'contact group' practices, which are demonstrably ineffective but to which they are nevertheless attached. The smaller Member States did not want to be, even indirectly, linked to decisions that they could not influence. Some probably preferred to leave crisis management, and the accompanying responsibilities, outside of the Treaty.

To be fair one needs to add that flexibility in the second pillar has an external dimension which does not exist in the other two pillars. Enhanced cooperation on social policy or drugs has no direct impact on the external image of the Union. An active policy on Ruritania that would bind only half the Member States is another matter. What would be the credibility, asked one negotiator, of an American policy that was known not to be approved by, or binding on, California, Texas and Massachusetts? Taken by itself the argument is perhaps not entirely convincing. But in the atmosphere just described it goes some way towards explaining why the Heads of State or Government finally decided to limit flexibility in the second pillar to a clause of constructive abstention: Article 23(1) TEU.

The trigger mechanism

The operational effectiveness of an enhanced cooperation clause is of course linked to the way it can be initiated. If unanimity is required it loses much of its interest, certainly for those who want such a clause precisely in order to avoid blockage by one or two Member States, or as a complement to the enhanced cooperation in the framework of EMU. On the other hand if it can be initiated by majority decision, the potential risk for those who fear being left out increases substantially. Naturally enough, once it became clear that some sort of flexibility clause would be introduced into the Treaty, debate concentrated on this issue, and it remained largely open until the Amsterdam European Council.

A related question concerns the number of participants: should the treaty specify, or should it not, a minimum number of Member States as a precondition for any form of enhanced cooperation? On the one hand, it could be argued that no grouping could bear a European Union label if it did not represent a sizeable majority. On the other hand, it was a fact that Schengen had been initially launched by a minority of Member States. Moreover, it had not always been clear in the past, and it would not necessarily be the case in future, that the participants in monetary union would be a majority of members. Yet Schengen and the consequences of monetary union were precisely the sort of initiatives one was trying to accommodate. The question was mentioned by the Irish Presidency in its report to the European Council in December 1996 as one of the open points. By March 1997 the Dutch Presidency was suggesting that any form of enhanced cooperation should concern at least a majority of Member States and this proposal was carried forward to Amsterdam without much debate. The fact that it was becoming apparent that a majority of Member States would in fact qualify for monetary union may have had some influence.

The question of the role of Community institutions in the initiating stage was an added difficulty.

The Commission, as guardian of the Treaties, would of course need to be closely associated to such a procedure. But some delegates made the point that an institution representing the collective interest of the Member States would be stepping out of its role if it were to initiate enhanced cooperation between some of them. They tended to conclude that, even in the first pillar, it should not, in this case, have the exclusive right of initiative that it enjoys in normal Community business. This departure from a sacrosanct treaty rule was rejected both by the Commission and by a number of Member States who were afraid of such a precedent. They were not unaware that the exclusivity of the Commission's right of initiative was under threat in other parts of the negotiation, so that utmost caution was necessary.

The way the European Parliament would operate in such cases was another point at issue. It would be unreasonable and unwise to exclude its participation altogether. But again some delegates made the point that it would be strange to allow members elected in countries not participating in enhanced cooperation to vote on what others might or might not do. The Parliament itself and most Member States considered that it was impossible to split up the Parliament in segments, and that the institution should, in all cases, function as a coherent whole, even at the cost of slightly paradoxical situations.

If the Court of Justice was enabled to pass judgement on the way an enhanced cooperation was being initiated, this might give some guarantee to the non-participating Member States. But the Court's competence was neither self-evident nor undisputed.

All these problems were further complicated by the distinctions to be made between 'pillars'. For a number of Member States majority voting on flexibility clauses in the second and third pillar would gravely adulterate the intergovernmental character of these pillars, and should be rejected as a matter of principle on those grounds alone. For the same reasons Commission, Parliament and Court should not have a decisive role. But another group of Member States had different views on both these issues.

The Dutch Presidency advanced with great caution in this institutional minefield. By March 1997 (document CONF 2500. Add 1) it was suggesting:

- decision by unanimity in the second pillar, by qualified majority in the third pillar and leaving the question open for the moment in the first pillar;
- on a proposal from the Commission, based on a request from the Member States concerned, in the first pillar, and on a request of the Member States, with an opinion of the Commission, in the second and third pillars (with slight nuances between the two);
- consultation of Parliament in the first pillar, transmission of the request to Parliament in the third pillar and no role at all, in the initiating phase, in the second (*ex post* information is foreseen in all cases).

Though the matter was quite actively discussed in April and May, including at a ministerial conclave on 20 May 1997, the text submitted by the Presidency on the eve of the Amsterdam European Council (document CONF 4000 of 12 June) is basically similar to that of March, with the notable exception that it opts for qualified majority decision in the first pillar.

At Amsterdam, Heads of State or Government deleted, as indicated above, the enhanced cooperation clause in the second pillar in favour of constructive abstention, which of course needs no trigger mechanism. In the first and third pillar they accepted the proposals of the Presidency, including qualified majority voting, but with an added clause indicating that a vote shall not be taken if a member declares that for important and stated reasons of national policy it opposes the granting of an authorization to establish enhanced cooperation (Articles 11(3) TEC and 40(2) TEU). This unexpected revival, and legal consecration, of the Luxembourg compromise of 1966 had been mentioned in the course of the negotiation without receiving much support. The Heads of State or Government apparently came to the conclusion that it was an acceptable price to pay for the introduction of qualified majority voting.

CONCLUSION

In the field of enhanced cooperation the Amsterdam Treaty puts in place a complex legal system based on:

- a general enabling clause: Articles 43 to 45 TEU
- an enhanced cooperation clause in the first pillar: Article 11 TEC
- a constructive abstention clause in the second pillar: Article 23(1) TEU
- an enhanced cooperation clause in the third pillar: Article 40 TEU.

The first question that comes to mind, by way of conclusion, is whether this system is likely to be put to practical use. It is always hazardous to comment on the future potential of legal texts but it seems reasonable to say that the Treaty does not make things easy for those who, in future, will want to practise closer cooperation within the Treaty. Conditions to be fulfilled, both in substance and procedure, are stiff. Françoise de la Serre and Helen Wallace note: 'There was a strong case for finding a way to allow the more determined to provide an integration dynamic ... without marginalising the slower or more hesitant member states ... It is not obvious that the text has reconciled and responded to these two very different objectives' (De la Serre and Wallace, 1997: 38).

Some observers attribute this weakness to a loss of dynamism in the final part of the negotiation. They consider that the British election had weakened the threat of blockage and that therefore 'the flexibility debate had run out of steam' (Stubb, 2001). This is demonstrated, in their view, by the relatively short time devoted to this issue by the European Council in Amsterdam. My personal view would be not that the debate had run out of steam, but that the negotiation had run out of time. The European Council was determined, in whatever circumstances, to close the Intergovernmental Conference at Amsterdam, and it had valid reasons for doing so. Now the number of issues that can be addressed, in a two-day session, by Heads of State or Government is large, but not unlimited, and choices need to be made. In this case the principle of an enhanced cooperation clause was practically undisputed and the point put to the European Council related to the use of qualified majority. Clarification and simplification of the conditions governing the use of these clauses would have been welcome for many delegations, but it implied a lengthy negotiation which was not compatible with the accepted agenda. These delegations then made virtue out of necessity: they were satisfied that the principle, initially disputed, had finally been accepted, and were confident that future Intergovernmental Conferences would find ways of enlarging the very limited opening offered by Amsterdam. Geoffrey Edwards and Eric Philippart note that enhanced cooperation 'remains a subject on which doubts and uncertainties are such that the issue is unlikely to be ignored' (Edwards and Philippart, 1997).

It seems to me that the results of the Amsterdam European Council confirm that some Heads of State or Government were ready to go to great lengths to ensure the inclusion of a closer cooperation clause. In Maastricht they had accepted, at the last minute, to go beyond the two-speed approach on differentiation and to accept a form of variable geometry. At Amsterdam they accepted, also at the last minute, something very similar to the Luxembourg compromise, which many of their countries had systematically rejected over the years, and which is an even greater departure from the norm. Community orthodoxy in these matters is not, as some of its critics pretend, an extension of dogmatic theology to European affairs. It is based on the conviction, substantiated by half a century's experience, that the basic institutional rules provided in the Treaties, especially on decision-taking, and the Community method of which they are part, are more effective and therefore, in the long term, more protective of the fundamental interests of the Member States, singularly the smaller ones, than the traditional practices of international diplomacy. The fact that both in Maaastricht and in Amsterdam Heads of State or Government were found ready, collectively, to depart, in a specific case, from these rules does not invalidate the reasoning which underlies the norm. But it does demonstrate the political commitment of the leaders to a flexible approach.

NOTES

1. See the chapter 'Subsidiarity and intervention', in De Schoutheete (2000: 41–51).
2. This comparison is developed by Hervé Bribosia (1998: 24–90). M. Bribosia was a member of the Belgian negotiating team.
3. The Chirac–Kohl letter is published in L'Union politique de l'Europe (1998: 410).
4. For the Franco-German document, see L'Union politique de l'Europe (1998: 439).
5. Speech by Jean-Luc Dehaene at the Fundación Carlos de Amberes in Madrid on 21 October 1996.
6. A detailed survey of the successive stages of the negotiation can be found in Stubb (2000). Mr Stubb was a member of the Finnish negotiating team.

BIBLIOGRAPHY

Bribosia, H. (1998) *'De la Subsidiarité à la coopération renforcée'*. In *Le Traité d'Amsterdam: Espoirs et Déceptions*. Brussels: Bruylant.

Club de Florence (1996) *Europe: l'impossible statu-quo*. Paris: Stock.

De la Serre, F. and H. Wallace (1997) *Flexibility and Enhanced Cooperation in the European Union: Placebo Rather Than Panacea*. Groupement d'Etudes 'Notre Europe'. Research and Policy Papers No. 2, September.

De Schoutheete, P. (1990) 'The European Community and its sub-systems'. In W. Wallace (ed.), *The Dynamics of European Integration*. London: Pinter.

De Schoutheete, P. *The Case for Europe: Unity, Diversity and Democracy in the European Union* (trans. A. Butler). Boulder: Lynne Rienner.

Edwards, G. and E. Philippart (1997) *Flexibility and the Treaty of Amsterdam: Europe's New Byzantium?*. University of Cambridge, Centre for European Legal Studies, Occasional Papers No. 3, November.

Ehlermann, C. D. (1995) 'Différenciation accrue ou Uniformité renforcée'. *Revue du Marché Unique Européen*, 3.

Hoffmann, S. and R. Keohane (1990) 'Conclusions'. In W. Wallace (ed.), *The Dynamics of European Integration*. London: Pinter.

'L'Union politique de l'Europe: jalons et textes' (documents rassemblés par Pierre Gerbet, Françoisede la Serre et Gérard Nafilyan). Paris: La Documentation française, 1998.

Major, J. (1984)'Europe: a future that works'. *Agence Europe*, No. 6312, 10 September.

McDonagh, B. (1998) *Original Sin in a Brave New World: An Account of the Negotiation of the Treaty of Amsterdam*. Dublin: Institute of European Affairs.

Stubb, A. (2000) 'Negotiating flexible integration in the Amsterdam Treaty'. In K. Neunreither and A. Wiener (eds,) *European Integration After Amsterdam: Institutional Dynamics and Prospects for Democracy*. Oxford: Oxford University Press, pp. 153–75.

Wallace, H. (1985) *The Challenge of Diversity*. Chatham House Papers, No. 29. London: Routledge and Kegan Paul.

CHAPTER 10

FLEXIBILITY AFTER AMSTERDAM: COMPARATIVE ANALYSIS AND PROSPECTIVE IMPACT

Eric Philippart and Monika Sie Dhian Ho[1]

INTRODUCTION

The evolution of the European Community is, according to Paul Pierson, an extraordinary political experiment in which, 'progressing sporadically but in a consistent direction, the Member States have pooled increasing areas of policy authority' (Pierson, 1996: 123). Until the European Council of June 1997 which agreed on the Treaty of Amsterdam (ToA), compelling empirical evidence was not lacking to back such a statement.[2] If the Treaty of Maastricht introduced new and possibly 'revolutionary' (Ehlermann, 1995: 191) forms of differentiation in the rights and obligations of the Member States, these innovations were nevertheless generally presented and regarded as expedients and anomalies. With an entire title dedicated to 'closer cooperation', the ToA has turned the anomaly into a constitutional principle, raising many uncertainties about the consistency of today's or tomorrow's trajectory of the European Union (EU). This dramatic amendment to the traditional Community system could indeed be interpreted as an implicit recognition of long-lasting, if not permanent divergence in the way Member States conceive the EU, or be considered as an instrument whose centrifugal dynamics will be clearly detrimental to the current coherence of the Union. It could, on the contrary, be seen as an alternative device to foster integration where, among other things, decision-making is blocked by procedures requiring unanimity. 'Closer cooperation' should, in this case, be considered as an intermediary step which, as a result of centripetal dynamics, would pave the way to full integration.

This chapter aims, through a contextual and comparative analysis, at interpreting the Amsterdam flexibility mechanism and evaluating its likely impact on the EU. It cannot be done in the abstract and supposes that various *contextual* elements are taken into account, such as current and future blockages to integration and cooperation, as well as the preferences and capabilities of incumbents and applicant Member States. The new provisions are an instrument to manage diversity within the Union. It is therefore useful to evaluate their prospective impact by *comparison* with other mechanisms designed for the same purpose, that is, other forms of flexibility existing in the EU and between Member States.

RESEARCH QUESTIONS, APPROACH AND STANDARDS FOR EVALUATION

Evaluation proceeds by measurement and comparison. Evaluating some- thing starts with assessing and scaling its value according to various yardsticks (monetary, aesthetic, etc. like the assessment of the costs and outcomes of a project in financial terms). It then goes on with determining the significance of this measurement by comparison with a set standard of achievement (like the target initially assigned to the project or the average cost-outcome ratio of similar projects in the same sector). In other words, an evaluation cannot be properly conducted without explicit reference points or norms. The fact that we are dealing with an *ex ante* evaluation – the new Treaty came into force only on 1 May 1999; its Title VII has never been applied and that is likely to remain the case for some time – makes no difference in that respect.

This study therefore requires a preliminary clarification of its variables. Evaluating effects of flexibility on the EU is indeed too vague. We cannot assess and evaluate these effects without explicitly defining what we mean by flexibility, setting a time frame (are we dealing with short or long terms effects?), and specifying standards of achievement.

Flexibility refers to various mechanisms designed to accommodate diversity among Member States. Flexibility is used here as the umbrella term[3] for institutional rules whereby not all EU Member States have the same rights and obligations in certain policy areas. The concept being quite broad, we will put the Amsterdam provisions on closer cooperation at the centre of our demonstration and choose them as our independent variable. Other forms of flexibility will be taken into account indirectly: their past performance will be compared with the prospective impact of Amsterdam enhanced cooperation.

The 1996–97 Intergovernmental Conference (IGC)'s main justification to discuss new forms of flexibility was to endow the EU with more effective mechanisms to overcome blockages to integrative–cooperative develop- ment in a number of policy areas in the short- and medium-term (i.e. before and after the next round of enlargement).[4] However, it is widely acknowledged that the result of this rather pragmatic assignment could well have considerable repercussions on the *finalités politiques* of the EU, i.e. the long-term orientations of the Union system as a whole. Apart from its short-/medium-term contribution in terms of functionality, this kind of flexibility might have more long-term (partially unintended) consequences. Both short/medium-term and long-term effects must then be included in our time frame.

The significance of the Amsterdam provisions will be evaluated against two standards: problem-solving capacity on the one hand, and prescriptions of general models of governance on the other. With regard to the first standard, we postulate that there are three fundamental problems which might call for some sort of structured and organized flexibility and are respectively linked to the development of the *acquis* 'in house', the development of the *acquis* 'by import', and to the adoption of the *acquis* by new Member States. Major differences oppose current and future Member States on the most 'adequate' form of flexibility to be used to resolve each of these problems. Their respective preferences percolate into the various demands formulated during the IGC. These demands are presented in a systematic way in the following section. In the evaluation part, we will see which demands have been eventually met and, in consequence, whose institutional preferences have been *de facto* embedded in the new system. Building on that informed assessment, we will evaluate the capacity of the new system to solve the three problems mentioned above (functional/managerial evaluation). To come back to the present section, the presentation of the problems calling for flexibility and the accompanying demands is followed by a concise description of the supply of flexibility. This simple enumeration is only intended to provide the contours of the alternative instruments of flexibility against which closer cooperation's problem-solving capacity/effectiveness will be compared.

The second standard – or rather set of standards – has to help us to evaluate flexibility in terms of its significance for the EU as a whole. Some problems have been solved in a specific way, others remain unanswered. The nature of this particular mix is not without importance for the course of EU integration. We still have to assess and evaluate its systemic consequences. That question has to be 'operationalized', i.e. relevant and measurable aspects on which the Amsterdam formula could have some bearing have to be selected. We will do so by focusing on the effects of closer cooperation on EU governance in terms of: (1) scope and depth of the EU policies; (2) methods of integration; and (3) institutional architecture and legitimacy.

The evaluation of the effects of flexibility on these dimensions depends on the 'vision' one has of the Union. We are confronted with various competing conceptions of what the EU is and should be. The palette of nuances is such that for our purposes we have chosen to use two ideal-types providing clear standards of evaluation: the 'Westphalian state model' and the 'Regulatory' ideal-type. The 'Westphalian' model conceives of the EU as a political system in the making, a system which – at its ultimate stage of development – should be similar to the Western-type liberal democracies. By contrast, the 'Regulatory' ideal-type conceives the EU's institutions and policies as diametrically different from those at national level (Caporaso, 1996: 39): the EU is seen as a highly developed 'special purpose organization . . . the primary task of which is to address a number of issues over which it can hope to achieve greater efficiency than the Member States acting individually' (Dehousse, 1998). Each of these models has different norms on what should be the EU's scope and depth of policies, method(s) of integration, institutional architecture and source of legitimacy. These norms or standards will be presented in a comparative table. On that basis, the systemic – or constitutional – significance of the various elements of the Amsterdam formula will be evaluated in order to answer the following question: are the solutions chosen to answer the problems of development and adoption of the *acquis* bringing the EU globally closer to the standards of the Westphalian or the Regulatory model?

Demand for flexibility

The debate on differentiation in the integration process is an old one. Various problems have, in the past, led to the successive development of methods to manage diversity, either by accommodating or decreasing it. This has been particularly true in the run-up to and/or in the wake of the four previous EC/EU enlargements, not only because the prospect of the incorporation of new Member States was synonymous with an increase of problematic heterogeneity, but also because it was seized as an opportunity for systemic renegotiation, deepening being imposed as a precondition to widening (Preston, 1995). The latest developments are, to a large extent, a continuation of this long-established feature.

New or unresolved problems leading to new or pending demands combined to place on the agenda of the 1996–7 IGC the question of the introduction of new forms of flexibility in the Treaties.[5] By the time of the European Council of June 1996 in Florence, a consensus was reached on the necessary 'institutionalization' of flexibility, i.e. the definition of clear rules regulating the use of flexibility and creating a 'regime' by which short-term interests are traded off against long-term certainties.

We have schematically identified three types of problem for which some sort of structured and organized flexibility could be needed: (1) the problem linked to the development of the *acquis* 'in house' (e.g. future harmonization in the field of tax policies); (2) the problem linked to the development of the *acquis* 'by import' (e.g. the 'import' of the Schengen *acquis*); and (3) the problem of the adoption of the existing *acquis* by new Member States[6] (e.g. by the candidate Member States from Central and Eastern Europe[7]). For each problem, one can imagine several systems providing different forms of procedural and/or substantive flexibility, which will eventually involve or affect many actors: national governments but also European institutions like the Commission, the Parliament and the Court of Justice as well as subnational public and private actors, at decision shaping, making, implementing and enforcement levels. We have chosen to focus on the governmental actors because the final decision on the design of flexibility systems is ultimately theirs. We have first categorized the 'demands' of the Member States – i.e. the elements which should be ideally included in the codification of flexibility from their point of view – according to their (objective socio-economic) inability/ability and (subjective ideological-political) willingness/unwillingness to participate in a policy development. For obvious reasons, a distinction has been made between Member States (MS) and candidate Member States (CMS) in the case of the problem of the adoption of the *acquis*.[8]

An inventory of demands for flexibility along these lines is by essence reductionist: the nuances within each government are smoothed out; the fluidity of the negotiation process and the communicative rationality which apparently played a significant role in the Amsterdam negotiation are not reflected. The picture given in Table 10.1 should be regarded as a simplified representation of the 'reality' with all the limitations of artificial reconstruction, but which nevertheless offers a useful heuristic and analytical device. It clearly shows that the background of the negotiations on flexibility was and will remain very complex, considering the number of antinomic demands and the shaky basis of some actors' preferences, who can be at the same time, depending on the policy area, unwilling, willing, able and/or unable. It also helps our understanding of the nature of the newly created mechanism and the evaluation of its potential.

As regards the development of the *acquis* in-house, the unable MS are relatively homogeneous in their demands.[9] Their interests are best served if they are involved in the decision-making process on closer cooperation, have the benefit of solidarity mechanisms (for instance through resource transfers) and automatic 'opt-in' in the vanguard group, as soon as they fulfil the objective criteria for participation in the closer cooperation. The fall-back position of the unable MS is the establishment of a defensive system which would at least include: the preservation of the EC/EU *acquis* (underlined by the separate status given to the 'flexibility' *acquis*) and of the single institutional framework,[10] veto right in the procedure triggering closer cooperation, an explicit recognition of the temporary nature of the latter, and the protection of their interests by independent institutions.

There are, by contrast, major differences among the groups of unwilling and willing MS. While all unwilling MS would ask for the protection of their interests by independent institutions, their additional demands would vary according to the nature and intensity of their underlying objectives, their relative size and central or peripheral situation within the Union (together with the resulting dependence *vis-à-vis* the EU), and/or the policy area involved.[11] Some MS would be satisfied with permanent exemptions of variable extent (e.g. Denmark), while others would insist in addition on monitoring rights on the course of closer cooperation or even veto right on the triggering procedure of closer cooperation. (e.g. the United Kingdom or Greece). Some would only disagree with the location of closer cooperation but not with its necessity or usefulness. In other words, they are unwilling to develop closer cooperation inside the EU, but keen to enter cooperative endeavour outside the latter's constraining framework, through *directoires* (e.g. in the field of defence) or exclusive clubs (e.g. in armaments production). Although EU membership does not preclude extra-EU international cooperation, this category of 'unwilling' MS would demand explicit provisions in the Treaties reasserting the authorization of extra-EU closer cooperation.[12]

The 1996–7 IGC negotiations saw for the first time a large group of 'willing and able' MS wanting to insert in the Treaties a general authorization to go ahead without having to cope with the veto of unwilling MS or being forced to integrate at the pace of the less advanced MS. Aspiring to establish a nursery where new policies would be nurtured by them before being eventually extended to the rest of the Union, they all wish to see this vanguard status recognized through some sort of *carte blanche* mandate. The other demands of the willing would mainly depend on the priority given to either effectiveness of the instrument for closer cooperation or protection of the integrationist dynamics of the EU as a whole. Where the first would, for instance, advocate a core of optimal size, a clear-cut exclusion of the outsiders, and a large potential scope for closer cooperation, the second would insist on a minimal critical mass to start closer cooperation, a (more or less limited) participation of the unable and the use of closer cooperation being restricted to important issues and as a last resort solution. The details of other demands (hard core versus temporary vanguard, tailor-made versus normal procedures, etc.) are likely to be also shaped by additional and overlapping cleavages, like pro-confederal/pro-federal and big/small willing MS opposition. One important exception to the effectiveness/commonality cleavage could emerge if some of the willing and able MS are excluded from the *de facto* 'hard core'. For instance, in the case of armament cooperation, small MS excluded from extra-EU cooperation schemes should logically seek the development of parallel or competing structures to non-EU exclusive clubs and would therefore demand an 'open-door' system even if their priority is effectiveness.

The demands relating to development of the *acquis* by 'import' and the adoption of the *acquis* differ from the demands linked to 'in-house' development for a simple but crucial reason: the detailed contents of the *acquis* to be imported or adopted are known, while the information on the contents of the *acquis* to be developed 'in-house' could well consist of mere references to more or less defined framework projects and open-ended objectives. This difference should logically affect neither the demands of the 'unable' MS and CMS who, in all cases, wish to avoid as much as possible their exclusion, nor the demands of the 'willing' MS who want additions to the *acquis* being yet to be designed or fully known. It could however change significantly the bottom line of the unwilling MS and CMS in as much as the detailed information available would allow them to determine more accurately the nature and the cost of the *acquis* concerned, and to adjust their demands accordingly. Specific parts of the *acquis* of a policy area could prove to be sufficiently attractive to bring them to revise their demands *vis-à-vis* flexible arrangements (for instance, MS might be unwilling to accept the Schengen package because of elements linked to freedom of movement and border checks but still be interested in exchange of information, police cooperation, extradition, etc.). If the cooperation envisaged by the willing is about attractive and costly public goods, the unwilling would be in a very advantageous free riding position.[13] It should reinforce their determination to remain totally outside, but also push them to relax their restrictive demands in order to facilitate the production of these goods. Conversely, the willing would be more amenable to 'protective' demands, 'open door' approaches and tailor-made procedures conducive to some sort of involvement of the unwilling, especially in terms of burden-sharing. If the cooperation concerns attractive club goods unaffordable for isolated MS, it should weaken the determination of the unwilling to remain outside and lead them to compromise some of their defensive demands against discrete opt-ins, i.e. the possibility to pick and choose in the *acquis* concerned. The negotiating position of the willing should be particularly strong either when the costs induced by the exclusion from the club goods are high, that is, when outsiders have to bear the weight of significant externalities (e.g. organized crime relocating itself out of the closer cooperation area and degrading the security previously enjoyed by non-participating MS) or when the benefits attached to the club goods are very attractive (e.g. organized crime is already established in the non-participating MS and the security enjoyed within the closer cooperation area is comparatively better).

If, at the end of the screening process of the first group of CMS, problems relating to the adoption of the *acquis* appear to be intractable, the EU will have to choose between two options: the classical method facilitating the adoption of the entire *acquis* (full inclusion and acceptance of free riding) or a new method limiting the adoption to specific parts of the *acquis* (partial exclusion and savings on solidarity expenses). The incumbent MS are likely to be rather inflexible *vis-à-vis* attempts of CMS to preserve their comparative advantages by securing undetermined postponement in the adoption of the *acquis* concerned (cf. social or environmental norms). They would instead offer strictly controlled transitory periods or demand other formulae, depending on the financial/effectiveness costs of the inclusion of unable CMS in each policy area. In other words, they might try to impose new forms of flexibility amounting to putting the largest share of the burden of adaptation on CMS shoulders in areas involving large transfers of resources[14] or to (partially) exclude CMS from areas where they present a risk in terms of policy effectiveness. One way to proceed would be to resort to new forms of flexibility in the territorial scope of EU law and the further development of the EU as a 'highly complex and differentiated set of territories', adding to the existing diversity of regimes for the countries and territories which have special relations with various EC Member States (the 'Overseas Countries and Territories') (Ziller, 2000). The idea of a multi-tier system or variable geometry, more difficult to reconcile with the preservation of a single institutional framework, is another variant. The situation in South Eastern Europe has triggered new thinking on forms of participation going beyond association but short of full integration. The Centre for European Policy Studies (Brussels) (CEPS) has, for instance, proposed the creation of 'Autonomous State of the EU' or 'Autonomous Region of the EU' constitutionally integrated in a European economic area based on the existing EEA model, a European monetary area, a European area of freedom, security and justice, and a European area of military security (CEPS, 1999).

Supply of flexibility

Before the constitutional entrenchment of the concept of flexibility decided in Amsterdam, diversity among Member States has been accommodated by differentiation in the *application* of EC/EU rules (category 1) and variation in their *participation* in EC/EU policies (categories 2 to 4). Besides, diversity also led to developments outside the EC/EU framework, insofar as membership of the Union does not preclude all intergovernmental cooperation between a limited number of Member States, together with third countries or not. In a number of cases, structural links have been established between the EU and these 'external' fora of cooper-ation (categories 5 to 6). What follows aims at listing, in the simplest and clearest manner, the flexibility options available before and beside the invention of 'structured' flexibility.

1. EC/EU policies with a differentiated application of common obligations and rights

This form of flexibility implies that, although Member States share the same rights and obligations, their application is subject to variation. Allowed by the Treaty establishing the European Community (TEC) and often referred to as 'differentiated integration' – in line with the initial Community orthodoxy (Grabitz, 1984; Ehlermann, 1984; Feenstra and Mortelmans, 1985), this mode of flexibility is based on the idea that temporary derogations justified by 'objective' differences – whether econ-omic, social or physical, on the one hand, and the Member States' commitment to the objectives and ongoing development of the Union on the other, are compatible with integration in the Community context. Underlying the use of transitional arrangements and safeguard clauses which exist since the onset of the Community, this idea is also explicitly formulated in TEC Article 15 (ex TEC Article 7c) introduced by the 1987 Single European Act. This article states that the Commission should take into account the differences of development among the Member States in the implementation of the internal market, provided that derogations allowing a Member State to catch up would cause the least possible disturbance to the functioning of the common market.

2. EC/EU policies incorporating an element of case-by-case flexibility

In a number of EC/EU policy areas, some or all Member States have the possibility to 'pick and choose' the measures which will commit them. This form of flexibility 'greatly oversteps the traditional bounds on differentiation in Community law' (Ehlermann, 1998: 3). It allows indeed for permanent and, to a large extent, discretionary exemptions, that is, based more on unwillingness than inability. Case-by-case flexibility can take the form of 'opt-out' or 'opt-up'. The possibility of a 'constructive abstention' introduced by the ToA in the domain of the Common Foreign and Security Policy is an example of case-by-case opt-out: according to Article 23 TEU, a Member State which qualifies its abstention with a formal declaration does not have to apply the decision of the Council, though it must accept that the Union is committed by the action or position in question. By contrast, the opt-ups mean that a Member State fulfils the general requirements but wishes to go further, which is closer

Table 10.1 Development and adoption of the *acquis*

Demands of the unable MS (unable CMS)	Demands of the unwilling MS (unwilling MS)	Demands of the willing MS (incumbent MS)[a]
	Development of the *acquis* 'in-house'	
Best formula • Involvement in the decision-making process • Solidarity mechanism • Automatic 'passerelle' *Second-best formula* • Preservation of the EC/EU *acquis* + separate status of 'flexibility *acquis*' • Preservation of EC/EU procedures and institutions + last resort • No competition between sub-groups • Positive list of areas or veto right in the triggering procedure (conditional veto) • High initial threshold of membership and 'open-door' based on objective criteria • Temporariness • Protection of the interests of the unable by independent institutions	• Protection of the interests of the unwilling by independent institutions • Discretionary opt-in *Depending on aims and dependence vis-à-vis the EU* • Permanent exemptions of variable extent • Monitoring right on the course of enhanced cooperation • Veto right in the triggering procedure (unconditional veto) • Authorization of extra-EU enhanced cooperation	*Depending on their priorities (effectiveness versus commonality)* • 'Automatic' versus consensual triggering procedure • Optimal size of the sub-group versus minimal critical mass • Large scope (short negative list excluding core *acquis* areas) versus restricted scope (short positive list of eligible areas) • No interference versus limited participation of the unable • Cooptation (subjective) versus 'open door' • Hard core versus temporary vanguard • Tailor-made versus normal procedures and institutional settings • No solidarity mechanism versus some solidarity
	Development of the *acquis* 'by import'	
Best formula • Solidarity mechanism • Automatic 'passerelle'	• Protection of the interests of the unwilling by independent institutions • Side-payments matching the externalities • Discretionary opt-in	*Depending on their priorities (effectiveness versus commonality)* • 'Automatic' versus consensual 'importing' procedure

Second-best formula
- Preservation of the EC/EU *acquis* + separate status of 'flexibility *acquis*'
- Preservation of EC/EU procedures and institutions
- No competition between sub-groups
- Veto right in the triggering procedure (conditional veto)
- High initial threshold of membership and 'open-door' based on objective criteria
- Temporariness
- Protection of the interests of the unable by independent institutions

Depending on the nature of the extra-EU acquis (club versus public goods)
- Partial exemptions (right to pick and choose) versus total exemption
- Veto right on the authorization of 'import' (unconditional veto)

- No fragmentation of the imported *acquis* versus some 'incentive' pick and choose offered to the outsiders
- No interference versus limited participation of the unable
- Cooptation (subjective)[b] versus 'open door'
- Hard core versus temporary vanguard
- Tailor-made versus normal procedures and institutional settings
- No solidarity mechanism versus some solidarity

Adoption of the *acquis*

Best formula
- Solidarity mechanism
- Automatic 'passerelle'

Second-best formula
- Preservation of EC/EU procedures and institutions
- No competition between sub-groups
- Veto right on the list of policy areas excluded from the *acquis* for new applicants
- 'Open-door' based on objective criteria
- Temporariness
- Protection of the interests of the unable by independent institutions

- Protection of the interests of the unwilling by independent institutions
- Side-payments matching the externalities
- Discretionary opt-in

Depending on the nature of the acquis (club versus public goods)
- Partial exemptions (right to pick and choose) versus total exemption

Depending on the cost of inclusion for the incumbent MS (high versus low)
- Fragmentation versus no fragmentation of the *acquis*
- Limited participation versus full participation of the CMS
- 'Open door' in both cases
- Tailor-made versus normal procedures and institutional settings
- Partial versus normal burden-sharing

[a] When dealing with the development of the *acquis*, the table focuses only on the demands of Member States. It includes the demands of candidate Member States when dealing with the adoption of the *acquis* (the names between brackets indicate the origin of the demands linked to the adoption of the *acquis*).
[b] Except for the 'willing excluded' who would insist on 'open door' only.

to some sort of 'participation and more' than the opt-outs straight 'non-participation'. An example of opt-up is given by Article 95 TEC (ex Article 100A (4) TEC) which allows Member States to maintain or adopt higher national standards in sectors relating to the environment and the working environment. The interested Member States notify the Commission which authorizes these standards or not, after verification that they neither establish arbitrary discrimination nor constitute a disguised restriction on trade. The request to go ahead is made by Member States individually and does not imply any kind of joint endeavour, even if parallel developments could occur (e.g. if the same higher standards are adopted by several Member States). Here lies a key difference with the 'closer cooperation' categories examined *infra*.

3. EC/EU policies established on the basis of *ad hoc* flexible arrangements

In this case, the exemptions granted to some Member States do not apply to individual acts or decisions (case-by-case flexibility) but to an entire policy (sub)area. Reference is often made to a 'pre-defined flexibility' method because the policy is established on the basis of a protocol detailing in advance all aspects of the flexibility arrangement (specific scope and procedures) for that particular area. The pre-Amsterdam European Monetary Union and post-Amsterdam Title IV TEC on 'visas, asylum, immigration and other policies related to free movement of persons' are two examples of this type of flexible arrangement. In the case of the EMU, one part of the monetary policy is run through 'normal' procedures, involving notably the (Ecofin) Council, while another part including the monitoring of government deficits or the adjustment of the Euro exchange rate is dealt with through *ad hoc* procedures and modalities, largely defined in protocols attached to the treaties. In the case of Title IV TEC, albeit explicitly mentioned by Article 3 TEC listing the activities to be undertaken by the Community, measures concerning the entry and the movement of persons will not be binding upon or applicable to all Member States.[15] In cases of pre-defined flexibility, a number of *ad hoc* procedures often allow Member States to renounce their general right to opt-out or to opt-in on a case-by-case basis, that is, to pick and choose the measures they are willing to accept.

4. Intra-EU closer cooperation established on the basis of *ad hoc* flexible arrangements

This form of flexibility authorizes Member States to use the institutional framework of the EU to develop a closer cooperation among them. Such cooperative developments take place inside the EU but are not considered as part of the common *acquis* or as EC/EU policies, even if they all build on an existing EC/EU policy or innovate in line with EC/EU objectives. Intra-EU instances of closer cooperation have been organized by specific Treaties provisions and/or protocols mostly. Their scope, objectives, rules and procedures were pre-defined on an *ad hoc* or 'occasional' basis. The main examples of this approach are found in the provisions of Title XVIII TEC 'Research and technological development' dealing with the additional research programmes, the Protocol and the agreement on social policy attached to the Maastricht Treaty, as well as the Protocol integrating the Schengen *acquis* attached to the ToA and deriving from the Schengen Agreements of 1985 and 1990 on the gradual abolition of checks at common borders.

5. Extra-EU closer cooperation

This form of flexibility refers to (intergovernmental) cooperation between EU Member States outside the framework of the EC/EU. This cooperation 'in parallel' can be informal (cf. the 'Contact Group', 'friends of the Congo', etc.) or formalized through an international agreement, be it bilateral (e.g. conventions for the avoidance of double taxation) or multi-lateral (regional cooperation pursued in 'subsystems' such as Benelux, or in policy-specific schemes such as the European Space Agency). EU Member States can also enter extra-EU cooperation which includes one or more third states (e.g. the Council of Europe and the Nordic Council).

6. EU-linked extra-EU closer cooperation

Some provisions are establishing direct links between instances of extra-EU closer cooperation and the EU. Extra-EU closer cooperation can be explicitly conceived, as the signatories of the 1985 Schengen agreement did, as a 'laboratory of EU policies' whose output is intended to integrate eventually the framework of the EU. It can also be considered as 'an integral part of the development of the Union', notwithstanding difference in the respective membership as in the case of the Western European Union. The EU can even go further by establishing on that basis a structural and functional link, when it stipulates that it 'will avail itself of the WEU to elaborate and implement decisions and actions of the Union which have defence implications' (Article 17 TEU, ex Article J.7 (3)).

Models and standards

Besides studying the comparative effectiveness of the Amsterdam provisions on closer cooperation in dealing with the demands for flexibility, we will assess in the final section the expected effects of closer co-operation on EU governance as a whole. While some demands for flexibility have not been met by the closer cooperation clauses, others have, albeit in a specific way. In order to evaluate the options underpinning closer cooperation provisions and to value their expected effects, we will use two ideal-types of EU governance: the 'Westphalian' model and the 'Regulatory' model.[16] These models do not pretend to represent the 'reality', but sketch in a stylized way a direction in which the Union could develop. Once again, they are a heuristic device for our evaluation, with all the limitations which come with it. We will deduce standards from each of them and assess in the next section whether the new flexibility tool is bringing the EU closer to or further away from those standards.

The *'Westphalian' model* conceives of the EU as a political system in the making, a system which – when reaching maturity – should be comparable with the model characterizing Western European states ('*Stato/Federatio*'[17]). The analogy with the Westphalian state implies that the EU is expected to evolve in the direction of an undifferentiated institutional order across policy-areas, covering all activities traditionally associated with the nation-state, including the provision of security and welfare (redistributive politics). As regards method and procedures of integration, the Westphalian model puts considerable emphasis on comprehensive participation by expanding numbers of Member States and uniform application of rules,[18] even if temporary differentiation in Member States' rights and obligations can be envisaged, provided that the centripetal dynamics of flexibility clearly prevail. Integration should proceed through constitutionalization, i.e. the intergovernmental agreements and treaties among the sovereign European states should convert into a classical set of rules binding those states, imposing limits on the power of the new entity, guaranteeing the rule of law and conferring rights to individuals. From the Westphalian perspective, the transfer of competences to the European level has to be accompanied by a much faster development of European democracy. The structures designed to regulate European affairs are seen as lacking transparency, and the European debate and party politics as underdeveloped. Wider opening to public scrutiny and extension of the power and competences of the European Parliament – the repository of democratic representation and legitimacy in the EU – are advocated as the sole remedy to overcome these deficits (input-legitimacy).

By contrast, the *'regulatory' ideal-type* considers the EU's institutions and policies as systematically different from those of national governments (Caporaso, 1996). The EU is seen as a highly developed '. . . special purpose organization . . . the primary task of which is to address a number of issues over which it can hope to achieve greater efficiency than the member states acting individually' (Dehousse, 1998: 1–3). The EU should not necessarily cover the whole gamut of policies national states usually operate: if some policies are more effectively managed at another level, that level should keep that competence; conversely, if the European level ceases to be the most efficient, the reallocation of competence should be envisaged. Consequently, there should be a clear, albeit not irreversible, division of labour between the Member States and the European Union, where European activities will logically tend to concentrate on market integration and 'risk regulation' (Dehousse, 1998: 3). In the regulatory model, the decision to enlarge EU membership and the choice of integration methods have to be made according to their contribution to the fulfilment of the functional objectives of the EU. There is no preconception in terms of variations in institutional settings and methods across issue-areas as long as they contribute to effectiveness and efficiency in that respect ('Consortio'). The regulatory model does favour delegation to supranational institutions for those policy areas which for reasons of efficiency have to be dealt with at the European level. These institutions and their special expertise are thought to be in a better position to guarantee the essential autonomy of decision and the non-discriminatory application of rules. The legitimacy of the system will be provided by clear mandates and objectives for which these autonomous institutions are held accountable, and through decision-making processes sufficiently transparent to allow stakeholders to express themselves (Dehousse, 1998: 4). Contrary to the Westphalian model, legitimacy is however not mainly derived from specific characteristics of the system or method of integration, but from the results produced by them (output-legitimacy).

In Table 10.2 we have summarized the standards which can be deduced from these two models in terms of scope of policies, method(s) of integration and institutional architecture.

Having listed the main demands for flexibility, the pre-Amsterdam tools supplying differentiation, as well as prescriptive general models of governance, we still have to describe – or assess – the new Amsterdam flexibility before eventually evaluating its problem-solving capacity and systemic significance.

The assessment of Amsterdam: anatomy of a compromise

The Treaty of Amsterdam has inserted a hybrid set of flexibility mechanisms into the Union's framework. The general regime for future 'closer cooperation' between Member States inside the EU is its main conceptual and procedural innovation. This latest system has been instituted by means of 'enabling clauses' set out in new Title VII TEU. They authorize Member States who are willing to engage in further cooperation among

Table 10.2 Assessment and evaluation of Amsterdam's flexibility

	Westphalian model	Regulatory ideal-type
Scope	• The EU should cover all policy areas traditionally associated with the national state (including defence) • Special importance of redistributive policies	• Policies where the EU is expected to achieve greater efficiency than the Member States (transborder issues; management of international externalities, ...) • Emphasis on market integration and 'risk regulation' • Clear division of competences between the Member States and the EU
Method	• Universal participation by expanding numbers of Member States • Uniform application of procedures; bias in favour of QMV voting coupled with solidarity • Methods incorporating democratic components • Extended transparency, including for the 'public' • Constitutionalization	• Controlled expansion of the 'club' according to functional standards • Pragmatism in terms of procedures and methods, resulting in a mix adapted to issue areas • Methods favouring a low-key (technocratic) approach • Transparency aimed at the representatives of interested parties
Institution	• Undifferentiated system of governance across policy-areas (*Stato/Federatio*) • The institutional architecture should resemble the parliamentary model dominant in European countries • Source of legitimacy (input-legitimacy): participation, political accountability, democratic control, solidarity • The European Parliament is the ultimate repository of legitimacy and should therefore play a substantive role	• Mixed system, possibly including sub-systems (which are close to *Consortio*), but short of a representative democracy for structural reasons • The institutional architecture should be functional and include delegation to autonomous supranational institutions (EC or autonomous administrative agencies) • Source of legitimacy (output-legitimacy): deriving from clear mandates, clear objectives and policy effectiveness and efficiency of the institutions

themselves to make use of the institutions, procedures and mechanisms laid down by the TEU and the TEC, provided that substantive and procedural conditions – see below – are met (Article 43 TEU). They regulate the procedures for the implementation of closer cooperation and its financing (Article 44 TEU), and stipulate that the European Parliament is to be regularly informed of its development (Article 45 TEU). These clauses are supplemented by specific provisions for the first pillar (Article 11 TEC) and the third pillar (Article 40 Title VI TEU). If the additional conditions set for the authorization of closer cooperation in the first pillar reinforce drastically the limitations outlined in the general clauses, those set for the third pillar are much less restrictive and more versatile. Specific triggering mechanisms and procedures for later adhesion are also provided.

Of the various forms of flexibility envisaged during the IGC for the second pillar, the only one eventually included in the Treaty was the possibility of 'constructive abstention' allowing for discrete opt-outs (see above on Article 23 TEU). Besides enabling clauses and case-by-case flexibility, Amsterdam resorted to pre-defined flexibility for matters concerning the constitution of an area of freedom, security and justice (several protocols attached to the Treaties determine the scope and the procedures of various possibilities for closer cooperation, such as the Protocol integrating the Schengen *acquis* into the framework of the EU (No. 2), or the Protocols allowing the UK and Ireland (No. 4), as well as Denmark (No. 5) not to be bound by the provisions of Title IV TEC). Finally, other forms of procedural and substantive differentiation, using multi-speed and opt-in features, were also introduced (cf. the system of 'rolling ratification' allowing for the entry into force of a convention in the third pillar once it has been ratified by at least half of the Member States – Article 34, (2)(d) TEU– or the optional declaration concerning the role of the European Court of Justice).

It is clear that parsimony has not been the main preoccupation of the Treaty makers. If the ToA has all the appearances of a complex patchwork, it should however not be regarded as a 'random' assemblage. The various forms of flexibility described above should even be seen as non-mutually exclusive.[19] Enabling clauses, and predetermined and case-by-case flexibility, can and are likely to be used in combination as suggested, for instance, by the contents of the Protocol integrating the Schengen *acquis*. The clauses provide a kind of 'standard lease contract' which, provided that all parties agree, can be optimized by a number of tailor-made rules according to the needs or opportunities different parts of the policy area concerned might present.[20]

This being said, we now turn to the assessment of the enabling clauses, the prime focus of our demonstration. Their mechanics are very much the result of a compromise we will dissect by comparing in some detail the Treaty provisions with the demands of the unable, unwilling and willing MS and CMS.

None of the major demands aiming at keeping the unable in the wake of the group ahead has been introduced in the system (no involvement in decision-taking, automatic *passerelle* or solidarity devices – even if the latter in particular could be rather easily obtained in exchange for the authorization of closer cooperation). Except for its openness, the system is also deprived of the other – more subsidiary – 'inclusive' features which would have reassured the unable MS and CMS: the triggering threshold is, for the time being, not high enough to oblige the willing to embark some of the unable from the start;[21] their eventual inclusion is not guaranteed by an explicit reference to the temporary nature of closer cooperation. However, the unable see most of the other 'second best formula' demands satisfied by an open, defensive and restrictive system. *Primo*, their demand for openness has been largely if not totally met. The principle of open-door based on objective criteria has indeed been clearly stated, allowing all MS to become parties to the cooperation from the outset or at a later stage, provided that they comply with its decisions. Differences between Article 11 TEC and Article 40 TEU concerning the triggering and late adhesion procedures suggest nevertheless that the openness of the system is better guaranteed for the first pillar – where the European Commission plays the key role in the enabling process – than for the third pillar – where the Council decides. *Secondo*, two of the main defensive demands of the unable, the preservation of the *acquis* and the single institutional framework, have been put at the core of the system in a rather maximalist way. Generally speaking, the defensive character of the enabling conditions has been deliberately reinforced at various stages of the IGC negotiation, choices being systematically made in favour of more conditions and more restrictive wording. Witness is the triggering procedure which contains a veto right in the form of a 'diluted version' of the Luxembourg compromise (Kortenberg, 1998: 850; De Zwaan, 1999: 20) or the condition requiring that enhanced cooperation 'does not distort the conditions of competition', while the initial proposal was only referring to a 'substantial' distortion of competition (Article 11(1)(e) TEC). If the defences against regressive flexibility are not absolute,[22] they are very strong. *Tertio*, a number of features, if interpreted literally, converge to reduce significantly the potential use of the new instrument (the 'last resort' principle; the conditions delimiting the 'non-forbidden' scope for enhanced cooperation[23]). The restrictive nature of the construction is a very positive element for the unable, insofar as any closer cooperation is for them synonymous with exclusion.

For partially different reasons, this triptych satisfies the interests and demands of the unwilling as well to an even larger extent. *Primo*, thanks to the openness of the system, the unwilling are not confronted with a 'now or never' choice which would have been very detrimental to their negotiating position in general. *Secondo*, their specific defensive demands have also been amply taken into account, with the possibility of permanent exemption, the monitoring right (the outs participate in the deliberation), and the right to veto the authorization of closer cooperation. (This last feature is not optimal though, insofar as the so-called 'emergency brakes' or *freins d'urgence* introduce some qualified majority and exchange the anonymity of a veto in the Council of Ministers with a veto aired at the highest level, with all the additional publicity that surrounds the meetings of Heads of State or Government; furthermore they are not fully discretionary – there is a possibility for the European Court of Justice to examine it – and can be used only once, during the initiating phase.) Of course, the unwilling will also welcome the other defensive characteristics already mentioned, especially those which have an obstructive potential and are politically cheaper than an outright veto (the condition stipulating that closer cooperation cannot affect no less than the 'competences, rights, obligations and interests' of non-participating MS is, *par excellence*, the sword of Damocles the unwilling can wave over the willing's head). *Tertio*, the restrictive nature of the enabling clauses is another source of contention, the unwilling being by definition above all interested by a stop in EU's task expansion. The fact that closer cooperation is restricted to policy areas already falling within the remit of the EC or, in other words, cannot be used to initiate common action in policy areas for which the Community has no competence, is crucial in that respect. The confirmation of the possibility for extra-EU closer cooperation[24] is also a positive element for them, in particular because the existence of external developments is *de facto* restricting the scope for intra-EU closer cooperation. In conclusion, the only reservation which the (maximalist) unwilling might have about the present system is that it does not envisage discretionary opt-ins or side-payments, but the EU has shown that almost everything is negotiable.

The balance sheet for the willing is much more contrasted. Their principal source of satisfaction is undoubtedly the constitutional entrenchment of a radical form of differentiation, acknowledging that, within the EU, it is no longer an absolute obligation 'for *all* member states to integrate in *all* policy fields at the *same* time' (Metcalfe, 1998: 18). In addition, some elements could be interpreted as an indirect recognition of their 'vanguard' status, like the possibility for Community financing or the use of the label 'closer cooperation' which implies a common *telos*, a shared objective (Snyder, 1998: 115). It could however be argued that the EU cannot at the same time practise variable geometry and pretend that all

MS still share the same objectives. The group of the willing could not then be considered as the vanguard, but simply as one sub-system co-existing with other sub-systems. Deliberate omission or not, the Treaties do not say if the CMS have to adopt as part of the Union's *acquis* what is developed in the frame of a closer cooperation,[25] which would have given a clear indication about the status of the group forging ahead. All in all, in another example of the well-known 'constructive ambiguity' technique, the dialectic solution chosen at Amsterdam seems to acknowledge without saying so explicitly that the willing are on some sort of reconnaissance mission.

Besides the introduction of a new principle breaking with Community orthodoxy and the uncertain recognition of a vanguard status which satisfies all willing, there is a sharp contrast in the extent to which the respective demands of the two sub-groups identified in Table 10.2 have been met. On the plus side, the system matches very few of the demands of the proponents of immediate effectiveness. They can take comfort from the fact that catch-up through self-help is the norm (in other words, solidarity is not an automatic obligation) and that the core of the willing and able can continue to exist for as long as necessary. On the minus side, the list is much longer. The triggering procedure is not automatic. With a minimal membership set on a conventional basis, the size of the group will not necessarily be optimal. The cooptation is not the main rule, even if the procedure for later adhesion to closer cooperation linked to the third pillar is partially satisfactory. The non-participants can interfere to a significant measure in the development of closer cooperation. The system makes a simple opening for burden sharing, but does not prevent free-riding (operational expenditures resulting from closer cooperation have to be borne by the participating MS, unless decided otherwise unanimously). The 'rigidity' currently embedded in the 'normal' procedures and frame-work is unchanged. The scope for enhanced cooperation is *a priori* rather restricted[26] – although this will not necessarily always frustrate the demands of the willing.[27] And, last but not least, the scheme is falling dramatically short of a hard core or a *directoire*. On the other hand, the demands of the proponents of cohesion have been better accommodated. Indeed non-antagonistic triggering, critical mass, cautiousness with the scope for closer cooperation, limited participation of the outs, open-door and preservation of the normal procedures[28] are among the characteristic features of the new system.

Such an output is not a big surprise in the eyes of negotiation theory. When the negotiating positions are very divergent and one party only (that of the willing) is really interested in a successful outcome, that party has to make the most of the concessions. The extent of the concessions, however, varies with the other parties' vulnerability to pressure, the unable being more vulnerable than the unwilling. It is therefore easy to explain *ex post* why within a rather narrow winset, the agreement corresponds to the 'second best' demands of the unable which were close to the pro-cohesion demand of the willing, combined with most of the demands of the unwilling – the willing ending up with a very high bill for the introduction of the new principle. The comparison of the demands of the parties and the Treaties provisions shows very clearly that closer cooperation is indeed a compromise based on mutual concessions and, incidentally, that the product of IGCs has little to do with lowest common denominator solutions.

The ensemble is not only free of ambiguities but remains silent on several key issues: how to end closer cooperation? what is the status of closer cooperation *acquis* for CMS? More importantly perhaps, is closer cooperation adding a new locus of power within the EU or a new level of power between the national and Union ones? (Bribosia, 1998: 23–92; Tuytschaever, 1999). Beyond these grey zones, the system is designed around the protection of the core elements of the Union, the recognition of the continued significance if not primacy of national interests, and yet some political versatility able to deliver, in a roundabout way, structural adjustments when deeper integration is needed. Extremely simplified, it can be conceived as multi-faceted and dialectically organized around a three-folded rationale – the prime rationale varying with the pillars: protection under pillar I; usefulness under pillar II; and necessity under pillar III (Philippart and Edwards, 1999: 102–3) It combines centrifugal and centripetal features, the latest being predominant thanks in particular to principles such 'open-door' based on objective criteria and acceptance of an *acquis* established by others.

The managerial evaluation of Amsterdam

Now that we have described the assemblage behind closer cooperation and assessed which demands were met, we will evaluate its expected problem-solving capacity (*vis-à-vis* the development of the *acquis* in-house, by import, as well as the adoption of the *acquis*) and compare it with the capacity of other forms of flexibility.

The provisions for closer cooperation were deliberately designed to deal with the problem of the development of the *acquis* 'in-house'. The result of a laborious compromise, they are said to have very little or no potential as a policy tool due to their multiple defensive and restrictive features. This corresponds in fact to a reading which implicitly uses the question of how to get around recalcitrant MS as the main criterion for evaluation – an obvious choice in the wake of an IGC battered for months by the defiant attitude of the UK Conservative government. If one considers the use of closer cooperation in a context of 'normal' disagreement, its potential is however greater than it first appears. Cases where, out of Union comity or to increase their political capital, Member States while lacking interest for a policy sub-area do not object to other MS cooperating more closely among themselves, are not unprecedented. A mechanism such as constructive abstention is based on that very expectation and has been welcomed by many as an experiment worth making. It would therefore not be justified to rule out that, despite its multiple vetoes and practical difficulties (Philippart and Edwards, 1999: 92–5),[29] closer cooperation could provide a reasonably attractive solution for problems involving uninterested unwilling and non-excluding willing.

Is closer cooperation then likely to be, from a managerial point of view, a good or a bad solution? In other words, what are its prospective efficacy and efficiency in the resolution of problems of integration, and for which policy areas? The ambiguity surrounding the exact scope of enhanced cooperation means that the answer to the second part of the latest question remains highly speculative. Public health, consumer protection, education, environment, international trade in services or fiscal harmonization and other EMU-linked cooperation are however commonly listed as possible cases for closer cooperation within the first pillar. For the third pillar, the use of closer cooperation in information exchange, harmonization of extradition and hot pursuit rules, etc. is mentioned as desirable and likely, but is seen as counterproductive in penal and criminal law where, for functional reasons, there is said to be no alternative to the constitution of a unified legal space. In all those policy areas, a superficial evaluation tends to show that the requirement for homogeneity is indeed dispensable or even harmful when pursuing integration. The introduction of closer cooperation is therefore a good thing insofar as, in a small number of cases, it introduces the first official possibility for flexibility and, in the other cases, increases the range of flexible managerial solutions. It also provides precious points of reference where *ad hoc* solutions to immediate problems have often been crafted without consideration of their wider repercussions. This is especially important for pillar I where hidden flexibility has been proliferating, including within core policies (De Burca, 2000).

A comprehensive evaluation would suppose comparing enhanced cooperation with the many policy-making instruments managing diversity by accommodating it but also by curbing it (through QMV, issue-linkage or side-payments, for instance). This is beyond the reach of a single chapter and we have restricted our comparison to the other forms of flexibility identified earlier. In spite of its obvious limitations, this approach puts clearly in evidence some of the specific managerial pluses and minuses of closer cooperation.

1. EC/EU policies with a differentiated application of common obligations and rights

Among all forms of flexibility, the 'classical' multi-speed differentiation keeps the increase in legal complexity at its lowest, with the preservation of one single *acquis*. Together with the two categories which follow next, it offers the advantage of having to manage only one policy within the Union framework. To be temporarily exempted from the application of a rule might, however, not satisfy opposing Member States. If the rule has to be adopted by unanimity such accomodation will not suffice to break a stalemate. In that respect, the new instrument is slightly more effective insofar as it only provides a one-off veto whose use is more costly. All in all, classical differentiation is more effective for 'all willing–some unable' situations, even if, on short-medium term, it is not the most efficient solution for the wealthiest MS footing the bill.

2. EC/EU policies incorporating an element of case-by-case flexibility

In terms of readability, especially for third countries not necessarily aware of the EU subtleties or keen to accept them, this formula is more predictable and less confusing than cases of a non EC/EU policy developed in the EC/EU framework. It is also more versatile: lighter to operate because, in most cases, it only supposes a unilateral decision of the unwilling (expressed through their qualified abstention) compared with requests for closer cooperation and proposals, information and procedures on it, etc.; easier to resort to because it is more secure or less stressful for the non-participants (their authorization is indeed needed for each decision while it is given once and for all in closer cooperation). If used parsimoniously, this form of flexibility is more compatible with the 'indivisible' nature of some policy areas (an argument often used for external policy). It could turn out to be more effective to manage situations where the blockage rests with hesitant, i.e. unwilling but non-recalcitrant, Member States. If used repeatedly, case-by-case flexibility could amount to some sort of jurisprudential development producing a more fragmented *acquis* than what would produce a limited number of clearly identified groupings (that is to say, in a Union practising restricted variable geometry, what Nordic, Southerner or other groups would develop for themselves in addition to a common *acquis*). The pick-and-choose approach is indeed, in theory, the most damaging option with respect to maintaining the coherence of a general scheme.

3. EC/EU policies established on the basis of *ad hoc* flexible arrangements (predetermined flexibility)

Tailor-made arrangements with *ad hoc* decision-making, burden-sharing, etc. procedures can be more complex or heavier to manage than arrangements designed according to the general rules for closer cooperation. They are indeed likely to include many expedients in order to meet all political considerations and exhaust all opportunities. As a result, this form of flexibility, together with the next one, can *inter alia* lead to monstrosity in terms of transparency and readability. On the other hand, it might prove to be a more effective policy tool than closer cooperation and its multiple safeguards and rigid features which some MS see as problematic. With predetermined flexibility, one does not have to demonstrate that the last resort has been reached, specific requirements can be minimized or maximized. If the EMU and the Schengen protocols had been drafted according to the provisions for closer cooperation, it is likely that the policy output would have been smaller and slower to come,[30] and most probably short of what is needed to solve the problems of the development of the *acquis*.

4. Intra-EU closer cooperation established on the basis of *ad hoc* flexible arrangements

This option has in theory all the advantages and disadvantages of the previous form of flexibility with one major additional complication: the management of one area then implies having to cope not only with a number of differentiated procedures but also with several policies and their respective 'blocks' of *acquis*. It is probably the worst managerial combination possible.

5. Extra-EU closer cooperation (including EU-linked extra-EU closer cooperation)

Unhindered by the constraints of the veto, the openness, the threshold, etc. this form of flexibility is more conducive to the development of regimes. It allows for the formation of optimal groups of like-minded MS able to agree more quickly on stronger sets of norms. But it also comes with particular managerial problems, such as the development of specific structures enjoying smaller economies of scale, this against a widespread reluctance to create new international bureaucracies. Extra-EU cooperation might in addition lead to duplication or emptying of existing EU/EC policies.

Among flexibility tools, closer cooperation is the least versatile but not the least effective. The system does not in particular compare well with the immediate problem-solving capacity of extra-EU or informal intra-EU management of cooperation. In a few specific configurations of MS preferences and policy area characteristics, it does however offer a better alternative to existing instruments. If it is not the solution to the general managerial deficit of the EU, it could partially alleviate it directly but also indirectly when used by the willing as a tactical negotiating instrument to undermine the legitimacy of the position of a blocking minority and put pressure on it. More generally, it could also reinforce the sectoral logic which prevails in the EU, strain the Union institutional resources and add to its deficit in horizontal coordination. In this respect closer cooperation represents a continuation of the post-Maastricht procedural and institutional proliferation, its multiplication of frameworks, diminished transparency and increased complexity, but this in a more precautionary way. From a managerial point of view, these are not necessarily negative developments, complex structures, for instance, having often a higher capacity to adapt to changes in their environment. In any case, closer cooperation ought to be revisited (in particular to see if policy areas in need of structured flexibility have not been left out of the scheme) and possibly revised.

The two other fundamental problems we identified as calling for some sort of structured and organized flexibility have not been directly addressed by the new system. As far as the problem of the development of the *acquis* by import is concerned, closer cooperation is nevertheless making a positive contribution, having provided some principles, norms and rules recognized by all as acceptable, if not totally equitable. In other words, a regime has been established which could contribute to decreasing the transaction costs for future imports: the new system provides indeed a starting point for the negotiation of specific arrangements, it sets minima and maxima, it narrows down the range of options or the size of the winset.

The contribution of closer cooperation to the problem of the adoption of the *acquis* by new MS is following a more circuitous route. To start with, this issue has been excluded from the design of the new system, this for two reasons: on the one hand, the postulate of the integrity of the *acquis* was reasserted in the conclusions of the European Council of Turin, on 29 March 1996; on the other hand, the Commission was mandated to address, in its Agenda 2000 propositions, the issue of the reform of the *acquis* with the perspective of the enlargement. In this very document, the Commission was nevertheless saying that 'The introduction of enhanced cooperation will also make it easier to take up the challenges of a broader and more heterogeneous Union'. This puzzled some commentators,

Andrew Duff wondering if it implies that 'even the existing MS will not have to complete their own integration agenda . . .' (Duff, 1998: 47). In the absence of clarification by the Commission itself, we propose another interpretation of its statement. Closer cooperation is only applying for further development of the *acquis* and consequently is not directly helping in the adoption of the existing *acquis*. But, if closer cooperation *acquis* turns out not to be a part of the *acquis* to be adopted by CMS, and considering that the next enlargement of the Union will not take place for some years, one could indeed argue that resorting to closer cooperation to develop the *acquis* over that period is a way to decrease the volume of the post-Amsterdam *acquis* to be adopted by the candidate MS. If enhanced cooperation *acquis* is considered as an integral part of the Union *acquis*, the new device does not help their accession by lowering the threshold in terms of the volume of the *acquis*, but it does facilitate the enlargement by contributing to reduce the anxiety of incumbent MS about the capacity to further develop the Union once enlargement will have taken place. It can also contribute indirectly to alleviate managerial concerns with the possible dilution of existing European policies. If applicants are not able to implement the *acquis* satisfactorily and if the postponement of enlargement is not an option, the only alternative solution would be to segment the *acquis* and fence some of its parts to prevent their decay. It can be argued that the constitutional entrenchment of closer cooperation has, depending of the point of view, broken a taboo or opened Pandora's box, and is legitimizing a number of principles which could be invoked in favour of such a regressive form of flexibility.

The systemic evaluation of Amsterdam

The repercussions of the Amsterdam flexibility go beyond the management of problems of integration and affect EU governance as a whole. Some are intentional, others not. Confronted with previous sterile or even counterproductive debates on the finality of the Union, many governments tend to put a managerial spin on their systemic objectives. Managerial solutions are for instance used as an opportunity to step up the pace to further (federal-like) integration or break down the dynamics of the initial pre-federal mould. This being said, the actors' information is limited and their capacity to foresee future developments is impaired by the fact that the Union is moving from one unstable equilibrium to another. Some consequences might therefore be simply unintended.

The impact of closer cooperation derives from the practical realities it might introduce one day, but also, and possibly more importantly, from the symbolic elements it brings with it. In that respect, its indirect contribution to the problem of the development of the *acquis* by import and the problem of the adoption of the *acquis* is not negligible. In this sub-section, the systemic consequences of the new provisions will be evaluated from the perspective of the Westphalian and Regulatory models, focusing on (1) the scope of EU policies, (2) the method of integration and (3) the institutional structure and legitimacy of the EU.

The new instrument has been explicitly restricted to existing EC/EU domains. It does not allow use of the Union framework for moving into new policy fields. So, for the Westphalian model postulating that the EU scope should widen to cover more and more areas traditionally associated with the national state, closer cooperation is *a priori* neither a gain nor a loss. On enhanced reading, the fact that solidarity has no part in the new scheme is sending a rather negative signal for the Westphalian objective of expanding the Union's redistributive policies (Wallace, 1990). On the Westphalian ambition to curb extra-EU cooperation which affects nega-tively the Union's scope (depending on one's reading of the ToA) closer cooperation is either a missed opportunity or a slight progress. For the Regulatory model which emphasizes the need to be able to deepen integration where functional reasons require it, it is on the contrary a systemic progress.

As far as the method of integration is concerned, the introduction of closer cooperation means a clear departure from the Westphalian model whose standards prescribe universal participation by expanding numbers of Member States, uniform application of procedures and extended trans-parency. One could however argue that the transgression of these West-phalian prescriptions does not automatically push the Union further away from its course to statehood. Another example of non-consequential trans-gression is given by Louis who argues that the possibility of withdrawing from the Union does not increase *per se* its international character insofar as the right to secede is embedded in the constitution of many federal states (Louis, 1996: 49). Furthermore the centripetal features of the new instru-ment could lead to the conclusion that closer cooperation should be conceived first and foremost as an intermediary stage. The departure from the Community method which is incorporating many of the Westphalian standards would then be only tactical, closer cooperation amounting to a new variant of the 'step-by-step approach towards an ever closer union'.[31]

A more significant breach in Community method would be the modifi-cation of ethos introduced by closer cooperation and its consequence on QMV. The actual implementation of the new provisions could indeed seriously erode 'the solidarity principle that is behind the extended practice of majority-voting in the Council' (Areilza Carvacal, 1998: 14). How far the EU will depart from the 'integration through solidarity' method advocated by the Westphalian model will depend to a large extent on whether future proposals for closer cooperation are designed in an exclusive or inclusive way. As mentioned above, a lot of things are open for negotiation in the new scheme. What is already certain is that closer cooperation offers an alternative to the strongly integrative QMV method and is therefore undermining the Westphalian hope for a strong extension of majority voting. The codification in the Treaties of a triggering mechanism which has similarities to the Luxembourg compromise is not helping either, if it is interpreted as a reaffirmation of the primacy of national interests over the 'European interest'. Let us note however that, according to the new provisions, the authorization to make use of the Union' structures shall be granted by a qualified majority, the veto being the exception.

Yet another serious hazard for the course of EU integration is linked to the non-solution of the problem of the development of the *acquis* by import. Precedents show that, in the process of importing, quite opposite things can be 'injected' into the system. To be imported in the EU, the European Monetary System had to go through a dramatic transformation which ended up with the introduction of a highly centralized and federative element in the Union framework. What the European Political Cooperation underwent was mainly repackaging, leading to the creation of a separate pillar for the Common Foreign and Security Policy and its considerable dose of intergovernmentalism challenging from inside of the TEU the Community method. The absence of 'structured flexibility' setting minimal procedural and institutional standards below which the import of any *acquis* would be forbidden means that the evolution of the system remains open or vulnerable to elements developed exogenously, possibly by some Member States only, through specific procedures and not necessarily in view of their eventual integration in the Union framework. This being said, this absence in itself does not make the system more vulnerable to Westphalian imports compared to Regulatory ones, and *vice versa*. The partial and indirect answer given by closer cooperation to this problem does not invalidate this observation. If accepted as transposable, the general terms of reference provided by the new scheme are indeed limiting the choice to existing procedures which already comprise Westphalian and Regulatory methods. As a last and most highly speculative consequence, the indirect argument provided by closer cooperation in favour of regressive flexibility in the context of the problem of the adoption of the *acquis*, is potentially the biggest threat for Westphalian aspirations but an acceptable development for the Regulatory ones.

If evaluated against the Westphalian methods standards, the general systemic consequences of closer cooperation are undoubtedly negative, but it is difficult to predict how much this is the case insofar as, on one side, these consequences might be of a temporary nature, and, on the other, there is more than one road to statehood. Closer cooperation might in time lead to a higher level of integration between all MS as envisaged by the Westphalian model, but through detours incompatible with its principle of equal rights and obligations for all MS. By comparison, the potential of closer cooperation is, from the Regulatory standpoint, very positive as a manifestation of pragmatism in terms of procedures and methods, laying the ground for policy mixes better adapted to issue areas and the rebuilding of more functional 'clubs'. The limited amount of supranationalism in the triggering of closer cooperation is acceptable for the Regulatory model. If it advocates supranationalism in implementation of policies, it does not necessarily favour it for policy-making.

In terms of institutional structure and legitimacy, the record for the two models is once more clearly asymmetrical. Closer cooperation is not creating new institutions in an organizational sense, altering significantly the inter-institutional balance of power which can be deduced from the other titles of the Treaties, or changing the pre-existing level of participation, political accountability and democratic control. In that respect, it is neutral with regard to the evolution of the Union towards a classical parliamentary system, the strengthening of the EP and the blossoming of input-legitimacy, all defended by the Westphalian model. It is, on the other hand, an innovation which, if used extensively, could dramatically affect the transparency *vis-à-vis* the general public and distract the EU from the ideal of an undifferentiated system of governance across policy-areas. If future developments result in the creation of new *loci* of power,[32] they could still be compatible with the *federatio* variant of the Westphalian conceptual world, as some forms of multi-level governance are with the German or the Belgian states for instance. If these developments go in the direction of a core Europe or a Europe of intersecting 'Olympic rings' (De La Serre and Wallace, 1997: 21), they will be simply antinomic with the Westphalian systemic objectives.

With the officialization of variable geometry, EU mixed governance is opening itself much further to a logic of sub-systems (*Consortio*) which is not ruled out by the Regulatory model. Besides that, closer cooperation is not contributing to the development of a representative democracy, which is Regulatory speaking positive, but either to the creation of supranational delegations and independent agencies, which is not positive. The Regulatory approach is here again the net beneficiary. A more flexible architecture and the reinforcement of sectorization are adding to the range of systemic solutions to a number of functional demands. If they are indeed producing effective and efficient policy results, closer cooperation would then help to increase output-legitimacy which would more than outweigh the possible loss of input-legitimacy (transparency).

CONCLUSION

The orientations of closer cooperation in terms of scope, methods and institutions are rather coherent and give a clear indication of its impact on the systemic direction taken by the Union: where not neutral or very marginal, it is rather detrimental for the Westphalian model and largely consistent with the Regulatory ideal-type.

The problem is that other parts of the Treaty of Amsterdam have a similar coherence but point in a different direction. Consequently, Amsterdam, as a whole, is not giving 'one' clear indication on the course of EU integration.

This may not be entirely surprising. Policies and public spaces are increasingly segmented. This segmentation equally affects IGCs: they tend to set up separate negotiation forums which communicate with difficulty and lack coordination. This absence of a clear direction is also related to the fact that the introduction in the EU of new managerial methods and systemic features through the IGC technique requires unanimity. The existence of competing camps with partially antithetic conceptions about the *finalités politiques* of the Union means that proposals which represent a clear step towards one specific model are very likely to be either vetoed, or reformulated ambivalently, or accepted in exchange for a step in the opposite direction. The players aim at creating reversible situations; they are wary of the ratchet mechanism or *engrenage* which acquired a bad connotation in some quarters. The outcome of the negotiations tends therefore to correspond to a new equilibrium set at a higher level but intrinsically unstable because it satisfies partially contradictory demands. The Treaty of Amsterdam's mixture is keeping most long-term options open: the move in the direction of the Regulatory model symbolized by closer cooperation is counterbalanced by other moves of a Westphalian nature (for instance, the extension of the co-decision procedure in favour of the EP, a reinforcement of the role of the Court of Justice, but also a closer association of national parliaments).

All in all, the probability of flexibility returning on the agenda of institutional reform for managerial reasons is not negligible. Some governments seem determined to keep the next IGC exclusively focused on the unfinished business of the 1996 IGC, that is, mainly on instruments intended to curb diversity (extension of QMV, reweighting of votes in the Council, number of Commissioners, etc.). If this reinforcement of the institutional and procedural framework is too weak, flexibility will once again be revisited as the only alternative formula to solve the Union's managerial deficit. If the reinforcement of the institutional framework is too strong it will generate new tensions, and flexibility could also be revisited as a more gentle technique of development – compared for instance with the 'brutality' of QMV and the resentment it can create. Finally, the screening process which candidate MS have to undergo might highlight new challenges which could well require new formulae for flexibility.

NOTES

1. This *ex ante* analysis was completed in April 1999, that is to say before the IGC 2000 put close cooperation on its agenda.
2. This is not to say that all theories on European integration share this reading of events. If, following W. Wessels' categorization, neo-federal/neo-functional and 'fusion' views see it as consistently linear, the 'governance' and realist views conceived it respectively as cyclical or on an ineluctable path towards decline. (Wessels, 1997).
3. For a discussion of the terminology, see Ehlermann (1998: 1). Many lawyers prefer referring to 'differentiation' as an overall term. We will use both terms interchangably.
4. Cf. TEU Article 2 (ex-Article B). The Union shall set itself the following objectives: 'to maintain in full the *'acquis* communautaire' and build on it with a view to considering to what extent the policies and forms of cooperation introduced by this Treaty may need to be revised with the aim of ensuring the effectiveness of the mechanisms and the institutions of the Community'.
5. See Chapter 9 by de Schoutheete in this volume and Stubb (1999).
6. This latest category corresponds to the 'Erweiterungsflexibilisierung' or 'enlargement flexibility' of the triptych proposed by Wessels, together with 'Abbauflexibilisierung' or 'decomposition flexibility' and 'Vertiefungsflexibilisierung' or 'deepening flexibility' (Wessels and Jantz, 1997).
7. Several commentators have expressed doubts whether the 'classical method of enlargement' is still appropriate to cope with the diversity of the applicants in terms of their social-economic development and judicial and administrative capacity (cf. Preston, 1997). According to the classical method, the applicants must accept the *acquis communautaire* in full. Transition periods and safeguard clauses may be granted to facilitate the adaptation process, but no permanent opt-outs are available.
8. Other lines of segmentation among the concepts and scenarios for flexibility are of course possible. Helen and William Wallace, for instance, are referring to 'core policies, core countries, core institutions, objective differences, differences of taste, differences of claim, and functional consortia' (Wallace and Wallace, 1995: 33).
9. The 'unable' refer to those MS which are willing to participate, but are for objective reasons unable to achieve common goals within a common time scale.
10. If one postulates that, inasmuch as the *acquis* has been developed in common, it represents something globally satisfactory for all MS. If one adds that it was developed through many side-payments and built on some elements of

solidarity, the wealthiest MS might be, relatively speaking, less satisfied and attracted by formulae-reducing EC 'cross-subsidization'. In that respect, it could be argued that, if all MS should *a priori* back demand for the preservation of the *acquis*, this might be more true for the unable insofar as they are among the net beneficiaries. The same logic is underlying the demand for the preservation of the EU institutional framework. The development of the latter has indeed always been very much preoccupied with the protection of the weaker and the overrepresentation of the smaller MS.

11. For readability's sake, Table 10.1 only includes one main variable per category of problem and actor, while variations in the demands are often the result of a combination of factors. The nature of the policy area plays, for instance, a role in almost all cases.

12. By integrating this element in the Union's primary law, these MS look to protect themselves from possible 'pro-integrationist' jurisprudence of the European Court of Justice (a kind of post-*ERTA* case syndrome).

13. The distinction between public and private (or club) goods refers to the possibility of excluding or not non-contributors from the benefits generated by the goods. Cf. Cornes and Sandler (1996); Mueller (1997); Padoan (1997: 107–33).

14. This type of flexibility can be interpreted as a case of crude discrimination or as the expression of a self-help philosophy pushed always further. (In the EMU system, the adjustments to meet the convergence criteria and accede to the Euro-zone have to be borne out by each Member State, but a Cohesion fund has been created to help the weakest members.)

15. Article 69 TEC refers to the Protocol on the position of the United Kingdom and Ireland (not participating in the adoption of the Schengen *acquis*) and to the Protocol on the position of Denmark (not participating either), without prejudice to the Protocol on the application of certain aspects of Article 7a to the United Kingdom and to Ireland (recognition of their 'Common Travel Area').

16. This dichotomy is *a priori* rather rigid and the analysis would benefit from the inclusion of a third and intermediary model of governance trying to make sense of diverging evolutions, i.e. the 'Multi-Level Governance' model. This has been developed further in Philippart and Sie Dhian Ho (2000).

17. Philippe C. Schmitter (1996: 121–50) has created four ideal types 'to provoke a discussion' on the future of the European polity. The four ideal types are defined by their specific mix of territorial and functional constituencies. In his typology, the '*Stato/Federatio*' ideal-type corresponds with the Westphalian model presented here, while his '*Consortio*' and '*Condomio*' ideal-types have much in common respectively with the Regulatory and Multi-level governance models.

18. This is particularly true for a very specific variant within the Westphalian paradigm, that is, the highly-centralized version of federalism used by A. Moravcsik and K. Nicolaïdis (1998: 16) as their term of reference.

19. In a letter of October 1996 to the president of the Council, Dick Spring, Hervé de Charrette and Hans Kinkel made that point very clear: 'The aim would be to adopt the simplest possible procedures, based on existing structures and machinery, avoiding competing circles while leaving enough flexibility for solutions on a case-by-case basis.' ('Closer cooperation with a view to

increased European integration: Joint Franco-German contribution to discussion in the IGC', CONF/395/96 Annex CAB, 18 October 1996.)

20. Just as Article 308 TEC (ex Article 235) gives a light alternative to the revision of the Treaty whenever action is required to attain one of the objectives of the Community and the necessary powers have not been provided, the enabling clauses are meant to provide a possibility to resort to flexible arrangements outside cumbersome IGCs. This advantage would of course be annihilated if the 'optimization' of the general system cannot be done without recourse to Protocols attached to the Treaties. Although the post-Maastricht practice shows that derogations to the Treaties are agreed by the European Council and immediately put in practice, their formal enshrinement in EU primary law is postponed to subsequent IGCs.

21. Closer cooperation should involve 'at least a majority of member states'. After the next enlargement, that threshold will satisfy the demand of most current unable MS.

22. The condition forbidding closer cooperation in areas which fall within the exclusive competence of the EC sounds final. The distinction between exclusive and shared powers is, however, in many cases, not clear-cut at all. The system puts independent institutions in a position to protect the unable and, by consequence, to prevent competition between sub-groups. But, here again, substantial discretion is left in the appreciation of the adequate level of protection to give. Institutions like the European Commission or the ECJ are sensitive or vulnerable to political considerations and are likely to take into account the balance of power between the ins and outs. They might also be biased in favour of specific cases of closer cooperation and ready to encourage them, be it to the (temporary) detriment of the unable.

23. Instead of determining *a priori* which policy areas would be opened or closed to closer cooperation (the option of the positive or negative list), the drafters have decided to define the scope of the new instrument through a set of negative conditions. This solution is introducing an element of ambiguity. (When is the stage of 'last resort' supposed to be reached? What means 'affecting' the interests of the non-participating MS or the *acquis communautaire?* etc.) This ambiguity could be exploited in an obstructive way, the unable insisting on a maximalist interpretation of these conditions.

24. There is no consensus on this interpretation. The fact that Member States '... *may* make use of the institutions ...' implies, many argue, that all the other options remain a possibility, including extra-EU cooperation (see, for instance, Gaja, 1998: 869). Others, building on various legal reasonings, are claiming that Amsterdam has largely foreclosed the use of the extra-EU option for the future (see Constantinesco, 1997: 755; Shaw, 1998). The suppression of former Article K.7 TEU could be seen as one of the indications pointing in that direction. ('The provisions of this Title shall not prevent the establishment or development of closer cooperation between two or more member states in so far as such cooperation does not conflict with, or impede, that provided for in this Title.')

25. This contrasts with Article 8 of the Protocol integrating the Schengen *acquis* stating that: 'For the purposes of the negotiations for the admission of new member states into the European Union, the Schengen *acquis* and further measures taken by the institutions within its scope shall be regarded as

an *acquis* which must be accepted in full by all States candidates for admission.'

26. As already mentioned in note 22, this is a moot point. The scope of closer cooperation's problem-solving capacity was initially seen as very narrow for the first pillar and rather vague for the third pillar, very few actors being able or ready to name policy areas potentially concerned. Suspicion and cautiousness progressively subsided. Getting accustomed to the idea and having gained a better understanding of the 'ins and outs' of the new scheme, the attitudes of many decision-makers including unenthusiastic countries like Spain were, at the time of the entry into force of Amsterdam, already more relaxed (cf. Deubner *et al.*, 1999, a report on hearings with government officials and parliamentarians in seven European capitals). Depending on the political context, the ambiguity inherent to the set of conditions defining the scope of closer cooperation can be used in an obstructive or 'constructive' way.

27. The record for the willing is indeed more ambivalent when considering the chronology of their demands. They were initially concerned exclusively with pillars II and III. They saw enhanced cooperation in pillar I as possibly counterproductive for them and their demand concerning pillar I only came as a tactical move to put pressure in favour of an extension of QMV. The narrow scope for closer cooperation in pillar I matters is therefore not necessarily a blow for the willing. As for the specific clause for pillar II, one could argue that its last minute dropping was, for them, the lesser of two evils. It maintains the existing extra-EU options albeit with their current shortcomings and preserves the willing from being locked in a possibly excessively constraining and not operational intra-EU new scheme.

28. When considering the triggering procedure, one could argue that closer cooperation is to some extent detrimental to the Commission, which has to share its right of initiative with the European Parliament, which is to be merely consulted (pillar I) or informed (pillar III). If one reckons however that the decision to initiate closer cooperation amounts to pooling or transfering more sovereignty at a higher level, the prerogatives of the Council and the MS only follow the logic of the current Treaty reform system. Once this decision has been taken, the Commission and the EP have the possibility to fully play their role which could be very significant as soon as closer cooperation involves costs to be borne by the Community budget or passing legislation. The impact on the interinstitutional balance is in fact rather neutral.

29. On 17 May 1999, the Council's Rules of Procedure have been adapted to answer some of these problems.

30. On the price paid for the extra-EU Schengen experience and on its relative success, see Monar (1997: 10–11, 15).

31. Devuyst (1999: 110). The Community orthodoxy was indeed always more a pious aspiration than a reality, the history of European integration being replete with 'tactical' transgressions.

32. Places where (some) federate units interact among themselves or with the federal level – what the federalist jargon called in a rather confusing way for specialists of international relations 'intergovernmental cooperation'.

BIBLIOGRAPHY

Areilza Carvacal, J.M. de (1998) 'Enhanced cooperations in the Treaty of Amsterdam: some critical remarks'. *Harvard Law School, The Jean Monnet Chair. Working Papers No. 13.*

Bribosia, H. (1998) 'Le Traité d'Amsterdam: Espoirs et déceptions'. In Y. Lejeune (ed.), *Le Traité d'Amsterdam: espoirs et déceptions*. Brussels: Bruylant.

Caporaso, J. A. (1996) 'The European Union and forms of state: Westphalian, Regulatory or Post-Modern?'. *Journal of Common Market Studies*, 34 (1).

CEPS (1999) 'A system for post-war South-East Europe'. *Working Document* No. 131, 3 May 1999.

Constantinesco, V. (1997) 'Les clauses de 'coopération renforcée'. Le protocole sur l'application des principes de subsidiarité et de proportionalité'. *RTD eur.*, 33(4), octobre–décembre, 751–67.

Cornes, R. and T. Sandler (1996), *The Theory of Externalities: Public Goods and Club Goods*. Cambridge: Cambridge University Press.

De Burca, G. (2000) 'Differentiation within the "Core"?: The case of the Internal Market'. In G. de Burca and J. Scott (eds), *Constitutional Change in the EU: From Uniformity to Flexibility?* Oxford: Hart Publishing, 133–73.

De La Serre, F. and H. Wallace (1997) 'Flexibility and enhanced cooperation in the European Union: placebo rather than panacea?'. *Research and Policy* (Groupement d'Etudes et de Recherches 'Notre Europe' – Paris), 2, September.

De Schoutheete, P. (1999) 'Closer cooperation: political background and issues in the negotiation'. In J. Monar and W. Wolfgang (eds), *The Treaty of Amsterdam*. London: Pinter.

De Zwaan, J. W. (1999), 'Flexibiliteit in het Verdrag van Amsterdam'. In *Flexibiliteit en het Verdrag van Amsterdam*. Asser Instituut Colloquium Europees Recht, T.M.C. Asser Press.

Dehousse, R. (1998) 'European institutional architecture after Amsterdam: parliamentary system or regulatory structure?' *RSC Working Paper*, No. 98/11.

Deubner, C. *et al.* (1999) 'Harnessing differentiation in the EU: flexibility after Amsterdam', SWP No. 5, 430. Ebenhausen: Stiftung Wissenschaft und Politik.

Devuyst, Y. (1999) 'The community-method after Amsterdam'. *Journal of Common Market Studies*, 37 (1).

Duff, A. (1998), In M. den Boer, A. Guggenbühl and S. Vanhoonacken (eds), *Coping with Flexibility after Amsterdam*. Maastricht: EIPA.

Ehlermann, C. D. (1984) 'How flexible is community law? An unusual approach to the concept of "two speeds"'. *Michigan Law Review*, 82, 1274–93.

Ehlermann, C. D. (1995) 'Différenciation accrue ou uniformité renforcée?'. *Revue du Marché Unique Européen*, 3, 191–218.

Ehlermann, C. D. (1998), *Differentiation, Flexibility, Closer Cooperation: The New Provisions of the Amsterdam Treaty*. Florence: European University Institute.

Feenstra, J. J. and K. J. M. Mortelmans (1985) *Gedifferentieerde integratie en Gemeenschapsrecht: Institutioneel- en materieelrechtelijke aspecten*. The Hague: WRR.

Gaja, G. (1998) 'How flexible is flexibility under the Amsterdam Treaty?' *Common Market Law Review*, 35 (4), 855–70.

Grabitz, E. (ed.) (1984) *Abgestufte Integration: Eine Alternative zum herkömmlichen Integrationskonzept?*. Strasbourg: N. P. Engel Verlag, Kehl am Rhein.

Kortenberg, H. (1998) 'Closer cooperation in the Treaty of Amsterdam'. *Common Market Law Review*, 35 (4), 833–54

Louis, J. V. (1996) 'Quelques réflexions sur la différenciation dans l'Union européenne'. In P. Manin and J. V. Louis (eds), *Vers une Europe différenciée? Possibilité et limite*. Paris: Pedone.

Metcalfe, L. (1998) 'Flexible integration in and after the Amsterdam Treaty'. In M. den Boer, A. Guggenbühl and S. Vanhoonacker (eds), *Coping with Flexibility and Legitimacy after Amsterdam*. Maastricht: European Institute of Public Administration.

Monar, J. (1997) 'Schengen and flexibility in the Treaty of Amsterdam: opportunities and risks of differentiated integration in EU Justice and Home Affairs'. In M. den Boer (ed.), *Schengen, Judicial Cooperation and Policy Coordination*. Maastricht: EIPA.

Moravcsik, A. and K. Nicolaïdis (1998) 'Federal ideals and constitutional realities in the Treaty of Amsterdam'. *Annual Review: Journal of Common Market Studies*, 36, 15–38.

Mueller C. (1997) *Perspectives on Public Choice: A Handbook*. Cambridge: Cambridge University Press.

Padoan, P. C. (1997), 'Regional agreements as clubs: the European case'. In E. D. Mansfield and H. V. Milner, *The Political Economy of Regionalism: New Directions in World Politics*. New York: Columbia University Press.

Philippart, E. and G. Edwards (1999) 'The provisions on closer cooperation in the Treaty on European Union: politics of multi-faceted system'. *Journal of Common Market Studies*, 37 (1), 102–103.

Philippart, E. and M. Sie Dhian Ho (2000), 'Flexibility and models of governance for the EU'. In G. de Burca and J. Scott (eds), *Constitutional Change in the EU: From Uniformity to Flexibility?* Oxford: Hart Publishing, 299–331.

Pierson, P. (1996) 'The path to European integration: a historical institutionalist analysis', *Comparative Political Studies*, 29 (2), 123–63.

Preston, C. (1995) 'Obstacles to EU enlargement: the classical community method and the prospects for a wider Europe'. *Journal of Common Market Studies*, 33 (3), 453–63.

Preston, C. (1997) *Enlargement and Integration in the European Union*. London: Routledge.

Schmitter, P. C. (1996), 'Imagining the future of the Euro-Polity'. In G. Marks *et al.*, *Governance in the European Union*. London: Sage.

Shaw, J. (1998) 'The Treaty of Amsterdam: challenges of flexibility and legitimacy', *European Law Journal*, 4 (1), 63–86.

Snyder, F. (1998) 'Comments'. In M. den Boer, A. Guggenbühl and S. Vanhoonacker (eds), *Coping with Flexibility and Legitimacy after Amsterdam*. Maastricht: European Institute of Public Administration.

Stubb, A. (1999), 'Negotiating flexible integration in the Amsterdam Treaty'. In K. Neunreither and A. Wiener (eds), *Amsterdam and Beyond: Institutional Dynamics and Prospects for Democracy*. Oxford: Oxford University Press.

Tuytschaever, F. (1999), *Differentiation in European Law*. Oxford: Hart.

Wallace, H. and W. Wallace (1995) *Flying Together in a Larger and More Diverse European Union*. Working Documents. The Hague: Netherlands Scientific Council for Government Policy.

Wallace, H. (1999) 'Flexibility: a tool of integration or a restraint on disintegration?'. In K. Neunreither and A. Wiener (eds), *Amsterdam and Beyond: the European Union on Its Way into the 21st Century*. Oxford: Oxford University Press.

Wessels, W. (1997) 'An ever closer fusion? A dynamic macropolitical view on integration processes'. *Journal of Common Market Studies*, 35 (2), 267–99.

Wessels, W. and B. Jantz (1997) 'Flexibilisierung/ Die Europäische Union vor einer neuen Grunsatzdebatte? Grundmodelle unter der Lupe'. In R. Hrbek (ed.), *Die Reform der Europäischen Union: Positionen und Perspektiven anläßlich der Regierungskonferenz*, Baden-Baden: Nomos Verlagsgesellschaft.

Ziller, J. (2000) 'Flexibility in the geographical scope of EU law'. In G. de Burca and J. Scott (eds), *Constitutional Change in the EU: From Uniformity to Flexibility?* Oxford: Hart Publishing, 113–33.

PART III

THE REFORMS IN MAJOR POLICY AREAS

CHAPTER 11

EU EMPLOYMENT AND SOCIAL POLICY AFTER AMSTERDAM: TOO LITTLE OR TOO MUCH?

Pier Carlo Padoan

INTRODUCTION

European governments have always been reluctant to give up their power in social policies and, for a long time, these have been firmly kept in the hands of national authorities. The idea of a European social policy gained some strength in the 1980s in the drive towards the Single Market and the Mediterranean enlargement. Discussion, however, dates back to the 1950s when, prior to the signing of the Treaty of Rome, the issue was whether harmonization of working conditions should be introduced along with trade liberalization. The Treaty of Rome endorsed the view that while improved working conditions were desirable no enforcement mechanism was necessary. Two areas were indicated for harmonization: equal pay for equal work for men and women and the maintenance of equivalence between paid holiday schemes, the former being introduced at the insistence of the French government.[1]

Little or no harmonization took place in the subsequent 15 years as no consensus was reached over the issue (only the French government was strongly in favour). Secondly, the high and stable growth environment which prevailed until the beginning of the 1970s coupled with the relatively limited amount of market openings produced little incentives for a supranational approach to social regulation (the so-called period of 'Adam Smith abroad and Keynes at home' which was based on strong national mixed economies and a substantial amount of trade liberalization, a largely different scenario from the present one where globalization and 'deep integration' are the dominant features). Finally, the characteristics of the early stage of European integration were such as to avoid major conflicts among Member States. Integration involved a similar economic system, which traded similar products (intra-industry trade) thus leaving little space for frictions such as the one that has been arising in the recent past, and likely to increase with the eastern enlargement, characterized by integration between different economies, leading to a larger share of trade between different products (inter-industry trade) where differences in labour costs and social conditions would, as we shall discuss below, clearly affect trade relations.

The high growth/smooth integration phase ended with the first oil shock. A new political consensus developed about the adoption of measures limiting regulatory competition within the Community. In 1974 the First Social Action Programme led to the adoption of a number of Directives concentrated in three areas: equal treatment of men and women with respect to pay, access to employment, vocational training and promotion, social security; labour law and working conditions; health and safety. Over the next decade two events changed radically the European scenario: the Single European Act and the membership of Greece, Portugal and Spain (1986), which significantly increased the diversity of Community membership in terms of per capita income levels and industrial specialization. The increased complexity of the Community also led to the substitution of unanimity with majority voting in a number of areas, such as health and safety at work. In 1989 the Commission issued the Community Charter of the Fundamental Social Rights of Workers, or Social Charter, which was adopted by all members with the exception of the UK, as the British Prime Minister argued that she would prefer competition among rules rather than common labour standards. The Charter led to a number of directives on health and safety and two harmonization directives, one on the duty of employers to inform employees in writing of employment conditions and another on more stringent conditions for collective redundancies. Another relevant decision was the doubling of the size of Structural Funds, which was to be complemented later, along with the start of the process on monetary integration, by the introduction of the Cohesion Fund in favour of the four poorest countries (Ireland, Greece, Portugal and Spain).

The next steps were the Agreement on Social Policy in the Maastricht Treaty (1992) and the Social Chapter (1997). The decision to include a social chapter in the Maastricht Treaty was mainly driven by the preoccupation that, with further deepening of the integration produced by progress towards monetary union, the risk of 'social dumping' was becoming more serious. Following the UK veto, with a Protocol on Social Policy annexed to the Treaty, the 12 member countries allowed 11 of them (with the exception of the UK) to sign an Agreement on social policy. The Agreement enlarged the possibilities of harmonization by extending qualified majority voting to: working conditions, information and consultation of workers, equality between men and women in labour markets, the integration of people excluded from labour markets. The Agreement was incorporated into the 'Social Chapter' (Chapter 1 of Title XI TEC, Articles

136–145 TEC) in 1997 when the new UK government put an end to this opt-out in the Amsterdam revision of the Maastricht Treaty.

The Social Chapter led to the adoption of four Directives: (a) the European works council directive, which gives to workers' representatives in multinational companies with at least 1000 employees within Member States, and at least 150 employees in each of at least two Member States, the right to be informed and consulted on management decisions through formal works councils or equivalent procedures; (b) the parental leave directive, which guarantees workers of either sex minimum unpaid leave of three months following the birth or adoption of a child, while keeping all their existing job rights; (c) the directive on equal treatment for part time employees, which grants them non-discriminatory treatment *vis-à-vis* full time workers though the proportionality of pay and benefits to time at work; (d) the directive concerning sex discrimination at the workplace, stating that once a case of sex discrimination has been established the employer is obliged to justify not having acted in a discriminatory manner.

The logic underlying the Social Chapter is simple: labour market regulation is basically left in the hands of national governments, with the role of the Union limited to a few minimum standards. This framework has to be completed with a brief description of the remaining aspects of EU social policy, especially if compared to the state of national regulations (CEPR, 1998). Most EU directives are generally less stringent than existing national laws. Three examples illustrate the point. In *workers' participation in business decisions* there is no relevant EU position. The main role of the Commission has been in supporting a dialogue between the Employers' Confederation of Europe (UNICE) and the European Unions Confederation (ETUC) and the main result has been their agreement on directive (c) recalled above. In *employment protection* there are only EU regulations regarding collective dismissals in which case managers must consult workers' representatives supplying them with information about the characteristics and justifications of the layoff plan. As far as *working hours* are concerned a directive on maximum working hours was adopted in 1993 (against UK opposition). The directive guarantees workers minimum daily and weekly rest periods, maximum weekly working time and minimum paid annual leave (four weeks). Directive levels are by far less restrictive than national ones in all countries with the exception of the UK, which had no regulation in this field. In addition, actual national levels are always far below/above the national legal maxima/minima in all countries. As a consequence EU directives do not represent a significant constraint in most labour contracts.

In the second place, even when EU-wide norms do represent an effective constraint, implementation into national laws is hardly straight-forward. As CEPR (1998) reports (European Commission, 1994), as of the end of 1993, of all directives applicable to employment and social policy Italy had transposed only 57 per cent into national laws, Luxembourg 59 per cent, Greece 67 per cent and Spain 68 per cent, while Portugal and the UK had reached 92 per cent. In addition, national enforcement mechanisms remain weak and tend to be looser when the norm is more binding (CEPR, 1998: 12).

The Treaty of Amsterdam introduced a new title into the EC Treaty dealing specifically with employment (Title VIII TEC). This is linked to the new general objective of promoting 'a high level of employment' (Article 2 TEU) and the extension of the Community's activities to the promotion 'of coordination between employment policies of the Member States with a view to enhancing their effectiveness by developing a coordinated strategy for employment' (Article 3(I) TEC). The new provisions define the promotion of employment as a 'matter of common concern' (Article 126(2) TEC) but are aimed only at the development of a 'coordinated strategy' (Article 125 TEC) and the encouragement of cooperation between Member States (Articles 127 and 129 TEC). Employment policies remain fully a matter of national competence. However, Article 128 provides for the adoption by the Council of annual *guidelines* that the Member States shall take into account in their employment policies. Each Member State has to draw up an annual report on measures taken to implement these guidelines. On the basis of these reports the Council, acting by a qualified majority on a recommendation by the Commission, may make specific *recommendations* to Member States (Article 128(4) TEC).

These rather vague new Treaty provisions were followed in the so-called 'Luxembourg process'. In the European Council held in Luxembourg, in December 1997, Member States agreed, under the pressure of a very dramatic employment situation in the EU,[2] to the definition of Employment Guidelines, which the Member States should follow, in setting their own National Action Plans for employment. These guidelines concerned, in particular, the support of young people in entering the labour market and the fight against long-term unemployment through extensive retraining. While these guidelines do not give rise to binding commitments they do signal the intention of the Union to strengthen collaboration and joint action in the area of working conditions. The Vienna European Council of December 1998 strengthened the approach (see below).

AN ASSESSMENT

The question one has to ask in assessing the contents of the Amsterdam Treaty with respect to its effects on the labour market and employment is:

is the Social Chapter appropriate to cope with the changes coming up in the new European environment marked by the establishment of Economic and Monetary Union and, in a few years time, enlargement to Central and Eastern Europe? The term 'appropriate' should be related to the two fundamental challenges the European Union will be facing in the years to come, unemployment and cohesion in a framework of monetary stability.

As it was made clear above, the idea underpinning the Social Chapter is that employment and labour market issues remain basically the responsibility of national governments. So our assessment requires consideration of a scenario where a supranational monetary policy coexists with national employment polices and, at the same time, countries with different social systems and labour market regulations come into much closer competition with one another. The problem with such a scenario is that is tangles up two different, if related, economic problems that have to be dealt with in the new European model: (a) the first one is to preserve monetary stability in such a way as not to constrain growth; (b) the second one is to preserve the competitiveness of national economies that have given up the exchange rate. These two economic problems are best dealt with by two different labour market models, neither of which is the one designed, if only implicitly, by the Amsterdam Treaty. Let us look at the two issues separately.

Labour markets and monetary stability

Economic and Monetary Union is built on the fundamental principle of monetary stability and one of the main pillars of EMU is the independence of the central bank, according to the widely held view that central bank independence is a necessary and sufficient condition for price stability.[3] This principle has been (partially) challenged in recent contributions (Iversen, 1998; Hall and Franzese, 1998) on the ground that the correlation between central bank independence and inflation has to be considered taking into account the characteristics of industrial relations and of the wage bargaining process in particular. More precisely, one result of these analyses is that the higher the level of wage bargaining coordination the more efficient and less costly in terms of unemployment is (independent) monetary policy in curbing inflation.

Wage coordination refers to a complex set of institutional arrangements, involving both trade unions and employer organizations that differ from country to country (Hall and Franzese, 1998). These actually involve five set of interactions: (a) the interaction, in each firm/sector (dyad), between workers' organizations and employers' organizations; (b) the interaction between the leaders of the bargaining organization and the rank-and-file members; (c) the interaction between the bargainers in each dyad and their counterparts in other dyads; (d) the interaction between the wage bargainers as a group and the policy authorities; (e) the interaction between monetary and fiscal policy authorities (which determines the actual degree of monetary policy independence).

It can be seen at a glance that all of these interactions are directly (the last) or indirectly (the first four) affected by the establishment of EMU. This point will be taken up later, let us now concentrate on the reasons why, for a given level of central bank independence, the structure of wage bargaining matters. To see the point, following Hall and Franzese (1998) consider the case where wage bargaining is not coordinated. In such a case each bargaining unit (a dyad of employer and union) has to reach an agreement while being uncertain about the results of agreements in other units. Three consequences follow. First, the union in each dyad will try to obtain an additional inflation increment in each wage settlement in order to protect itself from real wage losses resulting from other settlements that are more inflationary than its own. Second, as each bargaining unit is usually too small to have a substantial impact on the aggregate inflation rate, negotiators in each bargaining unit will not take into account aggregate considerations in their bargaining (free riding). Third, bargainers know that policy authorities will respond by adopting restrictive measures to *aggregate* inflationary wage behaviour, the result of which might be unemployment; however, they will not take into consideration this information in their behaviour as they know that policy action will be taken in response to an outcome (aggregate wage inflation) which is out of their control. In summary, in uncoordinated settings wage bargainers, both employers and unions, will be less responsive to threats of restrictive monetary policy even if central bank independence makes these threats credible.

Let us now look at the case of coordination where typically a 'lead bargain' sets the tune for the entire bargaining process. In such a case the lead bargain has a great influence over the level of economy-wide wage settlements. This leads to the following implications. First, as the members of each bargaining unit know what the results of other wage settlements are, they do not need to ask for extra inflationary concessions to protect themselves from unanticipated relative wage losses. Second, the lead bargainer is aware of the consequences of its actions over the whole economy both in terms of overall inflation and employment and, in particular, it will take into account in its bargaining the likely policy response. This makes the centralized bargainers highly sensitive in their settlements to signals coming from the central bank, especially if the latter enjoys a high degree of independence, which increases the credibility of monetary policy signals.

The implications of the above can be summarized as follows. If wage

Table 11.1 Monetary policy and wage bargaining regimes and results

	High unemployment	Low unemployment
High inflation	CBI low	CBI low
	CWB low	CWB high
Low inflation	CBI high	CBI high
	CWB low	CWB high

CBI = central bank independence, CWB = coordinated wage bargaining

bargaining is coordinated the central bank is able to influence the level of settlements, and hence of inflation, simply by signalling its policy intentions, so that monetary policy will not need to raise the level of unemployment. If wage bargaining is not coordinated, small bargaining units do not expect a direct response to their settlements and will not follow a self-restraint policy. In such a case the central bank will have to apply a stricter monetary policy stance, and hence produce higher unemployment, to reach its targets.

Following the considerations, Hall and Franzese propose and successfully test, the following three hypotheses: (a) there is a negative relationship between inflation and central bank independence (the traditional view about central bank independence and monetary stability); (b) the level of wage bargaining coordination has a direct effect on inflation irrespective of the role of central bank independence; (c) in cases where the level of wage coordination is low central bank independence lowers the rate of inflation only at the costs of higher rates of unemployment. Taken together, these three hypotheses determine a structure of monetary independence and wage bargaining structures leading to different macroeconomic performance patterns summarized in Table 11.1 and based on evidence, reported by Hall and Franzese, on the average performance of the OECD countries over the period 1955–90.

These results are, to some extent and as far as the rate of unemployment is concerned, confirmed by estimation results carried out by Nickell (1997), who also takes into account a wide range of institutional characteristics of national labour markets, and that will be discussed below. Before turning to this aspect we must look at some of the implications of the evidence discussed above for the operation of Economic and Monetary Union.

At first sight the implications are a source of concern. The framework set out by the Social Chapter introduces no incentive to increase the degree of wage bargaining centralization to match the degree of centralization and independence of monetary policy. As a matter of fact the establishment of EMU and of the European Central Bank *decreases* the level of wage bargaining centralization as it leaves it, in the best case, at the national level. The straightforward implication is that EMU will keep price stability at a higher cost in terms of unemployment with respect to cases where there is more wage bargaining centralization. In addition, according to this view, such higher costs would be unevenly distributed among different countries according to their levels of wage bargaining centralization, while facing the same degree of central bank independence; countries where this level is lower will suffer from higher unemployment.

Labour markets, flexibility and employment

The view just presented may be challenged, however. Another view (CEPR, 1995; Nickell, 1997) holds that the amount of unemployment, for a given level of monetary policy independence, is inversely correlated with the degree of labour market flexibility, itself dependent on the characteristics of the institutions regulating labour markets. In addition, with a supranational central bank, unemployment costs of monetary stabilization will be a function of the level of structural unemployment (i.e. the rate of unemployment not dependent on cyclical factors) which is the average of national levels of structural unemployment. In such a case what improves the smooth operation of monetary union is an increase in the level of labour market flexibility, itself dependent on national institutional characteristics.

A comprehensive review of this issue is presented in Nickell (1997) who studies the impact of labour market regulations on unemployment. To do so a set of indicators of labour market characteristics are calculated for a large number of OECD countries. A first inspection of such indicators (see Table 11.2) shows that continental European countries exhibit different degrees of labour market rigidities and that they are generally higher than in the UK and the US. These indicators have been regressed (Nickell, 1997) against different unemployment indicators (total unemployment, long term unemployment, short term unemployment) leading to results that can be summarized as follows. The unemployment rate is *positively* affected by: (unlimited) unemployment benefits, especially if associated with lack of incentives to accept jobs with lower pay rates and in different sectors; a high level of union militancy *without* a high level of coordination with employers' association in wage bargaining (which is equivalent to a *low* level of wage bargaining centralization as discussed above); high labour tax rates especially if associated with high minimum wages; a low level of workers' skills. The same analysis, however, shows that other labour market institutions do *not* affect the rate of unemployment, such as: workers' protection legislation and labour standards; unemployment benefits if they are accompanied by appropriate job search incentives;

Table 11.2 Labour market regulations in OECD countries

	Legal constraints on hiring and firing	Labour standards	Replacement rate of unemployment benefits (%)	Duration of unemployment benefits (years)	Active labour market policies (%)	Union coverage ratio (%)	Union coverage index	Trade union coordination in wage bargaining	Employers coordination in wage bargaining	Labour taxes paid by employers (%)	Overall labour taxes (%)
Austria	16	5	50	2	8.3	46.2	3	3	3	22.6	53.7
Belgium	17	4	60	4	14.6	51.2	3	2	2	21.5	49.8
Denmark	5	2	90	2.5	10.3	71.4	3	3	3	0.6	46.3
Finland	10	5	63	2	16.4	72	3	2	3	25.5	65.9
France	14	6	57	3	8.8	9.8	3	2	2	38.3	63.8
Germany	15	6	63	4	25.7	32.9	3	2	3	23	53
Ireland	12	4	37	4	9.1	49.7	3	1	1	7.1	34.3
Italy	20	7	20	0.5	10.3	38.8	3	2	2	40.2	62.9
Netherlands	9	5	70	2	6.9	25.5	3	2	2	27.5	56.5
Norway	11	5	65	1.5	14.7	56	3	3	3	17.5	48.6
Portugal	18	4	65	0.8	18.8	31.8	3	2	2	14.5	37.6
Spain	19	7	70	3.5	4.7	11	3	2	1	33.2	54.2
Sweden	13	7	80	1.2	59.3	82.5	3	3	3	37.8	70.7
Switzerland	6	3	70	1	8.2	26.6	2	1	3	14.5	38.6
United Kingdom	7	0	38	4	6.4	39.1	2	1	1	13.8	40.8
Canada	3	2	59	1	5.9	35.8	2	1	1	13	42.7
USA	1	0	50	0.5	3	15.6	1	1	1	20.9	43.8
Japan	8	1	60	0.5	4.3	25.4	2	2	2	16.5	36.3

high union militancy rates if associated with high levels of coordination with employers' associations in wage setting procedures (thus confirming evidence reported in the previous section).

The above results are relevant for our discussion especially from one point of view. While some labour market institutions may affect unemployment more than others it is their interaction that plays a relevant role. We can, therefore, draw some additional conclusions. Those reached in the previous paragraph are to some extent reinforced (with respect to the role of wage setting institutions) but they also shed only partial light on the issue as it is clear that the level of employment depends on labour market institutions other than those regulating wage setting procedures. Increased 'flexibility', understood as the appropriate combination of different labour market institutions, may increase employment perspectives for a given degree of monetary policy independence.

We are thus in a position to assess these results within the Social Chapter framework. By establishing minimum standards for working conditions, the above mentioned directives (b)–(d) do not introduce increasing rigidities that would negatively affect employment perspectives. Rather, the Social Chapter, within the EMU framework, may lead to an increase in institutional competition, the result of which might be an overall flexibility and, hence, lower unemployment costs of monetary stability with supranational central bank independence.

Institutional competition or social dumping?

The two elements we have been discussing above, the priority of a national as opposed to a European dimension in labour market policies and the relevance of the labour market institutions in affecting employment perspectives, have led many analysts and policy makers to describe the scenario that will prevail under EMU as one of 'institutional competition' or, even worse, of 'social dumping'. The point is simply clarified. Deeper international integration and 'globalization' increase competition between products and factor (especially labour) markets. To the extent that labour market regulations affect labour costs and hence competitiveness, the absence of a supranational labour market regulation, national (and subnational) regulatory bodies, often with the agreement of, or under the pressure of, workers' and employers' representative bodies, will tend to loosen labour market regulations in order to increase competitiveness. Better competitive positions, and hence better employment opportunities, could be the result of both cheaper domestic production costs and/or increased foreign capital inflows attracted by more favourable labour market conditions. As a consequence a 'race to the bottom' might result in labour regulations. This concern has been raised especially with respect to the EU's future enlargement to Central and Eastern European countries, which typically have much lower labour costs with respect to current EU members.[4]

The Social Chapter directive (a), mentioned above, partially deals with this issue to the extent that it calls for the consultation of workers' representatives in multinational companies and the right to be informed and consulted on management decisions. This directive would typically apply in decisions concerning plant relocation that is expected to take place as a consequence of 'social dumping'; however, consultation does not necessarily imply an impediment of any decision that workers' representatives would consider as hurting local employment oppor-tunities. In summary, although the directive points at the relevance of the problem, it does nothing to prevent the possibility of relocation and hence the risk of races to the bottom.

However, how real is this risk? Some empirical evidence might provide further insight. A first set of evidence (Padoan, 1997; CEPR, 1998: ch. 4) looks at the competition effect produced on the 'cohesion countries' of the European Union (Greece, Ireland, Portugal and Spain) and the core EU countries by the recent steps of European integration (the launching of the Single Market, the accession of Portugal, Spain and Greece, the launching of the Europe Agreements). Such evidence may provide some information about similar effects presumably generated by future enlargement waves. The changing environment in European integration over the 1980s has led to relevant changes in the trade specialization pattern of the European Union. In particular: (i) the peripheral ('cohesion') countries have gone through an intense process of restructuring in trade specialization; (ii) sectors where most changes have taken place have been the labour intensive and the labour and capital intensive ones (i.e. those sectors where three out of four peripheral countries – Greece, Portugal, and Spain – have their strongest competitive positions); (iii) an important process of geographical and sectoral trade restructuring has taken place over the period considered, and the peripheral countries have reacted positively to the changing trade environment; (iv) the core European Union countries have benefited from increased trade integration with Central and Eastern European countries in the period following the fall of the communist regimes.

Regional deepening in Europe has also led to an increase in the cross border activity of firms, both EU and non-EU, in terms of mergers and acquisitions as well as foreign direct investment (FDI). This process, however, has followed different patterns across sectors and countries. Knowledge intensive sectors have been characterized by stronger trans-national activities, which have led to polarization of production speciali-zation in core countries. Evidence (Padoan, 1997; CEPR, 1998) shows that

FDI and trade specialization patterns in core European countries led to polarization effects (i.e. concentration in the centre economies); nonetheless, diffusion of investment towards the peripheral EU countries is present and, in some cases, substantial. Some diffusion of production activities takes place in knowledge intensive and, especially, in more traditional sectors. However national (more than sectoral) differences emerge. Countries such as Spain and Ireland are successful in attracting FDI, which results in strengthening trade comparative advantages, while others, such as Greece, much less so, with Portugal taking an intermediate position.

Considering the European experience a more general conclusion could be drawn. Globalization leads to polarization effects, especially in knowledge intensive sectors, but important diffusion effects may also take place. The extent of this latter aspect in providing support to regional cohesion, i.e. whether peripheral countries benefit from increasing competition, depends on sectoral and, more importantly, on national characteristics as peripheral regions and countries compete with each other to attract FDI.

In summary, the possibility that races to the bottom may increase employment opportunities in peripheral countries at the cost of employment in core countries (to the extent that employment is directly correlated to trade competitiveness) is high in traditional, labour intensive sectors, while since advanced (knowledge, human capital, and R&D intensive) sectors tend to concentrate in core countries, races to the bottom would hurt much less these sectors and the countries where these sectors are concentrated. In other words, social dumping would be the consequence of conflicts between unskilled workers in 'core' and 'periphery' countries, both current and future members of the EU.

A second set of evidence (Padoan, 2000)[5] is related to the effects of international competition on employment and wage levels in manufacturing sectors in the core EU countries and it is useful in assessing the degree of exposure of these economies to competition from low wage countries. Estimation results[6] show that labour markets in continental European countries, irrespective of the manufacturing sector considered, react to international competition more through changes (decreases) in employment levels than through wage cuts, contrary to the case of the United Kingdom and of the smaller Nordic countries[7]. This can be taken as evidence of a generalized 'labour market rigidity' in continental Europe. Secondly, international competition exherts a stronger (negative) pressure on both wages and employment levels in sectors where the country exhibits a trade comparative *disadvantage*, while such a pressure is much weaker or absent in sectors where the country enjoys a comparative *advantage*. This implies that the assertion that international competition, which may be increased by forms of social dumping, will hurt especially unskilled labour intensive sectors must be qualified. (For instance Italy, which has a comparative advantage in traditional labour intensive sectors, does not show strong pressures on its labour markets in these sectors.) One important implication for the issue under discussion is the following. The role of labour market institutions which do affect performance of both wage and employment levels cannot be separated from the role of other factors (most notably, cumulated learning, scale effects, and specific knowledge) which determine the overall trade performance of a sector. In this respect social dumping could result in only limited benefits for low wage countries in the case in which *additional* competitive factors (such as e.g. infrastructure and fiscal incentives) are not available.

It might be argued, on the other hand, that the enlargement towards Central and Eastern Europe will put a much stronger pressure on western European labour markets to the extent that labour costs in the former countries are far below the EU average and, consequently, the effects of 'social dumping' would be much stronger. Should it be then appropriate that these countries upgrade their labour market and social regulations to the level of the most advanced EU economies? This is questionable. On the one hand, as CEPR (1998) shows, four of the five fast track Central and Eastern European Countries already have regulations of collective dismissals comparable to those of the EU countries. There are gaps between national regulations and the social *acquis* but the accession countries do not have to fill them in one go. On the other hand, upgrading of their regulation to EU standards too quickly might have the paradoxical effects of slowing down, rather than speeding up, the enlargement process as the possibility of these economies to compete successfully in an integrated market could be weakened.

To conclude this point, the central issue, both with respect to the 'cohesion' countries and with the Central and Eastern European ones, is whether upgrading social regulations in these countries would increase their labour costs thus hurting their competitiveness both in their domestic production and in their ability to attract FDI. The point may be restated in more general terms as follows. The shape and intensity of labour and social regulations is a component of national comparative advantages, in the sense that, for example, looser labour regulations in one country are equivalent to making labour more abundant, and thus less expensive, in that country. To what extent should an EU wide regulation alter these comparative advantages by imposing changes in domestic regulation?

The benefits of integration and social regulation

From a theoretical standpoint the benefits of integration are maximized when each country specializes according to its comparative advantage. To the extent that social regulations are a component of comparative advantage, any attempt to introduce common regulations would produce a distortion and a decrease in welfare as it would 'cancel out' differences in comparative advantage. So the issue becomes: to what extent should social norms and regulations be considered a determinant of comparative advantage? If one takes the view that the only effect of social regulation is to affect labour costs then the ultimate effect of changes in social regulation would be to make labour relatively more or less abundant. However this is only a part of the story. To the extent that elimination of labour market regulations has the effect of redistributing income across factors of production this might decrease efficiency.

In other cases, however, labour market regulations might prevent market failures. In the first case (distortions) comparative advantages would be strengthened by deregulation, in the second case (market failures) they would be weakened. For example, minimum wages and unemployment benefits that make workers less willing to accept some job offerings will redistribute income away from employers to workers. In such a case there might be a trade-off between efficiency and the level of social protection on which the policy-maker would have to pick a point, so legislation would have to be designed taking into account the effects of such a choice on national comparative advantage. In some other cases, however, social protection (e.g. high firing and hiring costs) imply a redistribution from unemployed (outsiders) to employed (insiders) thus decreasing overall employment opportunities while not raising the level of social protection. The effects of labour legislation on national comparative advantage are in such a case quite clear and the policy choices in favour of the insiders, for example, would reflect a rent-seeking pattern of policy making.

As an example of the second case (market failure), consider the case of unemployment insurance. If workers have an inadequate access to financial markets that prevents them from borrowing to sustain consumption in case of a job loss, then a mandatory state insurance scheme will spread risk across the population, thus increasing overall social protection, otherwise only workers with the higher risks of being unemployed will invest in an insurance scheme, making it overall more expensive to cope for the higher risk (adverse selection). Health and safety regulations are another example. If working conditions are not fully known to workers, they could not be fully covered by higher wages. In such a case compulsory insurance is needed both to protect workers and to avoid decreasing the incentives to find employment in innovative sectors where severe health and safety problems are often present.

This second example points to another aspect of the linkage between labour regulations and comparative advantage: sector specific aspects of labour market legislation. As Soskice points out (Soskice, 1998), the optimum amount of labour flexibility and mobility varies with product specialization. For example, electronic industries characterized by diffused network externalities and intra-firm complementarity will be best served by labour regulations favouring high mobility, and hence, for examle, personal employment insurance schemes and low hiring and firing costs will favour high mobility of specialized workers across firms. On the other hand, scale-intensive industries (for example, transport equipment) will be best served by legislation supporting longer term employment as this will favour investment in firm-specific skills. These considerations reinforce the view that labour legislation is, to some extent at least, a component of national comparative advantage. The implication is that a race to the bottom (social dumping) is not the most likely scenario in a diversified economy such as the European one. Rather one should expect the diversification of national labour standards according to national comparative advantages. In such a case 'institutional competition' is a desirable scenario to the extent that, given some minimum standards directed at preventing market failures, reinforces specialization and hence the benefits from integration. From such a point of view the 'minimalistic approach' taken in the Amsterdam Treaty is the appropriate one.

The Luxembourg Process

The Stability and Growth Pact guarantees that, once monetary convergence has been obtained and a single monetary policy becomes feasible, national fiscal policies are managed according to common guidelines. However, the sustainability of monetary union requires that some market adaptation is obtained. Consequently, as one cannot rely on market forces alone to produce this convergence, monetary union requires the adoption of appropriate micro (structural) policies to overcome labour and product market rigidities. The extent of harmonization or convergence of micro policies towards common standards required by EMU remains to be seen and evidence discussed above shows little sign in this respect over the recent past. The Luxembourg, Cardiff and Cologne processes[8] are based on procedures that might provide limited convergence in such policies.

This approach is still very much in its infancy and is, in many respects, still way behind the degree of implementation we observe for budget policies. To explore the implications of such an approach, we consider in more detail the case of employment policies within the Luxembourg process. This is particularly relevant (also taking into account the evidence discussed above) in that no 'institutional dumping' process seems to be at work in the EU, hence any convergence in social policies should be seen rather as a 'race to the top'. It is interesting to check, therefore, to what extent the existing policy framework can support such a process.

In a nutshell, the EU employment policy framework operates as follows. Each year every EU Member State sets out its National Action Plan (NAP) which contains the policy actions it has taken towards the improvement of employment opportunities. The general philosophy of the approach is that flexibility in European labour markets can be obtained by moving away from 'passive' employment policies, such as unemployment benefits, towards 'active' policies, such as welfare-to-work schemes, and active learning and retraining. Within the process, however, a wide range of policies is considered including policies targeted at supporting small and medium enterprises.

Policies are implemented at the national level, as only national governments have jurisdictions over such policies. They are classified according to a (long) list of 'policy guidelines' set out by the Commission and grouped under four headings: employability (employment policies in a strict sense such as the implementation of placing agencies), adaptability (policies aimed at adapting workers to the new market conditions such as retraining policies), entrepreneurship (policies aimed at improving the demand side of the labour market, such as incentives for small business), equal opportunity (policies aimed at increasing the employment opportunities for women).

Each year NAPs are presented to the Commission and reviewed by Member States through a 'peer review' procedure. A final 'score' is assigned to each government identifying the degree of fulfilment of policy guidelines as well as the identification of best practices. Policy recommendations are then directed to each Member State by the Commission and the Council. The early experience shows that countries differ greatly in performance, partially reflecting their specific market structures and institutions. Second, any evaluation process based on qualitative guidelines – rather than specific quantitative targets (such as in the Maastricht process) – can at best produce a 'scoreboard' but it remains unclear to what extent any national government feels compelled to adapt its policies according to Commission recommendations. In fact, only the first two guidelines, reduction of both youth and long-term unemployment, are associated with quantitative indicators and are also the guidelines which appear to have influenced national policy action more effectively.[9]

As mentioned, national governments retain full control of policy, are not subject to any explicit obligaton,[10] and failure to follow recommendations is not associated with any punishment and/or exclusion threat as was the case with monetary union. In other words, as we move away from policies in which the supranational element prevails the strength of the convergence process weakens.

It would inappropriate, however, to jump to the conclusion that in areas where there is no explicit obligation to adjust to a Union rule there are also no incentives for national policies to change. Two distinct incentive sets would be operating in a such a case: a 'competition' incentive and a 'cooperation' (regime building) incentive. The competition incentive derives from both the policy arena and from the market. A poor performing country in improving its employment policies, for example, would see her reputation weaken and, consequently, her leverage in the design and implementation of EU policies at large would diminish. This would be particularly worrying whenever the intergovernmental dimension is relevant. In addition, markets would punish a poor performer to the extent that inefficient policies would make that country less attractive for investment while good performers would presumably enjoy larger investment as their perceived profitability would be enhanced. This aspect will be increasingly relevant in a world of high capital mobility. In short, institutional competition will not go away, rather it may well produce a healthy improvement in EU economic performance as long as it takes the form of exchange of best practices and provides content to the principle of subsidiarity.

The cooperation incentive is relevant to the extent that poor performance in any member of EMU weakens the performance and attractiveness of Euroland as a whole *vis-à-vis* the rest of the world. In other words, poor policy and economic performance in any one member of the club decreases the quality of the club good (monetary union), generating a negative externality on the other club members. This will presumably lead to strengthened peer pressure on the poor performer from the rest of the club members (and from the Commission). In this case the supranational, rather than the intergovernamental, dimension would prevail.

To the extent that such an incentive structure is strengthened, policy convergence could well be the result of the interaction of intergovernmentalism and supranationality.

SUMMARY AND CONCLUSIONS

Is the Social Chapter, as designed by the Amsterdam Treaty, appropriate to cope with the new European environment marked by the establishment of Economic and Monetary Union and Eastern enlargement? The basic idea underpinning the Social Chapter is that employment and labour market issues remain the responsibility of national governments. So one should consider a scenario where a supranational monetary policy coexists with national employment polices and, at the same time, countries with different social systems and labour market regulations come into much closer competition one with the other.

We have first looked at the relationship between monetary policy independence and wage bargaining centralization. In the Social Chapter no incentive is present to increase the degree of wage bargaining centralization to match the degree of centralization and independence of monetary policy. Rather, the establishment of EMU decreases the level of wage bargaining centralization as it leaves it, in the best case, at the national level. The implication is that EMU will obtain price stability at a higher cost in terms of unemployment. In this respect, therefore the framework set out by the Amsterdam Treaty is not up to the new framework.

Another view maintains that the amount of unemployment, for a given level of monetary policy independence, is inversely correlated with the degree of labour market flexibility, itself dependent on the institutions regulating labour markets. However, evidence shows that while some labour market institutions may affect unemployment more than others it is their interaction that plays a relevant role. Increased 'flexibility', understood as the appropriate combination of different labour market institutions, may increase employment perspectives for a given degree of monetary policy independence. The provisions of the Social Chapter, to the extent that they establish minimum standards for working conditions, do not represent a risk of increasing rigidity, i.e. regulation that would negatively affect employment perspectives. Rather, the Social Chapter may lead to an increase in institutional competition, the result of which might be overall flexibility and, hence, lower unemployment costs of monetary stability with supranational central bank independence.

The possibility of institutional competition opens the way to a scenario of social dumping. Available economic evidence shows that the possibility of races to the bottom which increase employment opportunities in peripheral countries is strong in traditional, labour intensive, sectors. Conversely, innovative sectors concentrate in core EU countries, hence races to the bottom would hurt much less these sectors and the countries where these sectors are concentrated. In other words social dumping implies conflicts between unskilled workers in 'core' and 'periphery' countries, both current and future members of the EU. Relevant, in this respect, is the attitude that should be taken with respect to Central and Eastern European countries as it remains unclear whether upgrading social regulations in these countries would increase their labour costs thus hurting their competitiveness.

This leads to a more general point. As the shape and intensity of labour and social regulations are a component on national comparative advantages, to what extent should an EU-wide regulation alter these comparative advantages by imposing changes in national regulation? The approach taken in the Amsterdam Treaty clearly rules out this possibility by allowing fundamental autonomy to national policies. As a consequence one should expect an increasing diversification of national labour standards according to national comparative advantages. This implies that 'institutional competition' is a desirable scenario to the extent that, given some minimum standards, directed at preventing market failures, it reinforces specialization and hence the benefits from integration. Hence, from such a point of view the 'minimalistic approach' taken in the Amsterdam Treaty is the appropriate one.

This scenario, however, has been somewhat modified by the Vienna Summit which introduces a European dimension to employment and social policies. The strategy is consistent with the 'Luxembourg process', which calls for the definition of National Action Plans regarding employment policies and is based on a 'peer pressure' approach according to which each Member State is subject to scrutiny by the other Member States. It is still too early to see whether this process will lead to positive results in terms of higher employment and/or whether institutional competition will increase the degree of flexibility of European labour markets. It is however likely that institutional competition will raise the overall level of adaptability of the European economy. The implication is that, as this process evolves, the Social Chapter designed by the Amsterdam Treaty will probably need to be updated to cope with a new European Social Model that will result from the combination of institutional competition and 'peer pressure'.

NOTES

1. This introductory part draws on the excellent summary presented in CEPR (1998).
2. The average unemployment rate was well above 10 per cent, with much higher values in some member countries and regions.
3. For a recent reassessment of the issue see Eijffinger and De Haan (1996).
4. Central and Eastern European countries have hourly labour costs which are from one third to one tenth of EU average. See CEPR (1998), Table 4.4.
5. See Padoar (2000).
6. Based on a model suggested by Neven and Wyplosz (1996).
7. This is often referred to as the major difference between Anglo-Saxon (UK and US) and continental European labour markets.
8. The Cardiff Process involves the adoption of measures aimed at improving the performance of product markets. The Luxembourg process deals with employment policies. The Cologne Process calls for enhanced interaction between micro and macro policies.
9. The Lisbon European Council has set an explicit quantitative target for EU

employment and the Nice European Council has adopted a list of performance indicators to evaluate EU policies.

10. In some areas of course national governments must fulfill obligations emanating from Commission Directives such as those related to the prohibition of implementing state aids.

BIBLIOGRAPHY

European Commission (1994) *European Social Policy: A Way Forward for the Union.* COM(94) 333, Brussels.

CEPR (1995) *Monitoring European Integration 5: Unemployment Choices for Europe,* London.

CEPR (1998) *Monitoring European Integration 8, Social Europe: One for All?* London.

Eijffinger S. and J. De Haan (1996) *The Political Economy of Central Independence,* Special Paper in International Economy 19, Princeton, NJ: Princeton U.P.

Hall, P. and R. Franzese (1998) 'Mixed signals: Central Bank independence, coordinated wage bargaining, and European Monetary Union'. *International Organization,* 52, 505–35.

Iversen, T. (1998) 'Wage bargaining, Central Bank independence, and the real effects of money', *International Organization,* 52, 469–504.

Neven, D. and C. Wyplosz (1996) *Relative Prices and Trade Restructuring in European Industry,* CEPR Discussion Paper No. 1451.

Nickell, S. (1997) 'Unemployment and labour market rigidities: Europe versus North America'. *Journal of Economic Perspectives,* 11 (3).

Padoan, P. C. (1997), 'Globalization and European regional integration', *Economia Internazionale,* November.

Padoan, P. C. (ed.) (2000) *Employment and Growth in Monetary Union.* Cheltenham: Edgar Elgan.

Soskice, D. (1998) 'Openness and diversity in transatlantic economic relations'. In B. Eichengreen (ed.), *Transatlantic Economic Relations in the Post-Cold War Era.* New York: Council on Foreign Relations.

Internet

URL: http://europa.eu.int/council/off/conclu/dec98.htm

CHAPTER 12

REFORM OF THE CFSP: FROM MAASTRICHT TO AMSTERDAM

Dieter Mahncke

THE PROGRESS OF EUROPEAN INTEGRATION: MONETARY UNION WITHOUT FOREIGN POLICY INTEGRATION?

Next to defence and finance (military force and money) foreign policy is the third component of the hard core of national sovereignty, which is precisely the reason why the European Union, politically incomplete as it is, lacks both a common foreign policy and a common defence (at least in terms of a specifically *European* defence; of course, the European Member States of NATO do possess a common defence within the framework of the Alliance, and to no mean degree even a common foreign policy is often enough achieved within this framework).

Of course, the question arises of why this is apparently different for monetary policy – at least for those 12 Member States of the Union that have made the decision to introduce a common currency. Surely, the reason for this difference is not that the Europeans felt a particularly urgent need for unity in this area or that they simply for the sake of progress in European integration chose to begin with monetary union, hoping that advances in other areas would soon follow leading to further significant integration and ultimately to real political union.

It is true that there were two important *lobbies* that exerted pressure: first of all, the big international corporations, operating throughout Europe, in whose obvious economic interest a common currency is, and secondly, the 'integrationists' in Europe, i.e. those protagonists of European political unity who are not only willing to support all forms of integration but in particular expect from monetary union a decisive thrust toward political union. Ultimately, however, the road toward monetary union was opened up by two other factors. First, there is the motive on the part of many Europeans (perhaps particularly on the part of France) to limit, to control and ultimately to eliminate the strength and consequently the dominance of the German Mark. For this they are prepared to sacrifice their own, usually weaker national currencies.

The second factor was German reunification. The thesis has been expressed that France explicitly asked Germany for the introduction of a common currency in return for French support for German unity. Whether or not this was the case, it is correct that the German government in the process of reunification promised that united Germany would be irrevocably and firmly tied into the network of European integration, and that, indeed, German reunification should go along with the enhanced development of the European integration process. In the event this meant – under some pressure from France – monetary integration. As a matter of principle Germany, a consistently stalwart supporter of European integration, had no problem with this; it did insist, however, that the common currency should be a strong and stable currency, orientated along the concepts and guidelines of the German Bundesbank (Hefeker, 1997: 39–71).

In other words, the advent of the Euro probably reflects the current status of European integration to a much lesser extent than the intended common foreign policy does. True, monetary union may indeed lead to a significant thrust towards further integration as many of the supporters expect. That would necessarily also affect and influence the development towards a common foreign and security policy. But for the moment the goal of a common foreign and security policy is still in a field of its own, which in more ways than one highlights the core questions of integration facing Europe today:

- how much do the European states have in common,
- how can this common ground – in interests, attitudes and activities – be extended,
- do the European states in fact want to extend it,
- and, in particular, if they do want to extend it, how can it be done?

To put it differently: where do the Europeans want to go, and what needs to be done to achieve the desired end? Is there a clear objective, or is it the very lack of such an objective (or – worse – fundamentally different views on what the objective should be) that represents one of the main obstacles to further integration today? Are the majority of Europeans still convinced that political union is a desirable and necessary aim in the no longer divided and enlarged Europe of today? And what would be the immediate and longer-term implications for a common foreign and security policy?

MOTIVES FOR A COMMON FOREIGN AND SECURITY POLICY

Three main motives for the creation of a common foreign and security policy can be discerned. First, there is a feeling – mainly among the protagonists of further integration – that a uniting Europe would necessarily have to develop a common foreign and security policy, and in the long run also a common defence policy and ultimately even a common defence. It is, so the argument runs, simply logical and even inevitable that a uniting Europe would require a common foreign policy and a common defence (Gehring, 1995: 4–9). The weakness of this argument, of course, is the presupposition that the project of a united Europe is firmly on the agenda and will in fact come about.

A second motive is based on the expectation that a common European foreign policy is likely to have more weight in the world than the various policies of small or medium-sized European nation-states. This is plausible. Here, too, however, a reservation needs to be made, for most of the European states have obviously grasped that the extent to which they succeed in 'Europeanizing' their specific national interests, that is in 'selling' national interests as European interests, these (national) interests can be pursued with correspondingly more weight, namely the weight of having 'Europe' behind them. One can safely assume that at least some of the support for a common foreign policy comes from such expectations.

The third motive is more difficult to assess. It has to do with the end of the Cold War, the new complexity of global politics and new challenges as well as the somewhat uncertain feeling that in the future Europeans may have to rely more on themselves and may even be called upon to act independently. In such circumstances it may be wise to act together. Apparently, this motive has been reinforced by developments in the Balkans, specifically with regard to Kosovo, and was the background for the initiative taken by British Prime Minister Tony Blair in Pörtschach in October 1998 and St Malo in December 1998. In Pörtschach, Blair called for a strengthening of a European security and defence identity and, in particular, for the development of adequate European military capabilities that would allow the Europeans to act independently in situations where the United States might choose not to become involved. In St Malo these demands were repeated in a joint statement with France and with specific reference to the European Union (Adam *et al.*, 1999: 145–8).

It is worth noting that Britain and France came up with this joint statement, although their motives may not have been identical. While Britain clearly sees a necessity for the Europeans to prepare themselves for situations where action would be required – in the European interest – but not forthcoming from the United States, France, at least in the past, has shown an interest in reducing American influence in Europe and becoming 'less dependent' on the United States.

Of course, these three sets of motivations can be found in different blends and intensity among the different Member States, particularly as far as the first motive – a common foreign policy being a logical consequence of a uniting Europe – is concerned. These differences also become evident when looking at the question of how, in concrete terms, a common foreign and security policy is to be brought about. It is remarkable that one can detect two quite different approaches here.

The first approach – let us say the more reserved (or intergovernmental) one – argues that wherever common interests clearly exist close intergovernmental cooperation could and should lead to a common foreign policy. But common interests are not likely to be the norm; there would remain many, and perhaps substantially different, national interests. The Member States should be able to pursue these interests in a national context and perhaps in different ways. They should not be forced into a common foreign policy 'straitjacket', an effort that would be bound to fail anyway.

The other approach – one might call it the more optimistic (or integrationist) approach – proceeds from the assumption that common interests in foreign and security questions are in fact more encompassing and fundamental than is usually recognized. Moreover, the practice of cooperation would allow these common elements to grow further. Consequently (and this is where the real qualitative difference to the first approach is to be found), the Member States of the European Union should be tied into procedures that would assure common policies even in critical and difficult cases and even when there are initially different national viewsSuch a procedure would be acceptable because of the already existing broad common base, and it would be justified because there are 'higher' European interests, so to say a European *Staatsräson* which ultimately places the assurance of common European policies higher than the pursuit of particular national interests. To put it bluntly, the Member States should be pushed toward common policies by institutional arrangements (e.g. by qualified majority voting).

The significant difference between these two approaches can be illustrated by an example. One might imagine a democratic state defining its foreign policy not by the elected government, supported by a majority in parliament, but by negotiations between the different parties in parliament. Where common interests were found (or in this case, similar views on the common interest) a common foreign policy would be achieved. Where this was not the case each party would pursue its own foreign policy. Obviously, the supporters of the integrationist approach would call this madness, but the intergovernmentalists' response would be that, as far as Europe is concerned, this is simply the reflection of reality. The fact is, they would point out, that there is no common state in Europe – and many do not even want it. Hence, an area as important as foreign and security policy must remain under national sovereignty. Whenever common policies are to be pursued these must be negotiated and agreed upon in each case by national governments. This, the intergovernmentalists would argue, is not only realistic but also entirely sufficient. (In parenthesis it might be added that, although they do not find sympathy with the supporters of a united Europe, they can point with some justification to the experience within the framework of the CSCE in the 1970s and 1980s. Over a period of many years and on the basis of purely intergovernmental procedures – although supported by European Political Cooperation – the West developed a truly common foreign and security policy with substance, with coherence and with remarkable success. Of course, this was during the Cold War, there was pressure on all from the Soviet Union, and it took place largely in the framework of NATO and under significant leadership by the United States: singular circumstances that are now lacking, but which may partly explain the deficiency of a common European foreign policy.)

The crux of the issue is indeed whether the intergovernmental approach is sufficient. Certainly it seems that the events in Kosovo – with the almost negligible European performance in the spring of 1999 – may lead to (or has led to?) some rethinking on the part of Europeans. At least, there is a general feeling that European capacity must be improved, although, once again, capacity is seen more in terms of military capability than political performance, and even in the area of military capabilities the declaration of intentions on the European level stands in stark contrast to the development of defence budgets on the national levels.[1]

TASKS FOR A COMMON FOREIGN AND SECURITY POLICY

With regard to the common foreign and security policy the Amsterdam Treaty stipulates that such cooperation should cover 'all areas of foreign and security policy' (Article 11(1) TEU), a stipulation which can be fully appreciated only by those who know how long it took and how difficult it was to bring *any* foreign and security policy matters at all into the realm of the European Union. The Member States are committed to 'support the Union's external and security policy actively and unreservedly', and they 'shall refrain from any action which is contrary to the interests of the Union or likely to impair its effectiveness as a cohesive force in international relations' (Article 11(2) TEU). In particular, the common foreign and security policy 'shall include all questions relating to the security of

the Union, including the progressive framing of a common defence policy
. . . which might lead to a common defence, should the European Council
so decide' (Article 17(1) TEU). In contrast to Maastricht the improvement
is slight, though discernible, the 'eventual framing of a common defence
policy' having been replaced by the somewhat more intentional 'progressive framing'. Both a common defence policy and a common defence,
however, remain subject to a unanimous decision by the European Council, a result disappointing to some, but more could hardly have been
expected.

Specifically included in the Treaty are the so-called 'Petersberg tasks'.
This means that these tasks, defined in 1992 as tasks for WEU, have now
become tasks of the European Union. They 'include humanitarian and
rescue tasks, peace-keeping tasks and tasks of combat forces in crisis
management, including peace-making' (Article 17(2) TEU). This means
that the EU can now take decisions on the employment of combat forces,
although, at least as far as the Treaty of Amsterdam is concerned, the
actual task will not be carried out by the EU itself, but on request by
WEU. The Union 'will avail itself of the WEU to elaborate and implement
decisions and actions of the Union which have defence implications'
(Article 17(3) TEU). Of course, this primarily refers to the 'Petersberg
tasks', while collective defence would remain the exclusive responsibility
of the North Atlantic Treaty Organization. The common foreign and
security policy of the Union is indeed required to 'be compatible' with the
common security and defence policy established within the framework of
NATO (Article 17(1) TEU).

In the Maastricht Treaty, the WEU was already referred to as an integral
part of the development of European Union. In Amsterdam, France and
Germany among others asked for the full integration of WEU into the EU,
but this was firmly refused by Britain (Davidson, 1997: 66). The compromise (in Article 17(1) TEU) was the commitment to 'foster closer institutional relations with the WEU with a view to the possibility of the
integration of the WEU into the Union'.

At the time this seemed like a somewhat ambivalent compromise at
best, but it did not foreclose further movement. And indeed, at the EU
summit meeting in Cologne in June 1999 – after Kosovo and after the
movement in the British position as signalled by Pörtschach and St Malo
– the decision was made that by the end of the year 2000 the European
Union should take over all tasks of WEU in which case WEU 'as an
organisation' will have fulfilled its function.[2]

This seems like a logical move if the European Union is to develop a
clearer capability for action and if it is to become a more decisive actor in
crisis situations like Kosovo. Certainly, there may be difficulties in the
details, but they are likely to be less important than some observers expect:

- First of all, the quasi-automatic assistance clause in case of an attack, contained in Article V of the Brussels Treaty, which might form an obstacle for the neutral members of the Union, is not an essential requirement because those EU Member States that are NATO members have equivalent assurances in the Washington Treaty.[3] Furthermore, another *à la carte* element (allowing the neutrals to opt out) in the European Union is more than questionable, not only because 'neutrality' has become a disputable concept in today's Europe, but also because the European Union was not intended to be an organization in which members participate in those activities and undertake such commitments which seem immediately advantageous to them, while 'opting out' of all obligations that are burdensome or not immediately beneficial. The Union has allowed this development to become common in the past few years, but unless it stops this trend or at least returns to a firm core of political commitment it will continue on the 'slippery slope' towards something similar to an enhanced free trade area.
- Secondly, some of the organs of WEU could very well be taken over by the EU. WEU has set up a Defence Planning Cell, a Situation Centre and a satellite interpretation centre in Spain, has arranged for regular meetings of chiefs-of-staff and other military officers, and has developed procedures for military–political decision-making. In addition, it has earmarked certain forces for potential tasks and developed an exercise programme for these forces. All of this seems 'usable'. After all, the informal EU meeting of Foreign Ministers in Reinhartshausen in March 1999 declared that in order to fulfil the Petersberg tasks the Union would need a Defence Council, a Military Committee and a European military staff including a Situation Centre.[4] In most of these areas WEU has gained experience and undertaken some steps which the EU would not only require but could easily accept. Remarkably enough, this was taken up by the Finnish Presidency, which called for participation of EU Defence Ministers in the EU General Affairs Council meeting in November 1999.[5]
- Thirdly, the relationship with NATO is less problematical than it may seem. Again, the EU will benefit from the work already done by WEU. After all, the NATO Declaration, issued on the occasion of NATO's 50th anniversary in April 1999, expressly welcomes the intention of creating a European defence and security identity, including the capability for crisis control activities in situations in which the Alliance as a whole is not involved.[6]
- Finally, there is the question of the 'quasi members' of WEU: the observers (the neutrals: Austria, Finland, Ireland, Sweden as well as Denmark), the associated members (NATO members that are not EU members: Norway, Turkey, Iceland, Hungary, Poland, Czech Republic)

and the associated partners (the remaining central European states: Bulgaria, Estonia, Latvia, Romania, Slovakia, Slovenia). Here one could think of a programme similar to NATO's Partnership for Peace through which the non-members could adequately participate and remain involved. (In the Cologne Declaration it says: 'We want to develop an effective EU-led crisis management in which NATO members, as well as neutral and non-allied members, of the EU can participate fully and on an equal footing in the EU operations'.)[7]

MILITARY CAPABILITY

More than anything else the events in Kosovo seem to have brought home to the Europeans not only their limited role in critical situations in Europe, but their heavy dependence on the United States, both for political leadership and initiative as well as in simple terms of military capability. Since, as is often the case, it seems easier to talk about military hardware than about political initiative or European consensus on policy, at least some of the attention has concentrated on this issue, not the least reason being the initiatives taken by the British Prime Minister in Pörtschach and St Malo. At the summit meeting in Cologne in June 1999 the EU Heads of State or Government declared 'that the European Union shall play its full role on the international stage'.[8] And the statement continues: 'To that end, we intend to give the European Union the necessary means and capabilities to assume its responsibilities regarding a common European policy on security and defence'.[9]

This is to be achieved in three ways:

- Firstly, European military capabilities are to be enhanced both on the national and multinational levels, especially 'in the field of intelligence, strategic transport, command and control';
- secondly, by 'efforts to adapt, exercise and bring together national and multinational forces';
- and thirdly by 'closer and more efficient defence industry collaboration' (including 'harmonisation of military requirements and the planning of procurement of arms').[10]

Thus far two frameworks for improved European cooperation have been considered: the 'Forces Answerable to WEU' (FAWEU) and the 'Combined Joint Task Forces' of NATO (CJTF). The first, i.e. those forces that might be directly called upon by WEU are:

- the Euro-Corps with German, French, Belgian, Spanish and Luxembourg participation,

- the Multinational Division Central with German, British and Dutch participation,
- the British–Dutch Amphibious force,
- Eurofor and Euromarfor with Italian, French, Spanish and Portuguese participation.

All of these forces, with the exception of the French and Spanish, are 'double-hatted'. This means that their primary assignment remains with NATO, but they can be called upon by WEU to perform specific tasks which WEU may want to execute at the request of the European Union. However, on the occasion of the Franco-German consultations on 29 May 1999 the two sides stated their intention of transforming the Euro-Corps into a 'rapid reaction corps' (Adam *et al.*, 1999: 148–9). (Thus far the only rapid reaction corps available – and hence heavily relied upon in Bosnia and Kosovo – has been the Allied Rapid Reaction Corps.)

A second possible framework is the Combined Joint Task Force concept based on the NATO decision of June 1996.[11] Originally such task forces were not – contrary to what some Europeans like to think – intended specifically for European use. The purpose was to make NATO more flexible after the end of the Cold War and better able to deal with limited crises of the Yugoslav type. Nevertheless, it was also foreseen that a Combined Joint Task Force might be set up (by decision of the NATO Council) under European political control and military command.

The purpose of CJTFs is to provide procedures for withdrawing 'modules' from different headquarters, command structures or forces of NATO and to put them together as a separate task force. As the name implies, such a force shall have a specific task, and normally be limited in terms of objectives, extent and time. Once the task has been fulfilled, the task force will be dissolved and the different modules reintegrated into NATO structures. A separate or permanent European command structure is thus far not foreseen and has, in fact, been rejected by most of the allies because of its possibly divisive effect on NATO. Furthermore, the entire Alliance has to agree to the setting up of such a task force. That is to say, any member of the NATO Council has a veto, including the United States.

Two main reasons are usually mentioned why Europeans should have an interest in the CJTF concept. Firstly, it is possible that a situation might develop in Europe in which crisis control activities are required but the United States might prefer to stay out and leave these activities to the Europeans (for whatever reasons: the United States might be disinterested, might find it politically wiser to leave the activities to the Europeans or might find it domestically difficult to participate). Secondly, and probably more importantly, CJTFs would give Europeans the possibility of making use of so called NATO resources, in particular headquarters, communications, intelligence and long-range transportation. These are resources which the Europeans do not themselves possess, and which for financial reasons they do not feel in a position to acquire. Clearly, most of these resources are actually United States' resources (Gordon, 1997/98: 94), and it is not yet clear how, in case the NATO Council decides on a European CJTF, these American resources would be handed over to such a CJTF under European command and control. More importantly, it is likely that the United States would probably be rather reticent to hand over assets *and* control, possibly even running into a situation in which the United States would have to bail out the Europeans.

One can conclude, then, that any capacity of the European Union to back up diplomatic action 'by military means' is extremely limited at best (Gordon, 1997/98: 84ff; Roper, 1998: 1–6), and this is, of course, the reason both for the British moves and for the EU declarations of intent at Cologne. But any change in this situation will require not only a deter-mined political but also a significant financial effort. Thus far one might detect some of the former, but none of the latter. Probably, Europeans will hope to acquire more capability without more spending by increasing efficiency and cost effectiveness through improved multinational cooper-ation. But this, too, is easier on paper than in reality.

IMPROVED PROCEDURES FOR NEW TASKS?

Whatever one might want to say about the Treaty of Amsterdam and its deficiencies, in the area of a common foreign and security policy it did bring some improvement compared to the Treaty of Maastricht, certainly in terms of clarity, but also in terms of institutional procedures. As before, the Member States of the Union still have to *want* a common policy before such a policy can come about. But – and this is the main difference to Maastricht – the procedures to achieve such a common policy are more efficient and will possibly also prove to be more effective. In other words, procedurally it should be easier – provided that this is what is wanted – to achieve a common policy.

While the Maastricht Treaty confidently stated that a common foreign and security policy be 'established' (Article J TEU), the Treaty of Amster-dam – more modestly, and perhaps also more seriously – calls for more 'consistency' in the external activities of the European Union, calls upon the Council and Commission to ensure such consistency, and then limits itself to stating that the Union 'shall define and implement a common foreign and security policy' (Article 11(1) TEU). Perhaps this represents the lowest common denominator: that cooperation should be generally encouraged, and wherever a common foreign and security policy appears possible it should also come about. Differences exist not on the principle of cooperation where it is desired, i.e. where consensus can be reached, but on the expected extent of cooperation and on the procedures of coming to common positions.

According to Article 12 TEU the European Union's common foreign policy is to be based on five 'elements':

- on 'principles' and 'general guidelines', which the European Council (of Heads of State and Government) decides,
- on 'common strategies', also to be decided upon by the European Council,
- on 'joint actions', decided by the Council (of Ministers),
- on 'common positions', also decided by the Council (of Ministers),
- and finally on 'strengthening systematic co-operation between Member States in the conduct of policy'.

All of these elements are defined more clearly in the Treaty of Amsterdam than they were in the Maastricht Treaty. Overall, two – apparently contradictory – lines of thinking are recognizable. On the one hand, the European Council with its principle of consensus is reinforced; on the other hand, the way towards regular qualified majority voting in the Council of Ministers is opened up.

Clearly, the principles and general guidelines decided upon (unanimously) by the European Council are intended to have a determining character for any common foreign and security policy of the European Union. It is expressly stated (Article 13(3) TEU) that the Council of Ministers shall take all decisions 'on the basis of the general guidelines defined by the European Council'.

But an additional – and new – element is added, namely the concept of a 'common strategy'. This concept is not precisely defined; the Treaty states only that common strategies are 'to be implemented by the Union in areas where the Member States have important interests in common' (Article 13(2) TEU). Such common strategies 'shall set out their objectives, duration and the means to be made available by the Union and the Member States'. A 'common strategy', decided upon unanimously by the European Council, apparently has two purposes. Firstly, it is to form a more concrete, precise and directly applicable framework than the 'general guidelines' might provide for the decisions on common positions and joint actions by the Council. Policies might thus acquire more coherence. This purpose of binding common positions and joint actions into the framework of a common policy is supported by the sentence in Article 13(3) TEU: 'The Council shall recommend common strategies to the European Council and shall implement them, in particular by adopting joint actions and common positions'.

Secondly, and perhaps more importantly, the inclusion of this 'extra veto' (decisions have to be taken by consensus on the general guidelines and on the common strategies) provides an additional safeguard for those concerned about national control of foreign policy. But at the same time the added safeguard seems to have made it acceptable to have qualified majority voting as a general rule once there is a common strategy, thus no longer limiting such voting procedure to individual cases, each to be decided upon unanimously and related primarily to decisions of implementation. For the advocates of majority voting this must surely be seen as progress, even though the future will have to show whether the procedure will indeed bring about the desired result, namely to ensure, within the framework set out by the common strategies, that majority decisions are reached more rapidly, thus making a common policy and common action by the Union more effective. The obvious problem is that the European Council meets only twice a year: hence any common strategy would have to be rather farsighted and consequently couched in general terms, which appears to stand in contradiction to the detail expected from a common strategy as opposed to a general guideline. Indeed, one cannot ignore the fact that a common strategy will include the determination of the objective, duration and the means to be made available, thus ensuring that not only the overall format but even some of the details are decided upon in the European Council by unanimity.[12] This justifies some criticism. Not only have the protagonists of the intergovernmental approach made sure that the framework for the decisions of the Council of Ministers can be narrowly defined by the unanimous decisions of the European Council, but it is also questionable whether such a degree of detail is appropriate for the level of the European Council which, after all, meets only once every six months. Of course, this is no less than a reflection of the fear of the Member States to subject national freedom of movement to majority voting, but nevertheless – with this sheet-anchor to fall back upon – states have perhaps opened the door just slightly wider for majority voting.

Despite such reservations, the first 'Common Strategy of the European Union of 4 June 1999 on Russia' is a quite remarkable document.[13] It delineates goals and principal objectives, instruments and means, areas of action and specific initiatives. In a way, these are necessarily broadly defined, but they are not vague: they indicate remarkably clearly what the intentions are and what possible methods can and should be used to achieve them. The Common Strategy is to be of an initial duration of four years with regular intermediate reviews. It is also specifically stated that all decisions based on the Common Strategy will be taken by qualified majority. One will have to wait and see what practical results this Common Strategy will have, particularly when concrete activities are concerned (and to what extent these will in fact be co-ordinated or even be conducted jointly). But it is a start, and a further indication of success will be whether the foreseen common strategies for the Ukraine, the Mediterranean and the Balkans will come about soon and whether they will be equally successful in combining general objectives with relatively concrete means and activities.

Once a common strategy exists the implementation is left either to co-ordination between the Member States or to the *common positions* and *joint actions* of the European Union under the CFSP provisions. The basic difference between a common position and a joint action is that a common position delineates a common policy that is, however, to be implemented individually and through national means by the Member States (e.g. an embargo), while a joint action is, as the name implies, undertaken jointly by the Member States (under the 'EU flag', so to say, e.g. an EU delegation for election observation).

In general terms the concept of a common position can already be found in the Treaty of Maastricht (Article J(2) TEU). But in the Amsterdam Treaty it is now defined as 'the approach of the Union to a particular matter of a geographical or thematic nature' (Article 15 TEU), and Member States are called upon to 'ensure that their national policies conform to the common positions'.

While after Maastricht not very many common positions were in fact adopted (just over two dozen), since the Treaty of Amsterdam this instrument has been used much more frequently. Usually they have set out guidelines for economic sanctions or other restrictive measures, for example in the case of former Yugoslavia, Libya or Haiti.[14] In the case of the Sudan an arms embargo was involved. There have also been state-ments with regard to Ukraine, to Rwanda and to Burundi or, most recently, with regard to Indonesia and East Timor.

As for joint actions, they too were already introduced by the Maastricht Treaty, but are now defined more precisely in the Amsterdam Treaty. They 'shall address specific situations where operational action by the Union is deemed to be required' (Article 14(1) TEU). Again, objectives, scope and means are to be stated and, if necessary, duration and con-ditions for implementation. With regard to the implementation of a joint action the Council may request the Commission to submit 'appropriate proposals' (Article 14(4) TEU). In case of changed circumstances the Council can review a joint action; as long as the Council has not acted, however, 'the joint action shall stand' (Article 14(2) TEU).

There were a number of joint actions under the Maastricht Treaty (about three dozen), for example humanitarian aid for Bosnia, economic assist-ance to support the peace process in the Middle East, election observation in Russia and South Africa, export controls for 'dual use goods', or the joint preparation of certain conferences, such as the conference on the non-proliferation of nuclear weapons. Since then a number of further joint actions were decided upon, for example in July 1999 the appointment of a Special Representative of the EU to act as Co-ordinator of the Stability Pact for South-Eastern Europe, the installation of the structures of the United Nations' Mission in Kosovo (UNMIK) or the appointment of a Special Envoy for the African Great Lakes Region.

So there are efforts – under the provisions of the Amsterdam Treaty – to act together and to do so more frequently. The crucial question is, of course, whether this will also become possible and perhaps increasingly the rule in more critical areas.

DECISION-MAKING

Guidelines, strategies, positions and actions are thus the instruments of a common foreign and security policy. But how will decisions – for without the necessary decisions there will not be a common foreign policy regardless of the available instruments – on what to do (and whether to do anything at all) be taken in future, and what respective role does consensus or qualified majority voting have in these decisions?

The decisions not only of the European Council, but also of the Council (of Ministers), on foreign policy are as a general rule taken unanimously, that is to say, every member has a veto. This, according to some observers, is the critical point: it is the right of veto that in effect prevents the implementation of a common foreign policy. Consequently, they argue, the principle of consensus needs to be curbed; majority voting should take place more frequently or even as the rule. The intention, it is claimed, is not to force any Member State to do something against its will. However, experience has shown that simply the possibility of deciding by majority (and hence the risk of being outvoted) tends to make Member States more ready to compromise and to search for common ground more readily and effectively. Such a procedure would thus be a significant contribution to the achievement of a common policy even when there are initial differences between Member States. Moreover, only such a procedure would ensure quick and effective action.

The overall disappointment with the Treaty of Amsterdam has also affected the views on the changes with regard to the common foreign and security policy. Limitations continue to exist, particularly when measured against the integrationist hopes of achieving a truly common and effective European foreign policy despite all differences. Nevertheless, the Amsterdam Treaty has at least brought more clarity *and* more effective procedures, provided the Member States overcome their differences and choose to make use of the procedures. What has not been achieved – and could not be achieved – is a way of making members come to common policies against their will.

Of course, one could argue that a common policy will at least at times imply 'getting states to do what otherwise they would not have done' (Gordon, 1997/98: 82). In functioning federal systems, however, we seldom find individual Member States as such (as opposed to individual politicians) disagreeing fundamentally with the foreign policy conducted by the federal executive. The point is rather that two other conditions have been met: the conduct of foreign policy has been handed over to the federal executive (which in the case of the European Union would be the Commission), and, prerequisite to this, there exists a general foreign policy consensus determined by common interests, a common tradition and a common history. In other words, in such cases we are actually dealing with single, united political units.

In the case of the European Union we do not, however, have a federal executive as far as foreign policy is concerned (Gordon, 1997/98: 83).[15] Instead, the common foreign policy is negotiated between governments in the European Council which takes its decisions unanimously. This has not been changed. With regard to the Council, however, there are several agreements that could weaken the rule of unanimity. First, an abstention by a Member State does not prevent reaching a decision. This so-called 'constructive abstention' implies that as long as an explicit veto is not introduced, unanimity in the sense of positive agreement by each individual Member State is not required (Article 23(1) TEU).

Such an abstention can be quite informal and low-key. But a member may also, when abstaining, 'qualify its abstention by making a formal declaration', in which case, 'it shall not be obliged to apply the decision, but shall accept that the decision commits the Union' (Article 23 (1) TEU). At the same time the abstaining member is committed to refraining 'from any action likely to conflict with or impede Union action based on that decision'. If, however, several members qualify their abstention in this manner and 'represent more than one third of the votes weighted in accordance with Article 205(2) of the Treaty establishing the European Community' a decision shall not come about. On the whole this procedure seems reasonable – always taking into consideration the premise that the Member States continue to be reluctant to sacrifice foreign policy autonomy. In practice, substance rather than procedure may pose the more serious problem. For example, it may in certain circumstances be difficult for an abstaining state not to 'impede Union action', for example if the Union decides to break off diplomatic relations with a third country the exact policy to be followed by an abstaining member would turn out to be somewhat of a dilemma.

Beyond this procedure of a 'constructive abstention', however, there are now certain decisions which, as a general rule, will be taken by qualified majority vote. This shall apply (a) 'when adopting joint actions, common positions or taking any other decision on the basis of a common strategy' and (b) 'when adopting any decision implementing a joint action or a common position' (Article 23(2) TEU).

Whichever way one looks at it, this must be considered as representing at least some progress compared to Maastricht where the issues on which qualified majority voting was possible in the framework of joint actions had to be defined by the Council and thus by unanimous agreement in every individual case. Of course, it is correct that prerequisite to the now valid procedure is a common strategy, which not only has to be accepted by the European Council unanimously but will as a rule also contain some detail. But once this 'hurdle' is overcome, a presumably more efficient and effective procedure comes into play. The 'hurdle', of course, is agreement among the Member States. Without such agreement nothing goes: that is the reality of Europe's common foreign and security policy.

Decisions by qualified majority vote are taken by at least 62 votes, which must be cast by at least 10 Member States. However, here there is yet another possibility for a veto: 'If a member of the Council declares that, for important and stated reasons of national policy, it intends to oppose the adoption of a decision to be taken by qualified majority, a vote shall not be taken' (Article 23(2) TEU). The Council may then, 'acting by a qualified majority, request that the matter be referred to the European Council for decision by unanimity'.

Of course, one may criticize this provision of yet another veto. Some observers are concerned about what they see as a 'revival of the Luxembourg compromise', initiated by French president Charles de Gaulle in 1966, intended to ensure the ultimate supremacy of 'national interest' (Monar, 1998: 22). Indeed, in this way the entire procedure of qualified majority voting may once again be undone. This is undeniable, but one would also have to admit that it has become more difficult to do this. Any member wanting to proceed in such manner now has to state the reasons, and they have to be important. While there may be domestic pressures to opt out, it is likely that governments will be hesitant to bind themselves in such a manner publicly, and possibly to positions that may gain their own domestic weight and consequently be difficult to abandon later.[16] It is thus more likely than not that from the Amsterdam Treaty onward the rule will be qualified majority voting (on common positions and joint actions), the exception a return to unanimity (provided that states want to take common foreign policy decisions at all). Of course, the tendency in future may be that for the very reason of qualified majority voting decisions will either be taken at the highest level, where unanimity is required, or that generally fewer decisions will be adopted on the European level. While this does not seem likely, it remains true that the Amsterdam Treaty cannot and does not pretend to be able to force members to do something they do not want to do.

HIGH REPRESENTATIVE AND PLANNING STAFF

Two concepts developed in the Amsterdam Treaty have received a significant amount of attention: the idea of a planning staff and the notion of a High Representative for the common foreign and security policy. Many observers attach high expectations to these two new elements. The Policy Planning and Early Warning Unit is expected to deliver basic future-orientated concepts that would supposedly be so rational and convincing – and that would put Union-wide rather than national interests into the centre of its proposals – that members would find it difficult not to accept such concepts as common ground for a common foreign and security policy. The High Representative, on the other hand, would not only deliver ideas and take initiatives, but would indeed be *the representative* of a common policy and thus offer outsiders (to use an over-used cliché once more) that single telephone number that former United States Secretary of State Henry Kissinger once called for. These hopes were further nurtured by the appointment of former NATO Secretary-General Javier Solana as the first High Representative to take up the position in October 1999. Solana, it appeared, did not only have the personal prestige and political weight that seemed essential for the position, but as NATO Secretary-General had also acquired exactly the experience needed, namely to bring different national positions of sovereign Member States together to form a common position.

All of these hopes are valid, but at the same time one should be well aware that the Amsterdam Treaty circumscribes functions and authority of both Planning Staff and High Representative in a distinctly restrained manner. First of all, the High Representative is the Secretary-General of the Council, thus, strictly speaking, a civil servant in the services of the Council. He 'shall assist the Council in matters coming within the scope of the common foreign and security policy, in particular through contributing to the formulation, preparation and implementation of policy decisions, and, when appropriate and acting on behalf of the Council at the request of the Presidency, through conducting political dialogue with third parties' (Article 26). His function is thus primarily to assist the Council, which maintains full control. He may conduct a 'political dialogue with third parties', but only on behalf of the Council and at the specific request of the Presidency. The Council may, 'whenever it deems it necessary, appoint a special representative with a mandate in relation to particular policy issues' (Article 18(5) TEU). Whether this will weaken the Secretary-General in the area of the CFSP or whether, on the contrary, the Secretary-General will as a rule be the 'special representative' is uncertain at this stage. Perhaps it will in the end depend on the personality of the Secretary-General – which seems promising at this stage, but which is, after all, not particularly a sign of institutional strength.

The Policy Planning and Early Warning Unit will be the only administrative unit directly supporting the High Representative. It consists of 20 members (compared to, for example, the 3500 members of EU delegations in more than one hundred countries under the authority of the Commissioner for External Affairs), at this stage carefully selected by the 15 Member States (plus three members from the Council Secretariat, one from the Commission and one from WEU). Its tasks will be those of a conventional planning staff, that is the preparation of analyses on issues of importance as well as the presentation of political options – either at the request of the Council or the Presidency or on its own initiative. It is to cooperate 'appropriately' with the Commission, mainly to ensure coherence with the foreign trade and development policies of the Union. On the whole, so far there is little that points to this planning staff having a more significant or independent role than the planning staffs in national administrations. Moreover, if the nationally nominated representatives behave primarily as the representatives of their home foreign offices, the Planning Staff might end up to be no more than a 'sand box Council'. In the end, much will depend on quality. If the Planning Staff presents superior and convincing concepts and the High Representative takes the initiative, he may be able to gain status and even exert some leadership (particularly, of course, in a situation where the leadership in the Council or the Commission is weak or undecided).

LEGAL PERSONALITY, FINANCING AND THE EUROPEAN PARLIAMENT

Mainly in order to cope with such difficulties as arose in connection with the Union's inability to conclude an agreement with regard to the administration of Mostar, an attempt was made in Amsterdam to grant the EU legal personality in the framework of CFSP. Owing mainly to British resistance a compromise had to be and was finally found which will make it possible for the European Union to sign formal agreements with third parties, but the legal partner will not be the Union as a whole but all of its Member States (Article 24 TEU) (Nuttall, 1997: 3).[17]

Based on the negative experience with the Maastricht Treaty the financial and budgetary regulations are considerably more detailed and precise in the Treaty of Amsterdam. Administrative as well as operational expenditures will be charged to the budget of the European Communities 'except for such expenditure arising from operations having military or defence implications and cases where the Council acting unanimously decides otherwise' (Article 28 TEU). 'In cases where expenditure is not charged to the budget of the European Communities it shall be charged to the Member States in accordance with the gross national product scale' (*ibid.*). In the case of expenditures for operations having military or defence implications Member States which have abstained from a declaration (under Article 23(1) TEU) 'shall not be obliged to contribute to the financing thereof'.[18]

Finally, a detailed inter-institutional agreement has been concluded between the European Parliament, the Council and the European Commission, both on the financial regulations and the cooperation with the Parliament. The Parliament is to be informed on a regular basis by the Presidency on the development and implementation of CFSP activities, as well as receiving an annual report on the main aspects and options of a common foreign and security policy. On every decision involving costs the European Parliament is to be informed immediately.

CONCLUSIONS

On balance, then, one can well say that in the area of a common foreign and security policy – whatever one might say about other areas – the provisions of the Amsterdam Treaty do show some improvement over those of the Maastricht Treaty. These improvements run in the direction of more clarity, more modesty and some limited new opportunities. Such opportunities, when they arise, will do so within the existing restricted framework of CFSP. The Amsterdam Treaty has *not* created a structure which will inevitably lead to common policies. A common foreign and security policy will, in individual cases as well as in general, come about only if the members of the Union want such a common policy, i.e. when they perceive the advantages of a common policy as being bigger than the sacrifice of national autonomy in the specific case or where the differences in national attitudes or approaches have become so small that the sacrifice of national autonomy makes practically no substantive difference (Gordon, 1997/98: 80).[19] But, the European Union does now have at its disposal procedures that make the achievement of a common policy easier if it is wanted. The most hopeful or optimistic view may be that these same procedures, which at least in some areas and on some occasions make the accomplishment of a common foreign policy easier, may in the long run in fact lead towards a greater readiness on the part of governments to move along such a path more frequently.

The Treaty of Amsterdam did not achieve institutional arrangements by which the Member States of the European Union are forced to come to and to pursue a common foreign and security policy. In particular, it does not ensure that the Europeans can count on reaching common positions and undertaking joint actions in critical situations. There is no institutional magic that can conjure up a common European foreign and security policy. Moreover, the possibilities for institutional and procedural improvements now have been largely exhausted. If in future the Europeans want more (because they want more or because they need more) it will be difficult to avoid the core of the integration issue, namely to think about and decide what kind of Europe the Europeans need and want for the twenty-first century, and what will have to be done to achieve that Europe.

NOTES

1. Cf. *Financial Times*, 22 October 1999, p. 5: 'European Leaders Found Wanting when it Comes to Putting up Cash for Defence'.
2. European Council Declaration on Strengthening the Common European Policy on Security and Defence, Cologne Summit 4 June 1999, Annex III, paragraph 5, http://ue.eu.int/en/info/eurocouncil.index.htm.
3. It is correct that the NATO formulation is less automatic and more vaguely formulated (in view of the rights of the United States Congress), but the factual assurance is at least equivalent (or more so) to that of the Brussels Treaty.
4. Cf. *Agence Europe*, No. 7425, 16 March 1999, pp. 5–6.
5. Cf. Press Conference by Finnish Foreign Minister Tarja Halonen at the Saari-selkä 'Gymnich' [Foreign Ministers'] meeting of 4 September 1999, http://presidency.finland.fi/frame.asp.
6. NATO Washington Summit Communiqué, 24 April 1999, paragraph 9a, http://www.nato.int/docu/pr/1999/p99–064e.htm.
7. European Council Declaration on Strengthening the Common European Policy on Security and Defence, Cologne Summit 4 June 1999, Annex III, paragraph 3.
8. *Ibid*.
9. *Ibid.*, paragraph 1.
10. *Ibid.*, paragraph 2.
11. Cf. Final Communiqué of Ministerial Meeting of the North Atlantic Council, Berlin 3 June 1996, esp. paragraphs 6 and 7, http://www.nato.int/docu/pr/1996/p96–063e.htm.
12. See the critical and sceptical article by Simon Nuttall (1997: 1–3).
13. See *Official Journal of the European Communities*, Vol. 42, 24 June 1999, pp. 1–10.
14. On common positions and joint actions see European Commission, List of Common Positions adopted by the Council since the Entry into Force of the

Treaty on European Union (November 1993–September 1996), and List of Joint Actions adopted by the Council since the Entry into Force of the Treaty on European Union (November 1993-September 1996), in: *European Dialogue*, Brussels: European Commission, 1997, pp. 18–20.

15. Gordon makes the pertinent point that with the exception of foreign policy in the EU the term 'common' normally is reserved for policy areas that fall under the authority of EU institutions, the Commission, the Parliament or the European Central Bank.

16. One could think of the French position towards NATO: while it in effect damages French interests, every government since de Gaulle has found it difficult and indeed impossible to abandon the Gaullist commitment.

17. Nuttall calls this provision a 'potential landmine' because of lack of clarity, the 'reserve of sovereignty', and because the Presidency rather than the Commission will be responsible for negotiation.

18. This, of course, may be an incentive to abstain, but the political cost of such a motivated abstention may in the long run be higher than the financial cost.

19. See on this the detailed argument by Gordon (1997/98).

BIBLIOGRAPHY

European Commission (1997) 'List of Common Positions Adopted by the Council since the Entry into Force of the Treaty on European Union (November 1993– September 1996)'. *European Dialogue*.

European Commission (1997) 'List of Joint Actions Adopted by the Council since the Entry into Force of the Treaty on European Union (November 1993– September 1996)'. *European Dialogue*.

European Council (1999), Declaration on Strengthening the Common European Policy on Security and Defence, Cologne Summit 4 June 1999.

Official Journal of the European Communities (1999) Vol. 42, 24 June.

Adam, B. et al. (1999), 'La nouvelle architecture de sécurité en Europe. Le quadrilatère OTAN-Union Européenne-OSCE-UEO: un gage de stabilité?', *GRIP Cahier*, 233/235, Brussels.

Agence Europe (1999) No. 7425, 16 March 1999.

Davidson, I. (1997) *Challenge Europe, Making Sense of the Amsterdam Treaty*. Brussels: European Policy Centre.

Financial Times (1999) 'European leaders found wanting when it comes to putting up cash for defence', 22 October.

Gehring, T. (1995) 'Integrating integration theory. Neofunctionalism and international regimes', *EUI Working Paper RSC*, No. 95/39.

Gordon, P. H. (1997/98) 'Europe's uncommon foreign policy'. *International Security*, Winter 1997/98.

Halonen, T. (1999), Press Conference by Finnish Foreign Minister Tarja Halonen at the Saariselkä 'Gymnich' [Foreign Ministers'] meeting of 4 September 1999, http://presidency.finland.fi/frame.asp.

Hefeker, C. (1997) 'Between efficiency and stability: Germany and European Monetary Union'. In J. Pisani-Ferry, C. Hefeker and A. J. Hughes Hallett, 'The political economy of EMU: France, Germany and the UK'. In *CEPS Paper*, No. 69, Brussels, May 1997.

Monar, J. (1998) 'Der Vertrag von Amsterdam. Grenzen und Risiken des intergouvernementalen Verfassungsgebungsprozesses der Europäischen Union'. *Forum Politicum Jenense*, 3.

NATO (1996), Final Communiqué of Ministerial Meeting of the North Atlantic Council, Berlin 3 June 1996, http://www.nato.int/docu/pr/1996/p96–063e.htm.

NATO (1999), NATO Washington Summit Communiqué, 24 April 1999, http://www.nato.int/docu/pr/1999/p99–064e.htm.

Nuttall, S. (1997) 'The CFSP provisions of the Amsterdam Treaty. An exercise in collusive ambiguity'. *CFSP Forum*, 3, Bonn: Institut für Europäische Politik.

Pedersen, T. (1998) *Germany, France, and the Integration of Europe: A Realist Interpretation*. London: Pinter.

Roper, J. (1998) 'Wandel tut not Herausforderungen für Europas Sicherheitspolitik'. *Internationale Politik*, July.

CHAPTER 13

THE COMMON FOREIGN AND SECURITY POLICY OF THE AMSTERDAM TREATY: TOWARDS AN IMPROVED EU IDENTITY ON THE INTERNATIONAL SCENE?

Elfriede Regelsberger and Uwe Schmalz

INTRODUCTION

The view on whether or not the European Union is a major and credible actor in external affairs asserting a genuine identity on the international scene as foreseen in Article B of the Maastricht Treaty differs greatly in present European circles. Those involved in the daily CFSP business stress the importance of the collective framework to both formulate and implement the foreign policy interests of their respective countries while pursuing them individually is perceived a second best option.[1] Among the European public, most obvious in leading European journals,[2] a more critical view prevails which is strongly influenced by Europe's low profile in the management of recent crises, particularly in former Yugoslavia.[3] The United States, traditionally both supportive of and sceptical towards a decisive role of the EU in world politics, continues to criticize openly its European allies for their foreign policy performance[4] as do several other international actors, such as Israel, traditionally opposed to an active political influence of the EU in the Middle East conflict. In contrast, others, particularly the overwhelming majority of those actively involved in the CFSP at the national and European level, share a more positive view on the Fifteen's ability to play a significant international role.

The heterogeneous assessments of the CFSP originate in the mixed balance of the EU's performance on the international scene since the coming into force of the Maastricht Treaty including both progress and deficits.[5] Without any doubt, the CFSP contributed to the ongoing convergence of foreign policy positions on the part of the Member States through systematic information, communication and coordination between the national foreign ministries. Furthermore, the wide range of CFSP instruments such as declarations, common positions and joint actions allows the EU to develop an international weight and influence that exceeds by far the potential of its individual Member States. The importance that the EU has as an international actor not only for its Member States but also for external partners is reflected in the large variety of institutionalized dialogues between the EU and third countries (11 political dialogues with associated countries, 40 political dialogues with third countries or groups of countries) (Regelsberger, 1998: 2–3). Furthermore, the phenomenon of 'globalization' and the changed security challenges of the post-1989 international system (political and economic instability, migration, proliferation, organized crime, ecocide) even enhanced the EU's relevance as an international actor due to its potential to act in a broad range of policy fields such as economy, commerce, development aid, foreign and security policy, ecology as well as justice and home affairs. Consequently, the EU is increasingly perceived as the relevant level for coping with international challenges and threats that exceed the nation-states' capacities, particularly in the field of conflict prevention and stabilization of neighbouring regions such as the Mediterranean (Barcelona-Process), Eastern Europe (Stability Pact) and the Baltic region (Northern Dimension of the EU).

However, despite these achievements the EU did not yet manage to convincingly assert its identity on the international scene through the CFSP. On the contrary, the implementation of Title V of the Treaty on European Union (TEU) revealed in practice a number of legal, conceptual and institutional weaknesses. They include an insufficient forward planning and analysis capacity, an unsatisfying vertical and horizontal coherence, the incapability for speedy reactions, the declaratory character of CFSP decisions often lacking real substance, the highly disputed financing of joint actions, the low-profile external representation, the lack of legal personality and of a genuine treaty-making capacity, the inadequate cooperation in security and defence policy as well as the incapacity for military action.

The extensive list of deficits, the pressing challenges on the international scene, as well as the perspective of EU-enlargement (up to more than 20 members with the according paralysing effects on unanimous decision-making) required substantial reforms of the CFSP already a few years after its coming into effect. Accordingly, the Intergovernmental Conference of 1996/7 for the revision of the Maastricht Treaty included a fundamental review of the existing CFSP provisions of Title V TEU. Based on earlier considerations in the reflection group, a laborious negotiation process was set into motion which aimed at strengthening the political commitments of a collective foreign policy, bridging the gap between objectives and operational means, and at overcoming the problems resulting from the Union's pillar structure. Its results are to be found in Articles 11–28 of the consolidated version of the Union Treaty as amended by the Amsterdam Treaty, four declarations, the protocol on the Western European Union and the Inter Institutional Agreement on the financing of CFSP (Monar, 1997a; Nuttall, 1997).[6]

Whether reality will meet the aspirations of the signatory states, i.e. to achieve an 'effective and coherent external policy of the European Union' remains to be seen. The post-Maastricht experience has been less than promising (see above) and the 'collusive ambiguity' (Nuttall, 1997) of the Amsterdam provisions could produce uncertainties and irritations. On the other hand the Amsterdam Treaty offers certain dynamic elements which were inconceivable before, given the massive obstruction on the part of those governments, like the British, the Danish or Portuguese, who opposed any move towards some sort of a 'communitarization' of CFSP, for example the introduction of community-type decision-making procedures.[7]

OBJECTIVES, AGENDA, LEGAL STATUS AND MEMBER STATES COMMITMENTS

Articles 11 and 17(1) TEU reflect the Fifteen's approach towards a comprehensive foreign, security and defence policy, though the latter has to be understood as an incremental process which can be facilitated by an intensified cooperation of the Member States in the area of arms procurement without, however, imposing community competencies on it. The most concrete step is the inclusion of the so-called Petersberg tasks into the Union Treaty (Article 17(2) TEU) which gives room for specifying the EU's agenda in the area of security policy. Unfortunately, the Amsterdam Treaty does not provide for a coherent overall foreign policy strategy. Instead, European foreign policy objectives remain split in two distinct sets between the first and the second pillar. The results are the juxtaposition and the overlap of EC and CFSP objectives and the according procedures, means and instruments. One example illustrating this grey area are the objectives to develop and consolidate democracy and the rule of law and the respect for human rights and fundamental freedoms. Both are explicitly set out within the CFSP provisions (Article 11(1) TEU) and the community pillar (Article 177 (2) TEC). So far this dualism of external objectives has led to severe controversies about competencies and the pursuit of identical but institutionally distinct objectives, for example in the case of the MEDA-programme between the European Union and its

Mediterranean partners regarding the question of how to decide on the suspension of the agreement if a partner should violate human rights.[8]

One *conditio sine qua non* for effective action on the international scene is the ability to conclude international legal agreements. However, due to the Member States' reluctance to limit their national sovereignty the Maastricht Treaty provided the Union with neither a legal personality nor a treaty-making capacity. Instead, dualism prevailed with the Community being able to conclude international agreements on grounds of its legal personality whereas the Member States had to employ highly complicated legal arrangements in order to conclude international agreements on behalf of CFSP. Needless to say, such complex procedures and the according inability for effective action severely damaged the Union's international credibility. In view of this obvious imperfection a broad majority of Member States was in favour of providing the Union with legal personality. Yet, despite having almost achieved consensus on this matter during the Intergovernmental Conference, the according nego-tiations finally ended in deadlock due to the strict opposition of Denmark, France and the United Kingdom which regarded the establishment of legal personality for the EU as an unacceptable impairment of the inter-governmental character of CFSP. The undisputed need for reform together with the Member States' reservations of sovereignty once again led to an imperfect and indeed curious compromise (Monar, 1997a: 427). By virtue of Article 24 TEU the Union is equipped with a treaty-making capacity for CFSP without, however, having a legal personality. The Council may unanimously authorize the Presidency, assisted by the Commission, to open negotiations for the conclusion of an international agreement. Acting unanimously on a recommendation from the Presidency the Council shall conclude such agreements which are binding on individual Member States subject to their respective national ratification procedures. On grounds of these provisions it will be possible to conclude international agreements under the CFSP provisions with the Member States as contracting parties on behalf of the Union and – as explicitly stated in a declaration annexed to the TEU – without 'any transfer of competence from the Member States to the European Union'.

This complex legal compromise is not without risks for the delicate dual structure of European affairs. When applied to 'mixed agreements' involving the Community, the Union and the Member States, Article 24 TEU might serve the Council as a tool to expand these provisions to the treaty-making procedures of the Community. Such an intergovernmental-ization of Community procedures would impair the institutional balance thus provoking severe bureaucratic quarrels. Furthermore, it would ham-per the Union's external effectiveness due to an extension of the unanimity rule and due to the replacement of the Commission as a permanent body with long-standing experience in international treaty negotiations by the constantly fluctuating Presidency. On the bottom line, Article 24 TEU though providing for some progress for bridging the dualism in the Union's treaty-making capacity constitutes a number of risks for the institutional balance as well as for the effectiveness and credibility of European external activities.

Finally, Article 11 (2) TEU recalls already well-known principles stating that the Member States ought to support the policy of the Union 'actively and unreservedly in a spirit of loyalty and mutual solidarity'. This fundamental commitment has not always been adequately respected by all governments and hence could not prevent the CFSP from being impaired by a lack of vertical coherence. As a new element, Article 11 (2) TEU explicitly requires a strengthened mutual political solidarity. This could be interpreted as both a response to the emergence of conflicting blocks between the big and the small countries among the Fifteen as well as an indirect signal to governments blocking specific CFSP decisions due to alleged 'vital' national interests which the other partners were reluctant to acknowledge.[9] In addition, the Intergovernmental Conference agreed on an extension of the CFSP's objectives including the safeguard of the independence and integrity of the Union, the acknowledgement of the principles of the United Nations Charter, of the Helsinki Final Act and of the objectives of the Paris Charter with particular emphasis on the protection of external borders which was particularly desired by Greece (Article 11 (1) TEU).

OLD AND NEW ACTORS IN THE INSTITUTIONAL SET-UP

Some of the most fundamental novelties of the Amsterdam provisions on CFSP are the role of the European Council, the composition of the new Troika, the position of the Secretary General of the Council and High Representative for CFSP as well as the establishment of a Policy Planning and Early Warning Unit under the authority of the latter.

European Council

Compared to the very brief mentioning of the European Council in the former Article J.8 (1) TEU the new provisions contain a clear sophistication of the competencies of the Heads of State or Government: Article 17 (1) TEU defines the European Council's role as the initiator for the further development of a common European security and defence. Its current competence of establishing general guidelines for the CFSP is explicitly extended to all those cases in which the European Union avails itself of the Western European Union (Article 17 (3) TEU). Furthermore, the European Council is responsible for the definition of common strategies (Article 13 (2) TEU). This new instrument, invented by German diplomacy[10] to overcome French resistance towards majority voting in CFSP, aims at defining the fundamental long-term substance of the EU's approach in central foreign policy fields,[11] the details of which are to be implemented by qualified majority voting at a lower level. Whether or not the European Council will adequately fulfil this new guiding function remains to be seen, given the rare meetings of the Heads of State or Government over a year. Furthermore, this concept might hamper the effectiveness and efficiency of the CFSP due to the fact that the European Council is requested to define the objectives, the duration and the means for a common strategy in detail. This could lead to an arduous and time-consuming process if one considers that some Member States might wish to introduce as many 'safety clauses' as possible for the implementation process to be followed by qualified majority vote.

Since the European Council has an overall guiding function for all three pillars it could well be that common strategies of CFSP might touch upon competencies related particularly to first pillar issues. This might re-open the dispute about the 'contamination' of EC-competencies by CFSP and run counter to the requested 'consistency' of Europe's foreign relations.[12] Article 3 TEU reaffirms the responsibility of both the Council and the Commission for ensuring the EU's external consistency[13] and introduces an explicit obligation for them 'to co-operate to this end'. Furthermore, in cases where the cooperation would not function satisfactorily Article 14(4) TEU provides for a specific safe-guarding clause at least for the implementation of joint actions in which the Council may request the Commission to submit concrete proposals to it.

Finally, Heads of State or Government remain the 'last resort' for the solution of disputes which cannot be settled at the lower levels. This applies also to all those cases where a Member State claims vital national interests which make qualified majority decisions at Council level impossible and may place the issue with a qualified majority under the authority of a unanimous decision of the European Council (Article 23(2) TEU).

Council and Presidency

Article 13 TEU reasserts the key position the foreign ministers hold in the daily CFSP machinery. However, despite a considerable lack of coherence in the functioning of the Council's working level (Kiso, 1997) the preparatory procedures and institutions of Council decisions have not been subject of any reform in the Amsterdam Treaty. Proposals during the IGC such as the establishment of a permanent Political Committee composed

of the Deputy Political Directors and situated in the Permanent Represen-
tations in Brussels or the reinforcement of COREPER were rejected by
those Member States which opposed a weakening of the role of the strictly
intergovernmental Political Committee of the CFSP. The preparation of
CFSP decisions is thus likely to remain the highly contentious object of
well-known quarrels and bureaucratic infighting between rather communitarian oriented and strictly intergovernmental administrative cultures
within the Council's preparatory structure which have already in the past
prevented an adequate bridging of dualism in the preparation of CFSP.

The debate about an improved external representation of the EU led to
rather modest results. Innovative proposals like that of team presidencies
for a period of 12 months (Secretariat General of the Council of the
European Union, 1995) were unacceptable to those who feared shifts in
the balance of power between the big and the small Member States with a
re-weighting of the Council votes. Seen against this background it comes
as no surprise that the existing model of rotating presidencies was
confirmed (Article 18 (1) and (2) TEU). In order to allow nevertheless for
more 'visibility' and 'continuity' of the EU's external representation the
old troika system will be replaced by a new one. The Amsterdam troika
model will be composed of the Council Presidency, the Commission and
the High Representative for the CFSP, with the incoming Presidency
assisting the spokesman and the troika if needed. The preceding Presidency, a participant of the Maastricht troika model, will no longer be part
of the game. This new formula and particularly the participation of the
High Representative and the Commission suggests a greater coherence
and continuity of the external representation of the EU. However, the
three players are not on an equal footing: the Presidency is clearly highest
in the hierarchy assisted by the Secretary General of the Council (Article
18 (3) TEU). The Commission shall be 'fully associated' (Article 18 (4)
TEU) as already foreseen in the Maastricht Treaty. With the High Representative for the CFSP being subordinated to the Council and its Presidency, the Commission might strengthen its position as a
quasi-autonomous player in the troika particularly if it succeeds in mat-
erializing its intention to transfer all components of external relations
under the responsibility of a single Vice-President.[14]

The High Representative for CFSP

Since EPC and CFSP history tells us that the real weight of a new function
heavily depends on the chosen personality it is too early to say a final
word on the role of the High Representative at this moment. This key
appointment, originally foreseen for the Vienna European Council in
December 1998, was postponed to 1999 obviously to make it part of a

larger 'package' of other forthcoming vacancies of posts. After protracted bargaining the Member States were able to agree on the then NATO Secretary General Javier Solana Madaranga who was formally appointed by the Cologne European Council in June 1999. Though officially called 'High Representative for CFSP' the position as defined in the Amsterdam Treaty is a distinctly modest one[15] compared to French aspirations which favoured the concept of a political post directly responsible to the European Council. His role is by no means comparable to the autonomy of the Secretary General of NATO, i.e. to chair meetings at all CFSP levels – a task which remains with the Presidency[16] – or to have a right of initiative of his own. Hence, his 'place' in the CFSP decision-making structure will be largely determined by his relationship with the respective Presidencies and the quality of work that the Policy Planning and Early Warning Unit (which will work under his authority) will produce.

In the EU's external representation the High Representative could even find himself in competition with others speaking on behalf of the Fifteen and in particular with the special envoys which the Council may appoint (Article 18 (5) TEU) to show greater visibility and operability of CFSP policies in specific situations. Experiences with the EU administration of Mostar in Bosnia-Herzegovina, the role of Carl Bildt in the implementation of the Dayton Agreements and the Spanish Ambassador Moratinos as special envoy of the EU in the Middle East have already shown that this new instrument enhances the EU's visibility. Yet it also increases the number of 'faces' acting in the name of the EU and therefore requires considerable internal coordination.

The Policy Planning and Early Warning Unit

The often regretted lack of 'common visions' in CFSP (Secretariat General of the Council of the European Union, 1995) led the Member States to agree rather quickly on the necessity of establishing a long-term planning capacity for the second pillar. Consequently, the Amsterdam Treaty introduces a Policy Planning and Early Warning Unit (PPEWU) which shall provide a more in-depth and systematic analysis of distinctly 'European' perceptions of international developments as well as the formulation of policy options particularly to improve the EU's capacities for conflict prevention. However, the relevant declaration annexed to the Amsterdam Treaty[17] does not foresee the establishment of a separate new unit but an extension of the Council secretariat. Considerations at the time of writing suggest that the PPEWU will consist of 20 high-level officials ('A'-ranking), one from each EU-member state, one WEU representative, one from the Commission and three from the Council staff. Nominated for a three- to five-years term[18] they will be integrated into the existing

Directorate General's 'external relations', though the new unit will not be directly fused with the existing CFSP desks. This model – obviously chosen for budgetary reasons and for emphasizing the novelty of the PPEWU, but also for circumventing bureaucratic obstacles – will make a clear division of labour and guidance from the Secretary General imperative. Whether or not the PPEWU will live up to the expectations will not only depend on the recruitment of the personnel but also on the access to information particularly via the national diplomatic services and the Commission's delegations abroad (Dolan, 1997; van Ham, 1997; Schmalz, 1997b).

The European Parliament

The question of legitimacy and democratic accountability of the European foreign policy has never been of great concern to the architects of the EPC and CFSP. Only as a result of the unceasing efforts of the European parliamentarians certain rights of information were gradually transformed into treaty obligations. At first sight Article 21 TEU seems to merely confirm the identical wording of former Article J.7 of the Maastricht Treaty. However, the Amsterdam provisions on CFSP financing enhance considerably the European Parliament's influence on the second pillar. According to Article 28 (2) and (3) TEU, not only administrative but also operational expenditure shall be automatically charged to the EC-budget, except for expenditure for military or defence operations and cases where the Council unanimously decides otherwise. This extension of CFSP financing within the framework of the EC budget serves the interests of both the Member States and the European Parliament: the Member States can save their restricted national budgets; the European Parliament can use its central function as part of the budgetary authority within the EC budgetary procedures as a tool for preserving and even extending its influence in CFSP. This is particularly true with regard to the Inter Institutional Agreement on the financing of the CFSP annexed to the Amsterdam Treaty[19] which – after massive controversies between the two branches of the budgetary authority of the EU (Monar, 1997b) – now provides for an increased consultation and information of the European Parliament on all aspects of the CFSP financing.

The agreement contains detailed rules on the establishment of the annual CFSP budget, based on concrete proposals for the classification of CFSP expenditure[20] as well as the concrete obligation on the part of the Council to inform the European Parliament about every CFSP decision that is likely to entail expenditure including a detailed overview of the expenditure in each individual case. Taken together with the general obligation of the Presidency to 'regularly' inform the European Parliament about the developments and implementation of CFSP policies the Inter

Institutional Agreement on CFSP financing will definitely alter the European Parliament's traditional position as an 'underdog' in EPC/CFSP (Grunert, 1997). Hence, provided that the legal provisions are fully implemented, the new arrangements may be interpreted as a considerable step towards the realization of the European Parliament's claims for participation in CFSP decisions from an earlier stage onwards. Obviously as a *quid pro quo*, the CFSP budget no longer allows for building reserves which normally require parliamentary assent and therefore constituted another source of conflict between Council and Parliament since the very first days of CFSP. Furthermore, the Inter Institutional Agreement responds to the Council's plea for a certain flexibility by allowing the Commission on the basis of a Council decision to make autonomous transfers between the CFSP budget lines. To ensure an effective control and planning of the CFSP financing the Commission is obliged to inform both parts of the budgetary authority on the execution of the CFSP activities and any financial forecasts for the remaining funds on a quarterly basis.

REFINED CFSP DECISION-TAKING PROCEDURES

Despite certain weaknesses Article 23 TEU constitutes an important milestone on the road from strictly consensus-based decisions which governed EPC for more than two decades to qualified majority votes in CFSP. First pillar experience suggests that already the potential recourse to the principle of majority voting, without necessarily applying it immediately, might well have disciplinary effects and promote mutually shared policy solutions in due course. The extent to which qualified majority voting will be applied to the implementation of common strategies, joint actions and common positions will largely depend on the skills of the respective Presidency in a given situation and on the behaviour of those among the Fifteen which insist traditionally on a strict application of the unanimity rule.[21] As is current practice, qualified majority votes require 62 weighted votes in favour, cast by at least 10 Member States, while abstentions by members shall not prevent the adoption of decisions (Article 205 (2) TEC and 23 TEU). Not surprisingly the protagonists of an extension of majority voting had to offer 'safety clauses' for satisfying the concerns of the opponents of this approach. This led to the introduction of a modified version of the 'Luxembourg compromise' (Article 23 (2) TEU) according to which already a single member of the Council can block a qualified majority decision for 'important and stated reasons of national policy'. In this case, the only way out of the veto-deadlock is for the Council to delegate the issue by a qualified majority to the European Council for a unanimous decision.

The instrument of constructive abstention (Article 23(1) TEU) introduces an element of flexibility in the decision-taking mechanisms. It offers a way out in situations where one or a group of Member States representing less than a third of the weighted votes wishes to deviate from a common decision without, however, being able to block. Critics argue that the constructive abstention might turn out to be a 'destructive' one (Nuttall, 1997), since the required formal declaration of the reasons for which a Member State deems itself to be unable to follow the common line will make splits among the Fifteen obvious towards the outside.[22] Further-more, the inclusion of a rather simple possibility for Member States to deviate from a coalition of the 'able and willing' would expose CFSP more to domestic political pressure while EPC and CFSP so far offered a certain 'protection' against national interest groups and lobbies.

Not surprisingly, decisions with defence implications require unanimity as do all decisions by the European Council while procedural questions in the CFSP are to be taken by the majority of the member states (Article 23(3) TEU).

SECURITY AND DEFENCE

Matters relating to European security and defence have always been among the most contested ones in the Intergovernmental Conference negotiations of the 1990s and required final deliberations of the Heads of State or Government.[23] Traditionally, the dividing line lies between those in favour of a strengthened European Security and Defence Identity (the founding members of the EC plus Spain) and the protagonists of a continuation of the status quo (the United Kingdom, Portugal, Denmark, Sweden, Finland and Austria in particular).[24] The compromise between these two camps as reflected in Article 17 TEU reaffirms the role of the WEU as an integral part of the development of the Union and paves the way for the integration of the WEU into the European Union if the European Council so decides. However, a definite timetable as suggested by the seven protagonists of a gradual fusion of the two systems[25] did not find the support of the other partners who for various reasons (compe-tition between EU-WEU-NATO, non-acceptance of the EU as a security and defence union, status as non-aligned country) did not wish to go considerably beyond the *acquis* of the Maastricht Treaty.

With regard to the existing provisions, Article 17(2) TEU constitutes considerable progress and an important novelty by explicitly defining the fundamentals of a European Defence Policy within a treaty provision.

These so called 'Petersberg tasks' include 'humanitarian and rescue tasks, peace-keeping tasks and tasks of combat forces in crisis management, including peace-making'. The EU will avail itself of the WEU to implement the respective decisions having defence implications (Article 17(3) TEU). In this case, the European Council's competence for establishing general guidelines will include also the WEU. The new provisions signal the importance of a closer EU-WEU-cooperation, the details of which will have to be clarified during a one-year-period once the Amsterdam Treaty will be in force.[26] Experience tells us that the relationship between the two organizations will continue to be a difficult one (Jopp, 1994–8; Institut d'Etudes de Sécurité de L'UEO, 1998). However, the Pörtschach proposals of the British government[27] and the joint Franco-British declaration of Saint-Malo on European Defence[28] have marked a promising turning-point in this respect. Whether the Fifteen will succeed in improving their military crisis management, particularly in their immediate neighbourhood, will also depend on the WEU's own capacity to reform its consensus-based procedures (Missiroli, 1999), to improve its own operational resources and to better avail itself of NATO capabilities (particularly the combined Joint Task Forces).

OUTLOOK

Cautious optimism suggests that the revised CFSP provisions offer some dynamism for an improved EU capacity to act and to assert its identity on the international scene. It presupposes, however, that every single Member State has the political will to take its treaty obligations seriously, i.e. not to turn commonly agreed decisions to farce by counteracting them for the sake of national priorities as did the United Kingdom and Greece during the 1998 JAT flight ban (Schmalz, 1998a). Furthermore, the successful implementation of the Amsterdam provisions on CFSP requires the predominance of collective solutions over decisions achieved in smaller circles. This is not to say that the EU should be bound to total inactivity in situations where consensus cannot be achieved. As the 'Operation Alba' of 1997 demonstrated in Albania (Silvestri, 1997), coalitions of the willing may offer a way out of deadlocks in which no decision can be agreed on by all Fifteen. The Amsterdam Treaty modestly opens the way towards such forms of 'enhanced co-operation' by introducing constructive abstention and bi-/multilateral cooperation of Member States also in WEU and NATO (Article 17(4) TEU) (Janning, 1994–8). However, a predominance of such flexible 'core groups' over the normal CFSP proceedings would work to the detriment of CFSP. The activities of a restricted coalition of the able and the willing are not necessarily perceived from outside as truly EU-European and therefore might hamper the reputation and the credibility of the CFSP. Furthermore, the smaller EU members which – as illustrated by the Bosnia Contact Group – are more likely to be excluded from those smaller circles than the big ones are strongly opposed against the establishment of restricted core groups or 'directories' of the big Member States. The fact that several Member States publicly expressed their unease in this respect[29] underpins the seriousness of these concerns. Enlargement could work into the same direction by the simple fact that the growing number of participants changes the 'club' atmosphere and negotiating style which insiders deem decisive for the success of CFSP into something different labelled as 'UN-syndrome' (Ischinger and Kölsch, 1997: 10). The credibility of the EU as an international actor would then see another set-back. Hence, it is of utmost importance that the Member States share a joint foreign policy approach based on their political will and allowing them to fully use the potential which the Amsterdam Treaty offers for enhancing the EU's capacity for external action and for developing further a genuine foreign policy identity of the EU that meets the challenges of the international system at the threshold of the twenty-first century.

NOTES

1. Illustrative for this view is the assessment of the then German political director who became later state secretary of the German Foreign Office (Ischinger, 1998: 7–9); as well as the view of the Irish European Correspondent (O'Flaherty, 1997: 1–2).
2. See for example press comments on the EU action in the Kosovo Crisis of 1998 and on the Russian crisis of autumn 1998: with regard to the quarrels about the EU flight ban on JAT, the Yugoslav air carrier, the *Financial Times* judged that 'Belgrade's punishment threatened to turn to farce as it was undermined by foreign airlines and even EU governments' (*Financial Times*, 1998a). The Austrian *Standard* assesses the EU's role in the Kosovo conflict as that of a mere 'paper-tiger in security policy' ('sicherheitspolitischer Papiertiger') (*Der Standard*, 1998). The *Süddeutsche Zeitung* speaks of a 'political Punch and Judy show' ('politisches Kasperltheater') on which the Yugoslav President Slobodan Milosevic is smiling pityingly and which reveals the low profile of the EU Member States' diplomacy ('diplomatische Flachflieger') (*Süddeutsche Zeitung*, 1998). For the *Frankfurter Allgemeine Zeitung* the EU's reactions on the Russian political and economic crisis reveal a 'cluelessness and helplessness' ('Rat- und Hilflosigkeit') and demonstrate that the EU still has to go a long way to become mature in world politics ('Es ist noch ein weiter Weg, bis die Gemeinschaft die weltpolitische Reifeprüfung ablegen kann') (*Frankfurter Allgemeine Zeitung*, 1998).
3. For details of the EU's role in former Yugoslavia see Remacle and Delcourt (1998: 227–72). For a critical evaluation by the former High Representative for Bosnia see Bildt (1997: 23–31).

4. As did Richard C. Holbrooke, at the time Assistant Secretary of State for European Affairs, who claimed in January 1996, after a serious crisis between Greece and Turkey over the Imia Islet in the eastern Aegean Sea had been settled only under intense pressure from the United States: 'While President Clinton was on the phone with Athens and Ankara the Europeans were literally sleeping through the night. ... you have to wonder why Europe does not seem capable of taking decisive action in its own theatre' (quoted in Emmanouilidis (1996: 1). Another telling example for US criticism of the EU's inability for external action is the attack by Christopher Hill, US envoy to the Balkans, on the EU for 'fiddling while Kosovo burns' and for being 'absent in Kosovo, although it does nothing but congratulate itself on the coming introduction of the euro'. (See: *Financial Times* (1998b); *Agence Europe* (1998c).

5. See for the implementation of the CFSP: Durand and de Vasconcelos (1998); Regelsberger (1992–8); Regelsberger and Wessels (1996: 19–54); Ryba (1995: 14–35); Willaert and Marquès-Ruiz (1995: 35–95).

6. As for analyses of the Amsterdam Treaty provisions on CFSP see: Algieri (1998: 89–120); Regelsberger, and Jopp (1998: 155–170); Schmalz (1998b).

7. As for synopses on the positions of the Member States and institutions on CFSP during the Intergovernmental Conference 1996/7 see: European Parliament (1997); Piepenschneider (1996: 7–15).

8. Since January 1996 the coming into effect of the MEDA-programme was blocked by the open question of how to decide on a possible suspension of the programme in case a partner state should violate human rights. Whereas the United Kingdom insisted that such a decision would have to be taken by unanimity according to CFSP procedures, all other EU Member States and particularly Belgium and Germany favoured a decision-taking according to Community procedures with qualified majority voting. After longstanding quarrels, the MEDA-programme finally came into force on 2 August 1996. However, the principal question of how to decide on the suspension of agreements with third countries in case of the violation of human rights remained an open one. See *Agence Europe* (1996a; 1996b; 1996c; 1996d; 1996e).

9. Telling examples are the Greek reluctance to acknowledge the newly established state of Macedonia due to potential negative effects on its integrity, particularly with regard to the Greek province 'Macedonia' or the Portuguese obstruction policy in Asia as a means to enforce the self determination of East Timor. See in this context Wessels (1998).

10. As elaborated particularly by the leading German officials Ischinger and Kölsch (1997), 'Was Mehrheitsentscheidungen erreichen können. Zur Gemeinsamen Außen- und Sicherheitspolitik der EU'. *Frankfurter Allgemeine Zeitung*, 2 May 1997.

11. In December 1998, the Vienna European Council defined Russia as the top priority for the first common strategy to be followed by others on Ukraine, the Mediterranean region with particular emphasis on the Barcelona Process and the Middle East Peace Process and the Western Balkans. See: *Agence Europe* (1998d: 74).

12. For further details on the coherence of the EU external relations see: Schmalz (1998c: 421–42); Schmalz (1997a); Burghardt and Tebbe (1995: 1–20).

13. Whereas the French and the German versions of the TEU speak in Article 3 of 'cohérence' and 'Kohärenz' the English version still refers to the term

'consistency' instead of 'coherence'. The Amsterdam Treaty thus carries on with a semantic incoherence within the concept of coherence thereby constituting an unnecessary distortion in the wording of the legal foundations.

14. As provided for in the declaration on the organization and functioning of the Commission annexed to the Amsterdam Treaty.
15. Most recently, however, the official CFSP language speaks of a 'personality with a strong political profile'. See: *Agence Europe* (1998d).
16. The Franco-German proposal to give him the right to chair the Political Committee as suggested in the Kohl–Chirac letter of 9 December 1996 did not receive the support of the other partners.
17. Declaration on the establishment of a policy planning and early warning unit.
18. See: *Agence Europe* (1997b); *Agence Europe* (1998a).
19. Inter Institutional Agreement between the European Parliament, the Council and the European Commission on provisions regarding financing of the Common Foreign and Security Policy.
20. The Inter Institutional Agreement suggests the following lines: observation and organization of elections/participation in democratic transition processes; EU-envoys; prevention of conflicts/peace and security processes; financial assistance to disarmament processes; contributions to international conferences; urgent actions.
21. The United Kingdom, assisted by Portugal and Greece, was the most in favour of the unanimity principle while Germany, the Benelux countries, Italy and Austria wished an extension of the majority principle as laid down already in Article J.3 (2) of the Maastricht Treaty.
22. In contrast to current practice whereby Member States should abstain from blocking joint decisions in cases where a majority of Member States would already be in favour of it. See declaration no. 27 annexed to the TEU.
23. As for the negotiations of the Amsterdam Treaty see an insider's view: MacDonagh (1998).
24. As for an overview on the national positions and the chronology of events of the IGC see: European Parliament (1997); Gerbet, De la Serre and Nafilyan (1998); Piepenschneider (1996); *CFSP Forum* (1996); Weidenfeld (1998) (contains a CD-ROM with almost 400 official documents and a synopsis on Member States' positions).
25. As for this proposal see *Agence Europe* (1997a).
26. See the relevant protocol and the declaration on WEU both attached to the TEU.
27. According to the UK initiative launched at the informal summit of 24/25 October 1998 at Pörtschach, Austria, the WEU's political functions could be integrated as a 'fourth pillar' into the EU while the WEU's military capacity would revert to the NATO alliance. See: Blair (1998); Vernet (1998); *Financial Times* (1998c).
28. The declaration is printed in *CFSP Forum* (1998: 8).
29. By the Benelux countries in the course of the work of the Contact group. See: *Agence Europe* (1998b).

BIBLIOGRAPHY

Agence Europe (1996a), 27 January.

Agence Europe (1996b), 31 January.

Agence Europe (1996c), 28 March.

Agence Europe (1996d), 25 April.

Agence Europe (1996e), 1 August.

Agence Europe (1997a), 24/25 March.

Agence Europe (1997b), 'The Report of the Secretary General of the Council Jürgen Trumpf', 14 November.

Agence Europe (1998a), 'The Intermediary Report of the British Presidency', 2 April.

Agence Europe (1998b), 29 April.

Agence Europe (1998c), 7/8 September.

Agence Europe (1998d), 'Vienna European Council, 11 and 12 December 1998: Presidency Conclusions', 13 December.

Algieri, F. (1998) 'Die Reform der GASP: Anleitung zu begrenztem gemeinsamen Handeln'. In W. Weidenfeld (ed.), *Amsterdam in der Analyse: Strategien für Europa*. Gütersloh, pp. 89–120.

Bildt, C. (1997) 'The global lessons of Bosnia'. In The Philip Morris Institute for Public Policy Research (ed.), *What Global Role for the EU?* Brussels: Philip Morris Institute, pp. 23–31.

Blair, T. (1998) 'Time for Europe to repay America the soldier'. *International Herald Tribune*, 14/15 November.

Burghardt, G. and G. Tebbe (1995) 'Die Gemeinsame Außen- und Sicherheitspolitik der Europäischen Union: rechtliche Struktur und politischer Prozeß'. *Europarecht* 1/2, 1–20.

CFSP Forum (1996) 'Reforming the CFSP: Positions of Member States and Institutions'. No. 3/4, 7–15.

CFSP Forum (1998) No. 4, p. 8.

Dolan, A. (1997) The European Union's Common Foreign and Security Policy: the Planning Dimension. *International Security Information Service*, Briefing Paper No. 14, Brussels.

Durand, M.-F. and À. de Vasconcelos (eds), (1998) *La PESC: ouvrir l'Europe au monde*. Paris: Presses de Sciences Po.

Emmanouilidis, J. A. (1996) 'Imia Islet: an Ignored Test Case for the CFSP?', *CFSP Forum* 1.

European Parliament (1997) *Task Force 'Intergovernmental Conference': Summary of the Positions of the Member States and the European Parliament on the 1996 Intergovernmental Conference*. Luxembourg 12 July 1996 and 12 May 1997.

Financial Times (1998a) 'Belgrade's Punishment Threatened to Turn to Farce as it was Undermined by Foreign Airlines and even EU Governments', 9 September.

Financial Times (1998b), 12 September.

Financial Times (1998c), 'Euro Defence', 23 October.

Frankfurter Allgemeine Zeitung (1998) 'Es ist noch ein weiter Weg, bis die Gemeinschaft die weltpolitische Reifeprüfung ablegen kann', 7 September.

Gerbet, P., F. De la Serre and G. Nafilyan (1998), *L'Union politique de l'Europe: jalons et textes*. Paris.

Grunert, T. (1997) 'The Association of the European Parliament. No longer the underdog in EPC?'. In E. Regelsberger, P. de Schoutheete de Tervarent and W. Wessels (eds), *Foreign Policy of the European Union: From EPC to CFSP and beyond*. London: Lynne Reinner, pp. 109–131.

Institut d'Etudes de Sécurité de L'UEO (1998) *L'UEO à cinquante ans*. Paris.

Ischinger, W. (1998) *Die Gemeinsame Außen- und Sicherheitspolitik nach Amsterdam: Praxis und Perspektiven*. Discussion Paper C 14. Bonn: Centre for European Integration Studies, pp. 7–9.

Ischinger, W. and E. Kölsch (1997) 'Was Mehrheitsentscheidungen erreichen können. Zur Gemeinsamen Außen- und Sicherheitspolitik der EU'. *Frankfurter Allgemeine Zeitung*, 2 May 1997.

Janning, J. (1994–8), 'Differenzierung als Integrationsprinzip: Die Flexibilität im neuen EU-Vertrag'. In W. Weidenfeld and W. Wessels (eds), *Jahrbuch der Europäischen Integration 1993/94–1997/98*. Bonn.

Jopp, M. (1994–8), 'Westeuropäische Union'. In W. Weidenfeld and W. Wessels (eds), *Jahrbuch der Europäischen Integration 1993/94–1997/98*. Bonn.

Kiso, J. O. (1997) 'An uncosy relationship: COREPER, Political Committee and CFSP'. *CFSP Forum* 2, 3–5.

MacDonagh, B. (1998) *Original Sin in a Brave New World: An Account of the Negotiation on the Treaty of Amsterdam*. Dublin: Institute for European Affairs.

Missiroli, A. (1999), *Flexibility and Enhanced Cooperation after Amsterdam: Prospects for CFSP and WEU*. Paris.

Monar, J. (1997a) 'The European Union's Foreign Affairs System after the Treaty of Amsterdam: a strengthened capacity for external action?', *European Foreign Affairs Review*, 2, 413–36.

Monar, J. (1997b) 'The finances of the Union's Intergovernmental Pillars. Tortuous experiments with the Community Budget'. *Journal of Common Market Studies*, 1, 57–78.

Nuttall, S. (1997) 'The CFSP Provisions of the Amsterdam Treaty. An exercise in collusive ambiguity'. *CFSP Forum*, 3, 1–3.

O'Flaherty, C. (1997) 'A practioner's view of the CFSP'. *CFSP-Forum*, 2, 1–2.

Piepenschneider, M. (1996) *Regierungskonferenz 1996: Synopse der Reformvorschläge zur Europäischen Union. Working paper of the Konrad-Adenauer-Foundation*. 2nd rev. edn, St Augustin.

Regelsberger, E. (1992–8) 'Gemeinsame Außen- und Sicherheitspolitik'. In W. Weidenfeld and W. Wessels (eds), *Jahrbuch der Europäischen Integration 1991/ 92–1997/98*. Bonn: Institut für Europäische Politik: Europa Union Verlag.

Regelsberger, E. and W. Wessels (1996) 'The CFSP institutions and procedures: a third way for the Second Pillar'. *European Foreign Affairs Review*, 1, 29–54.

Regelsberger, E. (1998) 'Group-to-group dialogues: a prominent role in the EU's external relations?'. *CFSP Forum*, 2, 2–3.

Regelsberger, E. and M. Jopp (1998) 'Die Stärkung der Handlungsfähigkeit in der Gemeinsamen Außen- und Sicherheitspolitik'. In M. Jopp, A. Maurer and O. Schmuck (eds), *Die Europäische Union nach Amsterdam: Analysen und Stellungnahmen zum neuen EU-Vertrag*. Bonn, pp. 155–70.

Remacle, E. and B. Delcourt (1998) 'La PESC à l'épreuve de conflit yougoslave: acteurs, représentations, enseignements'. In M.-F. Durand and A. de Vasconcelos (eds), *La PESC: ouvrir l'Europe au monde*. Paris: Presses de Sciences Po, pp. 227–72.

Ryba, B.-C. (1995) 'La Politique Étrangère et de Sécurité Commune. Mode d'emploi et bilan d'une année d'application'. *Revue du Marché commun et de l'Union européenne*, 384, 14–35.

Schmalz, U. (1997a) *Kohärenz der EU-Außenbeziehungen? Der Dualismus von Gemeinschaft und Gemeinsamer Außen- und Sicherheitspolitik in der Praxis.* Working paper of the Konrad-Adenauer-Foundation. St Augustin.

Schmalz, U. (1997b) 'Setting up the Policy Planning and Early Warning Unit: a thorny path from idea to realization'. *CFSP Forum*, 4, 1–2.

Schmalz, U. (1998a) 'The Kosovo crisis: just another failure in CFSP crisis management?', *CFSP Forum*, 3, 1.

Schmalz, U. (1998b) *Zwischen Anspruch und Wirklichkeit: Die Amsterdamer Vertragsbestimmungen zur Gemeinsamen Außen- und Sicherheitspolitik.* Working Paper of the Konrad-Adenauer-Foundation. St Augustin.

Schmalz, U. (1998c) 'The Amsterdam Provisions on external coherence: bridging the Union's foreign policy dualism?'. *European Foreign Affairs Review*, 3, 421–42.

Secretariat General of the Council of the European Union (1995), *Report of the Reflection Group*. Brussels, 5 December 1995.

Silvestri, S. (1997), 'The Albanian test case'. *International Spectator*, July–December, 87–98.

Der Standard (1998) 'Sicherheitspolitischer Papiertiger'. 9 September.

Süddeutsche Zeitung (1998) 'Diplomatische Flachflieger'. 7 and 11 September.

van Ham, P. (ext.) (1997) *Informationsbedarf der Gemeinsamen Außen- und Sicherheitspolitik der Europäischen Union. Ansatzpunkte für eine Bewertung, SWP – IP 3046.* Ebenhausen. October 1997.

Vernet, D (1998), 'Paris accueille avec perplexité l'initiative de Tony Blair sur la défence européenne'. *Le Monde*, 23 October.

Wessels, W. (ed.) (1998) *National vs. EU-Foreign Policy Interests: Mapping 'Important' National Interests. Final Report of a Collective Project by the Trans European Policy Studies Association and Member Institutes.* Cologne/Brussels: Trans European Policy Studies Association.

Weidenfeld, W. (ed.) (1998) *Amsterdam in der Analyse: Strategien für Europa.* Gütersloh.

Willaert, P. and C. Marquès-Ruiz (1995) 'Vers une Politique Etrangère et de Sécurité Commune: Etat des Lieux'. *Revue du Marché Unique Européen*, 3, 35–95.

CHAPTER 14

JUSTICE AND HOME AFFAIRS AFTER AMSTERDAM: THE TREATY REFORMS AND THE CHALLENGE OF THEIR IMPLEMENTATION

Jörg Monar

INTRODUCTION

If it makes sense at all to qualify areas of policy-making as 'winners' of Intergovernmental Conferences then justice and home affairs have certainly been the biggest 'winners' of the 1996/97 Intergovernmental Conference and the Treaty of Amsterdam. The scope of the changes are spectacular, both in terms of sheer volume – over 100 new or amended treaty provisions, 6 protocols and 20 declarations in the annex – and substance: not only have the basic provisions of Title VI TEU been extensively amended but also major sectors of justice and home affairs have been moved into the EC Treaty, partly in the form of an entirely new Title of the EC Treaty governed by a whole range of new provisions. In addition, both the 'old' intergovernmental and the 'new' Community part of justice and home affairs have been opened to a wide range of actual or potential differentiated integration within the framework of the Treaties. The most substantial step taken towards differentiation within the EC/EU framework is certainly the incorporation of Schengen,[1] but the introduction of the possibility of 'closer cooperation' in all areas of justice and home affairs is of even greater political significance. All these reforms have been placed under the new heading of the Union as an 'area of freedom, security and justice' (hereinafter AFSJ) which adds a new programmatic element to the European construction.

These extensive changes are all the more remarkable since justice and home affairs entered the arena of European policy-making rather late. Intergovernmental cooperation in this area started, it is true, in 1975 with the development of the TREVI framework. Yet both TREVI and the large number of intergovernmental groups set up in the second half of the 1980s dealt only with a limited range of issues of justice and home affairs, lacked a clear legal basis, a stable institutional framework, regular procedures and, and above all, suffered from the absence of co-ordinated overall objectives. In 1993 the (Maastricht) Treaty on European Union marked a first major breakthrough by creating a comprehensive legal basis for cooperation in the fields of justice and home affairs which – in the context of intergovernmental Title VI TEU – were equipped with a single institutional framework and specific instruments and procedural rules. However, the Maastricht Treaty provisions on justice and home affairs had been the outcome of weak compromise between those Member States (like Germany and the Benelux) which favoured a communitarization of justice and home affairs and those (like the United Kingdom and Denmark) which wanted to keep policy-making on these issues as intergovernmental as possible. As a result the Maastricht Treaty did not define any objectives for cooperation between the Member States, provided this cooperation only with ill-adapted intergovernmental instruments and procedures and, last but not least, failed to establish adequate possibilities for democratic and judicial control.

Looking back to the nearly six years (1993–9) of the functioning of the 'old' Title VI TEU – the 'Third Pillar' – it seems fair to say that it paved the way for the dramatic reforms of the Treaty of Amsterdam through both its failures and its successes. Through its failures, because the slow and cumbersome decision-making under Title VI, its extremely limited legally binding output, the obvious shortcomings of its instruments and procedures convinced an increasing number of Member States that this 'Third Pillar' was unable to meet the growing challenges to the EU and its Member States in key areas such as asylum, immigration and the fight against organized crime. Yet also through its successes, because the build-up of a rationalized system of Council groups dealing with the various JHA issues, the emergence of a culture of cooperation between the national ministries, the large number of non-binding texts adopted and the signing (though subject to lengthy ratification) of a number of major conventions demonstrated since 1993 that there was after all enough common ground, capacity and political will to arrive at more substantial results. In both the literature and the evaluations by the EU institutions of the Maastricht 'Third Pillar' a lot of emphasis has been placed, and rightly so, on its numerous deficits. Yet enough real progress in terms of consolidating and expanding the basis of cooperation was achieved under Title VI from 1993 to 1999 to make the major overhaul of Amsterdam possible.

'Possible', however, did not mean inevitable, and such an overhaul was by no means certain at the beginning of the 1996 Intergovernmental

Conference. The constant opposition of the (Conservative) British Government to any major change, backed in a less prominent way by Denmark, and a number of disagreements even between the countries favouring major reform (such as between France and Germany over parliamentary control and the future development of police cooperation) made the chances for a major breakthrough look rather dim for many months of the negotiations. Yet during spring 1997 Austrian, French and German concerns about the internal security implications of the Eastern enlargement, the Schengen group's unflagging pressure for an incorporation of the Schengen system into the Union, and the more flexible positions adopted by the newly elected British and French Governments all effectively contributed to the critical mass of accumulated political will and compromises – both strategic and tactical – to make the Amsterdam European Council able to agree on the sweeping treaty changes which have now launched the Union into what many anticipate as a new era of policy-making on justice and home affairs.

In the following sections we will try to assess the main elements of reform introduced by the Treaty of Amsterdam[2] by looking not only at the new treaty provisions but also at the first steps taken to meet the challenge of their implementation.

A NEW RANGE OF OBJECTIVES

The Maastricht Treaty did not define any objectives for cooperation in the areas of justice and home affairs listed in Article K.1 TEU. These were rather vaguely described as 'matters of common interest' only. The Treaty of Amsterdam completely reverses that situation by establishing a range of new objectives in justice and home affairs.

The first and most important of the new objectives is enshrined in amended Article 2 TEU, fourth indent, which elevates the maintenance and the development of the Union 'as an area of freedom, justice and security' to one of the main objectives of the Treaty. This 'area' is defined as one 'in which the free movement of persons is assured in conjunction with appropriate measures with respect to external border controls, immigration, asylum and the prevention and combating of crime'. The wording chosen is clearly very broad and commits the Union to the adoption of measures in all of the core areas of the 'matters of common interest' of 'old' Title VI.

Yet the definition of the 'area of freedom, security and justice' in the Treaty is not as broad and ambitious as its ringing title may suggest: the 'appropriate measures' provided for with respect to external border controls, immigration, asylum and crime have been explicitly linked to the 'old' treaty objective of free movement of persons. This seems a rather narrow basis for any more comprehensive action in these fields. Here it is difficult to ignore the influence of the old rationale of the Schengen group. The primary emphasis here is clearly on guaranteeing the free movement of persons – the central objective of Schengen. The 'appropriate measures' to be taken in the other areas mentioned (external border controls, immigration, asylum and crime prevention) are explicitly related to this objective, and this in a way which is strongly reminiscent of the old 'compensatory measures' in the Schengen context. This definition of the central objective of Union falls short both of the broader scope that JHA cooperation had already reached before the entry into force of the new Treaty and of the needs of future action in JHA, especially in the areas of asylum, immigration and judicial cooperation, which would need to extend much beyond that of a mere flanking measure of ensuring free movement. Member States reluctant to engage in more extensive common measures in the areas of justice and home affairs could use the explicit link established between the objective of free movement and any 'appropriate measures' to obstruct any more comprehensive EU policies.[3]

With the exception of customs cooperation and the protection of the financial interests of the European Union all of the newly communitarized areas of the 'old' Third Pillar have been transferred into the new Title IV TEC on 'Visas, asylum, immigration and other policies related to free movement'. Its first Article, 61 TEC, links the general objective of progressively establishing an 'area of freedom, justice and security' with a whole range of measures to be adopted in the areas of justice and home affairs: according to Article 61(a) the Council shall adopt measures aiming at ensuring the free movement of persons in accordance with Article 14 TEC Treaty in conjunction with 'directly related flanking measures'. These are divided into two groups. Firstly, measures with respect to external border controls, conditions of travel of third country nationals within the territory of the Member States and asylum and immigration. These are to be adopted on the basis of the new EC Treaty provisions of Articles 62(2) and (3) and 63(1)(a) and (2)(a). Secondly, measures to prevent and combat crime that will have to be taken on the basis of new Article 31(e) TEU within the Third Pillar. Each of these provisions governs selected issues of justice and home affairs such as standards for carrying out checks at external borders, minimum standards for giving temporary protection to displaced persons from third countries, and the adoption of minimum rules relating to the constituent elements of criminal acts in the fields of organized crime, terrorism and drug trafficking. In addition, Article 62(1) provides in addition for measures ensuring, in compliance with Article 14 TEC, the absence of any controls on persons, be they citizens of the Union, or nationals of third countries, when crossing internal borders.

What is of major importance here is that for the first time measures in the areas of justice and home affairs are not only linked to specific objectives but also that the adoption of these measures must be completed within a clearly set deadline: under Article 61(a) TEC the Council has to act within five years. This means that the Community method of combining integration objectives with deadlines for their achievement, used successfully, for instance, in respect to the establishment of the Common commercial policy and the completion of the Single Market, is for the first time applied to justice and home affairs. It is important to note, however, that one finds here the same limitation as in amended Article 2 TEU: Article 61(a) TEC describes the above mentioned measures in the former Third Pillar areas as 'directly related flanking measures' to the aim of ensuring the free movement of persons.

Article 61(b) to (e) TEC requires for the Council to take measures in four other groups of fields.

- asylum, immigration and safeguarding the rights of third country nationals,
- judicial cooperation,
- the strengthening of administrative cooperation and
- (subject to the provisions of Title VI TEU) police and judicial cooperation in criminal matters.

These areas are not been explicitly linked to the aim of free movement. As part of the AFSJ, however, they remain subject to the general objective of Article 2 TEU with its emphasis on free movement related measures.

Articles 61(b) to 61(e) TEC do not establish a deadline for the Council to act. Yet each of these provisions refers to a different new provision of the EC Treaty, and one of these, Article 63,[4] dealing with measures on asylum, refugees and immigration, establishes the same deadline of five years as Article 61(a). Because of the political relevance of the subject matters covered this is clearly one of the most important new treaty provisions. The types of measures listed in Article 63 are described in considerable detail, ranging from criteria for determining which Member State is responsible for considering an application for asylum over minimum standards for giving temporary protection to conditions of entry and residence for immigrants. Together they bear much resemblance to an extensive legislative programme. This has both advantages and disadvantages. Many of the issues identified in Article 63 for Community action concern core areas of asylum and immigration policy. The fact that the Council will now have to take action on these within five years will certainly bring the Union closer to a common approach to major issues of asylum and immigration policy. Yet Article 63 does not provide for the establishment of a *common* asylum and immigration policy, nor does it create a general policy-making competence for the Community. The list in Article 63 is far from being comprehensive enough for providing a basis for a 'common' policy worth the name: it does not cover, for instance, the development of common aims in the area of immigration policy nor the question of social integration of asylum seekers and immigrants. The central issue of burden-sharing between the Member States, an issue which Germany has repeatedly brought up during the last few years, is only vaguely and inadequately referred to in Article 63(2)(b) as 'promoting a balance of effort' between Member States. The objectives set as regards asylum and immigration are therefore limited to a number of important individual issues only, rather than oriented towards comprehensive common policy-making.

This applies to an even greater extent to the policy areas mentioned in Article 63(c), judicial cooperation in civil matters, and Article 63(d), strengthening of administrative cooperation. Article 65 TEC, which governs judicial cooperation in civil matters, limits the scope of measures in this area to those having 'cross-border implications', and identifies five different areas ranging from improving the system for cross-border service of judicial and extrajudicial documents over the recognition and enforcement of decisions in civil and commercial cases to the elimination of obstacles to the good functioning of civil proceedings. Important as these areas are they are nevertheless unlikely to provide a basis for comprehensive policy-making in view of creating a common European judicial area. No reference is made, for instance, to cooperation in matters of customs, revenue and administrative law. As regards administrative cooperation, Article 66 only refers in rather general terms to measures ensuring cooperation between relevant departments. The objectives listed in Articles 65 and 66 are further weakened by the fact that no deadline is set for their achievement.

The measures in the field of police and judicial cooperation in criminal matters referred to in Article 61 TEC are 'aimed at a high level of security'. This objective is repeated in almost identical terms in amended Article 29 TEU which defines the general aims of cooperation under Title VI TEU and provides for closer cooperation between police forces, judicial authorities and other competent authorities as well as – 'where necessary' – approximation of rules on criminal matters. Articles 30 and 31 TEU specify in more detail the elements of 'common action' by the Member States in matters of police and judicial cooperation in criminal matters respectively. As regards the former a broad range of areas are listed in Article 30(1) which include, for instance, operational cooperation, data collection, training and common evaluation of investigative techniques. Yet no more precise objectives are set for cooperation in these areas and also there is no time constraint. Article 30(2) deals mainly with cooperation through

Europol. Although the new provisions do not provide for the introduction of operational powers for Europol, they nevertheless represent a clear step forward because a number of clear and deadline-linked objectives (five years) are set for the further development of Europol. By virtue of Article 30(2)(a), (b) and (c) TEU, the European police should be enabled to 'encourage' the coordination and carrying out of specific investigative actions by competent authorities of the Member States, to 'ask' the competent authorities of the Member States to conduct and coordinate their investigations in specific cases and to develop specific expertise which may be put at the disposal of Member States to assist them in investigating cases of organized crime, and to promote liaison arrangements between prosecuting/investigating officials specializing in the fight against organized crime. This goes clearly beyond the rather passive role – largely limited to information exchange – which Europol has had so far.

As regards judicial cooperation in criminal matters amended Article 31 TEU provides for 'common action' in a number of areas which include cooperation between ministries and judicial authorities, facilitating extradition, preventing conflicts of jurisdiction, and the progressive establishment of minimum rules relating to the constituent elements of criminal acts and to penalties in the fields of organized crime, terrorism and drug trafficking. Without any doubt the areas listed here are of major importance for more effective cooperation in criminal matters. Yet, again, they are far from comprehensive. There is no list of types of offences, such as fraud, money-laundering, corruption and disclosure of official secrets, on which Union action should focus. Issues of particular importance, such as the question of extraterritorial evidence, are not mentioned either. Last but not least, no deadline has been set for 'common action' to be taken. Article 31 may well ease progress on the issues specifically mentioned but it does not establish a comprehensive legal basis for the construction of a 'European judicial area' in criminal matters. It should also be noted that Article 32 TEU provides that the Council shall lay down the 'conditions and limitations' under which the authorities referred to in Article 30 and 31 may operate in the territory of another Member State. Having regard to the fact that cross-border cooperation and operation is going to be one of the central conditions of progress in the areas of police and judicial cooperation in criminal matters this provision appears as being rather negative and lacking in substance.

Looking at Title VI TEU one also wonders why there are no more specific objectives set in these provisions as regards the fight against drug-trafficking. After all this is an area of common concern of the Member States which has consistently figured high on the Council's agenda during the last few years.

There are two areas of the 'old' Third Pillar which are neither mentioned in Article 61 TEC nor in Title VI TEU: combatting fraud and customs cooperation. As far as it affects the financial interests of the Community the fight against fraud is covered by amended Article 280 TEC. One new element has been added to the objectives of Community action: Article 280(1) TEC now provides that measures taken 'shall act as a deterrent and be such as to afford effective protection in the member states'. According to Article 280(4) such measures shall be aimed at 'equivalent protection' in the Member States, but it is added that the measures shall not concern the application of national criminal law and the administration of justice. This can at best provide a better basis for the sanctioning of financial fraud through national penal law. Yet the provision comes in no way near to establishing a basis for a European penal law on financial fraud which many experts believe to be the only efficient response to the increasing problems of fraud (Delmas-Marty, 1997; Sicurella, 1998).

As regards customs cooperation a new Title X TEC with a single article has been introduced into the EC Treaty: Article 135 provides in very general terms for a 'strengthening of customs cooperation between the member states'. The only new element in comparison with the former Title VI TEU provision is that this now explicitly extends to cooperation between the Member States and the Commission. Having regard to the Commission's central role in Customs Union matters this seems a sensible addition, but it will not bring major change since in practice the Commission has already been associated with most of the Member States' customs cooperation measures.

The overall balance sheet of Amsterdam as regards the objectives in building up the AFSJ is a mixed one: on the one hand the former lack of objectives in Title VI TEU has been remedied, and the five-year deadline set for some of the measures to be adopted by the Council is clearly a major step forward. Yet the objectives cover a selection of issues rather than whole policy areas. This favours piecemeal problem solving rather than a comprehensive policy-making approach. It is significant that in spite of the whole debate about 'communitarizing' justice and home affairs during the IGC the ToA does not provide for the establishment of a 'common policy' according to the EC model in any of the newly 'communitarized' areas. In addition, the close link between the general aim of establishing an area of freedom, security and justice and the 'old' objective of free movement of persons betrays the influence of the old Schengen rationale with its much more restricted scope. Much will therefore depend on whether the Member States are willing to give a constructive and broad interpretation to the new objectives.

A NEW SET OF INSTRUMENTS

The 'old' JHA instruments introduced by the Maastricht Treaty had been largely taken over from the Common Foreign and Security Policy with its emphasis on co-ordinated political 'positions'. Yet justice and home affairs as a policy-making area are normally better served by formal legal acts rather than vaguely defined common political approaches. The application of the old Third Pillar instruments had been affected by uncertainties as to the nature and scope of 'common positions' and 'joint actions', and the clearly legally binding conventions proved to be an extremely heavy and cumbersome instrument because of their need for national ratification. The ToA brings major improvements in this respect. In the newly 'communitarized' areas the former Third Pillar instruments are now replaced by the EC legal instruments. Yet also the instruments in the remaining intergovernmental areas of Title VI TEU have been modified substantially.

With the 'framework decisions' of Article 34(2)(b) TEU a new instrument has been created for the purpose of 'approximation of the laws' which shall be 'binding upon the member states as to the results to be achieved but shall leave to the national authorities the choice of form and method'. Any direct effect is explicitly excluded. This means that 'framework decisions' are rather similar to EC directives, except that they are legal acts outside of the Community legal order and do not entail any direct effect. This instrument is doubtlessly more appropriate to the legislative needs of police cooperation and judicial cooperation in criminal matters than 'common positions' or the former 'joint actions'. It should be appreciated by the Member States for the greater margin of discretion it leaves them in the implementation and could become a useful instrument for the development of the legal *acquis* of cooperation under Title VI.

The former 'joint actions' have disappeared from the range of instruments. Instead Article 34(2)(c) now provides for the new instrument of 'decisions' for any other purpose than approximation of laws which is consistent with the objectives of Title VI. 'Decisions' are to be binding on the Member States, but, again, any direct effect is excluded. As general purpose instruments 'decisions' could become the standard instrument for matters of limited scope requiring legal action.

'Conventions' have been maintained as an instrument under Title VI TEU, but some effort has been made to shorten the period between their adoption and their entry into force. Article 34(2)(d) TEU provides that Member States shall begin ratification procedures within a time limit set by the Council. Since the Council will have to decide on the time limit by unanimity it seems unlikely to be extremely tight, but it can certainly help to speed up ratification procedures. It is also stipulated that, unless conventions provide otherwise, they shall enter into force as soon as they are adopted by at least half of the Member States. This can exercise additional pressure on Member States to proceed with ratification. It may not always be practicable, however, to start applying a convention with only some of the Member States participating.

One of the weaker instruments of the old Third Pillar – the 'common position' – has survived. In Article 34(2)(a) an effort has been made to clarify the scope of 'common positions' of which it is said that they 'defin[e] the approach of the Union to a particular matter', although the terms 'approach' and 'particular matter' are rather vague and the legal status of the act is not clarified. The vagueness of the definition and the fact that 'common positions' are the only acts listed in Article 34(2) which fall neither under the jurisdiction of the Court of Justice[5] nor under the right of the European Parliament to be consulted suggest[6] that a 'common position' has to be regarded as a decision on political strategy rather than a binding legal act. 'Common positions' could therefore become the preferred instrument of the Member States in all cases in which they want to avoid an act becoming legally binding and/or subject to formal consultation of the European Parliament.

The reformed instruments – both under Title IV EC and Title VI TEU – are likely to bring considerable progress in terms of the legal quality and potential effectiveness of instruments in EU justice and home affairs. Already at the end of 1998 it became clear that the European Commission would propose replacing existing intergovernmental acts in the newly 'communitarized' areas by Community legal acts for the sake of legal clarity and consistency after the entry into force of the ToA. The Commission announced, for instance, the replacement of the 1998 'Brussels II' Convention[7] by a Council Regulation and the 1997 Convention on the service of judicial and extrajudicial documents in civil and commercial matters by a Council Directive.[8] Yet also in the intergovernmental sphere the new instruments under Title VI offer for the first time the possibility of building up a clear-cut legal *acquis* at the Union level. As a result the legislative output of the EC and EU in justice and home affairs could increase quite considerably during the next few years, although under Title VI TEU Member States will still be able to make use of the non-binding wild card of 'common positions'. Together with the strengthened role of the ECJ[9] the refined set of instruments should also contribute to a higher degree of legal certainty in JHA.

NEW POSSIBILITIES OF EXTERNAL ACTION

One issue of justice and home affairs that was addressed by the IGC can be regarded as both a question of instruments and of competences. The old Title VI TEU provisions did not provide for cooperation of the Union with third countries. This imposed serious restrictions on the scope of EU action in justice and home affairs because in areas such as police cooperation, the fight against international organized crime, asylum and immigration the effectiveness of internal action often depends to a large extent also on parallel external action. The Union's deficits in this respect became all the more apparent because after 1993 many third countries, among these all the associated countries of Central and Eastern Europe, the United States and Canada, expressed considerable interest in close cooperation and even the conclusion of agreements with the Union in the fields covered by Title VI.

The ToA gives the Union for the first a time a capacity to act internationally on matters of justice and home affairs. According to the 'doctrine of parallelism' the Community's implied powers in external relations extend potentially to any subject matter which falls within the scope of the Community's explicit powers in internal matters. As a result it can be argued that on all those newly communitarized matters of justice and home affairs which will be covered by EC legislation the Community will also be in a position to enter into agreements with third countries. Especially in the areas of asylum and immigration – the negotiation and conclusion of readmission agreements with third countries may be taken as an example – this offers scope for effective external action complementing internal measures.

Yet in the remaining intergovernmental areas as well the situation has changed substantially. New Article 38 TEU provides that agreements referred to in Article 24 may cover matters falling under Title VI. This means that in the context of the Third Pillar the Council can make use of the new CFSP provision enabling it to negotiate and conclude agreements with third countries. The competence base and procedure are entirely different from the EC framework: international agreements under the Title VI are to be concluded by the Council acting unanimously on a recommendation from the Presidency, their binding effect on individual Member States being subject to any national ratification procedure that may be needed. It is rather peculiar, however, that a treaty-making authorization and procedure has been introduced without at the same time granting legal personality to the Union. This means that in the case of any future international agreement concluded under the CFSP provisions the formal contracting partners on the Union side will be the Member States only.

The Member States may still decide to attach a Union label to such an agreement by signing as members of the European Union or (in a political sense) on behalf of it, but the Union will not be a contracting party and there will be no transfer of competence to the Union.[10] Yet the fact that for the first time ever the Union will be in a position to enter into conventional relations with third countries on matters of justice and home affairs even in the intergovernmental sphere can be regarded as significant progress. It should also be mentioned that the 'old' provision on the defence of common positions by the Member States within international organizations (formerly Article K.5, now 37 TEU) has been strengthened by a reference to amended Articles 18 and 19 TEU that establish more precise rules on the external representation of the Union and the defence of positions in international fora.

THE NEW BORDERLINE BETWEEN THE FIRST AND THE THIRD PILLAR

The division of competences between intergovernmental JHA cooperation on the one hand and closely related Community competences on the other has in the past occasionally led to controversies as regards the appropriate legal basis for specific measures. By transferring major former Third Pillar areas into the EC framework the ToA removes a number of possible uncertainties and points of contention in respect to the scope of action taken within the two 'pillars'. This applies not only to the areas closely related to free movement of persons such as asylum, immigration and external border controls covered by new Title IV TEC but also to the full communitarization of the fight against fraud affecting the financial interests of the Community and of customs cooperation. Yet the ToA also creates a new potential for controversies over the borderline between Community and intergovernmental action. A few examples may demonstrate this.

Whereas measures against trafficking in persons and illicit drug and arms trafficking will still have to be adopted on the basis of Articles 29 and 30 TEU, external border control and customs cooperation measures, which are essential elements of any effective action in this respect, are now covered by TEC provisions. The fight against fraud affecting the financial interests of the EC is now a Community domain. Yet measures against fraud can also be taken on the basis of Article 29 TEU of the Third Pillar, and questions such as extradition and the prevention of conflicts of jurisdiction between Member States, which can be of considerable importance in the fight against fraud affecting the EC, are actually governed by Article 31 TEU. One may also regard it as rather unfortunate that whereas action against drug addiction has to be based on Article 152 TEC, the fight against drug trafficking remains fully within the scope of the Third Pillar. Drug addiction and drug trafficking should be regarded as two sides of the same coin, and comprehensive EU action on both sides may be more difficult if it requires two different legal bases and decision-making procedures.

It seems therefore fair to say that the ToA, while removing some of the existing problems over competences, has introduced new potential for friction by creating new artificial competence divisions in closely interrelated policy areas. These could in some important areas complicate and even delay effective Union action.

DECISION-MAKING STRUCTURES AND PROCEDURES

In the run-up to the IGC no other aspect of the 'old' Third Pillar had been the object of as much criticism as its decision-making system. A particularly cumbersome multi-level structure of decision-making, of the predominance of the unanimity voting rule and the limited role of initiative of the European Commission all contributed to a lengthy process of decision-making, the adoption of very few legally binding acts and a reduced substance of decisions due to agreements on the least common denominator. The scope for improvements was therefore large, and there was no lack in ambitious reform proposals in the run-up to the IGC. Yet, unlike in the sphere of objectives and instruments, the Conference failed to agree on a comprehensive overhaul of the decision-making system.

The transfer of a major part of the areas of justice and home affairs into the EC framework with its established single decision-making system offered the chance of a major simplification of the decision-making system. As a result of the transfer the role of the senior 'Article 36 Committee' (formerly 'K.4 Committee'), which introduced an additional level of decision-making between the working groups and COREPER, is henceforth formally limited to the few areas still covered by Title VI TEU. The fact remains, however, that the Committee has not been abolished, and this means not only that this distinctly intergovernmental feature of the Third Pillar has been maintained but also that distinct decision-making structures continue to exist in the communitarized and non-communitarized areas of justice and home affairs.

One would have expected that as a result of the communitarization the working structures of the areas now falling under Title IV TEC would be organized in accordance with the three-level system (working groups–COREPER–Council) existing in other areas of EC policy-making. It was easy enough to agree on the abolition of the Steering Groups. They had already ceased to meet during the second half of 1997. Yet several Member States insisted on retaining a special coordinating body for matters of asylum, immigration and external border controls. When new working structures of the Council were drawn up in April/May 1999 it was decided that this coordinating body should take the form of a 'Strategic Committee' working directly under the authority of COREPER. This solution – which was mainly due to the unwillingness of several national ministries to see certain supervisory and coordinating powers transferred to the Permanent Representatives – leaves the newly communitarized areas of asylum and immigration with a similar four-level structure as the remaining intergovernmental areas with their Article 36 Committee (see Chart 14.1). A further 'intergovernmental' feature in the revised working structure of the Council is the fact that the working parties dealing with the functioning of the SIS have all been included in the police and customs cooperation part of the working structure, although the SIS is arguably so far the Union's most important instrument in the newly communitarized area of external border controls. Equally noteworthy is that the working party on customs cooperation remains within the 'Third Pillar' working structure, although – as mentioned earlier – customs cooperation has been transferred to new Title X TEC. Some Member States took the view that it was so closely related to police cooperation it should remain in the context of the Title VI TEU working structures. Within the 'First Pillar' working structure The upgrading of the working party on civil law cooperation to a 'Committee on Civil Law' reflect the Union's increased agenda and legislative possibilities in this area.

As regards voting rules, one of the most controversial issues during the negotiations, the practice under the 'old' Third Pillar had shown that the requirement of unanimity for all acts under Title VI[11] led in most cases either to a compromise with far less than optimal results or no decision at all. One might have expected that the transfer of most areas of the 'old' Title VI into the EC framework would bring decisive change in this respect. However, at Amsterdam German Chancellor Helmut Kohl effectively blocked the introduction of qualified majority voting in the areas of asylum and immigration. The reasons behind the German position were anxieties about the particular asylum and immigration pressures on Germany and the involvement of *Länder* interests in this area. Yet there were other advocates of unanimity in the newly communitarized areas. The British Government, for instance, insisted on unanimity in the area of judicial cooperation in civil matters. As a result new Article 67(1)-(2) TEC, which establishes the decision-making rules for new Title IV TEC, now provides that the Council shall act unanimously within a transitional period of five years. After this period the Council shall then take unanimously a decision with a view to making all or parts of the Title on free

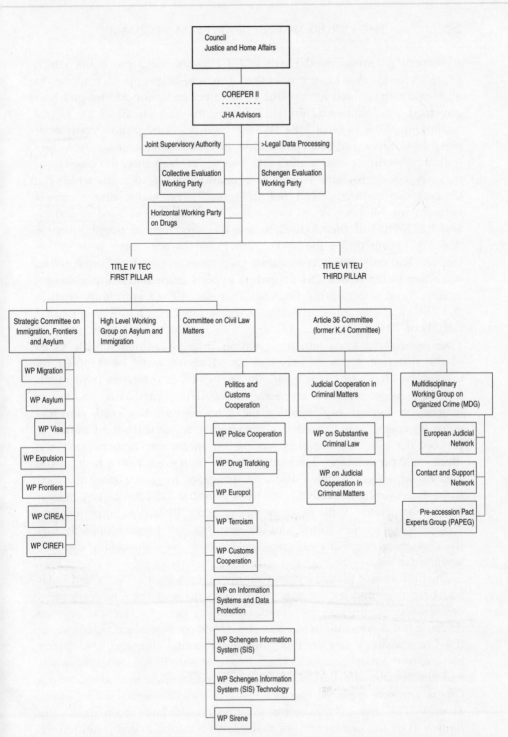

Chart 14.1 New working structure of the Council of the European Union in the area of justice and home affairs. The chart reflects the situation in September 1999.

movement governed by the Article 251 ('co-decision') procedure which provides for qualified majority voting. This two-stage approach applies to all measures provided for by Title IV with the exception of visa policy as governed by Article 62(2)(b) TEC.[12] It means that on all of the newly communitarized areas of Title IV TEC (asylum, immigration, controls at external borders, judicial cooperation in civil matters), majority voting will only become possible after five years. Yet even then the passage to majority voting remains subject to a unanimous decision on which the Council can perfectly well fail to agree.[13] The major disagreements between the Member States over key questions such as burden sharing and the failure of the Council to use the very limited possibilities for majority voting under the 'old' Third Pillar do not augur well in this respect. The only newly communitarized areas to which majority voting according to the Article 251 procedure applies immediately are measures against fraud affecting the financial interests of the Community (Article 280 TEC) and customs cooperation (Article 135 TEC), both being located outside of Title IV.

As regards the areas remaining within 'intergovernmental' Title VI all of the different types of acts mentioned above must be adopted by unanimity. However, Article 34(2)(c) provides that measures implementing a 'decision' shall be taken by qualified majority. This mandatory majority voting on implementing measures represents a small step forward because so far it needed a unanimous decision by the Council to proceed to qualified majority voting on measures implementing the 'decision's' predecessor, the 'joint action'.[14] Yet there is also a new hurdle because amended Article 34(3) now provides for a 'double' qualified majority requiring not only 62 votes but also that these are cast by at least 10 Member States. With majority voting being limited to implementing measures and subject to the 'double' qualification it seems unlikely that the changes will greatly enhance the Union's decision-making capacity under Title VI.

The limited role played by the Commission under the 'old' Third Pillar had been regarded by some as one of the causes of the Union's limited performance in justice and home affairs. Partly for tactical reasons (because it did not want to increase some Member States' suspicions about the Commission's role in this intergovernmental domain), and partly because of the weakness of its shared right of initiative,[15] the Commission had not developed a very active stance in policy-making under Title VI. One might have expected that as a result of the communitarization under Title IV TEC the Commission's position would have been drastically improved by the exclusive right of initiative it normally enjoys within the EC framework. Yet according to new Article 67(1) and (2) TEC the Commission still has to share the right of initiative with the Member

States in all the newly communitarized areas under Title IV during the transitional period of five years, and only after this period will its right of initiative become exclusive. This is clearly a serious restriction which will be made worse by the limitation of the Commission's margin to manoeuvre resulting from the maintenance of unanimity in the same areas during the transitional period. From an institutional point of view the transfer of asylum, immigration and external border controls to Title IV TEC therefore – at least during the transitional period – hardly merits the term 'communitarization'. It appears to be much closer to a massive (though in part temporary) import of intergovernmental procedures into the EC framework.

Yet some elements of progress can be found in the areas not covered by new Title IV TEC. The Commission has been granted an exclusive right of initiative in respect to the measures countering fraud affecting the financial interests of the Community (Article 280 TEC) and to customs cooperation (Article 135 TEC), the latter being an area in which the Commission so far did not have any right of initiative. Under Title VI TEU the Commission still has to share its right of initiative with the Member States, but by virtue of amended Article 34(2) TEU it now extends to all areas covered by Title VI. This represents a clear extension of the Commission's role because under the 'old' Third Pillar the Commission had no right of initiative in the areas of police and judicial cooperation in criminal matters. However, one should not expect immediate dramatic changes in the Commission's role in the Third Pillar because beyond all Treaty provisions it is also the 'climate' of the intergovernmental framework which tends to limit its actual possibilities of influencing decision-making.

Overall the reforms of the decision-making system have clearly led to a simplified structure and a slightly enhanced role of the European Commission. Yet during the transitional period the extension of majority voting will be limited to certain implementing measures, and the prospects for generalized majority voting thereafter remain uncertain. If one looks at the long list of newly defined objectives under Titles IV TEC and VI TEU one can only conclude that Amsterdam has created a new imbalance between objectives on the one hand and decision-making capacity on the other.

FLEXIBILITY

Whatever view one may have of the advantages and disadvantages of 'flexibility' its massive introduction into the EC/EU system is undoubtedly one of the most significant results of the 1996/97 IGC.[16] The AFSJ is going to be the main testing ground of this major move towards differentiation: in no other area of EU policy-making have so many and so varied forms of 'flexibility' been introduced.

The most substantial case is that of the incorporation of Schengen into the EC/EU framework. Its problems and implications are covered in detail elsewhere in this book.[17] The incorporation of Schengen not only represents a major success for the countries of the Schengen group but also provides a much more substantial basis for the development of the AFSJ than the rather limited legal *acquis* of the 'old' Third Pillar. Both under Title IV TEC and Title VI TEU the development of EU justice and home affairs will be able to benefit from the major progress the Schengen countries have achieved in areas such as border control procedures, information systems and police cooperation, from their extensive legal *acquis* and from their accumulated experience on difficult issues of cooperation. Yet there is also a negative side: with its focus on the abolition of internal border controls and 'compensatory' measures the rationale of the Schengen system falls well short of the more ambitious objectives which have emerged in EU justice and home affairs, such as the creation of a common immigration and asylum system or of a 'European judicial area' (see *The challenge of implementation*, below). The credentials of Schengen in terms of democratic and judicial control are also far from securing a positive impact on JHA integration in the EU context. Finally, the additional complexity generated by the differentiating effect of Schengen within the EU is also likely to create new legal, administrative and even political difficulties within the Union.

Of less immediate consequence but of perhaps even greater political significance is obviously the possibility for new frameworks of 'closer cooperation' being set up. Such 'closer cooperation' – which allows a majority of Member States to go ahead with deeper integration in certain areas of justice and home within the EC/EU context and full use of its institutions and procedures – can be set up both under Title IV TEC and Title VI TEU. Different legal procedures apply to both frameworks (Articles 11 TEC and 40 TEU) which are both linked to a new general clause on flexibility in Title VII TEU, Article 43. The differences between these doors to flexibility are quite pronounced.

The list of conditions that must be fulfilled is much longer in Article 11 TEC than it is in Article 40 TEU. One rather interesting difference in this respect is that the former Article provides that 'closer cooperation' should not concern the citizenship of the Union or discriminate between nationals of Member States. Yet the same condition is not provided for by Article 40 TEU. This seems difficult to justify because 'closer cooperation' in what is left of the intergovernmental pillar, i.e. police and judicial cooperation matters, can certainly have an impact on EU citizenship and lead to discrimination between nationals of Member States. The procedures for arriving at 'closer cooperation' are also rather different under these provisions: under Article 11 TEC the Commission plays a key role in the process due to its right of initiative, under Article 40 TEU it is the Council which is the decisive actor. Needless to say, the instruments and procedures after the establishment of 'closer cooperation' are those of the respective treaty frameworks and therefore substantially different. Should a group of Member States want to engage in a 'closer cooperation' covering areas of both pillars – which could well be the case because of the close interrelationship between some of the JHA issues – this division of instruments and procedures could cause additional complications.

In addition to the incorporation of Schengen and 'closer cooperation' a bewildering range of additional 'flexibility' is introduced into the AFSJ by what may be termed the group of the 'opt-ins' and 'opt-outs'.

The most significant of these is the 'Protocol on the position of the United Kingdom and Ireland'[18] which guarantees the UK and Ireland a complete 'opt-out' (the term is of course not used) from Title IV TEC. Yet Article 3 of the Protocol offers both Member States an opt-in possibility for the adoption and application of any measure proposed under this Title at the latest three months after the proposal has been made. Article 8 of the same Protocol gives Ireland a possibility to 'opt-out' from this 'opt-out/opt-in' protocol if it no longer wishes to be covered by it. Both Ireland and the United Kingdom have thereby secured an 'opt-out' combined with a selective 'opt-in' possibility which grants them a higher degree of 'flexibility' than any previous forms of differentiation (such as EMU or the British 'Social chapter' opt-out) within the context of the Treaties. It should be noted, however, that in a Declaration to the Final Act, Ireland declared that it intends to take part in the adoption of measures pursuant to Title IV TEC 'to the maximum extent compatible' with the maintenance of the Common Travel Area with the United Kingdom. Both provisions show to what extent the Irish position is under strain, torn between its commitment to maintain the Common Travel Area and its wish to participate in deeper integration in EU justice and home affairs.

There were even more special arrangements granted to individual Member States: Article 1 of the 'Protocol on the application of certain aspects of Article 14 of the Treaty establishing the European Community'[19] guarantees the United Kingdom the continuation of its right to exercise at its frontiers with other Member States controls on persons. Article 2 of the same protocol provides for a derogation given to the United Kingdom and Ireland to continue to make between themselves the necessary arrangements for maintaining the 'Common Travel Area'. The 'Protocol on the Position of Denmark'[20] grants Denmark an 'opt-out' from Title IV TEC which is in substance largely identical to the British and Irish 'opt-outs'. However, the Danish case is obviously more complicated because

Denmark is a member of Schengen. Article 5 deals with this problem by providing Denmark with six months to decide whether it will implement any Council decision building on the Schengen *acquis* into national law. If Denmark does so, this decision will only create an obligation under international law between Denmark and the other Member States. This is one of the most peculiar arrangements under the new Treaty because it effectively gives Denmark an 'opt-out' from the specific obligations of the EC legal order although the measure in question is a legal act of the EC. The special arrangements for Denmark are completed by an 'opt-in' possibility, similar to the Irish, if Denmark no longer wishes to avail itself of this Protocol. In a declaration attached to the Protocol on asylum for nationals of EU Member States Belgium declares that in accordance with relevant international conventions it will carry out an individual examination of any asylum request made by a national of another Member State. This is tantamount to a partial Belgian opt-out from the agreement reached in this Protocol that Member States shall be regarded as constituting safe countries of origin in respect of each other for all legal and practical purposes in relation to asylum matters. Still another case of 'flexibility' is introduced by the Declaration to the Final Act on Article 31(e) TEU which establishes that Member States whose legal system does not provide for minimum sentences shall not be obliged by Article 31(e) TEU[21] to adopt them.

There can be little doubt that without this amazing range of flexibility clauses most of the earlier mentioned elements of progress introduced by the ToA would not have been possible. In the area of justice and home affairs, more than in any other covered by the Treaties, 'flexibility' may have been the only way to prevent the reluctance of some Member States from blocking any positive developments within the EC/EU system. The costs of this 'flexibilization' of the AFSJ will only become fully clear over the next few years. They are likely to be high: fragmentation of the EC and EU legal orders, differentiation in legal protection and in the case-law of the ECJ, additional complexity in decision-making and democratic control, reduced transparency and potential tensions between the 'ins' and 'outs' (Monar, 1997: 9–28). A lot will depend on whether the Member States are going to make constructive use of their new 'flexibility' – and 'constructive use' may more often than not mean restrictive use.

THE CHALLENGE OF IMPLEMENTATION: THE VIENNA ACTION PLAN AND THE TAMPERE EUROPEAN COUNCIL

In order to realize the positive development potential of the AFSJ which Amsterdam undoubtedly provides the Union needs a set of pro-active priorities and a strategic agenda for the next few years which goes beyond the rather reactive and highly fragmentary approach to policy-making which prevailed under the 'old' Third Pillar. Although much time and energy was taken up during the ratification phase of the ToA by the protracted problems of incorporating the Schengen system, agreeing on the new working structures and finalizing some major texts like the Brussels II Convention the Member States nevertheless took some important steps to meet the challenge of implementation.

On the basis of a Commission Communication (COM(1998) 459) on the development of the new 'area of freedom, security and justice' submitted on 14 July 1998 the Member States agreed on a substantial 'Action Plan' on how best to implement the provisions of the Treaty of Amsterdam on an Area of Freedom, Security and Justice (OJ No. C 19/1 of 23.1.1999) which was formally adopted by the Justice and Home Affairs Council on 3 December 1998. The Plan clarifies, firstly, the rationale of the 'area of freedom, security and justice'. As regards the concept of 'freedom' the Action Plan emphasizes that the new Treaty opens the way to giving freedom 'a meaning beyond free movement of persons across internal borders' and that includes the 'freedom to live in a law-abiding environment' protected by effective action of public authorities at the national and European level. This marks a clear step beyond the old Schengen rationale with its focus on free movement and mere 'compensatory measures'.

On the meaning of 'security', however, the Action Plan takes a less progressive view, reflecting the concerns of several Member States about retaining control over internal security instruments. It explicitly states that the new Treaty – although aimed at developing common action in the fields of police and criminal justice cooperation and offering enhanced security to Union citizens – does not pursue the intention to create a 'European security area' in the sense of uniform detection and investigation procedures. The Action Plan also – rather restrictively – provides that the Member States' responsibilities to maintain law and order should not be affected by the new provisions.

On the concept of 'justice' the Action Plan is significantly more ambitious, declaring that Amsterdam is aimed at giving citizens 'a common sense of justice throughout the Union with an impact on day-to-day life which includes both access to justice and full judicial cooperation among member states'. The recently revived term of a 'European judicial area' has been avoided, but the wording used goes clearly beyond judicial cooperation as a mere accompanying process of economic integration.

The second important element of the Action Plan is the 'priorities and measures' listed in part II. These comprise both a number of strategic objectives (such as the development of an 'overall migration strategy') and a broad range of more concrete measures in each of the main fields of justice and home affairs most of which have to be taken either within two or within five years (i.e. until 2003).

In the area of asylum and immigration policy the Action Plan focuses largely on restrictive measures such as the implementation of EURODAC, the limitation of secondary movements of asylum seekers, common assessment of countries of origin in order to design common prevention strategies and a coherent readmission and return policy, all this in combination with additional measures to combat illegal immigration. There are some elements, such as the definition of minimum standards on the reception of asylum seekers, which go slightly beyond the pre-Amsterdam *acquis*. Yet some major issues, such as the social integration of legally resident immigrants and accepted asylum seekers and refugees or the potential use of external economic and CFSP measures to reduce immigration pressure, are not addressed at all. It should also be mentioned that due to the opposition of France and Spain precise objectives regarding the difficult question of burden-sharing in the area of asylum policy had to be dropped from the Plan. There is only a vague reference to a 'balance of effort between member states' in bearing the consequences of receiving displaced persons, which has left Germany, Austria and Italy, in particular, deeply dissatisfied. The Action Plan uses the term 'European migration strategy'. Yet it is difficult to see such a term having any meaning without adequate policies on prevention, integration and burden-sharing.

In the area of police cooperation and judicial cooperation in criminal matters the Action Plan envisages a number of measures to improve the position of Europol such as the examination of Europol access to investigation data of the Schengen Information System, the European Information System or the Customs Information System and a stronger focus of its work on operational cooperation. Yet on some of the more sensitive issues, such as the nature and scope of the new power of Europol to ask competent authorities of the Member States to conduct and coordinate their investigations the Action Plan remains vague and evasive. The same applies to the new possibility for Europol to participate in 'operational actions of joint teams' (Art. 30(2)) TEU). One cannot escape the impression that in spite of the very slight progress brought by Amsterdam as regards an operational role of Europol some Member States continue to regard it as an information exchange agency only and therefore try to delay (or even block) even the implementation of the modest Amsterdam reforms in this area.

Positive elements in other areas of police cooperation are the renewed emphasis placed on the evaluation of investigative techniques in relation to the detection of serious forms of organized crime and on the expansion of operational cooperation between law enforcement services. Yet the Action Plan again becomes vague (and even rather tortuous in its wording) when it comes to the sensitive issue of cross-border law enforcement. The Plan speaks only about 'consideration' to be given to the 'determination of the conditions and limitations under which the competent law enforcement authorities of one Member State may operate in the territory of another Member State, in liaison and agreement with the latter'. Such wording reminds one of the hesitant intergovernmental cooperation of the 1980s.

The emphasis in judicial cooperation in criminal matters is largely on the implementation and the improvement of instruments and mechanisms which have already been adopted such as the further development of the European Judicial network and the effective implementation of the two existing conventions on extradition. As regards the crucial issue of the mutual recognition of decisions and enforcement of judgements in criminal matters the Action Plan only provides for the 'initiation of a process with a view to facilitate' such recognition. Progress on this issue has proved to be very difficult during the last few years, and the absence of concrete objectives in the Action Plan does not augur well. The Plan is hardly more concrete on the question of the approximation of criminal law. True, the Plan provides for the identification of behaviours in the field of organized crime, terrorism and drug trafficking for which it is urgent to adopt measures establishing minimum rules relating to the constituent elements of crime and to penalties. No time limit is set for the adoption of such minimum rules, however, and as regards such important areas as rules on counterfeiting and fraud (important for the protection of the Euro) the possibility to approximate is only to be 'examined'. This is not to say that the Action Plan is devoid of substance in the areas remaining under Title VI TEU: there are a whole range of measures provided for which are likely to significantly improve data exchange, speed up and improve mutual assistance and to allow for better training and analysis of investigative techniques. Yet all this is unlikely to realize the full potential of the AFSJ and to fulfil the public expectations created by presenting this area as a major improvement and benefit for the European citizen.

It may be that the Heads of State or Government felt themselves that more was needed than the Action Plan to make some progress towards the new 'area'. At their Pörtschach meeting in October 1998 Commission President Santer's idea, launched a week earlier before the European Parliament, of convening a special European Council dedicated to justice and home affairs – the first ever in the history of European integration – found considerable support. The Vienna European Council in December 1998 then formally decided to convene the special summit in October 1999 in Tampere. In a joint letter to their colleagues of 18 March 1999 German Chancellor Gerhard Schröder and Finnish Prime Minister Paavo Lipponen emphasized their view that the aims of bringing the Union closer to its citizens and to develop the new AFSJ were closely interrelated and that 'significant political results' should be achieved at Tampere in order to meet citizens' expectations. As a result of this letter a 'tour of the capitals' was organized in April which explored – on the basis of a detailed questionnaire and extensive talks with ministers and senior officials – the Member States' views about the central issues which should be put on the Tampere agenda. As a result of the 'tour of capitals' the Member States were able to agree in April 1999 that the agenda should be focused on asylum and immigration, the establishment of a European judicial area and the fight against cross-border crime.

The preparations for Tampere and the summit itself which was held on 15 and 16 October 1999 revealed a considerable degree of consensus of the Heads of State or Government on the need to make an active use of the new possibilities created by the ToA and to develop the AFSJ. Yet there were also a number of diverging national priorities and some disagreements over questions of substance which are likely to remain on the EU's agenda during the next few years. Of particular importance were the following.

The German Government – concerned about Germany's position as a 'frontline' state as regards asylum and immigration pressure and refugee movements – was aiming at substantial progress towards a single asylum and migration policy which would involve a system of burden-sharing with other Member States. This was supported among others by Austria and Italy but met the resistance of some Member States less exposed to asylum and immigration problems, such as Denmark, Ireland and the UK which preferred a less communitarian approach without obligatory burden-sharing mechanisms.

The French Government was particularly keen on the establishment of a 'European judicial area' with common minimum standards and rules on European citizens' access to justice, cross-border litigation and enforcement of judgements.[22] This objective – which ties in well with the Jospin Government's efforts to reform the French judicial system – would involve a considerable degree of approximation and – ultimately – harmonization of national laws. The British Government, however, took the view that mutual recognition of judicial standards and judgements would be preferable to approximation and harmonization because it would take less time and require far less changes to existing national legislation.

The decisions adopted by the Tampere European Council[23] were largely related to the three priority areas agreed on earlier in the year.

1. The development of a common EU asylum and migration policy

During the last few years EU action in this sphere had concentrated on reducing the number of asylum applicants and immigrants by restrictive control, adjudication and returning procedures. This 'fortress Europe' approach had been criticized by human rights groups and the UNHCR. The Tampere summit agreed on a more comprehensive strategy which combines preventive measures outside of the EU with a greater emphasis on common standards and minimum rights for asylum seekers and immigrants. On the external side the green light was given for the use of EU external economic and political instruments for the purpose of cooperating with countries of origin in order to reduce asylum and immigration pressure. On the internal side agreement was reached on the establishment of a 'Common European Asylum System' providing for common standards for the examination of asylum applications, minimum conditions of reception for asylum seekers and the approximation of rules on the refugee status. This is intended to be accompanied by a more active EU policy on the integration of third country nationals aimed at improving their rights and legal status and measures against racism and xenophobia. More ambitious proposals aimed at creating a 'single' asylum policy with harmonization of basic national rules failed, however. Germany struggled in vain to secure an agreement on a system of burden-sharing in situations of mass influx of refugees.

2. The 'European area of justice': access to justice and mutual recognition of judicial decisions

The complexity, cost and often enough also inefficiency of litigation which involves individuals or businesses from different EU countries remains one of the most glaring deficits of over 40 years of economic integration within the internal market. At Tampere the Heads of State or Government agreed on a number of measures which should enhance both access to justice and the mutual recognition of judgements in cases of cross-border litigation.[24] As regards access to justice the Council of the EU was asked to establish minimum standards for an adequate level of legal aid in cross-border litigation and for the protection of the rights of victims of crime. Further measures include the mandate to introduce common rules for simplified and accelerated cross-border litigation on small consumer and commercial claims and common minimum standards for multilingual legal forms and documents used in cross-border court cases. The principle of mutual recognition of judicial decisions was endorsed by the Heads of State or Government as the future cornerstone of judicial cooperation in both civil and criminal matters, a major success for the British position. It was explicitly extended to a number of other areas such as pre-trial orders and lawfully gathered evidence. A comprehensive programme of measures to implement the principle of mutual recognition will have to be adopted by Council and Commission by December 2000. Yet those Member States arguing for more EU legislation and approximation and harmonization of national laws may have lost a battle, but not the war: the Commission has been invited to make proposals regarding fast track extradition procedures and on new procedural legislation in cross-border cases, including such important elements as the taking of evidence and time limits. The issue of the approximation of national legislation on civil matters will be the object of an overall study on which the Council will report back in 2001.

3. The fight against organized and transnational crime

As regards crime prevention the Tampere summit was not able to agree on more than the exchange of best practices and the strengthening of cooperation between national crime prevention authorities. National priorities and strategies on prevention continue to be very different and prevented a more comprehensive common approach. Yet the possibility was opened to support cooperation between national crime prevention authorities by a specific Community project. The results regarding cooperation in the fight against crime were more substantial. The Heads of State or Government agreed on the creation of two new institutions: a unit called 'EUROJUST', composed of national prosecutors, magistrates or police officers, will have the task to facilitate the coordination of national prosecuting authorities and to support criminal investigations in organized crime cases. The summit also decided to establish a European Police College for the training of senior law enforcement officials which will also be open to applicant countries. In addition the European Council put pressure on national authorities to set up without delay the joint investigative teams foreseen by the ToA and to create a special task force of European police chiefs for the exchange of experiences and for planning purposes. Money laundering was reconfirmed as a crucial issue in the Union's fight against organized crime. The European Council decided that legislation should be adopted to enable financial intelligence units to receive information regarding suspicious financial transactions regardless of secrecy provisions applicable to banking or other commercial activity. It also came out in favour of the approximation of criminal law and procedures on money laundering and for including money laundering in the remit of the European police organization EUROPOL.

In all but name Tampere was a summit on the implementation of the Amsterdam provisions on justice and home affairs and the build-up of the AFSJ. The risk of the Council contenting itself with a mere reaffirmation of general principles and the resolution of some unfinished JHA Council business was averted. The Tampere decisions were more substantial than many observers had expected. They provide the Union with a fresh impetus in major areas of the AFSJ, and substantial new legislation is to be expected over the next few years on asylum matters, access to justice, cross-border litigation and money laundering. EUROJUST could become the germ-cell of a European prosecution system.

CONCLUSIONS

As a result of the ToA there are now few policy-areas covered by the treaties which have a more wide-ranging set of objectives and offer more possibilities for action for the Community and/or the Union than justice and home affairs. The concept of an 'area of freedom, security and justice' is a major political innovation and marks a new extension of the integration process. Clear elements of progress like the time limits introduced under Title IV TEC, the refined set of legal instruments and the new scope for cooperation with third countries should enable the Union to give some substance to this concept over the next years.

Yet the flaws of the Amsterdam reforms are numerous, and some potentially damaging: the policy objectives focus on individual issues rather than comprehensive strategies, there is a highly artificial split between EC and intergovernmental areas of competence, the decision-making procedures retain much of the weakening features of the 'old' Third Pillar and, at least for the transitional period of five years, the areas 'communitarized' under Title IV TEC appear almost like an intergovernmental pillar within the EC framework. Perhaps most important of all, the enormous upsurge of flexibility means that there will be a major risk of legal fragmentation and political tensions between the 'ins' and 'outs' of Schengen and other frameworks of closer cooperation. The progress achieved in terms of new objectives, extended competences and the incorporation of Schengen has been bought at a hefty price in terms of fragmentation and old and new structural weaknesses.

The pressure on the Union to deliver effective policies is likely to increase during the few next years: not only because the problems in areas such as asylum, immigration and organized crime are becoming more pressing but also because the new objectives and competences introduced by the ToA will increase public expectation for the Union to take effective action. The ToA offers substantial possibilities to meet these expectations, yet most of these continue to depend on unanimity in the Council. This means that the ToA reforms relating to justice and home affairs comprise a major risk: should the Member States fail to agree on substantial measures under the new provisions the Union, not the Member States, will be blamed for another major political failure which it can hardly afford.

The Tampere European Council allows us to conclude on a more positive note. At least for the time being the Heads of State or Government have given the go-ahead for an active exploitation of the new potential created by the ToA for the future development of the 'area of freedom, security and justice'. This could become the starting point of a dynamic of integration in justice and home affairs similar to the one generated in the economic sphere by the launch of the Single Market programme in the mid-1980s.

NOTES

1. See the chapter by Monica den Boer in this book.
2. With the exception of the major issues of the incorporation of Schengen and of democratic and judicial control which are covered by the chapters of Monica den Boer, and Brendan Smith and William Wallace.
3. See on this point also Labayle (1997: 830).
4. Referred to in Article 61(b) TEC.
5. As provided for by amended Article 35(1) TEU.
6. As provided for by new Article 39(1) TEU.
7. Convention ... on Jurisdiction and the Recognition and Enforcement of Judgments in Matrimonial Matters, OJ C 221/1, 16.07.98.
8. See Europe No. 7459 of 6 May 1999, pp. 9–10.
9. On the new role of the ECJ in the context of the AFSJ see the chapter by Brendan Smith and William Wallace in this book.
10. Declaration No. 4 to the Final Act explicitly states that Article 24 shall not imply any transfer of competence from the Member States to the European Union.
11. The Maastricht Treaty introduced only one possibility for majority voting: according to 'old' Article K.3(2)(b) the Council can decide that measures implementing joint actions are to be adopted by qualified majority. Yet so far this provision has never been used.
12. The ToA provides in Article 67(3) TEC that the Council shall decide by qualified majority on the visa requirements for third country nationals and on the uniform visa format from the entry into force of the Treaty. Qualified majority on these two matters had already been introduced on 1 January 1996 by virtue of 'old' Article 100c(3) TEC. As regards the procedures and conditions for issuing visas by Member States and rules on the uniform visa, however, the Council – by virtue of Article 67(4) TEC – will act by qualified majority in accordance with the Article 251 procedure only after five years. This is the only real change.
13. As Franklin Dehousse rightly argues the (non-)use of the 'passerelle' of former

Article K.9 TEU can be seen as an unpromising precedent in this respect (Dehousse, 1997: 21).

14. See 'old' Article K.3(2)(b) TEU.

15. By virtue of 'old' Article K.3.2 the Commission had only a non-exclusive right of initiative which, in addition, was limited to six out of nine of the areas defined in Article K.9.

16. See the chapters by Eric Philippart/Monika Sie Dhian Ho and Philippe de Schoutheete in this book.

17. See the chapter by Monica den Boer.

18. Protocol No. 4.

19. Protocol No. 3.

20. Protocol No. 5.

21. Dealing with minimum rules relating to the constituent elements of criminal acts and penalties in the fields of organized crime, terrorism and illicit drug trafficking.

22. Since autumn 1998 French minister Elisabeth Guigou became the strongest advocate of making progress towards the creation of a 'European judicial area', pointing repeatedly to the difficulties citizens experience in finding out which judicial authority to approach, what they have to do to enforce their rights and how to obtain legal aid. See Ministère de la Justice: Colloque d'Avignon sur l'espace judicaire européen. Discours de Madame Élisabeth Guigou, Avignon, 16 Octobre 1998.

23. See the Conclusions of the Presidency of the Tampere European Council, Council Doc. SN 200/99.

24. Meaning litigation which involves parties from different states or cases in which evidence has to be received in a state other than where the proceedings take place.

BIBLIOGRAPHY

Dehousse, F. (1997) 'Les résultats de la Conférence intergouvernementale'. *Courier hebdomadaire*, Centre de recherche et d'information socio-politiques, No. 1565–1566, Brussels.

Delmas-Marty, M. (1997) *CORPUS JURIS portant dispositions pénales pour la protection des intérêts financiers de l'Union européenne.* Paris.

Lebayle, H. (1997) 'Un espace de liberté, de sécurité et de justice'. *Revue trimestrielle de droit européen*, 33 (4), 813–81.

Monar, J. (1997) 'Schengen and flexibility in the Treaty of Amsterdam: opportunities and risks of differentiated integration in EU Justice and Home Affairs'. In M. den Boer (ed.), *Schengen, Judicial Cooperation and Policy Coordination.* Maastricht: European Institute of Public Administration.

Sicurella, R. (1998), *Le Corpus juris: proposition d'un modèle d'espace judiciaire européen*, Cahier Chronique 22. Paris: Recueil Dalloz.

CHAPTER 15

THE INCORPORATION OF SCHENGEN INTO THE TEU: A BRIDGE TOO FAR?

Monica den Boer

INTRODUCTION: FROM TWO PARALLEL SYSTEMS TO ONE

The scenario to integrate Schengen into the European Union only emerged at the Intergovernmental Conference at a very late stage. The proposal – which was presented as a third horizontal item to be discussed at the Conference – was submitted at the end of 1996 by the then Dutch Minister of European Affairs, Michiel Patijn. Hence, even before the Dutch Presidency had started, a non-paper had been submitted to the IGC that proposed the integration of Schengen in three stages. The first stage would embrace a closer practical cooperation between the Schengen Secretariat and the Council Secretariat, the second would be the replacement of the Schengen institutions by Union institutions, and the third would be the actual conversion of the Schengen *acquis* (Piçarra, 1998). The underlying reason for submitting the proposal was the close relationship between the substance of the Schengen cooperation and EU Justice and Home Affairs (JHA) Cooperation (De Zwaan, 1998).

Patijn's proposal was at first not well received by the Intergovernmental Conference. In particular the United Kingdom and Ireland took an extremely reluctant view regarding the proposal. During the Irish EU Presidency, only five Member States endorsed a possible integration scenario.[1] Except for the political obstacles that had to be overcome, a number of delegations were concerned about the technical and institutional complexity of a potential incorporation. Certain partners were even of the opinion that individual Schengen texts had to be transformed into proper EU instruments before the IGC would be closed, and thus before the signing of the Treaty. In view of these political and legal-technical complications and the limited time available, the Dutch Presidency favoured a more modest and global approach. By proposing to agree on some basic principles, such as the principle of incorporation and the application of the Union's working methods and procedures as from the entry into force of the Treaty of Amsterdam, the allocation of Schengen texts to the TEU could be left to a later date (De Zwaan, 1998).

The mechanism for incorporating the Schengen *acquis* is a protocol (the 'Schengen Protocol') in which the 15 EU Member States authorize the 13 Schengen states to 'establish closer cooperation among themselves within the institutional and legal framework of the European Union'.[2] The institutional challenge that arises from this mandate is far from negligible, as the composition of the JHA Council may fluctuate in the future.[3]

The executive in the JHA hierarchy predominantly handles the incorporation process. Two Working Parties were convened under the Luxembourg EU-Presidency.[4] The first Working Party concerned itself with the distribution of the provisions of the Schengen *acquis* between the First and the Third Pillar, and the allocation of an appropriate legal base to each provision. In concrete terms, the mandate given to the 'Schengen I' group included: incorporation of the Schengen *acquis*, classification of the *acquis* to the First or Third Pillar (Article 2 (2) of the Schengen Protocol), and – at a later date – decision on the provisions of the Schengen *acquis* which may be adopted by the UK and Ireland (Article 4 of the Schengen Protocol) (EU Presidency, 1997). It was recommended by COREPER and the Presidency that the Working Party should consider these questions in a step-by-step approach; the latter issue would be dealt with in the future in a separate document. The problems that the Presidency and the Commission saw themselves faced with in the initial stages of the incorporation process probably look insignificant compared to the sizeable challenges that have arisen since. The main problems that had to be tackled included the examination of institutional questions (e.g. the role of the Central Group), problems in connection with the Schengen Information System (SIS) and its financing as well as with the SIRENE[5] system, the determination of the legal nature and legal form of the Schengen *acquis* if adopted within the framework of the Amsterdam Treaty, and questions regarding the translation and publication of the Schengen *acquis* (EU Presidency, 1997). In order to facilitate a rapid initiation of activities, the Luxembourg Presidency provided a provisional list of articles of the Schengen Convention (SIC) to be incorporated, and it advanced the opinion that the provisions of the 1985 Schengen Agreement had become redundant and should hence be excluded from the Schengen *acquis* subject to incorporation (EU Presidency, 1997).

The second Council Working Party examined the question of the position of Norway and Iceland, which are members of, or which have rights under, Schengen, within the new arrangements that flow from the ratification of the Amsterdam Treaty.[6] Under the British Presidency (first term of 1998), the Council failed to decide which of the acts of the Schengen Executive Committee and its subordinate bodies formed part of the Schengen *acquis* to be incorporated, and it was unable to propose an appropriate allocation to legal bases in the EU Treaties. This work continued under the Austrian EU Presidency (House of Lords Select Committee on the European Communities, 1998: Appendix 4) and was completed under the German Presidency of the second half of 1999.

THE RATIONALES BEHIND THE INCORPORATION OF SCHENGEN

It should be emphasized that the cooperation within the Schengen framework and the establishment of an area without internal frontiers to allow for the free movement of people are very much inspired by the same philosophy. The objective of establishing an internal market, which is provided by Article 14 TEC (formerly 7a), 'an area without internal frontiers in which free movement of goods, persons, services and capital', could apparently not be achieved without introducing so-called flanking measures that compensate for the security-deficit that has allegedly arisen because of the abolition of internal border controls (Elsen, 1996: 9–16). The 'third pillar', as the intergovernmentally footed Title VI TEU as introduced by the Maastricht Treaty on European Union is habitually referred to, comprises a series of provisions and instruments that compensate for the security deficit. Although the deadline for the realization of free movement of persons within the EU was originally fixed for the end of 1992, one can only conclude that nearly a decade after this deadline has passed the idea has still not been fully realized between all Member States of the European Union. Nevertheless – as the internal market has been infused with new life in the Amsterdam Treaty by launching an area of freedom, security and justice (Title IV TEC) – it remains a long-term programme for the whole European Union. Legally, the Schengen arrangement and twin-arrangement between Article 14 TEC and the third pillar have also been subject to convergence. The Schengen Agreement only allows the accession of states that are a full member of the European Union (Article 140 of the Schengen implementing corrections SIC) and the SIC is only applicable if its provisions are compatible with Community law (Article 142 SIC) (Den Boer, 1997a: 150). Hence, it was foreseen that Schengen rules would eventually be substituted by Community provisions. Moreover, incorporating Schengen would bring an end to Schengen as a 'laboratory' of free movement and a possible competition between two internal security regimes (Labayle, 1997: 124).

Except for the macro-political convergence of objectives, there are several other rationales for the incorporation of Schengen into the TEU. First of all, Schengen was by no means meant to be a definitive arrangement,[7] but its operationalization tended to take on an autonomous existence, which was neither politically desirable nor institutionally feasible. From a managerial point of view, the coordination of multi-speed integration is a costly and time-consuming exercise. A multiplication of decision-making bodies and procedures is hard to manage and it may reduce transparency and increase the administrative burden on national administrations (Monar, 1997: 11; Piçarra, 1998).[8] Although the same civil servants have been involved in the two policy-making systems, there has been a long-standing, cost-intensive co-existence of two bureaucratic systems (e.g. Executive Committee and JHA Council, thematically similar working parties, two secretariats with translation facilities) and two accountability systems with differentiated (national) parliamentary scrutiny for JHA and Schengen. All this has evolved while the designers of the Schengen Convention did not even want to create an international organization with a legal personality. Schengen was established as a field of experimentation, and the original objective was to integrate it into the TEU as rapidly as possible (Piçarra, 1998).

The co-existence of two internal security systems has resulted in considerable confusion for the citizens, who should benefit from a borderless Europe rather than be inundated with complex measures that have resulted from geographically differentiated and temporally limited arrangements. The absence of intelligible guidelines about whether or not to hold a passport when crossing an internal EU-border, the fluctuating visa-arrangements for extra-EU nationals, as well as the necessity to carry an identity document in a Schengen state itself should a citizen be subjected to 'internal security control', have been a source of uncertainty. Extra-EU businessmen and visitors for instance have to make a choice for either a visa to one of the Schengen countries or to the UK; most non-EU nationals will need an extra visa if they want to travel to the UK (Groenendijk, 1998: 2). Citizen confusion means a drawback on the social legitimacy of the Union (Weiler, 1991: 2469), and a lack of credibility may eventually undermine its effectiveness.

Second, the duality of cooperation in the field of internal security slowly became an untenable situation (Groenendijk, 1998: 3; *Tweede Kamer*, no. 19, 326: no. 167, p. 11, and no. 201, p. 9), because the substantive objectives of JHA under the EU-umbrella and Schengen began to converge. The accommodation of divergent interests of the Member States has made the search for more coherence between these two policy-making systems a very complex enterprise. Intergovernmental arrangements for bringing border controls, police co-operation, and visa, asylum and immigration policies into the ambit of the European Union are complex and confusing, and not well understood. The advantage for Member States is that by incorporating Schengen into the TEU, they do not have to renegotiate standards of security that were introduced by virtue of Schengen's external border policy. Moreover, integrating Schengen into the TEU compensates for the material failure of Justice and Home Affairs cooperation. Compared with EU JHA, Schengen has seemed to suffer less from bureaucracy. Although each of the internal security regimes has been organized on an intergovernmental footing, Schengen has not been bogged down as much by the multifarious levels of decision-making, the lowest common denominator effect propelled by the unanimity requirement, and the difficulty to negotiate effective legal instruments. Furthermore, unlike the vast majority of third pillar instruments, Schengen provisions have really been implemented, which has allowed for a more practical involvement of practitioners such as border control officials and police officers (Den Boer, 1997a: 148). Hence, the integration of Schengen implies the inheritage of its workability (Labayle, 1997: 125), and Schengen thus falls prey to its own (but not untainted) success (Monar, 1997: 14).

At the same time, however, much of the decision-making in the framework of Schengen has taken place outside the realm of democratic and judicial control. This situation has been deplored by many, who felt that the potential infringement of human rights that could be inflicted by the various Schengen security measures required a much better standard of protection and judicial redress. However, legal proceedings can merely be staged on a national level, which may easily result in a fragmentation of legal rights of EU citizens. The introduction of more solid and reliable accountability *vis-à-vis* the Schengen provisions and their operationalization have thus been imperative almost from the moment of its inception (De Kerchove, 1998: 200). The executive culture, which has dominated the Schengen process from the start, lacked this control, and it was thought that insertion of Schengen into the TEU would compensate for this shortcoming (De Kerchove, 1998: 200). Incorporation of Schengen diminishes its democratic and judicial deficit, as it introduces supranational democratic accountability and judicial oversight, and greater openness and accountability would be made possible.[9] Incorporation into the Treaty on European Union is thus expected to guarantee more consistency in judicial and democratic control (House of Lords Select Committee on the European Communities, 1998: 18). Furthermore, the Commission and European Parliament (which will have a largely consultative task) will have a formal role in shaping policy, and the European Court of Justice will exercise some degree of judicial control.[10]

The incorporation process embodies several aspects, which could be categorized as the institutional, the political and the legal aspects respectively. *Grosso modo*, the institutional incorporation involves the transfer of the Schengen 'institutions' to those of the European Union. The Schengen Protocol crucially provides for the substitution of the Executive

Committee – which is the 'supreme' Schengen institution – by the Council (Article 2(1) first paragraph Schengen Protocol). The Schengen Executive Committee consisted of the 13 signatories, the representatives of Norway and Iceland, as well as the observers from the European Commission and the Secretariat General of the EU. The meeting frequency of the Schengen Executive Committee was about six times a year. The task of the Executive Committee has been to adopt decisions and declarations that were taken on the basis of the Schengen Convention (Van de Rijt, 1998). The difficulty presented by the fusion of the Schengen Executive Committee and the JHA Council was that Norway and Iceland, which are associated with the Schengen Convention, should be able to participate. It was difficult to integrate these two countries into the Council, as they are not members of the European Union and required the negotiation of a quite complicated special agreement between the EU, Norway and Iceland, which was eventually concluded on 18 May 1999 (OJ L176, 10 July 1999, pp. 36–52) (Labayle, 1997: 128; Piçarra, 1998).

Some of the institutions which needed to be incorporated, such as the Schengen Secretariat (which had been accommodated by the Benelux Secretariat), did not even have a formal status in the SIC. In fact, the Schengen Secretariat received its first formal mentioning in the Schengen Protocol (Van de Rijt, 1998). The Schengen Secretariat functioned as the administrative, linguistic and logistic instrument of the Schengen states. The employees numbered about 60 in 1998, two thirds of whom worked in the linguistic service. The Secretariat had been managing about 200 meetings annually, with about 3000 documents numbering an average of 4500 pages (Van de Rijt, 1998). Although the incorporation of the Schengen Secretariat into General Secretariat of the Council of the European Union looked self-evident, the large number of Belgian nationals that work within the Schengen Secretariat and the incumbent surplus of translators made this transition less straightforward. Contentious issues included the question whether the integration should be gradual or *en bloc*, whether all or some of the Schengen staff ought to be transferred, whether or not Schengen staff should be subjected to Commission staff requirements and thus obtain the status of the European civil service, recruitment and competition procedures. Taking account of the size and the width of the integration of the Schengen *acquis* into the institutional and legal framework of the European Union and its conversion into the *acquis* of the Community and the Union, no particular administrative or logistic could be imposed (Piçarra, 1998). It was no trivial exercise for the Member States to agree on the integration of the Schengen Secretariat at once.

The function of the 'Central Group' of Schengen was comparable to that of the old K.4-Committee and of COREPER. The senior officials that were represented in the group met on average every month. They were in charge of directing the work undertaken in the Working Parties, again in the presence of the Commission and the Council. The activities of the Central Group were not essentially different from those of the Executive Committee (Van de Rijt, 1998). This implied that the Central Group effectively had powers in some cases where decision-making had been delegated. One of the questions that has arisen in the context of the incorporation process concerns the legal validity of the decisions of the Central Group, because the SIC does not provide in the formal attribution of these powers to the Central Group. An example of a mandate that was given to the Central Group concerns unilateral modifications in the list of visa-requiring countries, on the basis of a Communal Consular Instruction. For example, when a signatory of Schengen decided to simplify the issuing of visas to holders of a diplomatic passport in a certain country, approval of the Central Group was sufficient (Van de Rijt, 1998).

'Schengen' had not availed itself of parliamentary or legal control bodies, but a Joint Control Authority was created to control the exchange of personal data in the context of SIS (Article 115 of the SIC) (Van de Rijt, 1998). The Joint Control Authority consists of two representatives from each data protection board in the Schengen states (Van de Rijt, 1998). Again, the transfer of this task to an EU-body has been far from obvious. The European Commission and the European Parliament would prefer the European Commission to manage the Central Schengen Information System (C-SIS), instead of France, which has accommodated the C-SIS in Strasbourg until now. There have also been disparate views on whether to base the SIS on a coordinated dual basis (First and Third Pillar), which was favoured by the Commission, bringing it under a single legal basis in the Third Pillar, or maintaining it as an autonomous element without a specific legal basis (*Agence Europe*, 1998). At the time of writing this issue had not yet been resolved.

The second aspect of the incorporation process concerns political decision-making. The Dutch Presidency did not want to see a repetition of the earlier 'psychodramas' that were displayed during the negotiations and the entry into force of Schengen. Hence the Presidency sought to avoid a re-adoption of the Schengen *acquis* (Labayle, 1997: 126.). First of all, before signing the Amsterdam Treaty, macro-political agreement between EU Member States was required that the *acquis* had to be brought into the European Union. The price for unanimous approval at Amsterdam has been a thoroughly compromised, complex incorporation process that is larded with opt-ins and safety valves. Henri Labayle (1997: 135) typifies the situation that arises from the compromise text as *des morcellements matériels, temporels et géographiques*.

The United Kingdom and Ireland are, by virtue of a special arrangement

(Article 4 Schengen Protocol; House of Lords Select Committee on the European Communities, 1998: 9), allowed to request at any time to take part in some or all the provisions of the *acquis*. This opt-in arrangement does not, *inter alia*, apply to the accession states as they are required to apply the Schengen *acquis* at once and in full (Den Boer, 1997b: 1628). The special arrangement should be seen in the context of their obligations under the 'old' Article 7A TEC. The incorporation is likely to be a step-by-step process and the Council shall decide on a request from the UK or Ireland by unanimity of the Member States party to Schengen and the requesting State. It should be noted that this rule of unanimity exclusively applies to the existing Schengen *acquis*. The Community procedure of decision-making (qualified majority) shall apply when these two countries express their will to participate after a measure has been adopted. A Declaration[11] provides that the Council should seek the opinion of the Commission before it decides on a request under Article 4 of the Schengen Protocol by the United Kingdom and/or Ireland. This 'opting-in' process could potentially also be very political in character as certain Member States may use the unanimity requirement to block these two countries in participating in some or all of the Schengen *acquis*,[12] which forms an ideal opportunity to sabotage progress for those Member States that hold 'pre-Amsterdam' grudges against either of the opt-in countries. It is imaginable that a political stalemate could also occur *vice versa*, as it cannot be ruled out 'that aspects of enhanced cooperation in the areas of asylum, immigration, or the fight against international crime and drug-trafficking would lead to increased or even new problems in the sense that non-participating member states could provoke tension and possibly even unilateral protective measures' (Monar, 1997: 13).

Furthermore, the peculiar circumstance that is induced by this piecemeal integration calls into question the consistency of the jurisdiction of the European Court of Justice: will it not run the risk of getting terribly fragmented? (Monar, 1998a: 334) Representatives of the ECJ have observed that the instances in which it may be called upon to exercise its interpretative role resembles a jigsaw puzzle with incomplete pieces which may be supplied later and whose shape is unclear (Fennelly, 1998: 70). Pursuant to Article 2 of the Schengen Protocol, the European Court may be asked to exercise its jurisdiction in respect of the Schengen *acquis*, and then pursuant to potentially varying jurisdictional rules. All this should be read in conjunction with the Protocols concerning the positions of Denmark, Ireland and the United Kingdom under Title IV TEC, which comprehensively exclude those Member States from every aspect of the operation and application of Title IV except in the event that any of them should decide entirely of their own accord to accept any particular measure. Such may undermine the uniform application of (a new aspect of) Community law with the 'potential to affect the rights of individuals' (Fennelly, 1998: 80). Furthermore, the lack of specific provisions raises the question how the single institutional framework of the European Union can be preserved: the deliberations on Schengen shall presumably also be undertaken by the British and Irish judges and advocates general in the Court of Justice, as well as the members of the European Parliament from these two 'non-Schengen' states (Gialdino, 1998: 118).

Article 3 of the Schengen Protocol refers to the Danish position, which is further specified in a separate protocol (Protocol No.5) on the position of Denmark). According to this article, Denmark maintains the same rights and obligations with regard to the other Schengen signatories that it had before the integration of the Schengen *acquis*. This implies that in case an act adopted by the Council applies under the new Community title, Denmark reserves the right to decide whether or not to transpose this decision into its own law (Labayle, 1997: 132). Denmark, which is a member of Schengen but which objects to the incorporation of any Schengen provisions into the First Pillar, has the option to maintain its present obligations *vis-à-vis* its Schengen partners: it will remain bound to the provisions of the Schengen *acquis* and not under Community law (Article 3). In other words, Denmark will not take part in the adoption by the Council of measures on the basis of Title IV TEC. Insofar as these are measures building upon the Schengen *acquis*, Denmark shall decide within six months of the Council taking such a decision whether or not it will implement this decision in its national legislation (Demmink, 1998: 194). This complicated, disjointed incorporation poses considerable challenges to the various decision-making modalities that are at stake (De Kerchove, 1998: 202). Moreover, the Danish position has been characterized as 'a little perverse', given the fact that Denmark seems to have sacrificed democracy and transparency – which it values so highly – in exchange for the maintenance of its sovereignty, while the incorporation of Schengen within the framework of the EU exactly seeks to improve just those aspects (Shaw, 1998: 101).

Not merely the negotiations on the incorporation of Schengen into the TEU have had an extraordinarily political character, also the process in which the Schengen *acquis* has been defined and allocated is submerged in politics. Symptomatic for the political hesitation is the considerable number of footnotes to the draft Decisions that appeared during the incorporation process and included the Member States' reservations about the proposed definition and allocation (House of Lords Select Committee on the European Communities, 1998: 34). In particular, Spain was thought of impeding progress as it systematically recommended recourse to the Third Pillar alone by stressing the security purpose of the Schengen instrument (*Agence Europe*, 1998: 4). Several delegations as well as the

Commission were irritated by this stance, as it would undermine the progress that had been made in the Amsterdam Treaty.

In order to allow only a shimmer of democratic control by the national parliaments, however, Member States have had to accelerate the allocation process, so that drafts could be published in the *Official Journal* some time before the entry into force of the Amsterdam Treaty.[13] The progress on determining the content of the Schengen *acquis* has allegedly been slow.[14] Adherents of an intergovernmentalist conspiracy theory would perhaps argue that the slow progress and the self-imposed time-limits are deliberate in order to circumvent the communitarization of (large parts of) the Schengen *acquis*.

Last but not least, there was the *legal aspect* of the incorporation process, which primarily involves defining and allocating the Schengen *acquis*: on the one hand, the content of the Schengen *acquis* that has evolved over the past years needed to be delineated with exactitude, and on the other hand, the contents of the *acquis* had to be allocated to a legal base in the EC Treaty or the Treaty on European Union. Below we will discuss the details of these processes.

A VENTURE INTO THE UNKNOWN

In the Schengen Protocol, it was envisaged that some parts of the *acquis* would be integrated into the EC Treaty (First Pillar) and some into the revised Title VI of the TEU on police and judicial cooperation in criminal matters (Third Pillar) (House of Lords Select Committee on the European Communities, 1998: 21). The Council had the task of agreeing and defining, by unanimity, the appropriate legal base in either or both Treaties for each element of the Schengen *acquis*.[15] The definition and allocation processes had to be concluded before the entry into force of the Amsterdam Treaty (Article 2(1), first sub-paragraph, of the Schengen Protocol). If this process were not completed in time, or if the Council had failed to agree on a legal base, the contents of the Schengen *acquis* would have been automatically deferred to the (intergovernmental) Title VI (Article 2(1), first sub-paragraph, of the Schengen Protocol). It took the 13 Schengen states more than one and a half years to reach unanimous agreement on what should be included in the Schengen *acquis* for the purpose of its incorporation. The process was formally completed only on 20 May 1999 by the adoption of Council Decision 1999/435/EC concerning the definition of the Schengen *acquis* (OJ L 176 of 10/7/99, p. 1). The delineation process has been very difficult politically, not only because certain items were rather sensitive from a national sovereignty point of view, but also because the laundering process through the TEU-machine – by vesting the relevant Schengen provisions, decisions or declarations with a formal legal status – laid bare a number of different interpretations between the Schengen members as to the scope and binding legal effects of some of the provisions which had been agreed on in the intergovernmental context of Schengen.

Without entering into too much detail, it should be highlighted in the context of this chapter what is included in the *acquis*. The House of Lords Committee on European Affairs, which undertook a most useful and broad inquiry into the matter (House of Lords Select Committee on the European Communities, 1998), defined it as a body of law comprising the 1985 Schengen Agreement,[16] the 1990 SIC,[17] the Accession Protocols and Agreements and the Schengen Executive Committee Declarations and Decisions. The *acquis* also contains acts adopted for the implementation of the Convention by the organs upon which the Executive Committee has conferred decision-making powers. This last category has been somewhat puzzling, given the fact that the SIC never provided for the transfer of decision-making powers by the Executive Committee to other 'organs' (Groenendijk, 1998: 5). What was meant by it was probably (although we have officially not been told) the Central Group (see above) and not the Joint Control Authority that supervises the workings of the SIS.

According to the House of Lords European Communities Committee, the Schengen Executive Committee generated a substantial volume of *acquis* since it first adopted its Rules of Procedure in December 1993. The subject matter of these ranged from administrative and financial matters to operational guidelines for law enforcement and border control officials and weighty policy statements. No official list of this *acquis* was ever published (House of Lords Select Committee on the European Communities, 1998: 16).

It is far from exaggerated to claim that transparency problems were involved in the definition of the Schengen *acquis* and its allocation (i.e. finding a legal base in the TEU for these). The principle of confidentiality was applied to a not insignificant number of cases. Despite the fact that the Schengen *acquis* shall be published in the *Official Journal* of the European Communities, provisions will be excluded from publication 'which at the time of the adoption of the present decision are classified as "confidential" or "secret" by the Schengen Executive Committee' or by organs on which the Executive Committee has conferred decision-making powers.[18] At their meeting in June 1998, the Schengen Executive Committee decided that part of the Schengen *acquis* ought to remain confidential, after a request had gone out to the Schengen states to register comments with regard to a list of confidential documents. These documents were decisions and declarations of the Schengen Executive

Committee (respectively 164 and 57 in total) and decisions of the Schengen Central Group (11 in total).[19]

According to the decision, eight documents were to remain confidential, namely three annexes to the Common Visa Instruction, the Common Manual (on border control), the SIRENE Manual, and three documents concerning drug trafficking on controlled delivery, reinforced controls at external borders and the illegal exploitation of drugs.[20] Although it is conceivable that some information contained by the Schengen *acquis* should not be disclosed as criminal groups could exploit it, the self-invoked principle of confidentiality runs counter to the legislative process in the EC. The House of Lords European Communities Committee expressed its regret

> that the *acquis* will be formally published in the Official Journal only after it has been incorporated and taken effect within the framework of the EU Treaties. This is contrary to the usual practice of publishing binding legal instruments before they enter into force. (House of Lords Select Committee on the European Communities, 1998: 30)

There is no provision for a control body that has a mandate to observe whether these confidentiality procedures are legitimate. There is no provision in the Schengen Protocol for the European Parliament either to be kept informed, or to take part in the decision-making of the Council. Governments probably did not want a provision that would force them to enter into a debate with the European Parliament about an issue which was frequently the subject of fierce criticism because of its substance and undemocratic nature (Monar, 1997: 19). Hence, the participation of the European Parliament in the incorporation process was made dependent upon informal initiatives, for instance by EU Presidencies (House of Lords Select Committee on the European Communities, 1998: Appendix 3, p. 2). Furthermore, the jurisdiction of the European Court of Justice will have at least in part have to be exercised over a body of 'ill-defined material, much of it not even publicly available' (Fennelly, 1998: 83).

The decision-making rules that have been invoked to authorize 13 Member States to share a form of reinforced cooperation between them may resemble the trick of Baron von Münchausen, who propelled himself forward with a self-infused canon. Hence, the incorporation process was to a great extent self-executing (Piçarra, 1998) and self-legitimating. Although there was no further legislative intervention from the Council in the determination of the Schengen *acquis*, the role of the Council was paramount in the allocation process. This confirmed the significant role that the executive played throughout the whole process with only minor control to be exercised by parliamentary and judicial bodies (Groenendijk, 1998: 2).[21]

TO-ING AND FRO-ING: DEFINING AND ALLOCATING THE SCHENGEN *ACQUIS*

There was a succession of draft council decisions that contained various footnotes, which according to the House of Lords indicated the reservations some Member States continued to raise about the proposed allocation (1998, p. 34). Two draft Council Decisions were of paramount importance in this context, namely: (P)7233/1/98 REV1 ('Definition of the Schengen Acquis for the purpose of its incorporation into the EU', 8 May 1998), and (P)6816/2/98 REV2 ('Allocation of legal base for incorporation of the Schengen Acquis', 21 April 1998). Oddly enough, the draft decision concerning the allocation predated the decision concerning the definition, whereas one would have expected the allocation to follow the definition in chronological order.

The process by which the Schengen *acquis* to be integrated into the Union was being determined is hereinafter called the *definition process*. Thirteen EU Member States, namely those that are members of Schengen, had to adopt the Schengen *acquis* subject to integration, in accordance with Article 2(1) second paragraph first sentence of the Schengen protocol.

The definition process was to some extent an elimination one as it eliminated redundant or obsolete provisions or decisions of the *acquis* that were no longer operative, had been absorbed by provisions of Community law or other acts applicable to all Member States, belonged to the domain of exclusive national competence and were intended to have legal effects.[22] The various provisions and decisions of the Schengen *acquis* which were excluded from the incorporation process were regrouped in Annex B to Council Decision 1999/435/EC (OJ L 176 of 10.7.1999, pp. 10–16).

Excluded from the incorporated Schengen *acquis* were, first of all, the provisions of the 1985 Schengen Agreement.[23] These provisions of this first founding agreement have become obsolete because they have a programmatic character. As noted above, it was the Luxembourg Presidency which proposed to exclude the SIC. Secondly, certain provisions from the SIC[24] were excluded from the Schengen *acquis* to be incorporated as they have a long-term programmatic character and have as such already been integrated into the Treaty of Amsterdam (e.g. Articles. 7–28 were covered by Articles 29 TEU and 61 TEC) (Corrado, 1998: 28). Furthermore, excluded were the provisions of the Accession Agreements and Protocols to the Schengen Agreement,[25] and the decisions and declarations of the Executive Committee established by the Schengen Convention. Moreover, Schengen Convention provisions on the mutual recognition of short-term visas are not incorporated as they were replaced by community measures introducing a uniform format visa. However, other Schengen provisions on visas were allocated to the new Article 62(2)(b) of the EC Treaty that provides for the adoption of rules on short-term visas. Also the provisions on asylum in the SIC were excluded as these had been replaced by the Dublin Asylum Convention (Articles 28–38 and 135 of the SIC).[26] This contains rules similar to those in the Schengen Convention but has a wider geographical scope as it applies in all EU Member States. The problem is, however, that the common rules on this issue can only be integrated by a unanimous decision of the Council on the basis of the new Article 63(1)(a) EC Treaty. Until such a decision will be made, the system of the Dublin convention remains in force. It will continue to operate without any role of the Court and the Parliament and only an observer status for the Commission (Groenendijk, 1998: 7). Also excluded from the Schengen *acquis* to be incorporated were: provisions on extradition (Article 60, replaced by the Extradition Convention); provisions on firearms and ammunition (Articles 77–81 and 83–90 SIC, replaced by Firearms Directive);[27] provisions on cabin and hold baggage controls on internal flights (Article G SIC, replaced by a Council Regulation);[28] provisions concerning transport and movement of goods (Articles 120–125 SIC), which have been overtaken by Single Market legislation; and provisions on the role and functioning of the Executive Committee (Articles 131–133 SIC), which will be replaced by the JHA Council (House of Lords Select Committee on the European Communities, 1998: 22).

The second process, which we shall here call the *allocation process*, was set out to establish the legal base for each Schengen provision. The allocation had to be decided by all 15 Member States according to Article 2(1) second paragraph, second sentence of the Schengen Protocol. The provisions of the Schengen Agreement could be allocated to four different legal bases, namely: (1) the EC Treaty; (2) the Treaty on European Union; (3) the EC Treaty and the EU; (4) the Schengen Protocol (which is annexed to the TEC and the TEU) (House of Lords Select Committee on the European Communities, 1998). The allocation to any of these four legal bases had potentially far-reaching consequences for the legally binding character of the legal instrument, and for the respective competences of the EU-institutions. It is not surprising, therefore, that the allocation process gave rise to a host of political controversies: some Member States took the view that intergovernmental (Title VI TEU) legal bases should wherever possible be avoided in order not to undermine the move towards communitarization made at Amsterdam, others argued that the allocation of an EC legal basis for some Schengen provisions could infringe upon the remaining intergovernmental areas of EU justice and home affairs and threaten the preservation of national veto possibilities over internal security issues. These controversies delayed the process very considerably, so that contrary to the provisions of the Schengen Protocol the Council Decision determining the legal basis for each of the provisions or decisions which constitute the Schengen *acquis* was only adopted three weeks after the entry into force of the new Treaty, on 20 May 1999 (OJ L 176 of 10.7.1999, pp. 17–30).

According to the Home Office, which figured as a witness in the House of Lords inquiry, the allocation was made on the basis of

> the content of the Schengen provision, and its match with an appropriate Article in the Treaty establishing the European Communities, the Treaty on European Union, or the Schengen Protocol. Where the Schengen provisions contains both First Pillar and Third Pillar elements, a dual legal base is allocated. (House of Lords Select Committee on the European Communities, 1998)

Most Schengen provisions have been allocated a legal base in either the first or the third pillars. A large number of those have been given a double legal destination, such as Articles 39–69 SIC (police cooperation) which are based on Articles 34 and 31(b) TEU. Yet some have been given a base in both pillars,[29] and there are even several provisions that have been split between two legal bases, so that part comes under the first and part under the third pillar[30]. Obviously, this picture looks incredibly complex and hence there are increasing demands from Member States that one should be able to distinguish between different legal bases. The complexity of the incorporation will also have repercussions for the ability to exercise democratic control on the legislative process, as parliamentarians will need to follow decision-making in the different frameworks and to distinguish between EC Schengen and EC non-Schengen directives and between EU Schengen and EU non-Schengen decisions in Title VI (Monar, 1998b: 220). Indeed, it is quite probable that

> officials and perhaps also some ministers will be looking back with some nostalgia to the time when the Schengen *acquis* was not yet scattered over more than a dozen different legal bases across the Union Treaty and they did not yet have to struggle with the corresponding institutional and procedural requirements of the EU system. (Monar, 1997: 5–6)

Furthermore, there is the question regarding the procedures, such as qualified majority voting, which will apply to some, but not all, measures on visa in Article 62 (2) (b) of the TEC. The House of Lords raised the question whether they apply to each (relevant) element of the Schengen *acquis*. In this case, the legal base may be too broad (House of Lords Select Committee on the European Communities, 1998: 37).

There could also be a possible contamination effect. It could be caused by intergovernmental law – which also has connotations of secretly negotiated, soft or grey law – gradually inserted into EC law without a profound analysis of the compatibility with Community law in respect of fundamental rights. Incorporated Schengen rules will only be amended on the basis of the legislative rules in Title IV EC Treaty and Title VI EU Treaty, but given the fact that unanimity prevails in most cases, it is likely that Schengen provisions will continue to exist unaltered (Groenendijk, 1998: 6).

The allocation of a legal base to the SIS (Article 92–119 SIC) has been a rather contentious issue, mainly because quite a wide number of Member States saw considerable difficulties in assigning a dual legal base to a single system (House of Lords Select Committee on the European Communities, 1998: 35; Corrado, 1998: 31; Piçarra, 1998). The reason for the proposed schizophrenic solution is that the SIS has become a multipurpose system that contains data for the purpose of asylum and immigration control as well as criminal justice cooperation. On the other hand, since the SIS is financed intergovernmentally by individual contributions of the Member States, it should be subject to the governance system of the third pillar. The choice for a dual legal base for the SIS may invoke substantively identical provisions in two Pillars subject to different procedural requirements (House of Lords Select Committee on the European Communities, 1998: 37). Because of the contentious nature of these issues – which involves not only the question of the competences of Member States in the administration of the SIS but also that of the European Commission – the Schengen members were unable to reach a compromise in time for the adoption of the Council Decision of 20 May 1999: a blank ('pro memoria') was left in the text. At the time of writing (August 1999) these issues had still not been resolved. Especially difficult is the application of regulatory frameworks, for example the management of the system (see above) and the prevailing data protection regime. The data protection rules that apply to the SIS are contained in Article 126–130 SIC. Although these provisions will not apply to the chapters regarding the exchange of data of asylum seekers and the transmission of data in the framework of legal cooperation, there remains a substantial part of exchange of personal data through the system between police, customs and consular authorities. The European Union's directive on data protection[31] does not provide coverage for activities that are not within the scope of Community activities, i.e. criminal justice data (Corrado, 1998: 32).

It seems self-evident that all operational policing issues and judicial cooperation in criminal matters (Articles 48–68 SIC) have been automatically transferred to the third pillar, respectively Article 30 and Article 31, Title VI, TEU. However, the House of Lords report mentions some peculiar things here too:

Although most of the Schengen provisions on police co-operation are allocated to Article 30 (1) of the TEU, some are allocated to Article 30

TEU as a whole. This might suggest that a specific role is envisaged for Europol in some areas of Schengen co-operation but not in others. It also raises practical questions such as whether the United Kingdom, a full participant in Europol, may have equal access through Europol to information and intelligence held by the Schengen states. (House of Lords Select Committee on the European Communities, 1998: 38)

It is clear that academics, politicians and lawyers will have an interesting-looking bone to tackle for quite some time.

CONCLUSIONS

One of the introductory recitals to the Schengen Protocol is that 'it is necessary to make use of the provisions of the Treaty on European Union and of the Treaty establishing the European Community concerning closer cooperation between some member states', and Article 1 of the Protocol records that the named signatories to the Schengen Agreements have the authorization to establish closer cooperation, but says that 'this cooperation shall be conducted within the institutional and legal framework of the European Union and with respect for the relevant provisions of the Treaty on European Union and of the Treaty establishing the European Community'. Schengen thus becomes the first experiment of closer cooperation within the revised Treaty on European Union (Fennelly, 1998: 81–2). Paradoxically, it seems that we have substituted (multi-speed) flexibility with (case-by-case) flexibility, with the difference that it is now all incorporated by EU-decision-making procedures, EU-instruments and subjected to the powers of the EU-institutions.

The result of the merger between the Schengen and the JHA machinery is a very complex set of provisions that implicitly defies the agreed IGC-objective to bring the Union closer to the citizen by making it more transparent. Moreover, those who are relieved that it is now all behind us should be given a (mental) health warning, as – except for the political, legal and institutional complexity that is caused by the incorporation of Schengen[32] – there is still scope for a 'Schengen II' by means of the clauses on closer cooperation (Article 11 TEC and Article 40 TEU). It is argued, however, that even though this is being decided by qualified majority, reinforced cooperation may be suspended by the Council, and it can be effectively blocked by a Member State that invokes political reasons of national importance. Hence, the establishment of Schengen II may be difficult, except in cases where the subject has not yet been covered by other cooperative frameworks or when cooperation with states that have not been a member of Schengen is desirable

(De Kerchove, 1998: 201). Of course, we may have a remnant Schengen *acquis* that contains provisions that have not been incorporated in either the TEC or the TEU.

The limits of the flexibility process will undergo a practical test (Groenendijk, 1998: 7), as the incorporated Schengen *acquis* becomes Community law or Union law with respect to 12 EU Member States only, leaving three Member States (Denmark, the UK and Ireland) outside of this part of the acquis. This may invoke the JHA Council to adopt measures applicable to a reduced number of Member States (Curtin and Dekker, 1999: 37). The situation concocted by the executive in Brussels does not represent a legislative beauty. Throughout this chapter, we have found sufficient evidence of a mountain of legal problems that may potentially arise. As such, incorporation may diminish legal and procedural coherence as two different sets of rules may apply to various Schengen provisions.

The first attempts at improving JHA-transparency have certainly been thwarted by this patchwork exercise. The incorporation does not call a halt to the confusion for the citizens, because they will still be stuck with multi-speed integration in the future. Neither have formal promises of judicial control been fully realized. For a large number of incorporated Schengen provisions jurisdiction by the European Court of Justice will very much depend on the explicit and positive disposition of the EU Member States. Hence, we could argue that the incorporation of the Schengen *acquis* has only been of partial benefit to the integrity and institutional unity of the European Union.

NOTES

1. The BENELUX countries, Austria, Germany, Italy and Spain supported the idea. See Table 5.1 in Hix and Niessen (1996).
2. Article 1 of the Protocol integrating the Schengen *acquis* into the framework of the European Union.
3. '[I]t will also handle further cooperation with non-members Iceland and Norway (minus in any event the United Kingdom and maybe Ireland) pursuant to the terms of the Schengen Protocol (and subsequently adopted agreements with the non-members) of the Treaty of Amsterdam.' From: Curtin and Dekker (1999: 37)
4. Decided by COREPER (part 2) on 16 October 1997 (Note of the Presidency for the Group 'Schengen acquis', Brussels, 17 October 1997 (11480/97 Limite)); Piçarra (1998).
5. SIRENE = Supplementary Information Request at the National Entry.
6. Article 6 of the Protocol on Schengen provides for Iceland and Norway to be associated with the implementation of the Schengen acquis and its further

development. As a result two agreements had to be concluded on the future relationship, one with the Member States party to Schengen, the other with the United Kingdom and Ireland. The final of those two agreements was concluded on 17 May 1999 (OJ L176 of 10 July 1999, p. 35).

7. Opinion expressed by the then Dutch Junior Minister of Foreign Affairs, Mr M. Patijn, in: *Tweede Kamer*, vergaderjaar 1995–1996, 19 326, no. 141, p. 10.

8. Monar, (1997: 9–28); on p. 11.

9. 'The Schengen Convention enlarged the scope for executive action by establishing an Executive Committee empowered to adopt measures, largely in private, in areas having a direct impact on individual rights and freedoms. It made no provision for systematic parliamentary scrutiny of executive measures prior to their adoption. And although complaints could be brought before national courts, there was no mechanism for obtaining rulings on the interpretation and application of Convention provisions.' The House of Lords Select Committee on European Commmunities (1998), *Incorporating the Schengen Acquis into the European Union*. 31st Report. Session 1997–98 [HL Paper 139], p. 17.

10. According to Groenendijk (1998: p. 6), this judicial control could be extremely limited if the restriction contained by the second sentence of Article 2 (3) of the Protocol on Schengen, namely that the 'Court of Justice shall have no jurisdiction on measures and decisions relating to the maintenance of public order and the safeguarding of internal secrecy', would be applicable to measures and decisions in the incorporated Schengen *acquis*. The clause – which was inserted in Amsterdam at the very last moment to prevent the Court from challenging the legality of the maintenance of the border controls by France with Belgium and Luxembourg – presumably refers to measures and decisions of national authorities.

11. Declaration (45) on Article 4 of the Protocol integrating the Schengen *acquis* into the framework of the European Union.

12. *Europe*, No. 7014, 11 July 1997, p. 2, claims that this unanimity rule was introduced at the Amsterdam summit on the insistence of Spain, which was engaged in the Anglo-Spanish dispute over Gibraltar (Monar, 1997: 27).

13. Groenendijk (1998: 10). The Immigration Law Practitioners Association claims that no other national parliament was undertaking the kind of analysis which was undertaken by the House of Lords Select Committee on the European Communities; the ratification of the Amsterdam Treaty seemed to include a blanket acceptance of the Council's allocation process (evidence submitted to the House of Lords Committee, 2 June 1998).

14. *Agence Europe* (1998), 'Integration of Schengen Treaty and its Protocols in EU progresses, but certain basic issues remain on the table', no. 7202, 17 April 1998; *Statewatch* (1998: 28); participants in the negotiation process tend to be more optimistic however (see e.g. Piçarra, 1998).

15. The voting procedure that applies to the definition process is by the Council acting by unanimity of the EU Member States with the exception of the UK and Ireland, in accordance with Article 2(1) second paragraph, first sentence; the voting procedure that applies to the allocation is by the Council acting unanimously at 15 in accordance with Article 2(1) second paragraph, second sentence of the Schengen Protocol. From: Explanatory Note on Two Draft Council Decisions concerning the Incorporation of Schengen into EU/EC

Structures, as provided for in the Treaty of Amsterdam, submitted by the Home Office on 21 May 1998.

16. Agreement signed by France, Germany and the Benelux countries in Schengen on 14 June 1985.

17. The Convention implementing the Agreement of 14 June 1985 between the Governments of the States of the Benelux Economic Union, the Federal Republic of Germany and the French Republic on the gradual abolition of checks at their common borders, signed in Schengen on 19 June 1990.

18. Article 1, paragraph 2, Document No: 7233/1/98, SCHENGEN 14 REV 1.

19. Note of the Belgian Presidency concerning the determination of the Schengen *acquis* with a view to incorporating it into the European Union – confidentiality, SCH/Tr-Rego (98) 15, Brussels, 14 May 1998, and Note of the Belgian Presidency concerning the determination of the Schengen *acquis* with a view to incorporation into the European Union – decisions and declarations of the Executive Committee and decisions of the Central Group, SCH/Tr-Rego (98) 12 herz., 25 May 1998. It is unclear what the legal foundation is of decisions made by the Central Group as no official competence is provided in the Schengen Implementing Convention to issue binding legal decisions.

20. Decision SCH/Com-ex (98) 17, adopted by the Executive Committee on 23 June 1998.

21. Lord Wallace of Saltaire, Chairman of the House of Lords Committee, said: 'It is shocking that EU Member States have all agreed to incorporate "Schengen" into the EU without first deciding what it is. More and better information is needed urgently, not just for citizens, but for Governments, to help them understand what they are signing up to. Individuals and governments need to know whether their rights and obligations are based on national, Community or international law.' House of Lords Press Information, 'Lords shocked by confusion about EU Border Controls and Police Co-operation', 8 September 1998.

22. According to the evidence given to the House of Lords, there is no clear explanation of this category. (House of Lords Select Committee on the European Communities, 1998: 21–2).

23. The Agreement, signed in Schengen on 14 June 1985, between the Governments of the States of the Benelux Economic Union, the Federal Republic of Germany and the French Republic on the gradual abolition of checks at their common borders (Article 2, paragraph 1 (a) of Document No. 7233/1/98, SCHENGEN 14 REV 1).

24. Provisions of the Convention, signed in Schengen on 19 June 1990, between the United Kingdom of Belgium, the Federal Republic of Germany, the French Republic, the Grand Duchy of Luxembourg and the Kingdom of the Netherlands implementing the Schengen Agreement and its related Final Act and declarations ('the Schengen Convention'). For a listing of provisions, see part 1 of Annex B of Document No. 7233/1/98, SCHENGEN 14 REV 1.

25. Listed in Part 2 of annex B to Document No. 7233/1/98, SCHENGEN 14 REV 1 (Article 2, paragraph 1 (c)).

26. A Protocol agreed in Bonn on 26 April 1994 provides that the Schengen rules on asylum will no longer apply upon the entry into force of the Dublin Convention determining the State responsible for examining applications for asylum loaded in one of the Member States of the EU. Detailed provisions on

the criteria for determining the State responsible for examining asylum applications no longer apply since the entry into force, on 1 September 1997, of the Dublin Convention.

27. Council Directive 91/477/EEC of 18 June 1991 on the control of acquisition and posession of weapons.

28. Council Regulation (EEC) No. 3925/91 of 19 December 1991 concerning the elimination of controls and formalities applicable to the cabin and hold baggage of persons taking an intra-Community flight and the baggage of persons making an intra-Community sea-crossing.

29. An example is the Schengen Executive Committee Decision SCH/Com-ex(93) 22 Rev on the Confidential nature of certain documents, which has been based on both Article 207 TEC and Article 41 TEU.

30. An example is Article 76 SIC (monitoring of narcotic drugs), part of which has been based on Articles 95 and 152 TEC, part on Articles 30(1)(a) and 34 TEU.

31. Directive 95/46/EC of 24 October 1995, *relative à la protection des personnes physiques à l'égard du traitement des données à caractère personnel et à la libre circulation de ces données.* JOCE l 281/31 of 23.11.95.

32. Rationalization is also required between the provisions in Title IV and Schengen, which could be one of the subjects for the next IGC. In: Kortenberg (1998: 833–54)

BIBLIOGRAPHY

European Presidency (1997), Note of the Presidency for the Group 'Schengen acquis'. Brussels, 17 October 1997 (11480/97 Limite).

Agence Europe (1998), 17 April, No. 7202.

Belgian Presidency (1998), Note of the Belgian Presidency Concerning the Determination of the Schengen *acquis* With a View to Incorporating it into the European Union – Confidentiality, SCH/Tr-Rego (98) 15, Brussels, 14 May 1998.

Belgian Presidency (1998), Note of the Belgian Presidency Concerning the Determination of the Schengen *acquis* With a View to Incorporation into the European Union – Decisions and Declarations of the Executive Committee and Decisions of the Central Group, SCH/Tr-Rego (98) 12 herz., 25 May 1998.

Corrado, L. (1998), *l'Integration de Schengen dans l'Union Européenne: problèmes et perspectives*, Mémoire présenté pour le Diplôme d'études européennes approfondies. Bruges: Collège d'Europe, 1997–1998.

Curtin, D. M. and I. F. Dekker (1999), 'The European Union as a "Layered" international organization: institutional unity in disguise'. In P. Craig and G. de Búrca (eds), *European Union Law: An Evolutionary Perspective*, Oxford.

De Kerchove, G. (1998) 'Un espace de liberté, de sécurité et de justice aux dimensions incertaines: Quelques réflexions sur le recours aux coopérations renforcées en matière de justice et d'affaires intérieures'. In M. den Boer, A. Guggenbühl and S. Vanhoonacker (eds), *Coping with Flexibility and Legitimacy after Amsterdam*, Current European Issues. Maastricht: European Institute of Public Administration.

De Zwaan, J. (1998) 'Schengen and its incorporation into the New Treaty: the negotiating process'. In M. den Boer, *Schengen's Final Days? Incorporation into the*

New TEU, External Borders and Information Systems. European Institute of Public Administration.

Den Boer, M. (1997a) 'Travel notes on a bumpy journey from Schengen via Maastricht to Amsterdam'. In M. den Boer (ed.), *The Implementation of Schengen: First the Widening, Now the Deepening*. Maastricht: European Institute of Public Administration.

Den Boer, M. (1997b) 'Hollen of stilstaan? Justitie en Binnenlandse Zaken in het nieuwe Verdrag van Amsterdam'. *Nederlands Juristenblad*, 35 (3 October), 1625–30.

Demmink, J. (1998) 'Flexibility and legitimacy in JHA after Amsterdam'. In M. den Boer, A. Guggenbühl and S. Vanhoonacker (eds), *Coping with Flexibility and Legitimacy after Amsterdam*, Current European Issues. Maastricht: European Institute of Public Administration.

Elsen, C. (1996) 'Rechtlicher Rahmen und Grundsatzprobleme der Zusammenarbeit von Polizei und Justiz'. In K. Hailbronner (ed.), *Zusammenarbeit der Polizei- und Justizverwaltungen in Europa*. Heidelberg: Kriminalistik Verlag, pp. 9–16.

Europe (1997), 11 July, No. 7014.

Fennelly, N. (1998) 'Preserving the legal coherence within the New Treaty'. In M. den Boer, A. Guggenbühl and S. Vanhoonacker (eds), *Coping with Flexibility and Legitimacy after Amsterdam*, Current European Issues. Maastricht: European Institute of Public Administration.

Gialdino, C. C. (1998) 'Schengen et le troisième pilier: le contrôle juridictionnel organisé par le traité d'Amsterdam'. *Revue du Marché Unique Européen*, 2, 89–123.

Groenendijk, K. (1998) *The Incorporation of Schengen: Continuation of the Democratic Deficit of a Fresh Start?* Mimeo.

Hix, S. and J. Niessen (1996) *Reconsidering European Migration Policies: The 1996 IGC or the Reform of the Maastricht Treaty*. Brussels: M.P.G., C.C.M.E., S.L.G.

House of Lords Press Information (1998) 'Lords Shocked by Confusion about EU Border Controls and Police Co-operation', 8 September.

House of Lords Select Committee on the European Communities (1998) *Defining the Schengen Acquis*. Session 1997–98. 20th Report. HL paper 86. London: HMSO.

House of Lords Select Committee on the European Communities (1998) *Incorporating the Schengen Acquis into the European Union*. Session 1997–98. 31st Report. HL paper 139. London: HMSO.

Kortenberg, H. (1998) 'Closer cooperation in the Treaty of Amsterdam', *Common Market Law Review*, 35, 833–54.

Labayle, H. (1997) 'Un espace de liberté, de sécurité et de justice'. In *RTD. eur*, 33 (4, oct.–déc.), 105–73.

Monar, J. (1997) 'Schengen and flexibility in the Treaty of Amsterdam: opportunities and risks of differentiated integration in EU Justice and Home Affairs'. In M. den Boer (ed.), *Schengen, Judicial Cooperation and Policy Coordination*. Maastricht: European Institute of Public Administration.

Monar, J. (1998a) 'Justice and Home Affairs in the Treaty of Amsterdam: reform at the price of fragmentation'. *European Law Review*, 23, 320–35.

Monar, J. (1998b) 'Legitimacy of EU action in Justice and Home Affairs: an assessment in the light of the reforms of the Treaty of Amsterdam'. In M. den Boer, A. Guggenbühl and S. Vanhoonacker (eds), *Coping with Flexibility and Legitimacy after Amsterdam*, Current European Issues. Maastricht: European Institute of Public Administration.

Piçarra, N. (1998) 'La mise en oeuvre du protocole intégrant l'acquis de Schengen dans le cadre de l'Union européenne: règles et procédures'. In M. den Boer, *Schengen's Final Days? Incorporation into the New TEU, External Borders and Information Systems*. European Institute of Public Administration.

Shaw, J. (1998) 'Flexibility and legitimacy in the domain of the Treaty establishing the European Community'. In M. den Boer, A. Guggenbühl and S. Vanhoonacker (eds), *Coping with Flexibility and Legitimacy after Amsterdam*, Current European Issues. Maastricht: European Institute of Public

Statewatch (1998), May–August, Vol. 8 (3–4).

Tweede Kamer, vergaderjaar 1995–1996, 19326, no. 141.

Tweede Kamer, vergaderjaar 1995–1996, 19326, no. 167.

Tweede Kamer, vergaderjaar 1995–1996, 19326, no. 201.

Van de Rijt, W. (1998) 'Le fonctionnement des institutions Schengen. 'Pragmatisme, toujours' In M. den Boer (ed.), *Schengen's Final Days? Incorporation into the new TEU, External Borders and Information Systems*. European Institute of Public Administration.

Weiler, J. (1991) 'The Transformation of Europe'. *Yale Law Journal*, 100, 2403–83.

PART IV

THE WAY AHEAD

CHAPTER 16

CONTINUING AND BUILDING ON AMSTERDAM: THE REFORMS OF THE TREATY OF NICE

Jörg Monar

Just ten months after the entry into force of the Treaty of Amsterdam the European Union engaged in a new round of treaty reforms. This new round – which formally started on 14 February 2000 with the convening of a new Intergovernmental Conference – was focused on the so-called 'left-overs' of Amsterdam. These were primarily the institutional issues of the composition of the Commission and the re-weighting of the votes in the Council which Amsterdam had failed to resolve but which were acquiring a dimension of urgency with the approaching next enlargement. Yet the new IGC agenda went beyond these questions. Already, in a Declaration to the 'Protocol on the institutions' attached to the Treaty of Amsterdam, three Member States – Belgium, France and Italy – had expressed their view that Amsterdam had not met the need for 'substantial progress towards reinforcing the institutions' and that a 'significant extension of recourse to qualified majority' should be part of the necessary reforms. This view found strong support by most of the other Member States, the Commission and the European Parliament, and became therefore another key issue of the IGC which inevitably also raised the question of an extension of the European Parliament's co-decision powers. In addition, a couple of other items which were strictly speaking not Amsterdam 'left-overs' – such as the adoption of the Charter of Fundamental Rights, the strengthening of the role of the Commission President, the reform of the European Court of Justice and progress towards the Common European Security and Defence Policy – came on the agenda so that the new IGC ended up as being more than just an exercise in 'fine-tuning' the changes introduced by the Amsterdam Treaty although covering much less ground than its predecessor.

After difficult negotiations and a near failure the previous evening, the new IGC ended in the early hours of 11 December 2000 on the Acropolis of Nice with the agreement on a new treaty – the Treaty of Nice – which after Maastricht and Amsterdam is the third EU reform treaty agreed in less than a decade. The Nice Treaty introduces a range of changes to the existing Treaties some of which are of a major nature and will need a comprehensive and careful political and legal analysis. This is not the place to engage in such an analysis – it would require another book – but since this is a volume on the Amsterdam Treaty it seems useful to provide here a brief survey and preliminary assessment of the Nice Treaty as a follow-up to its predecessor. The Nice reforms can be conveniently regrouped under three major headings: reform of the institutional system, strengthening of policy-making capacity and 'constitution-building'.[1]

REFORM OF THE INSTITUTIONAL SYSTEM

The Treaty of Amsterdam had clearly failed to resolve the two already mentioned institutional issues – the composition of the Commission and the re-weighting of votes in the Council. This was in essence a question of the balance of powers between the Member States and entailed almost inevitably also a renegotiation of the allocation of seats in the European Parliament for which Amsterdam had only set an overall ceiling of 700. The Treaty of Nice provides a 'package solution' which consists of four interrelated elements: the reform of the Commission, the re-weighting of votes, the new qualified majority and the reallocation of seats.

The reform of the Commission

Article 4(1) of the 'Protocol on the enlargement of the European Union' provides that from 1 January 2005 the Commission shall consist of one national of each of the Member States. This takes up the option envisaged in the Amsterdam Treaty 'Protocol on the institutions'. Yet Article 4(2) of the Nice Treaty Protocol goes a step further by providing that when the Union consists of 27 Member States the number of members of the European Commission shall be less than the number of Member States and that the members of the Commission shall then be chosen according to a rotation system based on the principle of equality. This rotation system remains to be defined, but this can be done unanimously by the Council and does not require an IGC context. For the time being, therefore, the strong nationality element in the composition of the Commission will be preserved with only the larger Member States having to give up one of 'their' Commissioners. An effort has been made, however, to strengthen the internal efficiency of the Commission by giving its President more extensive powers as regards its internal organization, the reshuffling of responsibilities among Commission Members and even the forced resignation of Members which the President will be able to obtain, this however only with the collective approval of the Commission (amended Article 217 TEC). The crisis of the Santer Commission has clearly left its mark on this part of the reform.

A further significant element of reform is provided by amended Article 214 TEC which now provides that both the President of the Commission and then (in the second stage) the other Members of the Commission shall be nominated by a qualified majority of the Heads of State or Government, meeting in the Council. Although the Member States may still prefer to aim at a consensus on nominations, this provision should put an end to agreements on least common denominator candidates as President of the Commission and could therefore lead to the appointment of stronger candidates. It could also mean, however, complex bargaining between potential 'presidential' majorities in the European Council and the European Parliament whose outcome may be far from obvious. Finally, it could mean new challenges for the President of the European Commission if he should be appointed against the explicit wishes of one or more national governments. So far the 'common accord' system meant that the President appointed was (at least in principle) the candidate of all Member States and could therefore, at least to some extent, count on initial goodwill from all capitals.

While the reforms strengthening the role of the Commission President may actually strengthen the institution internally, it should be noted that otherwise a stronger role for the Commission was clearly not on the Nice agenda. The Commission's weak position in the context of the Common European Security and Defence Policy (CESDP) was not strengthened and – with the exception of the area of non-family law related judicial cooperation in civil matters – the Commission will at least until 2004 still only have a shared right of initiative in justice and home affairs, the most dynamic area of legislative activity since Amsterdam. The Commission has also not been given any role as regards the establishment of the new consultative Social Protection Committee (new Article 144 TEC) and the functioning of Eurojust (amended Article 31 TEU). It may even be argued that some of the new provisions in the area of the Common commercial policy (see below) could weaken its position in one of its traditional areas of strength.

The re-weighting of the votes in the Council

After the difficulties this point had raised in the Amsterdam negotiations it was no surprise that this issue – crucial to the balance of powers between the Member States in an enlarged Union – was also one of the most contentious of the Nice Treaty. It not only opposed bigger and smaller Member States but also bigger Member States (such as France and

Germany) and smaller (such as Belgium and the Netherlands) struggling over their relative weight. According to Article 3 of the 'Protocol on the enlargement of the European Union' Article 205(2) TEC will, from 1 January 2005 on, reallocate the number of votes in the Council as follows: France, Germany, Italy and the UK 29; the Netherlands 13; Belgium, Greece and Portugal 12; Austria and Sweden 10; Denmark, Finland and Ireland 7; Luxembourg 4. The Conference also agreed on the vote allocations for the candidate countries (with the exception of Turkey), rejecting earlier proposals of the French Presidency which would have given existing member States more votes than candidate countries of the same size.[2] This compromise clearly marks a step towards a reduction of the over-representation of smaller Member States which has become unsustainable in view of the next enlargement. Yet the vote allocations continue to be a negotiated political compromise, do not follow a coherent system, and in some cases the disproportional elements have even been increased. The relative weight of Germany and Spain may be taken as an example. Currently Germany – which has more than double the population[3] – has 25 per cent more votes than Spain.[4] Under the new arrangements this margin, rather than increasing, will shrink to 7.4 per cent. Some of the decisions on votes in the Council were counterbalanced, however, by those on the new qualified majority and on the reallocation of seats in the European Parliament (see below).

The new qualified majority

The negotiations on the new qualified majority were closely linked to the re-weighting of the votes and no less difficult. The compromise which was achieved in the end adds another dimension of complexity to the EU system. The new qualified majority which will apply from 1 January 2005 on will consist of three elements. For the EU-15 the threshold will be at 169 out of the total of 237 votes, i.e. it will remain at the long-standing roughly 71.3 per cent.[5] According to amended Article 205(2) TEC, however, the votes of this qualified majority must be cast by a majority of the Member States if the Council acts on a proposal by the Commission and by at least two-thirds of the Member States in all other cases. To this, new Article 205(4) TEC adds the provision that when a decision is to be adopted by the Council by a qualified majority, a member of the Council may request verification that the qualified majority comprises at least 62 per cent of the total population of the Union. If that condition is shown not to have been met, the decision in question shall not be adopted. This third element introduces a strong demographic factor and significantly increases the weight of the larger Member States. Any combination of three of the current largest four (France, Germany, Italy and the UK) will in fact be able to form a blocking minority. It also explains why Germany accepted in the end to remain on a par with France, Italy and the UK as regards the number of votes in the Council. Germany will need only the support of one other of the biggest four and of one of the smaller (with the exception of Luxembourg) to arrive at a blocking minority. It should be noted that this 62 per cent threshold is higher than the current (informal) one which is around 4 per cent lower, so that the qualified majority threshold has actually been increased.

This system will obviously have to be adapted as Union membership grows, and on this aspect the Heads of State or Government got into some confusion which may be explained by hours of middle-of-the-night negotiations. In the 'Declaration on the enlargement of the European Union' it is provided that after the enlargement to all twelve of the applicant countries with whom whole negotiations have started (with the exception of Turkey) the qualified majority threshold is to attain 258 out of a total of 345 votes, i.e. 74.78 per cent. Yet this provision is in contradiction with the 'Declaration on the qualified majority threshold' which establishes 91 as the minimum number of votes for a blocking minority after completion of the accession of all twelve candidate countries. This would mean a qualified majority minimum of only 255 instead of 258 being equivalent to only 71.26 per cent. To increase the confusion further the 'Declaration on the qualified majority threshold' provides that after enlargement the percentage of votes constituting a qualified majority will be 'lower than the current percentage' and that it will 'increase until it reaches a maximum of 73.4 per cent' which means that the qualified majority threshold will have to be adapted with each wave of the next enlargement. Rather interestingly the figure of 73.4 per cent is both higher than the 'current' one and lower than the one which results from the 258 votes threshold in the 'Declaration on the enlargement' and clearly requires further clarification. It will no doubt find its place among the memorabilia of badly prepared last minute deals at the level of the EU Heads of State or Government.

The reallocation of seats in the European Parliament

The changes to size and composition of the Parliament are among the most puzzling of the Nice negotiations. The first surprise is that the ceiling of 700 MEPs agreed at Amsterdam in order to keep the EP workable has been breached. By virtue of amended Article 190(3) TEC the maximum ceiling will now be 732. This is unlikely to be helpful for a parliament which will anyway have to cope with an increasing diversity of languages and national backgrounds.

As regards the allocation of seats, both Germany and Luxembourg have come out as the winners of the compromise package because they are the only Member States that will keep their current number of seats in spite of enlargement. According to revised Article 190(2) TEC, seats among the current Member States are to be allocated as follows from 2004 on, based on an EU of 27 Member States: Germany 99; France, Italy and the UK 72; Spain 50; the Netherlands 25; Belgium, Greece and Portugal 22; Sweden 18; Austria 17; Denmark and Finland 13; Ireland 12; Luxembourg 6. These figures are likely to be higher for the next EP elections in 2004, though, because the 732 ceiling is going to apply regardless of the number of new Member States that may have joined by then, with current Member States having proportionably inflated numbers of seats if not all of the twelve applicants have joined by then.

The second rather surprising element of the 'seat package' is the numbers of seats allocated to the accession countries. These are Poland 50; Romania 33; Czech Republic and Hungary 20; Bulgaria 17; Slovakia 13; Lithuania 12; Latvia 8; Slovenia; Estonia and Cyprus 6; Malta 5. These numbers obviously breach in at least four cases the principle, agreed on at some stage during the negotiations, that representation in the European Parliament should be broadly proportionate to the size of the population. The Czech Republic and Hungary have each more people than Belgium and Portugal but have each ended up with two seats less. Estonia has more than three times the population size of Luxembourg but has the same number of seats. Cyprus is as well significantly under-represented in comparison to Luxembourg.

It should also be noted that the new allocation of seats will increase rather than decrease the differences in the numbers of citizens represented by each MEP. Currently the two extremes are Germany (828,667 citizens per MEP) and Luxembourg (71,500 citizens per MEP), after completion of the enlargement to 27 these will be still Germany (same figure on current basis) and Malta (63,167 citizens per MEP), an increase from 11.59:1 to 13.12:1.[6] Overall, therefore, the EP democratic representativeness will decrease with the implementation of the Nice reforms.

Looking at the 'institutional package' of Nice altogether it seems fair to say that its primary merit is to have found some sort of solution to the Amsterdam left-overs at all. Any failure to do so would have been a major blow to the Union's political credibility and its capacity to proceed with enlargement. Yet the package clearly defeats some of the original purposes of the reforms in the sense that it actually increases the qualified majority threshold, creates new elements of disproportional Member State representation in both Council and Parliament, and further reduces the democratic representativeness of the EP. The relative winners are the bigger Member States (although they have lost, in line with the solution suggested at Amsterdam, one Commissioner), and, as regards representation in the European Parliament only, the two smallest, Luxembourg and Malta. The Commission President will find his position strengthened, but this in the context of an institution whose relative decline in importance has not been reversed by Nice. The Parliament's new composition raises further question marks over its internal workability and its democratic representativeness, but it may find modest consolation in the qualified majority voting on the Commission President in the European Council (which is likely to give more leverage to its own powers in the appointment process), its now explicit *locus standi* to bring actions before the ECJ under amended Articles 230 and 300(6) TEC, and in the modest extension of the application of the co-decision and assent procedures (see below).

Not strictly enlargement related and not formally a 'left-over' of Amsterdam are the extensive institutional reforms decided on the reorganization of the EU's judiciary which are aimed at a new division of competence between the Court of Justice and the Court of First Instance, and better working methods, and will allow for the setting up of special judicial panels for hearing and determining certain classes of actions.[7] These changes are amongst the most detailed of the Treaty of Nice and could significantly reduce the caseload for the Court of Justice and the time of proceedings.

STRENGTHENING OF THE POLICY-MAKING CAPACITY

Broadly speaking two major issues came on the Nice agenda as regards the increase of the Union's policy-making capacity: the extension of qualified majority voting and the rules regarding 'closer cooperation'. Behind both of them were the concerns of most of the Member States that the Union's policy-making capacity could grind to halt if individual Member States – current or future – were allowed to prevent others from further developing and deepening EU policies in the enlarging Union.

Qualified majority voting

Discussions in the IGC on voting requirements were limited to only 45 out of the around 70 treaty bases currently still subject to unanimity.[8] In the end qualified majority voting was extended to 35 of those, of which 22 will come under qualified majority voting with the entry into force of the Treaty, the others at later dates or after a separate decision of the Council. Some of the areas newly coming under qualified majority voting are of considerable importance. On the internal side these include, for instance, incentive measures to promote non-discrimination (Article 13(2) TEC), facilitation of the right to freedom of movement and residence

(Article 18(2) TEC), judicial cooperation in civil matters (by virtue of new Article 65 TEC), Community financial assistance to Member States in difficulties (Article 100 TEC), measures for the rapid introduction of the euro to new Member States (Article 123(4) TEC), and the reform of the structural and cohesion funds (from 2007 on; Article 161 TEC). On the external side – a traditionally rather 'hostile' territory for majority voting – the extension of QMV has been quite substantial. The new areas include the appointment of the Secretary General of the Council (who since Amsterdam is the High Representative for the CFSP, Article 207(2) TEC) and of special representatives for the CFSP (Article 23(2) TEU), international agreements implementing a joint action or common position (Article 24(3) TEU), international representation of the Community as regards EMU matters (Article 111(4) TEC), trade in services and the commercial aspects of intellectual property (with exceptions; Article 133 TEC), and economic, financial and technical cooperation with third countries (Article 181a TEC). In addition, qualified majority voting has also been introduced to a range of institutional decisions of considerable importance such as the appointment of the Commission (see above), the decision of the statutes of MEPs (Article 190(5) TEC), the appointment of the Secretary-General and Deputy Secretary-General of the Council (Article 207(2) TEC), the adoption of the rules of procedure of the Court of Justice and of the Court of First Instance and the Court of Auditors (Articles 223, 224 and 248 TEC), and the appointment of the members of the Court of Auditors, the Economic and Social Committee and the Committee of the Regions (Articles 247, 259(1) and 263 TEC).

In terms of sheer numbers the extension of qualified majority voting might appear like a major breakthrough, and it can be regarded as a step forward in the direction of transforming the EU into a two-chamber system. It should be noted, however, that in particularly sensitive areas – such as treaty changes, common CFSP strategies, many areas of justice and home affairs, tax harmonization, culture, and four substantial areas of social policy[9] – unanimity has been maintained. In addition some of the extensions have been limited by important exceptions. Qualified majority voting on aspects of freedom of movement and residence, for instance, will not apply to provisions on passports, identity cards and residence permits, and provisions on social security or social protection (Article 18(3) TEC). As regards the introduction of the euro to new Member States, unanimity will continue to apply on the crucial issue of the fixing of the conversion rates (Article 123(4) TEC). The application of qualified majority voting in the area of judicial cooperation in civil matters looks much less impressive if one considers that family law matters – arguably the most substantial part of civil law cooperation – remain excluded from this 'breakthrough' (Article 67(5) TEC). In the important area of asylum policy the German Government (very much under pressure from the German Länder) successfully insisted that measures in these areas will only be adopted by qualified majority once 'common rules and basic principles' have been adopted by unanimity (Article 67(5) TEC). On the whole the Treaty of Nice, therefore, continues the line of a gradual extension of qualified majority voting which had also prevailed at Amsterdam without making it the standard procedure. Nevertheless there is some distinct qualitative change in the sense that majority voting has now become the predominant procedure on questions of major appointments and a number of statutory rules for the institutions, and that majority voting has also been significantly extended in some of the areas of external representation of the Union, traditionally one of the main strongholds of unanimity.

The European Parliament has only to a very limited extent benefited from the extension of qualified majority voting. The automatic link it had proposed between the extension of qualified majority voting and co-decision was not accepted by the IGC. As a result, the co-decision procedure will only be extended to five new areas upon the entry into force of the Nice Treaty: incentive measures to promote non-discrimination (Article 13(2) TEC); measures relating to the freedom of movement and residence (with the already mentioned exceptions; Article 18(2) TEC); judicial cooperation in civil matters (Article 65 TEC); specific measures in support of actions in the field of industrial policy (Article 157 TEC); specific actions for social and economic cohesion outside of the structural funds (Article 159 TEC); and regulations governing political parties at the European level and the rules regarding their funding (Article 191 TEC). Co-decision can be extended earlier than provided for by the Amsterdam Treaty to a number of 'first pillar' justice and home affairs areas (Article 67 TEC) and also to some social policy areas (Article 137 TEC), but only if the Council decides unanimously to do so. This is clearly a rather meagre result for the Parliament if one considers the comparatively much larger extension of qualified majority voting. Yet its legislative powers have also been strengthened through an extension of the assent procedure to the determination of the existence of a clear risk of a serious breach by a Member State of fundamental rights (Article 7 TEU); the establishment of an 'enhanced cooperation' in areas falling under co-decision (Clause G on 'enhanced cooperation'); and the reform of the structural and cohesion funds (only from 2007 on; Article 161 TEC). The growth the of EP legislative powers continues therefore, but at a slower pace than at Amsterdam.

'Enhanced cooperation'[10]

Although not yet tested in practice – if one excepts the special case of the incorporation of Schengen – the Amsterdam Treaty provisions on 'closer cooperation' have already generated at least as much political debate as academic literature. In the run-up to the IGC several Member States pushed very strongly the idea that the national veto possibility against the establishment of such forms of flexibility would need to be dropped in order to keep this instrument operational for the 'willing' against the 'unwilling' or the 'unable'. The result is a set of sixteen amended or new rules – 'Clauses' A to P to be inserted into Part 1 of the TEC and Titles VI and VII TEU – which try to strike a new balance between the interests of the 'willing' and the protection of the EU/EC acquis and of the 'unwilling' or 'unable'. Primary innovations to be mentioned are the abolition of the national veto possibility against the establishment of 'enhanced coopera-tion' in the 'first' and 'third' pillars through the introduction of qualified majority voting (Clauses G(2) and O). Such cooperation can now also be established in the context of the CFSP, although it will be limited to joint actions or common positions and cannot relate to matters having military or defence implications (Clause J). The minimum number of Member States participating has been fixed at eight which means that after enlarge-ment (unlike the Amsterdam provisions) fewer than half of the Member States may engage in such a cooperation framework (Clause A(g)). As new conditions, it has been added that enhanced cooperation must be aimed at 'reinforcing the integration process' (Clause A(a)) and that it must not undermine the internal market or economic and social cohesion (Clause A(e)). The 'last resort' provision has been strengthened. Enhanced cooperation may now only be engaged in when it has been established within the Council that its objectives cannot be attained within a reason-able period by applying the relevant provisions of the Treaties (Clause B). Commission and Council have been vested with the task of ensuring the consistency of activities carried out within enhanced cooperation with the policies of the Union and Community (Clause F). Overall this appears as a fairly balanced compromise which makes the instrument more oper-ational while at the same time increasing the safeguards against a poten-tial negative impact on the institutional and legal acquis. The risks of a further fragmentation of the legal order and potential conflicts between 'ins' and 'outs' will remain, however.

Overall the changes regarding qualified majority voting and 'enhanced cooperation' reduce the risk of a paralysis of the Union's policy-making capacity. Yet, as indicated above, unanimity still governs crucial policy issues, and 'enhanced cooperation' is only a last resort measure which carries its own risks. The political will for a fundamental overhaul was clearly not present at Nice. This is also demonstrated by the tortuous compromise negotiated on the reform of Article 133 TEC (Common Commercial Policy). The scope of Article 133 TEC (and thereby also qualified majority voting) has been finally extended to trade in services and the commercial aspects of intellectual property. Yet the exceptions added deprive this step forward of much of its substance. The Council will decide unanimously on matters where unanimity is required for the adoption of internal rules, on matters on which the Community has not yet exercised its powers and on horizontal agreements (Article 133(5) TEC). An agreement cannot be concluded if it includes provisions which go beyond the Community's internal powers; agreements relating to trade in cultural and audiovisual services, educational services and social and human health services will continue to fall within the shared competence of the Community and the Member States and will therefore need the 'common accord' of the Member States (Article 133(6) TEC). Here again the defence of national competences and interests has clearly prevailed over the interests of an effective common policy-making, and this in spite of the increasing pressures on the EU in the international trade negotiations.

'CONSTITUTION BUILDING'

Although there was some political debate during the year of the IGC (partly triggered by German Foreign Minister Joschka Fischer's 'private' speech at Humboldt University (Berlin) on 12 May 2000)[11] about laying the foundations of a constitutional organization of the EU, the negotiations never entered into the fundamental questions of the Union's constitutional design. There were, however, some issues on the IGC agenda which had a certain constitutional significance or, at least, potential.

The most important of those was the adoption of the Charter of Fundamental Rights which was prepared outside the IGC by an extraordinary Convention of representatives of national governments and parliaments, the Commission and the European Parliament. A majority of the Member States, the Commission and the Parliament would have liked to incorporate this Charter, which was finalized on 2 October 2000, in one form or another into the new Treaty. Yet, due to firm opposition by the British Government and the reluctance of some other Member States, the Charter was in the end only 'solemnly' proclaimed at the Nice summit with no reference at all made to the Charter in the Treaty of Nice. The opportunity to formally add a constitutional rights dimension to the Treaties has therefore been missed and further controversies and uncertainties as to the status and legal effects of the Charter are to be expected.

A further element of constitutional significance would have been the incorporation into the Treaty of new provisions on the CESDP on which much, and indeed constitutionally potentially very relevant, progress has been achieved since the Amsterdam reforms. Yet there were already disagreements over the need to do so at that stage, and the IGC was overshadowed by disagreements between France and the UK about the relationship of the CESDP and NATO. In the end the Heads of State and Government limited themselves to the elimination of some provisions of Article 17 TEU which could have been obstacles to the further development of the CESDP in its current form and to the adoption of a Declaration (in an annexe to the Treaty) which provides, inter alia, for the opening of negotiations with NATO.

Another much more modest constitutional issue which appeared on the agenda was that of the potential funding out of the Community budget of political parties at European level. After it had been made clear that this would not imply any transfer of competence to the European Community and that such funds may not be used to fund, either directly or indirectly, political parties at national level, it has been possible to include a provision to that effect (Article 191 TEC). It could make a significant contribution to the strengthening of the trans-European party landscape whose weakness continues to be among the main factors contributing to the absence of a political culture at the EU level.

Overall the Treaty of Nice has clearly not much to show in terms of the further constitutionalization of the EU construction. One can take the view, however, that this was indeed not the task of this latest round of Treaty revision, which had to deal with the Amsterdam 'left-overs' in view of the next enlargement, and required institutional and procedural engineering rather than big constitutional designs. Yet the Heads of State or Government themselves seem to have felt that the Union is in need of – and this even before the next enlargement – a thorough consideration of its fundamental constitutional bases and rationale. They added a 'Declaration on the future of the Union' to the final act of the IGC which calls 'for a deeper and wider debate about the future development of the European Union' and provides for the the Laeken European Council in December 2001 to indicate a way forward on fundamental questions such as the delimitation of competences between the European Union and the Member States, reflecting the principle of subsidiarity, the status of the Charter of Fundamental Rights, the simplification of the Treaties, and the role of national parliaments in the European architecture. They also decided that a new IGC will be convened in 2004.

This prospect for a wider debate and another IGC puts the Treaty of

Nice into perspective. Far from invalidating the Treaty of Amsterdam it answers, although in an imperfect and provisional form, some of the questions it left open; builds, although in a rather modest way, on some of the progress achieved at Amsterdam (such as the comprehensive Amsterdam provisions on justice and home affairs); and continues some of the great lines of reform – such as extension of majority voting and co-decision by the European Parliament – which were on the EU reform agenda throughout the 1990s.

The Treaty of Nice has its disappointing side, as indeed had its Amsterdam predecessor. Jean-Louis Bourlanges has vigourously made a case for its non-ratification by pointing to its failure to reinforce the supranational character of the Commission, its failure to provide a break-through towards majority voting in some of the most crucial policy-making areas, the increased qualified majority voting threshold, and its more than questionable reallocation of seats in the EP.[12] One may indeed raise the question whether the Treaty of Nice is not a proof that the Union and its Member States have not yet reached the necessary mental pre-paredness for a further major enlargement. The emphasis at the Nice negotiations was clearly on the protection of acquired interests *against the effects of enlargement* rather than on a constructive preparation *for enlargement*. Yet in terms of consolidating and further developing what had been achieved by the far more extensive reforms introduced by the Treaty of Amsterdam, this was obviously the maximum which could be achieved for the time being. The fact that at Nice the Heads of State or Government spent more than three days and, in the final phase, the better part of a long night hammering out a compromise can be taken as a proof of how crucial and vitally important the European construction has become for all of the EU governments.

The Treaty of Amsterdam was a bigger step in the development of the Union, its successor of Nice a smaller one, but both are milestones on a road whose final destination is as much as ever in need of clarification. With every new IGC and treaty reform the questions of the final objectives and the final shape of the 'ever closer union'[13] become more pressing. Both the effectiveness and the legitimacy of further rounds of reform will depend on whether the Member States which remain the masters of the Treaties can agree at least on some common answers to these questions. The losses from any further postponement may never be retrieved.

NOTES

1. The following brief analysis is based on the provisional version of the Treaty of Nice of 22 December 2000 which includes corrections agreed on by CORE-

PER but is currently still undergoing legal and linguistic revision (Council document SN 533/1/00 REV 1).

2. Poland 27; Romania 14; Czech Republic and Hungary 12; Bulgaria 10; Lithuania and Slovakia 7; Cyprus, Estonia, Latvia and Slovenia 4; Malta 3.
3. 82.0 million to 39.4 million (1999 figures).
4. 10 to 8.
5. Currently the threshold is 71.26%, the new one will be 71.30%.
6. Source for basic figures: European Parliament: Projet du Traité de Nice, 10 January 2001, PE 294.737, p. 13.
7. Amended Articles 220 to 225a, 229a and 245 TEC.
8. European Parliament: Projet du Traité de Nice, 10 January 2001, PE 294.737, p. 17.
9. Social security and social protection of workers, protection in case of redundancy, representation and collective defence of interests of workers and employers, conditions of employment of legally resident third-country nationals. By virtue of amended Article 137 TEC the Council may decide, however, to use qualified majority voting under the co-decision procedure for all of these areas with the exception of the first one. This decision, however, must be unanimous, a point very much insisted on by the British Government.
10. The English version of the Nice Treaty replaces the term *closer* by *enhanced* cooperation.
11. Text: www.auswaertiges-amt.de.
12. Jean-Louis Bourlanges 'Il ne faut pas ratifier Maastricht', in *Le Monde*, 13 December 2000.
13. Preamble TEU.

INDEX